Waterhouses

Ohio University Research in International Studies

This series of publications on Africa, Latin America, Southeast Asia, and Global and Comparative Studies is designed to present significant research, translation, and opinion to area specialists and to a wide community of persons interested in world affairs. The series is distributed worldwide. For more information, consult the Ohio University Press website, ohioswallow.com.

Books in the Ohio University Research in International Studies series are published by Ohio University Press in association with the Center for International Studies. The views expressed in individual volumes are those of the authors and should not be considered to represent the policies or beliefs of the Center for International Studies, Ohio University Press, or Ohio University.

Waterhouses

LANDSCAPES, HOUSING, AND THE MAKING OF MODERN LAGOS

Mark Duerksen

Ohio University Research in International Studies
Africa Series No. 99

Ohio University Press
Athens

Ohio University Press, Athens, Ohio 45701
ohioswallow.com
© 2024 by Ohio University Press
All rights reserved

To obtain permission to quote, reprint, or otherwise reproduce or distribute
material from Ohio University Press publications, please contact our rights
and permissions department at (740) 593-1154 or (740) 593-4536 (fax).

Printed in the United States of America
Ohio University Press books are printed on acid-free paper ∞ ™

Library of Congress Cataloging-in-Publication Data
Names: Duerksen, Mark, 1989– author.
Title: Waterhouses : landscapes, housing, and the making of modern Lagos /
Mark Duerksen.
Other titles: Research in international studies. Africa series ; no. 99.
Description: Athens : Ohio University Press, 2024. | Series: Ohio University
research in international studies, Africa series ; no. 99 | Includes bibli-
ographical references and index.
Identifiers: LCCN 2023057375 (print) | LCCN 2023057376 (ebook) | ISBN
9780896803312 (hardback) | ISBN 9780896803329 (paperback) | ISBN
9780896805156 (pdf)
Subjects: LCSH: Urbanization—Nigeria—Lagos. | Housing—Nigeria—
Lagos. | Dwellings—Nigeria—Lagos. | Natural resources—Nigeria—
Lagos. | Nigeria—History.
Classification: LCC HT384.N52 L343 2024 (print) | LCC HT384.N52
(ebook) | DDC 966.9/1—dc23/eng/20240412
LC record available at https://lccn.loc.gov/2023057375
LC ebook record available at https://lccn.loc.gov/2023057376

Contents

List of Illustrations
vii

Acknowledgments
xi

Introduction
Èkó: Mapping What a House Is in Lagos
I

1
Bar
Houses as Gateways to Status: Lagos Colony
42

2
Canal
Trenches in Land, Labor, and Sanitation Struggles: Imperial Lagos
76

3
Swamp
Foci in Land, Labor, and Sanitation Struggles: Interwar Years
III

4

Lagoon

Hidden Depths across Independence

139

5

Atlantic

Gatekeepers of Wealth and Power: The Oil Years

172

Conclusion

Flooding: Barometers of Human Security in a Fractured Global Landscape

199

Notes

223

Bibliography

271

Index

297

Illustrations

Figures

I.1. Lagos's housing landscapes, 2014–17	3
I.2. Estate in Victoria Garden City, Lekki, 2016	5
I.3. Map scanning, 2016	28
1.1. Lagos's channel, 2016	43
1.2. Lagos from West End of Marina, 1885	43
1.3. Ilojo Bar and Orange House, ca. 1911	44
1.4. Payne's Orange House, 1878	52
1.5. Ilojo Bar	54
1.6. Ebun House, ca. 1920	55
1.7. Taiwo Olowo's palace, 1970s	57
1.8. Water House, 1970s	63
1.9. Government House under construction, ca. 1896	75
2.1. MacGregor's Canal, ca. 1908–12	78
2.2. House construction by African laborers, ca. 1900	87
2.3. Embankment of the marina, ca. 1900	87
2.4. Pre-reclamation Alakoro, February 1908	89
2.5. Post-reclamation Alakoro, July 1908	89
2.6. Alakoro's thatch and clay buildings, 1908	90
2.7. Epe houses, ca. 1900	91
2.8–2.9. British officers' quarters, early 1900s	92

Illustrations

2.10–2.11. A sanitary report on an Afro-Brazilian house, 1908   93

2.12. A multistory "Lagos-style" house beyond Alakoro, 1908   98

2.13. British colonial quarters, ca. 1900   107

2.14. Jaekel House, 2017   107

2.15. Government House, early twentieth century   108

2.16. Government House contrasted with African house, early 1900s   108

2.17. Colonial housing in Ikoyi, 1923   109

3.1. Makoko floating school   112

3.2. Koolhaas's Makoko, 2006   113

3.3. Aerial views of Lagos, 1929   113

3.4. Oko Awo house models, 1928   127

4.1. Ditch to prevent flooding, 1952   140

4.2. Gropius House (1938), 2015   146

4.3 House at Ikoyi, 1940s   149

4.4. Lagos Executive Development Board House, ca. 1958   156

4.5. Central Lagos, ca. 1958   157

4.6. Lagos Executive Development Board estate, ca. 1958   157

4.7. Lagos skyline, 1967   167

5.1. Lagos and the Atlantic Ocean, 1975   173

5.2. I-face floor plan, ca. 1986   180

5.3. Compound walls, 2014   197

5.4. A city of walls, 2014–17   198

C.1. Flooding, 2016   200

C.2. Vacant plot, 2016   204

Maps

I.1. Glover's map, 1859   37

1.1. Lawson's map, 1885   45

1.2. Prominent Lagosians on Lawson's map   48

1.3. Cadastral map of Lagos, 1891   67

Illustrations ix

2.1. Stephens and Christophers's mosquito spot map, 1900   86

2.2. Roofing regulation map, 1911   89

2.3. Ikoyi plots, 1919   109

3.1. Town of Lagos, West Africa, 1926   117

3.2. Map of Lagos and Environs, 1932   119

3.3. Town planning scheme near Oko Awo, ca. 1928   124

3.4. Plan of Lagos, 1942   128

3.5. Colonial expropriations mapped, 1946   135

4.1. Corporate Lagos, 1968   144

4.2. Lagos Executive Development Board citywide schemes, 1958   155

4.3. Lagos Executive Development Board's Central Lagos
      Slum Clearance Scheme, 1955   159

4.4. Metropolitan Lagos, 1964   164

5.1. Walking tour of new Lagos, 1975   177

5.2. Walking tour of old Lagos, 1975   177

5.3. A patron's neighborhood network of clients, 1970s   182

Table

1.1. Prominent nineteenth-century Lagos-style houses   53

Acknowledgments

This book is the cumulation of a decade of learning from Lagos, including of my limits as a historian. This manuscript is a start, and one that—in trying to dredge and hold 150 years of Lagos's unyielding currents—draws on countless colleagues, kindnesses from friends and family, conservations with Lagosians, and a vast body of secondary works on the city. I owe these many people and predecessors everything. My hope is that in identifying a few through currents, these pages can help map out new branches and new ways of looking at a city that needs histories as full and forceful as itself. Each of its chapters is an outline in need of further surveying and shading in from future historians of all varieties and methods. I cannot wait to read their findings and interpretations.

I owe several people particular thanks. My dissertation committee, Emmanuel Akyeampong, Suzanne Blier, and Michael Hooper, encouraged me to pursue my unconventional way of seeing history while pushing me to define and refine my ideas constantly. They shared the tools of their own fields, listened to my thoughts, and showed faith in my research through its most rudimentary phases.

This kind of interdepartmental collaboration was made possible by my graduate school home in the Department of African and African American Studies at Harvard. There I had the opportunity to learn from a rare combination of brilliant and generous professors, including Vince Brown, Walter Johnson, John Mugane, Jacob Olupona, and Jim Sidanius, and to engage (and commiserate) with fellow students, including Khytie Brown, Chambi Chachage, Bradley Craig, Jessica Dickson (without whom I would not have made it through my first two years of grad school), Kathleen Jackson, Moses Xu Liang, Sarah Lockwood, Erin Mosley, Anna Neumann, Ayodeji Ogunnaike, Nicholas Paskert, Kevin Tervala (who, along with Jess Williams, made commuting from New York to Cambridge every week for a semester less painful), and Jason Warner. The Department of African and African American Studies and Harvard generously funded my research through grants and fellowships, including a Philippe Wamba Grant and a Frederick Sheldon Fellowship.

My experience in the Department of African and African American Studies continued my privilege of learning from excellent teachers. As an undergraduate at the University of Virginia, several professors shaped my interest in African history and my appreciation for what makes good scholarship. Joseph C. Miller, my adviser, was first and foremost in this journey, and he continues to be my standard of a scholar. Other UVA professors and instructors to whom I owe a great deal in steering me toward this dissertation are Cynthia Hoehler-Fatton, Adria LaViolette, Allan Megill, Elizabeth Schoyer, Michael Smith, Jared Staller, and Benjamin Ray. My original calling to historical research was kindled at Woodberry Forest School by the passion and rigor of Matthew Boesen and Karen Jordan.

While researching houses in Lagos, the city truly became my second home thanks to my hosts "mum and dad" Ajayi who shared their country with me and taught me far more than I could ever learn from reading about Lagos. Other generous Lagosian friends include Chibueze "Chibu" Amanchukwu (who, as an MIT PhD student taking Yoruba classes with me at Harvard, taught me everything I know about Nigerian politics and soccer), John Godwin and Gillian Hopwood, Nike Davies-Okundaye, Olayinka Dosekun, Ed Keazor, Ayodeji Olukoju, and Kehinde Thompson.

I am also grateful to the National Security Education Program for funding my research through a Boren Fellowship, which took me on a memorable detour to Benin. The Boren program led me to the good fortune of my current role at the Africa Center for Strategic Studies, where I have been surrounded by passionate public service–minded colleagues. A heartfelt thanks to everyone along the way on the Research and Strategic Communications team, steered by the incredible vision and mentorship of Joseph Siegle, and for the great comradery

Acknowledgments xiii

of Alix Boucher, Candace Cook, Daniel Eizenga, Eric Kingsepp, Paul Nantulya, Katie Nodjimbaden, Wendy Williams, and Susan Quinn. A special shoutout to other Africa Center colleagues whom I continue to learn from, including Amanda Dory, Daniel Hampton, Nate Allen, Joel Amegboh, Anouar Boukhars, Carolyn Haggis, Catherine Kelly, Assis Malaquias, and Daisy Muibu.

I am appreciative of all the creative support and patience from the excellent team at Ohio University Press.

Finally, my family and friends are the bedrock of this dissertation. I continue to lean on my close friends Leon Frati, Trevor Lawson, Luke Perry, and Steph and Aditya Fontana-Raina. The Stewarts have been a second family, and they all now know who Jane Jacobs is. The Scaifes have always been there for me and have supported my intellectual pursuits in so many ways. I would not be a PhD without the love and enthusiasm of Allen Ross and Anne Lounsbery. My sisters, Emily and Laura, are special in countless ways, and I know I will hang up feeling energized and happy after calling them. My dad, Matthew Duerksen, was there for me throughout grad school in big and small ways from going to baseball games to building wedding altars. My mom, Susan Scaife, kept me on track throughout the process of writing this book, always ready with a smart and sympathetic ear while also prodding me to just finish the thing already. She has found her match in Greg Blake, whom I am thankful to have in my life. My wife, Meredith Stewart, who committed to years of long distance and traveled to at least nine countries with me (including a post-Bar trip to Nigeria) during graduate school, has been there in every single way, helping me keep perspective, rhythm, and priorities throughout the long process of writing a book. Thank you.

Introduction

Èkó: Mapping What a House Is in Lagos

The breeze is blowing, the great lagoon sleeps. Twenty-one million people are in whatever form of shelter they call home, these human energies at rest, numerous as the stars above the endless city.

—Teju Cole, "One Night in Lasgidi"

So overdetermined is the nature of this sign [of Africa epitomizing the intractable, the mute, the abject, or the other-worldly] that it sometimes seems almost impossible to crack, to throw it open to the full spectrum of meanings and implications that other places and other human experiences enjoy, provoke, and inhabit.

—Achille Mbembe and Sarah Nuttall, "Writing the World from an African Metropolis"

Riding through Lagos—speeding over the sleeping lagoon on the Third Mainland Bridge or inching down clogged commercial streets during a rush-hour rainstorm—brings shelters of countless styles and states of repair into sight. These are the structures twenty-some-million Lagosians call home. Some glimmer over gates and walls studded with broken glass. Others are architecturally eccentric gems coated with pollution and grime. Many provide inadequate shelter, exposing tenants to flooding, forceful evictions, and other threats of violence. Yet together they form the moorings and pilings of a city built on a sandbank half-submerged into the Atlantic, a city that has flourished for hundreds of years and grown ferociously in the past fifty. Across Lagos's history, houses have had many meanings and assumed innumerable forms, but they have always held a paramount place in the city, its systems of value, and its residents' visions for the future.

Seven photographs I took between 2014 and 2017 convey a sense of the homes that make up the city's landscapes, the upheavals they have undergone, and the histories they hold. These photos can be seen in figure I.1. At top left in this figure, nestled near the front gates of the University of Lagos, is the compound of a local *baálẹ* (neighborhood chief). It is a cement and iron structure wrapped around a communal patio with architectural roots going back to when Lagos was called Èkó (thought to mean "farm" or "war-camp," depending on the Awori or Edo interpretation). Many of its denizens still use the term.[1] In the courtyard, children play, women cook, and in a nearby room the baálẹ greets and assists his constituents. Banners on the front of the house welcome visitors "to the palace of baale, Abule-Oja [the neighborhood], Chief M.K.I. Adedeji Balogun-Eletu."

Down the road in Yaba stands an Afro-Brazilian bungalow built in the 1920s or 1930s, a time when Lagos stretched into the mainland and British officials decreed a settlement there for the overspill. The front of the home operates as a small shop, advertising Coca-Cola to accompany the hot meals prepared by the woman in the blue and yellow dress (*top right*). Inside, rooms radiate from a central passage, like the flow of a Yoruba courtyard. The painted warning "This House Is Not 4 Sale: Beware of 419" is everywhere in Lagos, a necessity in a housing market fraught with homeownership scams.

Continuing east and crossing the Third Mainland Bridge, the longest bridge in sub-Saharan Africa, brings the city's famous water-straddling community, Makoko, into view (*second row left*). As many as one hundred thousand people call Makoko home, but they and other waterfront "slum dwellers" are constantly under threat of expulsion by Lagos State security forces backed by powerful landowning families that make claims under both customary and statutory laws. Families in Makoko live in single-room homes constructed of wooden planks milled from logs floated into the lagoon from up-country.

FIGURE I.1. From top, left to right: Chief Balogun-Eletu's compound; an Afro-Brazilian bungalow in Yaba; Makoko from the Third Mainland Bridge; "face-me-I-face-you" tenements; "I-face" low-rise with laundry drying; view of Lagos Island's skyline from Dolphin Estate in Ikoyi. Author's photographs.

4   WATERHOUSES

Back on land, traffic slows in Isale Eko (the base of Lagos), one of the oldest settlements on the city's central island and one of the densest commercial hubs in West Africa. Compacting the sides of the narrow streets are apartment buildings nicknamed "face-me-I-face-you" for their symmetrical layouts along central hallways (*second row right*). These utilitarian structures are a large part of how Lagos accommodates its millions. Made popular as the population soared in the 1960s and 1970s, they were economical for landlords to build and comfortable enough for families who expected both privacy and an outdoor space (the balconies) for cooking and doing laundry.

Passing eastward into the formerly segregated colonial reserve, Ikoyi, lots become larger. Rows of "face-me" tenements in eastern Ikoyi date to the postcolonial government's attempt to increase the housing stock, often replicating colonial patterns of elite privilege and "slum clearance." Longtime residents were pushed out while replacement stock was funneled to the well connected. These "Jakande houses" (named after the Lagos State governor who commissioned them) remain some of the only semi-affordable housing in the most expensive area of Lagos (*third row left*). They are anomalies amid the walled mansions of the wealthiest Lagosians (*third row right*).

Exiting the islands and following new money eastward down Lekki Peninsula, traffic bottlenecks as vehicles converge onto a congested highway. Victoria Garden City offers a taste of suburban tranquility for Lagosians willing to spend hours commuting (fig. I.2). The residents of these homes employ houseboys and housegirls who live in tiny guard shelters, sleep on kitchen floor, or commute from precarious accommodations in surrounding "shadow" settlements.[2]

Crossing the city by car means constantly confronting Lagos's immensity and commotion. It can take an entire day of stops and starts to navigate the city's sixty-mile coastline from Lekki in the east to Badagry in the west and nearly as long south from the Atlantic to the Ogun River that feeds the lagoon in the north. Along the way, buildings, homes, and people can be swallowed by the scale of humming settlements sprawled across a seemingly endless patchwork of lagoons, estuaries, peninsulas, and islands.

Lagos's coils of packed and ceaselessly flat streets have bewildered Europeans for centuries. Their complaints and epithets about the city have appeared in countless publications.[3] Finding one's bearing in Lagos

Introduction

FIGURE I.2. Estate in Victoria Garden City, Lekki, 2016. Author's photograph.

has long challenged outsiders. European surveyors struggled to arrive at a geographic sense and take precise measurements (which requires elevation) of a town at sea level. The British midcentury modernist Maxwell Fry perceived a stagnant landscape that had "slumbered on for centuries" like a hardened crust needing to be broken off and replaced carte blanche. In the twenty-first century, the Dutch architect Rem Koolhaas provoked unending controversy when he turned his attention to Lagos and called its neighborhoods "giant rubbish heaps" before retreating to a helicopter tour to gaze beyond his street-level perception of "apocalyptic violence."[4] Such visual and temporal myopia has shaped how Lagos has been seen and the interventions it has undergone. The intensity and apparent inscrutability of Lagos's landscapes have been both celebrated and feared, but they have not stopped observers from working backward to find an explanation for what they assumed they saw and to develop—through the city's historical power imbalances between Europeans and Africans and between elites and the masses—influential plans for the place they wanted Lagos to become.[5]

It can take an effort to avoid this kind of impressionistic and prescriptive reflex and instead to picture—going slowly like the city's traffic, street by street and house by house—Lagos as a place, like cities everywhere, made up of people moving, working, exchanging a few words on a stoop, laughing, reminiscing, enjoying a bowl of *garri* or pepper soup, worshipping, and resting. Somewhere between the city's landscapes and these everyday places is the movement of history: the space between how Lagos has been seen, imagined, explained, and plotted over and the smaller, more intimate local and domestic spaces—like the unremarkable houses in my photographs—through which Lagosians have built the city and kept it moving. How do historians distill and describe this nondimensional "third space," as some urbanists have articulated it, where history unfolds in "the ongoing negotiation between . . . what is and what could be"?[6]

Much of the literature on Lagos—and recent studies of African cities generally[7]—has explored the place of movement and interchange in the production of the city. In its crudest and most common form, this motion is written about as "chaos," "anarchy," and "disorder." While often under the spell of Lagos's energy, these perplexed observers perceive the city's flows of movement as irrational and frame Lagos and other African cities as "*apart from the world,* or as a failed or incomplete example of something else."[8]

More nuanced studies overturn these assumptions about Africa and see African metropolises not as aberrations but as world metropolises with sophisticated actors and complex layers of cultures, aesthetics, and meanings that make up their "citiness."[9] The photographs I took of Lagos homes were taken from the street—a privileged vantage point for thinking about both everyday spatial practices in Lagos and the larger historical flows of people, ideas, and capital behind the growth and power of the city as a port of exchange and circulation. Daniel Agbiboa's work on social mobility and the "production of security and insecurity" in Lagos shows how road checkpoints are connected to the political bosses who control and benefit from the money extorted from motorists.[10] Historian Ayodeji Olukoju and others have examined Lagos's circulatory infrastructures, with its ports, markets, railways, bridges, buses, and tramways, and how the city's development has been inextricable from its macro-economic node as a transportation hub undergirding an entrepôt economy.[11] Looking farther back, Kristin Mann has shown how Lagos's nineteenth-century rise from relative obscurity was tied to its exploitation as one of the last remaining points of exchange of enslaved people between West Africa and the Atlantic World.

Introduction

She traces how systems of bondage were reworked as the port became a colonial depot and profitable palm oil market. Mann's *Slavery and the Birth of an African City* is the history of the city's human infrastructures and the instrumentalization of its labor.[12] The messy struggles over how it was arranged, exploited, resisted, and put into productive motion to serve accumulation by elites laid the foundations for the city's expansion, inequalities, and global importance.

In organicist and cybernetic analogies of urbanism, transportation routes and other infrastructures of movement and production are cities' arteries—their lifeblood and energy. However, during my stays with two generous and protective octogenarian Lagosians, our conversations often turned to ostensibly static places, particularly houses and their ownership, exorbitant costs, security, and supply shortages.[13] Like Agbiboa's checkpoints, homes are discontinuities—spaces that disrupt and redirect flows of movement. They also provide respite from those flows. Like many Lagosians, I spent much of my time in the city's homes, visiting, waiting for traffic to calm, enjoying a meal, meeting contacts, or catching my breath after a long day navigating the city. If Lagos is a body, its heart is its houses, which pump, drive its movement, and hold the warmth and affections that can be difficult to see in the bustling streets. Lagosians spend so much time in traffic because they are trying to get home, to someone else's house, or to places of work that may lead them to secure decent housing and the accompanying prospects for respect, family, and future. Yet most studies of Lagos only mention houses in passing, and even then they are either relegated to the background or placed into typologies that my photographs could simply fall into: "Yoruba compound," "Afro-Brazilian bungalow," "face-me tenement," or "detached new construction." Despite being an omnipresent and cherished part of the city's fabric, houses are frozen while so much of the Lagos literature focuses on movement and change.

This book places houses in historical motion with the city's histories and its shifting landscapes. One way to bring houses and the city's spaces and pasts together to reveal historical processes is through mapping. Photographs of homes and even descriptions and stories about them can be matched to coordinate systems and placed on geographic representations that show transportation networks, neighborhoods, ecologies, businesses, and even people's names. This would be simple enough to do for my photographs by adding digital layers of historical maps and photographs, revealing a history. With the Harvard Design Studio, my early attempts to understand Lagos involved creating a spatiotemporal timeline of the city by combining scanned historical maps, photographs of buildings and landscapes, and digitized renderings to see how its footprint had changed over time.[14]

But a problem emerges in these types of projects when they are not combined with critical history: images like the photographs I took can render a vivid sampling of the compositions, colors, and textures of Lagos homes and their visual changes over time, but alone they are merely phenomena. They are physical facades, which, like human faces, often reveal as much about what the viewer or society imposes on the image as it does about the place or person.[15] The problem is amplified at the scale of the city—landscapes speed up our optical processing of a place, its peoples, and its histories but can be easily manipulated through (sub)conscious choices in visual scapes and cartographic representations to evoke awe, romanticism, or revulsion.

In their study of Johannesburg, Achille Mbembe and Sarah Nuttall warn "of the limits of classical theories of the metropolis, which hold that the most revelatory facets of modern metropolitan life lie on the *surface*, in the ephemeral and the visible."[16] *Looking*—that is, reading surfaces—has been the preferred urbanist method since writers began wandering Paris and London while searching for what metropolises could reveal about society and how its condition might be improved. When critiques have been leveled against "high modernists" or "states" seeing from above or looking with too wide an aperture at city forms, the urbanists' reflex is to redouble efforts to examine from the street level. However, there are limits to this in Lagos. Without residents' perspectives of the places being perceived and of their meanings, and without an exploration of how facades are not always representations of reality, even street-level surfaces can become houses of mirrors reflecting back the viewer's assumptions about a place. Outsiders, especially Europeans aiming to exploit and impose colonial control, have for centuries inscribed African urban spaces and aesthetics with alterity, linking them with semiotic meanings meant to devalue and thereby justify European confiscation and control over them.[17] This "surface" reading of the city that Mbembe and Nuttall describe was practiced over a century of

Introduction

colonial rule in Lagos, where appearances—how African landscapes and dwellings looked and were made to appear through the European lens—were privileged over African forms of cosmopolitanism. Yet because of these imperial and Western perceptions and reproductions of urban landscapes, there are troves of visual sources—maps, buildings plans, and photographs—across Lagos's history. The challenge of this book has been to examine these records from a different perspective, to engage visual archives in ways not originally envisioned.

In seeking the elusive and ignored personas of Johannesburg, Mbembe and Nuttall cite David Pike in suggesting that "there is no surface without an underground." They argue that, indeed, "one of the characteristic features of a metropolis is an *underneath*." In Johannesburg this imagery alludes to its mining origins and the "subterranean" classes who pulled the ore out of the earth, the historically repressed "buried life of the black body."[18] In Lagos, *underneath* is also *around*: creeks, floodplains, lagoons, and undertows—the soup Lagos is sunk in—and the marginalized peoples these waters sustained: characters like Wole Soyinka's "swamp dwellers." Historically and still today, these layers and lairs of Lagos have been written off as rural anachronisms or impediments to the city's development. They have been seen as spaces to be tamed to produce a sufficiently urban and modern landscape.[19] Visual archives have documented these places on maps, panoramic photographs, and reports, but have framed them in ways that silence and speak for them. By rereading these images from new angles and alongside diverse historical sources, a wider and deeper story of Lagos's homes starts to surface, one that captures houses as more than just shelter or financial instruments and begins to see them in all their human meanings, uses, and forms.

Cities today will continue to be mediated, evaluated, and judged by their appearance. In trying to see old archives in new ways, this book suggests how we might explore the fullness of the meanings of Lagos's houses in ways that reveal how they—through all their changing forms and all the shifting historical perceptions of them—have animated the city.

A Megalopolis of Houses and Water

This book is about the places the people of Lagos have inhabited, imagined, and made home for the past two centuries. It asks what a house in Lagos is and explores how the answer to that question has been historically constructed and reconstructed in tandem with the city's urban landscapes.

The title is taken from Antonio Olinto's classic 1970 novel, *The Water House*, based on a real nineteenth-century Afro-Brazilian home in the heart of Lagos.[20] Olinto's account describes the reintegration of a formerly enslaved family that has returned from across the ocean to find in the emerging Black cosmopolitanism of Lagos (before it was amalgamated with the rest of British Nigeria) a world transformed yet still familiar to the one the family's matriarch was taken from years before. After struggling and renting, the family is inspired to seek out a loan to purchase the house and to dig a well in the property's yard to sell fresh water to the neighborhood. The business thrives, and the family invests in a furniture shop to outfit the fashionable hybrid-style homes sprouting above the hustle of the port's crowded streets. In the house's name and story, so much of Lagos's history is encapsulated—Africa's great city on a sandbar is a place made from the alchemy of water and houses, their enduring cultural significance, constant proximity, gradual commercialization, and the human struggles to gain a hold over them that constantly made and remade the city's urban landscape.

My central argument in *Waterhouses* is that in the coastlands from which Lagos rose, housing architectures were the single most important social, material, and political instrument for people hoping to contour the city's landscapes—both its ecology and its image—and its historical course. As a result of housing's significance, the meanings and forms of houses in Lagos have shifted dramatically over time and in ways that reveal how power, house-making, visual perception, and environment are entangled in modern cities.

As its Portuguese name implies, Lagos ("lakes") is a city built on, in, and around water: the riverine trading networks that gave rise to its original African polity; the Atlantic that brought slavers and eventually returnees; the shipping canals dredged to drain the resources from British Nigeria; and the marshes that, like the city's African residents, were maligned and misunderstood by European planners—yet kept the city afloat. The historical currents of Nigeria and West Africa are found in Lagos's waterways and in what inhabitants envisioned they could give rise to. This book's chapters tell this story across six eras and through the six waterscapes that flowed through them: sandbars, canals, swamps,

Introduction

lagoons, oceans, and floods. These spaces guide the book's exploration of how people saw and attempted to remake Lagos's environs in a process that invariably involved housing architectures.

Amid the ebbs and flows of water and the mercurial tides of commerce it carried, houses have been the bedrock of Lagos. At its human core, Lagos is a city built through the materials, relations, and powers contained in the dry, solid, and hospitable spaces of homes, which have long been scarce and culturally celebrated resources in the city's water-constricted setting. While sheltering and sustaining people is integral to any city's development, houses have been particularly important and sought after in Lagos because of the city's land shortages and because of the societal influence and physical footprint of traditional Yoruba *ilé* (family compounds) in which all activities—from production to politics to social reproduction—were historically organized and centered. As Akinwumi Ogundiran writes in *The Yorùbá: A New History*, "More than any other social attribute, the *ilé* (House) [has formed] the primary basis of Yorùbá social organization and the fulcrum of its social reproduction."[21] When British administrators arrived in the Bight of Benin, they in turn viewed houses as essential technologies to keep Europeans alive amid tropical disease and to position them in exclusive positions of power above their African subjects. In Lagos it has been through real estate, especially housing stock, that both individual strategies to belong and to get ahead as well as political calculations for control over the city's populations have run. For this reason, ideas and forms of urban dwelling in Lagos underwent a quick succession of changes as political, legal, and economic systems and possibilities shifted and were imposed over the century covered in this book. From waterfront Afro-Brazilian mansions that could be replastered annually with the season's most fashionable patterns from around the Atlantic, to rows of postcolonial apartment blocks that adapted the spatial sensibilities of vernacular compounds, the homes of Lagos have included a brilliant—if bewildering—diversity of structures and housing estates.

Through dozens of maps, photographs, and housing plans found in the British and Nigerian archives, this book traces the relationship between Lagos's residential spaces and its urban landscapes across the rise, fall, and aftermath of British colonization. These sources illuminate how British officials learned to use housing plans to tighten their control over land, labor, and status and to bend society and ecology toward colonial ideals of what a city should look like, repeatedly stressing visual appearances over historical or actual field inquiry. But these superficial Eurocentric readings of the city's landscapes often clashed with its environmental realities and the ways African residents experienced and imagined the city's relations and functioning. In examining visual sources "against the grain" in counterintuitive and careful ways, the book reveals how the city's African quarters used homes to claim a place in Lagos and to resist displacement and expropriation. Likewise, it shows how African political figures used housing to expose injustice and hypocrisy in segregation and clearance plans. The struggles in Lagos over Nigeria's independence reached a crescendo when thousands of women marched in protest of plans to raze the city's old central neighborhoods and replace them with a modernist skyline—and to move the residents into replacement housing on the outskirts of the city. The power of housing architectures—the histories and the people they would hold and privilege and the role they would have in physically and ideologically configuring the postcolonial city—were clear to all when Nigeria gained its independence in 1960.

In postcolonial Lagos, housing only grew in importance as landlord-tenant patronage relationships structured and sustained everyday life while a succession of military dictatorships neglected the booming city's municipal functions. These relationships and the city's exponential population growth increased the value of homes. Houses have become financial instruments used to park and launder cash in Nigeria's "vampire" economy of elites funneling off petroleum rents. Despite court injunctions, housing estates with centuries of history and community are again being demolished and their residents pushed out to make way for fortresslike mansions monstrously disconnected from social and civic life. These forced evictions and a dire shortage of affordable housing are pushing long-term residents and newcomers alike into the rising waters around the city.

Conflicts over how to view and inhabit Lagos's watery landscape, questions about who could dwell in the city, and the resulting schemes, razings, and hybrid housing forms combined to create Lagos's current conditions. These processes are one of the critical historical forces for understanding the city—its buoyant vibrancy and its two-headed problem of housing shortages and rising seas—today. By showing how African

Introduction

visions of "home"—though often forgotten or misunderstood today—coexisted with European notions, this book offers ideas about how the definingly human act of inhabiting a place might be regrounded in practices of continuous custodianship rather than extractive possession.

More has been written about Lagos than perhaps any other West African city. This body of excellent scholarship provides the historical context and framing needed to tell a *longue durée* story that—through new and underutilized visual sources—threads together a history of Lagos across the waterways and houses that connect the city's eras. By bringing houses and landscapes to the fore and exploring how people saw and strategized over their production and place in the city, a comprehensive history of Lagos takes shape, which, while providing a temporal throughline, leaves room to understand the peculiarities and fissures between the city's various eras. This book illustrates how Lagos's houses—through their scale-crossing and sociomaterial constructions as homes and housing—have been a hinge for tracing these historical and political processes.

The House and the Housing Question in African History

In his global history of bungalows, Anthony King writes, "The design of dwellings, the materials and manner of their construction, their size and contents, and their arrangement in settlements are perhaps the most visible signs of any civilisation and culture."[22] King is remarking on something universal: that societies, families, and individuals, whether subtly or forcefully, show what they value, how they think, and how they organize through the places in which they live. Whether singular homes or entire settlements, houses are visible signs of what matters to people and who has power to make that declaration.

What King leaves unpacked is how the reading of houses as signs has been profoundly skewed toward a kind of seeing evoked by his use of the word *civilization*. The concept of a world made up of developed or modern "civilizations" and less-developed or traditional "cultures" reflects a deeply held assumption of a historical timeline in which there are progressive stages of building and house-making. The conventional if unsaid supposition in works like King's is that societies naturally, and therefore rightly, strive to build more spacious, durable, landscape-altering, and visually striking abodes as they accumulate agricultural surpluses, engage in trade, devise occupational specializations, and increase in sociopolitical stratification and advance toward the "civilization" end of the spectrum. These views of architecture as signs of advancement are the lenses through which influential (mostly Western) theorists and decision-makers have for centuries evaluated dwellings and the people who built them.

No way of seeing—other than racist perceptions of skin tone—I suggest, has been more detrimental to the modern history of the African continent and to our understanding of it. Universalist theories of civilization's preset order and progression, whether eighteenth-century ideas of a great chain of being, nineteenth-century evolutionist views of racial orders, or twentieth-century modernization metanarratives, have devised hierarchies of houses and landscapes corresponding to perceived hierarchies of civilization.[23] Dwelling categories such as "huts," "hovels," "rattraps," "shacks," "shanties," "slums," and "ghettos" have served as the euphemisms for "primitive," "non-White," and "undeveloped" peoples. Terms like "mud hut," so thoroughly associated with popular images of the African continent, have been used to signify dwellings presumed to be so basic as to be ahistorical—providing little more than the shelter that prehistoric man would have used to avoid the elements—and home to people who are presumably nonhistorical actors who can easily be dismissed.[24]

Paintings, maps, photographs, and travelers' descriptions of non-Western houses and landscapes as primitive and stagnant underwrote colonial claims to occupy and administer foreign lands.[25] They served as the "visible proof" that non-White peoples were not only less advanced but were actually "stuck" and required European intervention and direction. Recycled images and descriptions of African "huts" and "bush" were the groundwork for each iteration of imperialism: views of African dwellings at the bottom of or even outside history helped establish legal concepts such as "terra nullius" (land unoccupied and thus there for the taking) at the time of the Berlin Conference; views of African neighborhoods as epidemiologically and socially unsanitary enabled widespread residential segregation schemes and pass systems during the interwar era; and views of African countries as helplessly rural helped market a push to intensify colonial oversight premised on lending expertise for urbanization and development of African countries after the Second World War.

Creating and circulating a view of African housing as backward, rural, and undeveloped devalued Africans' ways of dwelling and justified taking dominion over their lands and settlements. Descriptions like those made by a European visitor of Lagos as a "filthy, disgusting, savage place" with hundreds of "huts" making up "wretched native tenements" legitimized naval bombardment (1851) and rebuilding according to British building codes.

This pattern recurred throughout Africa as European armies and administrators seized, occupied, and overturned existing landscapes. In 1897, frustrated that the ọba (king) of Benin refused to cede his trade monopoly, British officials sent soldiers several hundred miles to the northeast of Lagos to sack Benin City. During the invasion, they looted the city, including its famous Benin bronzes. We now know that Benin was likely larger than Lisbon, built over centuries on an intricate design based on sophisticated mathematical principles, and home to some of the world's most stunning works of art. However, beginning in the early 1890s British photographers had begun producing images that, according to the art historian Christraud M. Geary, "created a myth about Benin as a degraded, wretched country, where human sacrifice was rampant and horrors abounded." Images in a popular book about Benin showed "a crucifixion tree," where criminals were impaled, and "a juju altar in the king's compound."[26] These portrayals of Benin's landscapes and domestic spaces helped to justify military orders to raze the city and claim it as British territory, erasing evidence of a place and people contrary to those depicted in popular lore.

Hierarchies of houses and landscapes have persisted even as "the rise of civilization" narrative has been intellectually dismantled as imperialist cheerleading in the past fifty years.[27] Views of Africa's contemporary and historical cities and landscapes as lacking, undeveloped, stunted, and *urbanizing*—not urbanized—also persist. Norbert Schoenauer's still widely cited *6,000 Years of Housing*, first published in 1981 (and most recently published in 2003), traces a linear evolution of housing from preurban (ephemeral, episodic, periodic, seasonal, and semipermanent) dwellings to urbanized permanent ones.[28] Perspectives like these that fail to consider other trajectories of housing or African houses on their own terms offer little actual information about the continent's cities, their inhabitants, or their architecture.

If much of the inherited views of African housing is the residue of European projections and colonial campaigns to devalue foreign lands, what is actually known about African houses and their histories? Knowledge of African houses is scattered throughout several academic fields, including architecture, landscape architecture, urban planning, and the social sciences.[29] The following two sections review the historiography and insights of these bodies of literature.

The Housing Question

The older and much larger body of academic literature concerns what Frederick Engels termed "the housing question" in 1872.[30] Housing—used as a gerund for the process of how society produces and organizes shelter—has become a well-researched quantitative topic for planners, geographers, and political scientists. Scholars in this tradition have grappled with vexing questions: How should shelter be provided and distributed within a society? Who or what entity should own land and the buildings on it in which people reside? What form should a household's composition take, and what are its members' individual and collective prerogatives and obligations? How should land acquisition and the construction of houses be financed, and how should materials and designs be regulated? What responsibilities does a society or a city have to people who find themselves homeless or unable to afford housing?

These are difficult questions, as shelter is a basic need that is spatially scarce in a way that other necessities are not. While water, food, electricity, and other supplies can be shipped, wired, or piped into cities, square footage is finite, increasable only by building out, up, and down. Engels noted that housing's tie to economic class creates unintended consequences to many well-intentioned housing solutions that seek to transfer property rights to precariously housed people.[31] Yet the scale of the world's housing shortage today means there is a pressing need for instrumentalist literature to inform policy, even if it is imperfect. Over five million households in Lagos alone lack adequate shelter.[32] Without stable and secure homes, these households struggle to survive, and their life outcomes are threatened. This dire challenge affects not just rapidly urbanizing parts of Africa but overcrowded and growing urban centers around the world.[33]

While housing studies has no perfect solutions, the literature has been characterized by a narrow frame of inquiry—especially in

Introduction   17

geographic contexts like African cities. Housing studies, like the literature on African cities more generally, as Mbembe and Nuttall write, has shown a "lack of comparative depth, the paucity of its theoretical reach, and its overall dependence on political economy."[34] A lack of historical context could be added to this list. Each chapter in this book discusses the housing literature that informed how Lagos's settlements were viewed, reimagined, and regulated in each era of the city's history. Until the occasional sociological study in the 1950s began to describe a more nuanced and complex picture of African houses and housing needs, the majority of housing literature treated Africa's homes as unsanitary, outdated, and structurally unsound—and deserving of being razed and rebuilt. The perceived problem that African housing needed to be completely reformulated was rarely questioned by leading academics before the 1950s. According to the studies that shaped the opinions of generations of colonial policymakers, nothing was to be learned from looking at African dwellings. Over time, plans to remake African housing progressed in tandem with imperial power. In Britain's African colonies, plans expanded in ambition from regulation to segregation to clearance and reconstruction. Absent from these stages was any historical evaluation of the previous era's assumptions and schemes.

In the decades after colonial rule, housing literature boomed as demand for living space in urban settings soared. The focus of housing studies changed from clearance and master planning to more localized approaches that limited displacement: the shift from "supply to support" in housing theory and praxis.[35] Yet it remained predominantly technical and concerned with appraising existing housing and devising programs to replace or upgrade it from "informal" to "formal." Many of these studies did privilege the place of residents' perspectives and preferences through participatory approaches, collecting and analyzing the views of African dwellers through surveys. Yet then and today, this housing literature rarely cites or engages the historiography of the field or the history of houses in Africa. Housing studies often present the issues they are surveying, such as in a recent study of displacement in Kigali, as resulting from the "novelty of urban space transformations in Sub-Saharan African countries" as "many old inner-city neighbourhoods are being demolished to give way to modern commercial and residential developments, and generally, to a more modern living environment."[36]

These trends are centuries long, yet subscribers to journals like *Habitat* would not know it from the articles that assume Africa has been predominantly rural and thus "premodern" until recently. The conclusion of this book engages some of the more imaginative and provocative housing literature that has reevaluated the place of housing in traditional political economy models as the global housing shortage becomes more pronounced and as prescriptions to create secure housing stock continue to falter.

The House and African Urban Landscapes

It is not surprising that most housing studies stick to tightly designed evaluations, surveys, and the present moment. Contemplating the historical and metaphysical relationship between houses and humanity can raise daunting questions. Wondering about humanity's dwellings can lead to Heidegger and essential if often semi-unintelligible considerations of "being" and human experience.[37] Yet these intellectual paths—often much less tethered to theories of teleological trajectories for humankind—can provoke reevaluations of widespread assumptions about houses and housing. Why and when did humans begin building houses? How have humans altered their abodes over time, and how have homes in turn affected humanity? Likewise, how have these familial vessels influenced the relationship between humanity, the concept of time, and the surrounding ecosphere? These questions push us to examine messy historical spaces and processes and the possibilities they can suggest for the future. Thinking through these issues might be more than is required for a family looking for a solid roof and running water, even if these questions are relevant to the larger societal and aesthetic questions of how housing is organized, delivered, and inhabited. Considering how closely the popular image of Africa is tied to its housing landscapes, dismayingly little attention has been given to African houses on these questions. Likewise, precisely because of the perception of a rural continent without anything approaching "Architecture," there has been a dearth of research in African studies on the continent's houses despite the field's central themes of kinship, wealth in people, and security. There is, however, a small but important body of house studies in Africa, and recent scholarship is starting to expand our ways of seeing African houses and landscapes—and their deep histories.

Introduction

Before the founding of the field of African studies in the 1950s, few writers looked with interest at the design of the continent's homes, with two notable exceptions: Samuel Johnson and Leo Frobenius in southwest Nigeria. Johnson was a Yoruba historian and preacher who spent the last decades of the nineteenth century researching and writing *The History of the Yorubas from the Earliest Times to the Beginning of the British Protectorate*. The manuscript was mysteriously lost by its London publishers in 1899, but a version reconstructed by Johnson's brother from notes and drafts was published in 1921. The book's short sixth chapter, "Yoruba Towns and Villages," sketches a picture of the cities of Yoruba country and their structures, laying out both a model of Yoruba urbanism ("All Yoruba towns with very few exceptions are built on a uniform plan") and a process for its formation ("As soon as houses begin to spring up and a village or hamlet formed, the necessity for order and control becomes apparent. The men would thereupon assemble at the gate of the principle [*sic*] man who has attracted people to the place and formally recognize him as the Bale [baálẹ]").[38] The landscapes Johnson painted bore little to no resemblance to the places that had been described for decades by European agents and travelers. Dying in 1901, Johnson never saw his project come to fruition, but he had launched one of the first pieces of international literature to treat African cities and housing as places of order, historical processes, and ingenuity. The publishing delay allowed a European to beat him to sharing glimpses of Yorubaland's urban histories and landscapes with the wider world.

When the famous German ethnologist Leo Frobenius traveled to the Colony and Protectorate of Southern Nigeria in 1910, he visited a shrine to the Yoruba deity Shango in the city of Ibadan. He wrote, "[The] originality of the building ... struck me dumb."[39] When describing urbanism and houses in Yoruba-speaking areas, he marveled that

> nature has smiled upon Yorubaland. . . . The clustering of houses form the cities, which are built amidst Nature's fairest pictures. . . . The city population . . . is counted in hundreds of thousands and millions of heads. . . . Cities, which in the sense we, too, give to the term, deserve to be called "metropolitan." . . . Every one of these towns resolves itself into a definite number of astonishingly large compounds, all of which are severally built on a clearly organized system and in themselves

again give expression to an extended, powerful, systematic and social ideal. Each city has its own special divinity, and every compound within it has its own particular God.[40]

Frobenius was particularly struck by Yoruba houses and saw them as signs of a sophisticated society, commenting, "[It] is a self-evident proposition that a nation ruled by such a remarkable religion and philosophy ... should show some individual symptoms in the forms of its housing arrangements," and going on to closely describe the features of Yoruba compounds:

> Every Yoruban compound is surrounded by a great wall, to which all kinds of edifices, in the shape of elongated chambers, are attached inside, but in its centre there is before all other things a double-fronted chief edifice. All the dwelling-rooms really consist of long clay boxes. Every separate apartment is ceiled with rafters and covered with beaten clay. Over this cover there is the mighty saddle-back roof made of poles and foliage, which drops far beyond the walls and is supported by posts. This makes a veranda, through which one must go to get to the actual rooms.... But the relation of the roof—timber covering the clay box-buildings—to the edifice in the middle, is very singular. This always has two little yards next to each other at right angles to the surrounding buildings. Those parts of the roof which overhang this part of the building form galleries and two water-sheds inwards. These rain-collecting constructions ... are the main feature and characteristic of the Yoruban style.[41]

So awed was Frobenius by Yorubaland's architecture, culture, and art that he described it as a civilization. This was a radical statement at a time when European claims to colonize Africa rested on the supposed absence of anything approaching civilization. Most European travel writers dismissed African shrines and shelters—such as in the widely circulated works on Benin City—with terms like "juju," "rubbish," and "fetish." Frobenius resolved the incongruity between what he saw and the assumed status of Africans by devising a theory attributing Yorubaland's "civilized" features to the residue of an ancient Phoenician settlement that he claimed once existed in southwest Nigeria. Describing Yorubaland as

Introduction 21

the lost Atlantis, Frobenius went to great length to trace a connection between its style and religion to a branch of the Caucasian race while making clear that by 1910 it had "retrogressed" to the "miserable level it occupies now."[42] He concluded, the "culture of Yoruba is the crystallization of that mighty stream of Western civilization which, in its Eur-African form, flowed from Europe into Africa, and, when it sank in volume, left behind it the Etruscans as its cognate and equally symphonic exponents."[43]

For Frobenius, water-collecting "impluvia" courtyards were the defining feature of Yoruba houses and the first piece of evidence he cited for his claim of an Etruscan connection in the volume's final chapter, "Atlantis." The water systems reminded him of those found in Moroccan and Algerian homes, and he concluded that their presence in Yoruba houses must have been the result of an ancient Phoenician imprint. In the end, rather than conveying dignity and respect, Frobenius's view of Yorubaland reinforced colonial claims by contending that an ancient Europeanized settlement had lit a civilizing ember in southwest Nigeria—one that could be rekindled by colonial settlement.

Johnson, Frobenius, and countless other observers of nineteenth- and early twentieth-century Africa were influenced by what became known as the "Hamitic hypothesis." This line of thinking had many iterations but was bound together by a quest for European origins for anything of value in Africa.[44] Foremost among these assuredly Caucasian residues that Hamitic hypothesizers accounted for were monumental architectures and prosperous cities. The stone walls and towns of Zimbabwe and Mombasa, the hilltop capital and palaces of Buganda and Rwanda, and the walled cities and "astonishingly large compounds" of Yorubaland, Dahomey, Benin, and Asante all had to be traced back to White protagonists, otherwise the colonial promise of (re)civilizing the continent crumbled. African scholars, especially the educated elite in late nineteenth-century Yorubaland like Samuel Johnson (who saw Yoruba cities as Mecca-inspired), adapted these theories, seeing them as routes to connect their heritage and culture to the grandeur of Egypt and the status of religious centers In the Middle East.[45]

By the 1950s the Hamitic hypothesis was out of favor as colonized people challenged its grotesque caricature of African history and as imperial powers sought to stave off independence movements by casting colonialism as a "partnership." At this point, housing studies on the continent conveniently turned away from history and focused on the proclaimed urgent need to create urbanized African abodes for modern workers. Ironically, the image of Africans drowsily dwelling in frozen-in-time rural huts was as strong as ever in the final decades of colonialism. This image both stirred a postwar European nostalgia for a lost preindustrial pastoralism and was used to induce a sense of anxiety in African subjects as to whether they were capable of building and inhabiting great First World cities and nations. Early African anthropologists reified this image, almost exclusively studying a romanticized sliver of African cultures in the countryside. When midcentury scholars looked at cities in Africa, they were not anthropologists studying humans in their natural environments but sociologists seeing through the lenses of urbanization and adaptation, which was assumed to be necessary for Africans to adjust to urban homes and lifestyles.[46]

During this era, a subfield of sociology sprang up to debate Yoruba urbanism. Like Frobenius, writers in the field viewed Yorubaland's dense and visually prominent habitation patterns as a problem to be solved. Southwest Nigeria's housing structures and their socioeconomic patterns—the "devious nature of Yoruba cities," as one sociologist called it[47]—were a source of puzzlement for these midcentury observers. The landscapes and structures they saw and measured were inconsistent with prevailing models of urbanization. They pointed to family compounds that dominated urban landscapes in southwest Nigeria and to the close connections their members kept to the countryside (where families often had farmhouses) as evidence that Yorubaland had no actual cities or, more charitably, that Yoruba urbanism "represent[ed] a relatively early developmental phase of city evolution."[48] Again, African landscapes were cast as behind the curve, relegated to the early stages in a time line to modernization. Places that met the criteria for "cities," declared these sociologists, were not organized by kin-groups (corporate descent groups), and city slickers did not keep farms. Time and again, they categorized Yoruba urbanism in terms of what it was not. Few looked carefully at African homes or their designs without reference to their own definitions of urbanization.

Researchers who did study African houses on their own terms found a rich world of creativity and purposeful innovation with people and their agency, visions, and priorities at the center. These scholars saw

Introduction 23

a system of building and dwelling much more suited to Nigerian society than the "purely rational" plans of midcentury architects. Ulli Beier, a folklorist and expert on Yoruba oral traditions and culture, flipped the term that European travel writers were fond of applying to African landscapes, describing the rectangular modernist plans for the University of Ibadan as "frozen" in comparison to Yoruba architecture, the barb being that European society was stuck in its views and its restrictive building structures, while Yorubaland was in motion, adaptive and inventive.[49] Around the same time, a case for the value and suitability of "traditional" African architecture was made by the Egyptian architect Hassan Fathy, who designed the New Gourna housing complex. Fathy criticized the importation of steel, concrete, and modernist aesthetics in the settlements that were being built in Egypt, choosing at New Gourna to fashion rounded homes from clay blocks and to construct a community that was informed through consultations with the future residents.[50] As modernist housing projects faltered in later years, scholars looked to Fathy's work as one of the first bold assertions of the value of closely studying vernacular African architecture, particularly houses and their layers of cultural meanings, as antidotes to the intentional emptiness of modernist spaces.[51]

One of the first widely read theorists to examine the design of African houses and perceive a subject worthy of serious analysis and reflection was Pierre Bourdieu. His 1970 study of Algeria's Kabyle House, coauthored with the Algerian Abdelmalek Sayad, has become a classic structuralist interpretation of the meanings rooted in domestic spaces and of the ways homes can mirror the order and values of their society. Bourdieu and Sayad's study was influential in the historiography of African houses in treating the continent's domestic spaces as complex, symbolic (rather than simply functionalist), and decipherable. As others have noted, the study is influenced by a sense of longing both on the part of Bourdieu and his informants for an agricultural lifestyle that was being lost amid the rapid changes in Algeria.[52] Additionally, Bourdieu read the Berber house as a series of binary oppositions (high/low; light/dark; male/female). This interpretation did not escape the kind of boundary drawing and hierarchizing that European observers had similarly drawn for centuries in making macrocomparisons between European and African dwellings.[53]

In the 1960s, predating Bourdieu's work on the Kabyle House, the Nigerian architectural historian G. J. Afolabi Ojo situated traditional Yoruba compounds within the societies that built them by paying careful attention to their forms and symbolism. Ojo relied on interviews and the descriptions of Johnson and Frobenius to outline the significant architectural features of Yoruba houses. Embedded in his descriptions is a stunning call to see Yoruba houses as commensurate to the famed Ifẹ bronzes:

> The little that is known about Yoruba architecture has tended to make people doubt the originality of Yoruba art itself.... One would have expected that with the sort of simple local materials being used for Yoruba houses, the architecture would have been naive and unworthy of the attention of the art and architectural world. This is not simply because the humanistic, rather than hieratic nature of Yoruba art causes it to seek expression in objects of everyday life, *among which houses are of dominant importance.* Consequently, Yoruba houses have architectural peculiarities which vary in importance depending on the rank or status of the occupants. The house of the ordinary man, a commoner, conforms with the descriptions of Yoruba houses so far given. That of a chief, who is the head of a quarter of the town, possesses additional features such as carved posts, instead of ordinary wooden posts, more than one courtyard, and in a few cases, a background forest. Still higher on the scale is that of an oba (a ruler who wears a beaded crown): his residence is known as an afin, that is, a royal residence or palace. At the apex of the scale is the temple, the residence of an orisa, or deity.[54]

What Ojo was describing is how the architecture of houses served as signposts in Yoruba society. Though he only touched on this point, Ojo offered a glimpse into how built landscapes appeared in southwest Nigeria to those who knew how to look at them.[55]

Ideas of houses reflecting their societies and serving as maps for how to move through the world opened new doors in the understanding of African houses into the 1970s and 1980s. By the early 1980s, Claude Lévi-Strauss had sharpened the structuralist interpretations of houses by describing "house societies": societies organized around belonging to a dwelling rather than a lineage or descent group. His views did not escape

Introduction

an evolutionist timeline, as he placed house societies between "elementary" and "complex" social structures. Drawing on structuralism but more ready to challenge presumed stages of dwelling, architectural scholars had since at least the 1960s taken up "primitive architecture" (non-Western and overlooked everyday structures), recasting it as "vernacular architecture" and interpreting its design and aesthetics as purposeful and expressive rather than rudimental and functional.[56] By the end of the century, vernacular architectural and anthropological studies framed through the theories of Lévi-Strauss, Bourdieu, and others had established houses in Nigeria, Madagascar, Kenya, Ghana, and South Africa as a rich locus for examining social, symbolic, and cosmological structures.[57] However, as Janet Carsten and Stephen Hugh-Jones point out in their 1995 edited volume, *About the House*, much of this work peered inward to the self-contained relationship between houses and their occupants, limiting broader inquiries of house forms as processual and situating them within their shifting political, ecological, and historical surroundings.[58]

Seeing beyond colonial discourses and erecting the intellectual scaffolding to hold up African houses as architecture rather than just shelters was a giant leap in learning how to look perceptively at African landscapes. Moving beyond African houses as stand-alone and static cultural idioms and to perceive the historical motion between them and their environments required an arguably even greater reworking of inherited assumptions about houses, cities, and Africa. Few studies have taken this step, but several stand out for opening up new ways of seeing African houses in relation to their political, ecological, and temporal contexts.

Now well known beyond West Africa, the work of Roderick McIntosh and Susan McIntosh changed the way we think about urbanism. Their archaeological digs at Djenné-Djenno (in present-day Mali) beginning in the 1980s showed how the people of the middle Niger Delta had built a densely populated settlement that spanned more than a millennium starting several hundred years before the current era. The region's riverine lattice of swamps, rivers, channels, and flooding was marked by extreme unpredictability and ecological constraints. Rather than erecting monumental architecture to awe residents into submission and centralizing power in a royal court, the builders of Djenné created clusters of smaller, interconnected settlements made up of specialized guilds of artisans, traders, fishermen, and hunters who collaborated to manage the landscape and coax out a shared livelihood. People in Djenné lived in clay brick homes that were rebuilt over time until their accumulated foundations piled into "tells," mounds six meters high, representing generations of knowledge and stability. That cities could be decentralized, nonhierarchical, and home to the kind of long-term security of tells hinted at not only different trajectories for urbanization outside the primitive-to-civilized model but also of one that offered possibilities for reimagining how contemporary cities could be built and occupied more humanely.

Examining contemporary West African landscapes, architectural historian Suzanne Blier's first book (1987) was a detailed study of Batammaliba houses: clay structures that Frobenius described as "genuinely and rightly small castles" in northern Togo and Benin. Influenced by the linguistic structuralism of Lévi-Strauss, Blier read African buildings as "a kind of text or language system whose meaning can be understood through its orientation, form, materials, construction process, and details."[59] Standing out in her work is the careful documentation of the Batammaliba house "as an active, living, organism."[60] The homes she saw built, dedicated, populated, repaired, and left to ruins shifted in meaning over time and underscored the need to study, as she wrote, "architecture in process."[61] This was a critical intervention and implied that African architecture could be read historically. Going into the countryside was not to go back in time to see "Africa" as it had been centuries before. While Blier's writing on Batammaliba houses recorded these changes as an abstract cyclical process, her later work on Dahomey and West African clay architecture, along with the research of scholars like Steven Nelson and Prita Meier, examined the longer histories of building traditions that had been removed from their historical context and frozen as cultural images.[62] Their research on famous structures, including Teleuk houses of Cameroon and Swahili stone houses, examined how their creators had altered the buildings over time in response to changing sociopolitical pressures. They also traced how the images of these buildings were circulated by postcards and travel brochures as symbols of exotic and unchanging Africa but were adapted by Africans as signs of belonging to international traditions.

Today, the picture of West Africa's historical landscapes is coming into clearer focus thanks in part to the work of scholars imagining where and how people dwelled, what types of structures they built and how people changed those structures over time. Historians are following the

Introduction

lead of archaeologists in seeing these houses as historical sources. This need not be confined to the distant past or to the iconic African houses that anthropologists and art historians have prized. Rather, it can be applied to more mundane and recently built homes in cities and towns.

Archives of Land, Houses, and Scapes

Historians of modern Africa are now using houses as archival sources for understanding how Africans engaged, and often challenged, visions of urban modernity through the politics of house-building and homemaking. The material, memories, and images of where people lived and how they lived in those places are excellent records of historical process: every house is an archive of personal, local, and global changes, of the aspirations and struggles that went into dreams of homeownership, of house design, financing, construction, ritual dedication, actual day-to-day inhabitation, of attempts at eviction or removal, of alteration and appropriation, and of eventual destruction, abandonment, or attempts at preservation.[63] The stages of houses make an enticing archive for the exploration of cities from perspectives that are rarely privileged in official archives.

David Morton's 2019 book, *Age of Concrete: Housing and the Shape of Aspiration in the Capital of Mozambique*, is a pathbreaking use of houses as historical archives.[64] As Morton elegantly describes, "Each neighborhood in Maputo and each yard is a specific place with a specific past. Taken together, the countless gambles, disputes, impositions, half measures, achievements, and failures inscribed on the landscape constitute an enormous, open-air archive."[65] He traces how residents living in *subúrbios* on the margins of Maputo, Mozambique, sought to solidify their place in the city across the three decades since independence (1975) by covertly converting the walls of their homes from dried reeds to concrete blocks, arguing convincingly that "house builders and home dwellers of the subúrbios of Mozambique's capital helped give substance to what governance was and what governance should do."[66] Few historians have treated houses as archives in this way, particularly not in urban Africa. As Morton describes, there are very few reed homes left in Maputo—this disappearance is part of the historical story, which required the use of photographs, plans, and occupants' memories to piece together the past of these impermanent materials and how residents saw and replaced them.

Part of the challenge of undertaking research on houses in a city like Lagos is that very few old homes are still standing in a city that bears little resemblance to what it was 150 years ago. As this book shows, colonial agents in Lagos were thinking about houses and landscapes as holders of history, as historical evidence of colonial malfeasance, and as counterpoints to the claim of a "rural" African past, and were thus razing or carefully altering them, foreshadowing the epistemological urges behind the now infamous written archival erasures that would accompany independence. Examining how the houses of Lagos changed over more than a century of upheaval has required a concerted effort to recover and build a record of older house forms that were forgotten or demolished by urban growth and by colonial and postcolonial schemes.

In the course of several research trips (2014, 2016, and 2017), I gathered dozens of maps and hundreds of photographs (see fig. I.3) to create an archive of Lagos houses and housing. Read alongside secondary sources, primary written sources (including colonial records, newspapers, and reports on housing and urban development), and hundreds of informal oral interviews and conversations, these maps and

FIGURE I.3. Author scanning a 1932 map (after the building's generator was turned on) at the Federal Survey Department, Lagos, 2016. Author's photograph.

Introduction

photographs provide a deeper understanding of the visual and spatial reordering that the houses of Lagos have undergone.

This archive influenced the direction of my project and the ideas I pursued. Working with historical images of Lagos's cartography and visual scapes brought me into engagement with studies of "landscape" and the use of maps and photographs as mediums of landscape. Not only does an archive of maps and photographs recover the surfaces of house forms and their emplacements within the city but it also gives insights into how housing was shaped by the interplay between changing landforms (ecologies, urban plans, and systems of owning and managing space) and scapes (ways of perceiving the city as shaped through the aesthetics and technologies of representation). Reading a landscape archive gradually revealed a historical dynamic between the city's landforms and visual scapes.

The work that most closely theorizes a similar understanding of historical processes is W. J. T. Mitchell's landmark volume, *Landscape and Power*. In the introduction, Mitchell describes landscape as "a dynamic medium, in which we 'live and move and have our being,' but also a medium that is itself in motion from one place or time to another," and as a "medium of exchange between the human and the natural, the self and the other."[67] Landscapes are constantly in motion between the changing physical environment and evolving human experiences, perceptions, and representations of the surrounding world. Maps and photographs of cities are visual mediums of landscape—"in the middle" between a "site" and "sight," as Mitchell suggests—and therefore give insights into the "motion" between phenomena and perception. Robert Pogue Harrison's especially insightful essay, "Hic Jacet" in *Landscape and Power*, argues that houses occupy similar "in-between" zones, "dwelling" between the natural and the human.[68] As both "in" and "in-between" land and scapes, house forms are not only revealed by maps and photographs but have been influenced by them. Maps and photographs were handled by architects, planners, aspiring homeowners, inspectors, landlords, tenants, and administrators whose images of Lagos and their ideas for what a "house" was and could be were influenced by the terrain on which Lagos was situated and the cultural perception and human production of that terrain, of which houses were part, as mediated through maps and photographs.

Images proliferated in Lagos between 1885 and 1985, circulating as part of colonial dispatches, newspaper articles, postcards, travel accounts, sanitary reports, and tourist guides. This was Africa's "imperial century," and as Mitchell argues, mediums of landscape were "intimately bound up with the discourse of imperialism."[69] Colonial maps and photographs were part of the "'dreamwork' of imperialism": the imperial fantasy to make foreign spaces into familiar places, rolling them into the "homeland" for the colonial occupiers and into familiar hometown spaces for African, Asian, and South American migrants.[70] While the genre of "landscape" often involved a colonial pursuit (and claim) of "pure objectivity and transparency," maps and photographs require skepticism about the extent to which they actually reflect the city. More often they were blueprints and aspirational documents showing how their creators imagined and intended the city to look and what they wanted to highlight in its environs. Often, what does not appear on a map is just as important as what does appear.

Each chapter in this book centers on a handful of maps and images from the era in question. In chapter 1, an 1885 map created by Theo Lawson, a West African resident of Lagos, shows how the city's elite community of Black cosmopolitans imagined Lagos as an atoll floating between Africa and the Atlantic. The names printed on the map (representing their residence) signified a presence among the port's power brokers of culture and commerce. These elites cultivated an affective aesthetic through their homes' floor plans and facades that rose above the flat, congested landscape. They took the opportunity to reshape the city's character into something that drew from several cultures, but the window of possibility would slam shut as British engineers hastily mapped and opened the channel to the city's harbor by circumventing and leveling the sandbar that blocked large European ships.

The early twentieth-century mitigation of Lagos's infamous sandbar was part of British efforts to remake the colony. This was made possible by scientific and bureaucratic innovations, including the proliferation and circulation of detailed photographs and maps. From these documents emerges a picture of how British officials began to view Lagos as a mechanized geography built for the export of goods from what would become the capital of an amalgamated Nigeria in 1914. Yet, as becomes clear from the reports and dispatches in which colonial

Introduction   31

maps and photographs were included, the housing plans to assist in the transformation of the city were not shaped solely or even predominantly by scientific methods and experiments but were guided more often by Europeans' long-held imprints of African landscapes as visually disordered, diseased, and depraved. With this cultural image in mind, colonial planners sought to enclose African settlements behind a canal and tramway, quarantining the "dangers" lurking in the "dirty thatch" of African "huts" to the northern half of Lagos Island (chapter 2). House forms became signifiers of the division between European rulers, with their second-story verandas and manicured lawns, and their African subjects, who were packed into single rooms and subjected to intrusive sanitary inspections.

A striking confrontation occurred in 1910 when Nigerian nationalist Herbert Macaulay stood at the foot of Governor's House—the grandest symbol of British power and injustice—and demanded native rights to land in perpetuity. Legal and political battles over interpretations of land rights would henceforth dominate Lagos history.

Chapter 3 shows the continued influence of visual scapes in struggles over Lagos's future as the first aerial photographs of the city distanced the imperial eye from ground-level processes and flattened African "slums" into shapes that appeared as impediments to a visually sanitized urban order. Eradication was the preferred colonial solution for these blots, but this required seizing greater control of land through new schemes and alliances made possible in part by the outbreak of plague in 1927. The global depression interrupted the demolition of "slums," giving African communities a renewed degree of autonomy. In this environment, Africans developed new house and household forms, reimagining the use of communal and market spaces in the congested city that no longer could accommodate the ever-additive family compound model of dwelling. Depression brought migrants from across Nigeria who sought out the El Dorado of Lagos at the railway's terminus. Inspired by the city's cowboy cultures, young migrants experimented with new living arrangements that gave them greater independence. Even without an extensive state-built infrastructure, a dynamic African side of Lagos was developing by the early 1940s, but with the end of World War II on the horizon, colonial schemes would once again find their way into the African side of the city.

32   WATERHOUSES

Indeed, in the postwar crisis of empire, as chapter 4 describes, a new generation of colonial planners proposed extensive clearance plans, insisting that their modernist designs adhered to purely rational principles. The writings and plans of Tropical Modernists like Maxwell Fry and Jane Drew show that beneath the veneer of their technocratic manuals were old European stereotypes of African landscapes as "jumbled" and "stagnant" scapes where Africans "slumbered" in a "village mentality." These images of a primordial landscape combined with planners' empiricist mindset to produce a planning ideology that devalued historical inquiry and any local considerations other than climate. Ignoring history allowed the Colonial Office to distort a century of colonial neglect into the justification for continued and intensified imperial rule. This was not lost on Lagos protesters, many of whom were market women whose homes in Central Lagos had provided a valuable spatial niche to sell their wares to the traffic crisscrossing the city. The women marched by the tens of thousands in protest of the bulldozing of their homes to turn Lagos into a "citadel for foreign commercial interests."

Chapter 5 covers the postcolonial years into the 1980s, when Nigeria's federal government relocated from Lagos to Abuja. Using a guidebook from the 1977 FESTAC celebrations and other housing reports and newspaper stories, the chapter illustrates how elites continued to see the city as split into a modern section which was connected to the national Nigerian state, and a traditional and "African" section. Lagosians saw houses as liminal spaces between these two sides, as foundations of support in a city without robust legal protections and as springboards for landlords into positions that connected them and thus their clients to the state and to the petro-economy. Eventually, realizing the value of houses in Lagos, state-connected actors hoarded housing like they did oil profits, unmooring home values from use or exchange. The conclusion argues that this trend has continued since the end of military rule in 1999, under the influence of international capital, pushing the city's non-elite residents away from its wealthy core and into, the rising waters around it.

Èkó before 1885

What we can piece together of the origin tales and early history of Lagos has been written by historians using oral histories and accounts of Europeans who intermittently visited the port.[71] Settlements near contemporary

Introduction 33

Lagos were formed out of what local traditions describe as the "war of the world."[72] Before the sixteenth century, this conflict brought a group of men and women who spoke Awori (a dialect of Yoruba) to the edge of the known world, far from the heartland and Yoruba holy city of Ilé-Ifẹ (city or house of abundance), to the shores and islands of a great lagoon that deposited into the Atlantic abyss. The refugees left behind their homes (ilé), but they soon rebuilt similar structures on Iddo Island northwest of what would become Lagos Island. What was more difficult to replace was the presence of ancestors (buried under the floors of the houses that they had abandoned) and the unborn (the eternal inheritors of family homes) and deities (òrìṣà) who had inhabited their family shrines. By putting up new houses, interring those who passed within them, and building new shrines, the settlers reconstituted their kinship relations and found a semblance of stability in the chaos of fleeing.[73] As was the urbanization pattern throughout Yorubaland, from a cluster of ilé, a small town (which is also called ilé or ilú in Yoruba) soon took form beside the lagoon.

As fertile soil became scarce on the small Iddo Island, some residents crossed the lagoon's rough channel to establish farms on the low plains of what they are thought to have called Oko ("farm" in Yoruba) and what would become Lagos Island.[74] Spread between two spacious islands and surrounded by a lagoon, early Lagosians prospered by trading pepper, fish, and dried salt to the canoes that plied the intercoastal rivers and creeks stretching from Allada (and later Dahomey) in the west to the Kingdom of Benin in the east.[75] The homes shared by lineage groups on the islands were earthen, oblong, and not unlike their counterparts in the numerous Yoruba cities and towns dispersed wide and far from their tenth-century prototype, Ilé-Ifẹ.

The Lagos settlement pattern deviated from the Ifẹ model and was unique among Yoruba urbanism by virtue of its littoral setting. In Yoruba culture, an ideal city is circular and centered on the ọba's palace—the king's compound—which is surrounded by similar, but inferior, compounds usually headed by the eldest male (baálẹ) in the lineage. The town is protected by raised earthworks and a ditch.[76] Two trade roads run east–west and north–south, dividing Yoruba towns into four districts, each under the authority of a chief. These patterns did not apply to early Iddo and its extension at Oko because commerce was by water, and it was not possible for all residents to cluster on the small

34 WATERHOUSES

Iddo Island around the local leader known as the *ọlọfin* (later known as the *ọlọgun* or ọba).[77]

In the second half of the sixteenth century, the regional hegemon, Benin, established a war camp (*Èkó* in Benin's Edo language) on Lagos Island. In one version of the story, Benin military commanders convened a council comprising the heads of local settlements—the landowners still known as *ìdéjọ* chiefs. These leaders today claim a shared Awori identity and descent from of the original *ọlọfin* of Iddo.[78] Additional chieftaincy titles passed to influential men in Èkó, establishing a power structure of military chiefs (*àbàgbọn*), administrative chiefs (*àkárígbéré*), religious chiefs (*ògáládé*), and landed chiefs (*ìdéjọ*). The last three are known collectively as "white cap" chiefs because of their ceremonial head coverings.[79] These men met as a council and accepted visitors in the courtyards of their compounds.

The compounds themselves were made of seven layers of foot-thick clay topped by thatched roofs of palm leaves. The walls were windowless; the roof overhung them nearly to the ground, where it was supported by carved columns to create an exterior veranda. Inside, through a single entry point, a central impluvium courtyard was encircled by sleeping rooms and an internal veranda formed by a roof overhang. Together these rooms and courtyards are called an *agbo ilé* (flock of houses), referring to the privacy of each wife's rooms, and an *ilé tiwo* (house of ours), in reference to the entire household headed by a baálẹ and occupied by his sons and their wives who married into the compound. Sets of adjoining rooms occupied by a mother and her children are known as *ilé temi* (house of mine). In the courtyard, these kinship groups (*ẹbí*) mingled, cooked, produced goods for market, and welcomed visitors. This familial space was the heart of precolonial production, politics, and social life in Lagos.[80] Under the Benin Kingdom, Èkó family compounds adopted elements of Edo architecture such as the addition of a second outer courtyard, which held the family shrine and rooms for non-kin dependents, while the inner courtyard was reserved for *omo'le* (the children of the house) of the baálẹ.[81]

Dependents or associates of an *ilé tiwo* could also live outside the compound without losing their affiliation with the household. As historian Akinwumi Ogundiran describes, although *ilé* means "house," it also refers to "a multi-sited kinship network that transcended blood and

Introduction

marriage ties [to encompass] other types of interpersonal and social bonds, including patron-client relationships, friendships, and fraternities."[82] These affiliates were often newcomers, orphans, slaves, or strangers who arrived in town from elsewhere and were offered protection in exchange for loyalty to an established household. Around Èkó these affiliates lived in smaller structures, including rectangular single-room homes made of bamboo or later timber frames. Fishermen and canoe men often put up temporary shelters of this type on sandy areas or over the water's edge on stilts. The space for these small plots was granted by the ìdéjọ chiefs, and dependents' access to the allotments usually came through connection to a baálẹ on good terms with an ìdéjọ. This was not a complicated process for dependents, as baálẹ and ìdéjọ valued the labor and allegiance of followers more than land, which was still plentiful on and around Lagos Island. Those who were allowed to occupy a piece of land pledged loyalty to their patrons. The ìdéjọ chiefs continued to control access to the land (as executors for the òrìṣà deities dwelling in and around the land) but allowed unrestricted use of plots lent out to baálẹ and their dependents so long as these households met certain obligations such as good behavior, allegiance, and small annual gifts—understood as offerings to the òrìṣà spirits of the land—of palm, kola, or other goods. During colonial rule, the nature and extent of ìdéjọ's control of land became a matter of controversy as real estate became more valuable. But prior to the imposition of British private property rights, powerful men in Yorubaland displayed their prestige by summoning legions of followers who showered them with praise poems (oriki) during festivals and other public appearances. These loyal followers gained social standing, protection, and political representation in the community from their association with a household. Not belonging to a household in early Lagos meant poverty.[83] Being homeless was less about physical shelter than a lack of affiliation with a household.

During the first centuries of the Atlantic slave trade, Lagos was a mediator of people and trade goods across the inland waterways of the Bight of Benin to major production centers in Benin and the Ijebu kingdoms and slave ports like Ouidah and Badagry. It was not until the middle of the eighteenth century that European slave traders began consistently seeking to purchase human beings from Lagos. Once this occurred, these people became commodities that could be traded or sold for other commodities such as cloth, ceramics, and iron, which local slavers could then use to increase their household's prominence—and attract more followers. Èkó was a marginal city-state under the yoke of Benin Kingdom when Portuguese and Brazilian slavers began arriving and offering cowry shells as well as rare and unique goods to local men in exchange for slaves. Èkó ọba (Lagos kings) made imported glass, marble, tiles, and bricks the exclusive propriety of their residence, but they also continued to allow private individuals to compete for a piece of the slave trade, creating a cutthroat entrepreneurial ethos that appealed to European buyers who encountered high-priced royal monopolies in other West African markets.[84]

This culture and the island's protected intercoastal harbor made Lagos an attractive slave port, and the trade in humans grew in the nineteenth century, exceeding seventy thousand departures of enslaved people in the 1840s. The wealth and power Èkó derived from this trade allowed the ọba to begin refusing tribute to Benin, reestablishing the autonomy of the kingdom. The ọba and major chiefs who also benefited from the trade expanded their households to include enslaved attachés (a symbol of wealth and power), and expanded their compounds to include four courtyards in the style of Benin plus an additional open space for large public ceremonies. In time Èkó became preferred by slavers as one of the only West African deepwater ports with an outlet to the Atlantic. Chased by anti-slaving naval squadrons once the British and French outlawed the trade at the beginning of the nineteenth century, the Portuguese turned to the city they called Lagos as a hideout, establishing residences, slave barracoons, and trading stores.

The port quickly earned notoriety in Britain and elsewhere as a haunt for the horrors of the slave trade. In the 1840s, British politicians and citizens mounted campaigns to intervene. Missionaries headed the efforts to create an abolitionist footprint in Yorubaland, establishing outposts at Badagry (1842) and Abeokuta (1846), towns near Lagos, and bringing former slaves from Sierra Leone, many of whom, like Samuel Ajayi Crowther and Joseph Wright, were from Yorubaland. Pressure mounted in London from Consul Beecroft and naval officers patrolling the Bight of Benin for a military operation to chase the slavers from Lagos and to establish a consulate where British law, property, and palm merchants would be protected.[85]

MAP I.1. Glover's 1859 map showing the districts of Lagos Island, plans for a railway terminus, and depth markers. *Source:* The National Archives, Kew, UK.

In December 1851 their pleas were heard. But the British bombardment of the town destroyed more than half of its homes. Ọba Kosoko fled and Britain reinstated his rival uncle Akitoye, whom Kosoko had exiled to British Badagry. This was the first time Europeans had resorted to military force to conquer an African polity and impose European law. Previously, Africans had controlled port cities and the terms of the trade, often to Europeans' frustration. With the bombing of Lagos to "protect Africans," the upper hand passed to Europeans as the British established a tenuous foothold in the Bight of Benin.

An 1859 British map drawn by Lieutenant John Glover, governor of Lagos from 1863 to 1872, illustrates the layout of the town in the early years of British rule (map I.1).[86] The map does not include roads but does show four districts on the island, in which the town's diverse array of settlers from around the Atlantic clustered.

Isale Eko. The first district is the "old town" of Èkó, which Governor Glover labeled "District of Egga" in the northwest peninsula of the island. This part of town was known as Isale Eko. In this district, the ọba continued to live in his *igá idunganran* (pepper palace), labeled "King's Palace" on the map, the hub around which chiefs and other residents built their compounds, which are not shown on the map. Missionaries used the palace's courtyard for the first Christian service on the Island, the symbolic heart of the city.[87] Increasingly, refugees from other Yoruba cities fleeing civil wars or bondage arrived in Lagos and took up residence in Isale Eko, creating their own distinct, ethnically defined neighborhoods. Glover's map shows no other landmarks or houses in Isale Eko aside from the palace. The map is not drawn to scale by contemporary standards owing to the difficulty of finding sufficiently high ground from which to survey the town. The District of Offee (Offin on later maps) southwest of Egga is particularly distorted and enlarged. This area was also home to native Yoruba speakers.

Olowogbowo and Oko Faje. Southeast of Offee is the District of Olubowo (written Olowogbowo elsewhere, and later Saro Town), which means "he who asks for his money back" in reference to Europeans and Sierra Leonean returnees who introduced practices of moneylending secured with property. The use of land and homes as collateral was new in Yorubaland, but by the 1860s merchants demanded liens on property in exchange for credit, replacing former Yoruba practices of "pawning" people who would work for the creditor until the loan was repaid. Most of the immigrants to Olowogbowo were Saros and European missionaries from the Church Mission Society and Wesleyan Missionaries and palm merchants who originally built single-story earth and thatch homes not unlike the stand-alone structures in

Introduction   39

the Yoruba quarters.[88] This area of town grew from about 400 or
500 Sierra Leonean returnees in the 1850s to hundreds more after
the British took possession of Lagos in 1851, giving the district a
population between 1,500 and 2,500 by the 1860s when the town
population reached 25,000.[89] Further east, the District of Oko
Faje (elsewhere Oke Faji, Faji, Portuguese or "Popo" Town, and
later the Brazilian Quarter or Oke Ite)[90] and the areas north and
east of this district ("the fields") were home to Portuguese and
Brazilian merchants, Brazilian "Aguda" returnees or *emancipados*,
and a Roman Catholic mission. Among these returnees were
craftsmen who would become sought-after builders of the city's
grand late nineteenth-century homes.

The Marina. Along the southern waterfront, in an area that became
known as the Marina, European factories are labeled on the
map. These include merchants from Sardinia, Hamburg, France,
and England who were attracted by the palm trade and British
protection after 1851. Their number totaled little more than forty
or fifty throughout the 1850s and 1860s. Most lived in timber
or clay dwellings, but in 1857 a Sardinian named Giambattista
Scala founded a masonry and tile factory (seen on the map in the
southeast outskirts of the town), allowing some Europeans to
build small brick homes, a development that displeased the ǫba,
who had banned the use of bricks on all residences other than
his palace. Lagos administrators lived in the British Consulate,
labeled between the Church Mission and the "Hamburgh Factory."
The consulate was an iron structure imported from Britain that
Richard Burton famously described as "a corrugated iron coffin or
planklined morgue, containing a dead consul once a year," owing to
the tropical climate and prevalence of disease in Lagos.[91]

The 1859 map also illustrates faintly outlined but firm British in-
tentions for Lagos's future, plans that would take decades to materialize.
Likely added to the map decades later in red ink, perhaps in the 1870s
or 1880s, plans for a railroad terminus and docks are drawn along the
mainland, the construction of which would not be undertaken until the
turn of the century. The map includes detailed depth markers in the
channel and lagoon as well as considerable comments on the mouth of

the channel,[92] an obstacle to large ships entering the port that British engineers would alter with the construction of two "moles" (barriers to block the surf and thus deepen the channel) in the early twentieth century. Clearly, even under the Lagos Consulate, British agents were planning to extend the sphere of the settlement and facilitate the ease and cost of getting goods to European markets.

In 1861 the British took another step toward consolidating these plans by annexing Lagos. By then Ọba Akitoye had died and his son Ọba Dosunmu had signed the Treaty of Cession, ceding all the land in Lagos to the Crown, although the document's legitimacy would become a major source of anticolonial disputes in the twentieth century. A description from John Whitford, who visited Lagos in the 1860s, gives a sense of how perceptions of Lagos's landscape, plans for housing, and power over the city's future were already becoming part of the same contemplation:

> The huts of the town extended to the water's edge, and it was a filthy, disgusting, savage place, and unsafe to wander about the streets. In 1861 the British Government pensioned off the King [Dosunmu] with £2,000 yearly, and turned Lagos into a colony. The governor immediately cleared the filthy beach of the wretched native tenements and for a considerable distance back from the Lagoon border destroyed them and formed a wide promenade.... He also pulled down hundreds of huts behind the promenade and constructed wide streets for the sea-breeze to blow through. The consequence is that, on the promenade fronting the lagoon, merchants have erected brick stores, with comfortable luxurious dwellings above, fronting the glorious life-sustaining sea-breeze. . . . Markets have been regulated, Houssa Zouave-dressed soldiers and a police force organized, a race-course established, churches, schools, court-houses, Government-house, and barracks built; and lastly a cemetery (which drives a brisk trade) has been walled in outside the town, but rather too near to the houses. It is not a pleasant place, for you can tell in which direction it lies, long before seeing it.[93]

Between Glover's 1859 map and Lawson's 1885 map, Lagos became built up and crowded. Yet, despite the presence of a few British outposts,

Introduction

including a courthouse and government house, much played up in the pejorative views of Europeans like Whitford, Lagos was still a city of opportunity for a cosmopolitan class of Black Lagosians who constructed their own view of the landscape and of housing's place in it in the decades before a fusion of Whitford and Glover's visions for a racially organized export center could be expanded on a wider scale. Chapter 1 reconstructs the landscape of this lost era through the city's "Lagos-style" houses.

1

Bar

Houses as Gateways to Status: Lagos Colony

For the year prior to visiting Lagos for the first time I pored through books checked out from libraries and ordered from obscure presses, watched choppy YouTube clips on the city's urbanism, and streamed the Nigerian pidgin radio station Wazobia into my apartment. Then, after a year of immersing myself in screens and paper, I was finally in Nigeria, and everything I saw—from the plane's descent over the haze of the city's peri-urban limits to the occasional Molue bus still glimpsed on back streets—conjured the histories I had spent months imagining.[1] Flickers of the past were everywhere present in the city's famously frenetic landscape, animated in my gaze through hours of soaking in the descriptions of path-laying historians like Patrick Dele Cole, Kristin Mann, and J. D. Y. Peel.[2] This way of seeing, wide-eyed but widely read, stilled my field of sight with the weight of Lagos's previous lives while bringing those histories into motion.

The strongest experience I had of this sense, what Helen Macdonald calls "history collapsing,"[3] was standing on the banks of Victoria Island one afternoon, looking out at the channel connecting Lagos Lagoon to the Atlantic (figs. 1.1 and 1.2). The water was visibly thick with

FIGURES 1.1 AND 1.2. Lagos's famous channel in 2016 (author's photograph) and 1885 (The National Archives, Kew, UK).

power, twisting silently as the pressure of the lagoon basin's only point of escape met the resistance of an ocean. Looking right toward Lagos Island's modern skyline, and left where I knew the submerged sandbar lay within the channel, history was forcefully present. This was the space that had given Lagos its opening to become globally consequential. But it was also the chasm where enslaved people had seen everything they knew disappear, where forests of Nigeria's resources had vanished in transit to Europe—a river of death like the Fon meaning of Lagos's smaller rival city to the west, Cotonou. Untold numbers of people had departed and arrived through this slit in the coast, and many others had been lost, their boats breaking up on the bar or capsized by the currents. The channel's history was no more stable, and I had to remind myself that what I was looking at had been drastically altered due to its logistical and strategic importance. This is one of the tricks and, for many imperialists and nationalists, the appeal of landscapes: their ability to silence radical upheaval through their quiet immensity. The surrounding city, tranquil from a distance but unambiguously humanmade in the form of transoceanic freight ships and glass skyscrapers, spilled the channel's secrets. This was not a timeless landscape but a place of constant change.

From the outset of British rule, visitors and engineers had obsessed over how to mitigate the underwater bar that blocked deep hulls from passing and loading directly in the marina beyond the threat of ocean surges. Explorer Richard Burton called it the "bugbear of the Bights [of Benin and Biafra]."[4] Organizing the technological machinery and the political apparatus to make the deepening of the bar (and Britain's footprint in the Bight

FIGURE 1.3. A landscape of late nineteenth-century "Lagos-style" houses. Ilojo Bar's distinctive arched windows can be seen in the left foreground. Payne's Orange House (with the later addition of dormer windows) can be seen to the far right, ca. 1911. *Source:* The National Archives, Kew, UK.

of Benin) possible and more profitable began in earnest at the close of the nineteenth century. Extensive dredging would allow heavy boats to enter the harbor by 1908.[5] In the decades between the last slave ships anchoring south of the bar off the coast in the 1840s and British steamers traversing it to occupy modern Nigeria in the early twentieth century, Lagos evolved into a unique cosmopolitan enclave with a landscape dominated by distinctive "Lagos-style" houses that dotted the island (fig. 1.3).

Centered on an 1885 map of the island (map 1.1), this chapter examines these homes and the more precarious mass housing that developed in their shadow toward the end of what might be thought of as the town's "fluorescence period"—between the British bombardment in 1851 and the intensive colonial expansion of the 1890s.[6] These years were by no means uneventful[7]—it was quite the contrary in terms of administrative turnover and legal disputes—but they were not dominated by British ambitions.[8] It was a time when the African and immigrant social and commercial scene flourished, embodied by the construction of multistory homes peppered with flowers carved in plaster. The 1885 map captures a landscape awash with new ideas for what a house and city could be in addition to new ideas from around the Atlantic about constructing and claiming a place in the city. Private property is established on the map's cartography with the names of more than a hundred individuals and trading companies labeled on specific plots. Roman Catholic, Church of England, and Wesleyan churches in gothic, baroque, and austere architecture dot the streets. A savings bank, social

MAP 1.1. "Plan of the Town of Lagos West Coast of Africa, Prepared for the Lagos Executive Commissioners of the Col. And Indian Exhibition 1886 . . . , by W. T. C. Lawson, C. E., &c. (Native of West Africa), Asst. Colonial Surveyor—Lagos. 30 December 1885. Corrected to June 1887." *Source:* The National Archives, Kew, UK.

hall, race course, and telegraph station offer new services and connections; hospitals and cemeteries hint at the prevalence of disease and, for Lagos, novel forms of burial.

The map frames Lagos Island alone, a colony in itself, only a few square miles but Britain's crucial wedge between the Atlantic and the vast interior. The town occupied a sphere of its own, an encircled landscape in which a strong-willed but sophisticated frontier culture developed in the nineteenth century. Scholars in several disciplines have written about the forms of cultural experimentation happening in Lagos during this era. Art historians Charles Gore and Olubukola Gbadegesin have shown how photography, especially the images made by the West African photographer Neils Walwin Holm (1866–ca. 1927), became a means of "self-fashioning," of carefully manipulating elements from Yoruba and Victorian clothing, poses, and entourages to express fluency, fluidity, and a common dignity.[9] As Gore argues, this legitimization of African culture was a radical act and speaks to the ways Lagos was an unusual space on the fringes of two worlds. J. C. Echeruo in a classic study of Lagos and Nara Muniz Improta França in her more recent work explore how literacy in English and Yoruba was essential to elite lifestyles and the ways in which newspapers and print culture proliferated as the direction and values of the colony were debated.[10]

Another expressive social outlet was local associations—recently described by Nozomi Sawada—which included dozens of sporting, religious, and educational clubs as well as several prominent floral-themed groups such as the Flower of Lagos Society and the Afro-Brazilian Flor de Dia Society.[11] However, the blend of a volatile middleman economy dependent on European demand, a flow of export goods through sparring interior polities, outbreaks of smallpox, yellow fever, and malaria, and an astounding amount of imported liquor (not all of which was consumed)[12] was the less-than-verdant backdrop against which these creative exploits grew. It was a setting of productive turmoil on the margins of life and death, wealth and poverty, Atlantic and Africa. Fortunes were made and lost in the scarcely regulated palm trade, and a spirit of male bravado, ambition, and self-aggrandizement solidified in this environment of rampant opportunities and pitfalls.

As seen in map 1.1, by 1885 the four distinct Lagos "towns" where Yoruba, Brazilians, Saros, and Europeans once clustered had collided

Bar

and permeated one another. Refugees from the Yoruba Wars streamed in along with returnees and fortune seekers from around the Atlantic. Lagos was becoming crowded. In this climate, three critical developments affected the way houses were thought about and used. The new density alongside the growing recognition of individual private property rights drove up the value of space. As property values rose, privately owned and architecturally prominent residences became central to being counted among the city's elite and powerful: status through a legally titled house was an economic stake and a cultural statement in the unstable city. Finally, this rise in the scarcity and importance of titled property helped turn housing into a powerful vehicle for social and political control as the social distance increased between those with authority over shelter (landlords and British administrators) and the untitled majority of the city, the latter finding themselves vulnerable to evictions, new obligations, and limited power to challenge abuses arising from their dependency. In other words, securing and maintaining housing became a burden for most and a primary objective rather than a secondary benefit derived from the traditional association with a powerful lineage. Yet there were opportunities for those individuals savvy and fortunate enough to find a way to acquire titled property.

The British drive for colonial expansion and entrenchment in the late nineteenth century clashed with the emerging African elite scene in Lagos, disrupting it before it coalesced. What did emerge was housing as a means of asserting authority and coercing others. The conclusion of this chapter discusses how houses were part of how Europeans pulled the rug out from under elite Africans by calling their loans and foreclosing on their property as British agents began to consolidate power in the growing colony. Today, the handful of houses remaining from the nineteenth century are some of the best records of that other Lagos, of a small opening between the modern city and precolonial Èkó, a space like the one the channel's sandbar once occupied.[13]

The Dominant, Domiciled Class

The 1885 map of Lagos was the first detailed street-by-street depiction of the city. It was surveyed and drafted by a West African named W. T. G. Lawson for the 1886 Colonial and Indian Exhibition in London.[14] Born in Sierra Leone to the exiled royal family of Little Popo and Aneho

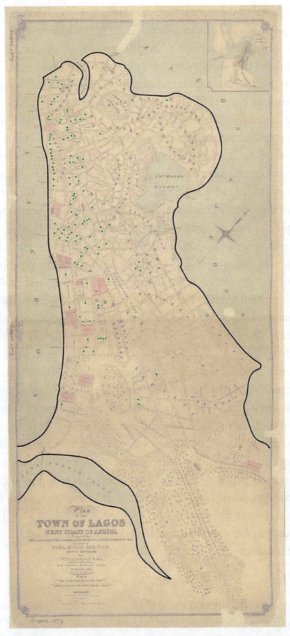

MAP 1.2. Digitized version of Lawson's 1885 map using green dots to show the locations of the elites.

Bar   49

(Togo) in 1855, Lawson had qualified as a civil engineer in England.[15] He was the first African to become a British colonial surveyor, serving in Sierra Leone and the Gold Coast before settling in Lagos in 1877.[16] Once there he was frequently mentioned in the local newspapers in connection with his professional and philanthropic activities and when his wedding was attended by the city's most prominent citizens.[17] As a man of means, Lawson was part of a new generation of cosmopolitan Lagosians who navigated Yoruba, Afro-Brazilian, and Victorian cultures and institutions. This fascinating collection of nineteenth-century Atlantic elites is the subject of much of the first wave of scholarship on Lagos.[18] These foundational studies and their successors presented arguments for who merited inclusion as an "elite" in the Colony of Lagos, listing the names and analyzing their traits and habits.

What these studies omit is the role of houses in consolidating the status of elites and the way a person's physical place in the city's landscape affected his or her social standing. It is intriguing that the 1885 map itself includes small inscriptions for the residences of approximately 125 people who were clearly considered important enough to be mentioned in a document that would represent Lagos at a major international event and, as noted in Lawson's obituary, "which remained for many years a standard work of reference."[19] Lawson's map testifies to what it took to be somebody in the Colony of Lagos (map 1.2).

The two definitive works on Lagos elites are Patrick Dele Cole's *Modern and Traditional Elites in the Politics of Lagos* (1975) and Kristin Mann's *Marrying Well: Marriage, Status and Social Change among the Educated Elite in Colonial Lagos* (1985). Both draw on Weber's distinction between class (conferred by economic power) and social status (defined by the conscious ability to exclude others from high society) to underline the importance of the elite status in nineteenth-century Lagos.[20] Status was both an economic currency for occupying a lucrative position in the commercial city and a sociopolitical currency for entrance and influence in decision-making arenas. Cole writes that "to lose status in colonial Lagos was to lose everything."[21] Both Cole and Mann described the ways in which a person could cultivate status in the eyes of the community through lifestyle and consumption patterns. For Mann, marriage was "a fundamental part in the consolidation of elite status."[22] Cole suggests the role of visual cues in policing status lines, writing how status "gave individuals the 'right' to be addressed reverently, to wear certain kinds of clothes or other distinguishing jewelry."[23]

Mann and Cole draw different boundaries around elites. Mann conceives of elite society in the Lagos of the 1870s, 1880s, and 1890s as a singular stratum and traces the group's prominence to its members' ability—through Western education and familiarity with British manners and customs—to be appointed to prestigious roles by possessing the skills and talents that British colonial rulers valued.[24] She identifies 200 lawyers, doctors, ministers, high-ranking colonial servants, and educated merchants based on their education and professional records.[25] For Cole, beneath "the top social class of Lagos in the 1880s [that was] dominated by the Europeans," all III of them in a city of 30,000 (and as many Germans as British), he paints a more pluralistic, less hierarchical picture, describing two poles of non-European elites: those whose status was derived from "traditional" titles and offices and those belonging to Mann's newer, educated "modern" elites.[26]

Cole's narrative is more reflective of the fact that nineteenth-century Lagos was not yet a hegemonic space dominated by British influence, due in part to the fact that inland Yoruba polities like Ibadan-Oyo, Ijebu, and Egba still controlled the production and supply of palm oil, the cornerstone of the export economy.[27] This reality would, by the 1890s, motivate British expansion into the interior and the imposition of a racial colonial hierarchy. In the meantime, chiefs, wealthy African landowners, moneylenders, and especially the intermediaries or "lobbyists" for the interior states, the bàbá ìsàlẹ, commanded prestige and respect in Lagos at a time when nascent ethnic-nationalism was beginning to stir against creeping British discrimination.[28] Some educated elites took Yoruba names, adopted elements of traditional dress, held Yoruba and Christian marriage ceremonies, and aligned with inland states, even becoming a bàbá ìsàlẹ, to bolster their standing and influence in Lagos.[29] The "elite" encompassed more than just those who "created a distinctive style of life built around Christianity, Western education and British manners and customs."[30]

In the later poststructuralist work of Pierre Bourdieu, with which neither Cole and Mann could engage (publishing before or at approximately the same time), Weber's separation of social status from economic class is challenged and condensed into an all-encompassing stratification of "class." For Bourdieu, class was the product of both economic and cultural "capital," with capital defined as "the set of actually usable resources and power."[31] In this framework, social and economic pursuits and standing are two sides of a single coin, important only insofar as they translate to authority over others. In Bourdieu's theory, class is manifested through "habitus," how one physically and cognitively inhabits the world. The "dominant class" in society possesses abundant economic and cultural capital, conveyed by expensive and sophisticated habitus.[32] This is true in the capitalist societies Bourdieu describes as well as nineteenth-century Yoruba society, in which the highest regard was reserved for those who combined the status of both a wealthy (olórò) and honorable person (olólá)—as culturally defined by generosity and dignity—to become bòròkìní (an influential person) or gbajúmò (a prominent person).[33]

The idea of a combination of cultural and economic capital defining a "dominant class" is a better explanation of elevated standing in nineteenth-century Lagos than the dichotomy of "traditional" and "modern" elites in Cole or the reduction of elite status in Mann to those with the closest approximation of Victorian values and tastes. At the top of society, neither "traditional," "modern," nor "educated" elites were stable groups, nor did any of them have a monopoly on claims to "elite" standing. Rather, the monikers (e.g., "civilized native," "educated native," "Black Englishman")[34] used in newspapers at the time and later adopted and modified by scholars were used to classify these individuals as part of the struggle to define, and thus to convert into capital, the culture of city's dominant class against "other" groups.

From rival and overlapping pools of elites jostling for esteem, what had emerged by the 1880s was a dominant class with a habitus marked by the shrewdness to code-switch between dueling but intertwined economic and cultural systems.[35] Lagos was a cosmopolitan entrepôt, where culturally those who thrived were the men who absorbed elements of the several societies operating in the city, showed the ability to move among them depending on venue and audience, and possessed the ability to reinvent themselves in a rapidly changing environment.[36] These men included names on Lawson's map like J. A. Otunba Payne (Orange House [fig. 1.4]) and J. J. Thomas (on Lawson's map in Olowogbowo) who embarked on numerous careers and business ventures.[37]

FIGURE 1.4. J. A. Otunba Payne's Orange House. *Source:* John A. Payne, *Payne's Lagos Almanack and Diary for 1878* (London: W. J. Johnson, 1878), 3. The etching of Payne's house was included above the author's introduction in every addition of *Payne's Lagos Almanack* throughout the 1870s and 1880s.

Payne and Thomas were among the elite Lagosians who helped curate the Lagos exhibit, which included Lawson's map, for the Colonial and Indian Exhibition in London.[38] Their exhibit was explicitly cosmopolitan: seven tables of artifacts showcasing Lagos's history and culture through Yoruba heirlooms with deep stories and meanings; Lagos's access to modern technology through photography and cartography; and Lagos's elements of sophistication through refined furniture that refuted European images of primitive African dwellings.[39] As residents of a commercial city, those who dominated Lagos economically enjoyed access to credit in order to link transactions between the hinterlands and the Atlantic, which by the 1880s required titled property as security in Lagos.[40] In this setting, a grand, privately owned house of a hybrid architectural style was the ultimate repository of both cultural and economic capital, something possessed only by the city's most esteemed and powerful, outside of the small number of European administrators and merchants. Among the culturally and economically elevated houses of the late nineteenth century were famous Lagos residences like those listed in table 1.1.[41] Houses were omnipresent in nineteenth-century Lagos but, like water, easy to overlook.

Bar

Table 1.1. Prominent nineteenth-century Lagos-style houses

House	Other names	On Lawson's map?	Date built	Owner
Branco House			1880s	Joaquim Branco
Campos House			1885	Ramon Campos
Caxton House			1880s	R. B. Blaize (owner of several other prominent houses)
Doherty House			1890s	Josiah H. Doherty (later: A. W. Thomas)
Elephant House			1900	S. H. Pearse
Elias da Silva House	Lion House		1880	Santan da Silva
Fernandez House	Olaiya House, Ilojo Bar	Yes	1846	J. A. Fernandez (later: Napoleon Rey Couto)
Lumpkin House	Leventis House	Yes	1890	W. E. Lumpkin
Maja House			1895	Oni Gbaragbo
Orange House	Henry Carr House (unconfirmed)	Yes	1870s	J. A. Payne
Savage House				J. A. Savage
Taiwo's Palace	Taiwo's *Iga*	Yes	1860s	Oloye Daniel Conrad Taiwo
Tapa House			1886	Tapa Oshodi
Vaughan House			1895	J. C. Vaughan
Water House		Yes	1875	João Da Rocha
Wilberforce Hosue				
Willoughby House			1880s	I. H. Willoughby
Yoyo Araromi House			1900	Borges da Silva

Houses as Economic Capital

Between the start of British rule in 1851 and the 1880s, land and housing went from secondary considerations to the most valuable forms of economic capital in Lagos. The primary drivers in this transformation were the rising population density on the island and the introduction and protection of private property rights by British administrators and courts. Cole cites the importance of this shift in the first lines of his study: "It was in land transactions that the most profound changes took place [in early colonial Lagos]."[42] Casa do Fernandez (later Fernandez House, Olaiya House, and then Ilojo Bar), bordering Payne's Orange House in Tinubu Square on Lawson's 1885 map, is symbolic of

FIGURE 1.5. Ilojo Bar, 1954. *Source:* Gillian Hopwood.

the transformations in nineteenth-century Lagos (fig. 1.5). Built in the 1840s by a merchant named Fernandez who had arrived in Lagos from Brazil,[43] the structure was originally a barracoon used for holding and possibly selling Africans destined for enslavement in the Americas.[44] With the arrival of the British and the outlawing of slave exporting, the Fernandez family fled for Badagry along with the exiled ọba Kosoko, who opposed the British antislavery agenda. The consulate government then seized the house and sold it. Years later the house was auctioned again, and the auctioneer, Andrew W. U. Thomas—listed among the educated elite in Mann's earlier study—sold it to himself, part of a lucrative personal estate totaling £9,500, six times the value of the average Lagos merchant's estate.[45] Thomas knew the value of a unique and centrally located house in Lagos, having showcased his own wealth by constructing Ebun House (1913), the grandest Lagos-style house ever built (fig. 1.6).[46]

The conversion of space and structures into tangible and fungible economic assets was a piecemeal and contested process. This transformation was set in motion in the 1850s when Kosoko's rival and overthrower ọba Akitoye (and then Ọba Dosunmu) issued land grants around the marina and elsewhere in town to Europeans and repatriated slaves or their descendants from Brazil and Sierra Leone. Europeans

FIGURE 1.6. Ebun House, ca. 1920. *Source:* Allister Macmillan, editor and compiler, *The Red Book of West Africa; Historical and Descriptive, Commercial and Industrial Facts, Figures & Resources* (London: Cass, 1968, first published in 1920).

and immigrants arrived familiar with private property rights and interpreted the grants as permanent.[47] The recipients of these grants began treating them as conferring fee simple title, and a cash market for property quickly developed. After British annexation in 1861, the understanding that the sale of property entailed absolute alienation of rights solidified, an interpretation reinforced by the British administrators. Appointed in 1863, a panel of three British land commissioners upheld claims to private property, issuing Crown grants to those who could prove ownership of property through conveyances or testimony of possession for longer than three years.[48] Many of the prominent houses of Lagos, including Da Silva House, Water House, Elephant House, and Doherty House, were constructed on land titled in the 1860s through

Crown grants.[49] The rights conferred by Crown grants were not clearly defined, but the Supreme Court of Lagos (established in 1876) usually interpreted them to confer fee simple title unless family members could prove a legitimate claim to the property under native custom, such as when an individual had originally applied for a Crown grant on behalf of an extended family.[50]

As Lawson's 1885 map shows, Lagos was crowded by the 1880s, nearing forty thousand residents, short on habitable land, and hemmed in by large swamps, factors that intensified demand and competition for land and housing.[51] This combination of growing land scarcity and the gradual entrenchment of private property rights led to several novel functions for land and housing. In *Slavery and the Birth of an African City* (2007), Mann describes three new uses of particular importance in her discussion of property's central role in the renegotiation of relations between former slaveowners and rising entrepreneurs and former slaves, refugees, and dependents:[52]

Mortgages. The first new use was property as mortgaged collateral in exchange for credit, a practice that became standard in the 1860s when lenders started demanding that loans be secured with real estate rather than "pawned" people (a practice uncomfortably similar to slavery for the British).[53]

Rental Income. The second was as a source of rental income from rooms and buildings that were let out to the growing number of people looking for accommodations on a transactional rather than a relational basis.

Investments. The third novel use of houses was as a speculative investment once Lagosians saw land values soar as practices of mortgaging for credit and renting for cash became widespread.

Financial capital never lasted long in Lagos. Merchants constantly reinvested funds abroad or inland for new shipments, which meant that credit was king, and property was the key to acquiring it. Mann describes how in Yorubaland "a great chain of credit linked all of the participants in the new international trade, from the local producers and consumers to the European, Sierra Leonean, and Brazilian exporters and importers."[54] Property, especially a house where creditors knew they could locate the loan recipient, became the entrée to this system, giving small traders a chance to expand their enterprises. A neighbor of Fernandez House and Orange House, and one of the most prominent African merchants of nineteenth-century Lagos, Taiwo Olowo ("Taiwo the Rich" or "Taiwo, man made of money"), illustrates the importance of land and a house in the process of ascension to the city's dominant class.[55] Taiwo came from a mainland town and appears to have begun his life in Lagos as little more than an enslaved basket weaver.[56] His break came when as a follower of ọba Kosoko in the 1840s he was invited to acquire land in the center of the growing city on which build a home.[57] This property appears under the name "D. C. Taiwo" on Lawson's 1885 map in the district of Faji (named after Fajimilola, the wealthy woman from whom Taiwo received the original plot) on Taiwo Street, reflective of his rise in the intervening years. The plot and the house (fig. 1.7), which Taiwo expanded into his ìgá (palace), gave him the space to house his growing number of children, slaves, and dependents, thus allowing him to mobilize their labor and command their

FIGURE 1.7. The exterior of Taiwo Olowo's palace in the 1970s, over one hundred years after he constructed it. *Source:* Joane Nagel Shaw, "Historic Buildings of Lagos, Nigeria" (unpublished manuscript, 1980), Oak Grove Library Center, Northwestern University.

allegiance.[58] This base of support gave him connections and standing in the community, a reputation that helped him build his palm trading operations with credit from the German firm G. L. Gaiser in the 1863.[59] With profits from trade, Taiwo speculated early and often once Crown grants became available, acquiring fourteen such grants between 1863 and 1870, and over twenty more before 1892.[60] He rented some of these investments to European firms at a large profit and collateralized others to receive trade goods and currency from the French firm Regis Ainé, which he then channeled through middlemen in the interior for huge amounts of palm oil.[61]

Taiwo often extended credit in exchange for security in the form of property to his network of followers and small traders, a practice that made it possible for him to acquire additional real estate holdings when the recipients defaulted and surrendered their property.[62] Using his initial plot of land and house as a foundation, Taiwo built his unequaled status in nineteenth-century Lagos by leveraging property at every turn through long-established spatial functions of accommodating kin and dependents, and by utilizing newer property functions of mortgaging, renting, and speculating. His house-sized stone mausoleum, which still stands on Taiwo Street, is a fitting tribute to his life and status—an eternal piece of Lagos's most valuable commodity: urban real estate.[63]

Just as important as—and to—a house's tangible economic value were the more abstract forms of cultural capital they signified, prized in an era when the city's elites were consciously constructing cosmopolitan tastes. If land and a residence were the ticket to commerce in Lagos, a mansion was the entrance to elite status and the power that came with it. Two elements distinguished the city's prominent homes during the era: their size and opulence and the composite nature of their architecture, which drew on Yoruba, Brazilian, and British influences to create a distinctive "Lagos style." By the 1880s, important houses in Lagos sat on several acres and were typically two stories, well over twenty feet high. The first floor usually contained workshops, storage spaces, trading shops, servants' quarters, and parlors.[64] The upstairs levels consisted of small rooms used as personal and sleeping quarters. Houses on Lawson's map like that of I. H. Willoughby (1880s)—whose mother had recognized the value of property and squatted on the future site of his house[65]—were described as a "gigantic edifice rear[ing] its lofty

Bar
59

roof above the neighboring houses." R. B. Blaize's Caxton House (1880s) was called "the new mansion—for such it is—which is of itself a most imposing piece of architectural beauty, exhibit[ing] the scientific skill of the colony to the highest advantage."[66] These and similar houses were built of brick covered inside and out with painted plaster (white, ocher, or gray)[67] and topped with an iron roof. Arched windows, balusters, and elaborately carved cornices were common and often adorned with plaster or cast-iron flower and plant motifs. The homes of Taiwo, Payne, Willoughby, Blaize, Lumpkin, and others on Lawson's map exemplified refined examples within this mold.

An imposing house decorated with flamboyant trimmings fit the cultural ideals of nineteenth-century Yoruba society and the city's commercial ethos. In business circles such a house signaled creditworthiness via the collateral value of the structure alone and the capital reserves it took upkeep such a home. In the 1870s a prominent house could cost upward of £1,000, double the net annual income of prominent merchants (four times that of professionals), with prime plots of land costing as much if not more by the 1880s.[68] Costs were high because a large quantity of material like galvanized roofing and nails had to be imported and a customs duty had to be paid on these supplies.[69] Also, a limited number of master craftsmen were capable of building large houses. Continual upkeep of plaster, foundations, and roofing in the humidity of Lagos added material and labor expenses. Creditworthiness was also signaled by the fact that the owners had sunk roots (and just as importantly, capital) into the transient and chronically undercapitalized city and were not likely to disappear. Trust was a scarce commodity, and a house went a long way to building it.[70] This allowed owners of prominent houses to rise literally above the "mushroom gentlemen" caught between rapid fluctuations in commodity prices, who, as historian Antony Hopkins describes, were "distinguished for their rapid appearance and equally swift exit."[71]

A titled house put one's name on the map, specifically Lawson's 1885 map. This brought respectability and the opportunity to host social functions and to accommodate visiting dignitaries. Payne had the honor of doing so when Edward Blyden, "Greatest Defender of the Negro Race," visited Lagos in 1890 and again when the Awajale of Jebu (Payne was the bàbá ìsàlẹ̀ for Ijebu) visited for the 1897 Queen's Diamond

Jubilee Lagos celebrations he held at Orange House.[72] Social functions within one's domain brought the power to exclude, to draw the lines of the elite class, and to arrange connections for business opportunities. So frequent and intense were social gatherings in Lagos that, as Cole writes, the "administrators of Lagos found it impossible to keep up with the high level of social entertainment Lagos demanded and requests for increases in table allowances and salaries were frequent."[73]

The cultural ideals of stately homes and ostentatious hospitality were revered in many nineteenth-century Yoruba towns, a well-documented cultural trait often characterized under the umbrella of "conspicuous consumption." Ayodeji Olukoju describes how riches were important to one's standing in Lagos, but equally important was using one's wealth conspicuously and generously, as personified, again, by Yoruba native D. C. Taiwo Olowo. His 1901 obituary stated, "Chief Taiwo was a true type of African 'big man.' With him money became wealth in the fullest sense of the term for he so utilized it so as to make it so, and the result was that his name was a household word in all the surrounding country, while he was respected far and wide."[74] The palace Taiwo built on his original plot of land in Faji grew to be a sprawling compound with two large courtyards fronted by an elegant, arcaded veranda. His rise from humble origins to the owner of a palatial estate in Lagos, and the fact that he was celebrated for this accomplishment, suggests the ways Yoruba society was changing in the late nineteenth century as young African men and returnees of Yoruba origin defied hierarchies of age and lineage to establish compounds of their own, a process facilitated by new sources of wealth like titled land.

In her study of *oríki* praise poems from the nineteenth century, Karin Barber analyzes the cultural values venerated in Yoruba society, finding "a large and splendid house" a reason to be lauded but also an increasing focus on the self-made nature of the recipient of praise in later dated poems. This shift reflected the decline of traditional titles and offices in the merit-based cultures emerging in cities like Ibadan, a city founded by warriors after the collapse of Oyo.[75] Many refugees from the upheavals of the interior fled to Lagos, where by the 1880s over thirty-two thousand of the city's thirty-thousand residents were Yoruba.[76] In this changing culture there was every incentive to establish one's own abundant domestic space, rivaling or even surpassing those of ǫbas and chiefs (unheard of before the middle of the nineteenth century), and utilizing the most expensive, novel, and high-quality materials, to be seen as a "big man."[77] In Lagos, customary social obligations to kin and the community mixed with new ideas of merit and individualized private property, allowing wealthy men to express enduring Yoruba values outside traditional channels and restrictions. A breach of tradition was especially easy for Saros and Brazilian returnees who saw their roots in Yorubaland but without the constraints of familial bonds.

The houses of prominent men were a symbol of their personal status rather than the honor of their lineage, but often, at the bequest of the patriarch or the interpretation of the courts, land and homes reverted to family property upon the death of the owner, restoring the property to the lineage. This meant that homes were often divided up, tied up in litigation, or sold off after the death of the original owner. Yet even under new owners, many of the grandest houses retained the surnames of the men and families who had established them, such was the degree to which they were tied to their identity in the community. Like their cultural uses, the appearance and construction of Lagos houses reflected a hybrid style of systems of seeing and being seen.

The Architecture of the Lagos Style

The architectural style of Lagos houses evolved over the nineteenth century as several waves of migrants arrived, each one bringing new aesthetics, construction skills, and materials. Afro-Brazilians had been trained as artisans and craftsmen in the building industries of Bahia, Olinda, and Recife, and arrived with a desire to reproduce the architecture of the Portuguese colonial "sobrados" of those cities. Sobrados were ornate middle-class houses of several stories with slaves occupying the first floor and the household family occupying the upper floors, in a microcosm of Brazil's socioeconomic structure. Initially, the Aguda, as the Brazilians of Lagos were known, faced material limitations and applied molded plaster to single-story dried-clay buildings.[78] Europeans and missionaries like Giambattista Scala and Joseph Harden introduced burnt brickmaking and established several brick factories.[79] This allowed Brazilians to reproduce their Brazilian homes, as with the model of Water House (fig. 1.8).[80] European missionaries likewise sought to build multifloor homes in Lagos's tropical environment with the belief that elevated living quarters removed occupants from the threat of malaria, thought to be the result of "bad air" seeping up from the ground.[81] In 1852 the British missionary Reverend Gollmer actually relocated the first "storey house" forty miles from Badagry to Lagos when the Church Mission Society headquarters relocated.[82] The mission had originally imported all the prefabricated planks, nails, and glass windows for the structure from Britain in 1845 along with four carpenters to erect the structure.[83] Lagos residents named the mission house *ilé alapako* (house of planks) while coining the term *ilé petesi* (upstairs house) for the two-story homes Brazilian returnees introduced in their quarter of town later in the 1850s.[84] Material, labor, and occupant's country of origin drove much of the aesthetics of early colonial Lagos.

By the 1880s the town's quarters had fused, facilitating the exchange of building techniques and styles in increasingly cosmopolitan spaces like Tinubu Square, where Payne, Fernandez, and Taiwo were neighbors on the edge of Portuguese Town. Master craftsmen like Juan Baptist da Costa trained Yoruba carpenters and brick masons, some of whom, like Sanusi Aka, became more skilled than the Brazilians.[85] In the 1880s notable craftsmen passed on their knowledge by establishing several institutes to train local craftsmen.[86] This new generation of homegrown builders found plentiful work in the 1880s as the city underwent a building boom with the houses of many prominent citizens being constructed or expanded.[87]

A minor debate in Lagos historiography concerns the origins, influences, and architectural "essence"—Yoruba, Brazilian, Afro-Brazilian, or Victorian—of these houses. Two Portuguese scholars who spent significant time in Lagos in the 1970s and 1980s, Marianno da Cunha and Massino Marafatto, found substantial elements of Yoruba architecture in prominent nineteenth-century Lagos homes, particularly the organizing principle of a central communal space.[88] Da Cunha describes the houses of the era as "a covered Yoruba compound in miniature," and another scholar echoes him in calling them "vertical Yoruba compounds."[89] Others, like Marjorie Alonge, argue that any decorative or spatial similarities to Yoruba compounds are "coincidental" and view them as fundamentally Brazilian sobrados.[90] Still others argue that Lagosians made the architecture "profoundly their own."[91]

While certainly some houses leaned more toward Brazilian precedents like Fernandez House, toward traditional Yoruba compounds like

Bar

FIGURE 1.8. Water House in the 1970s. *Source:* Joane Nagel Shaw, "Historic Buildings of Lagos, Nigeria" (unpublished manuscript, 1980), Oak Grove Library Center, Northwestern University.

Taiwo's ìgá, or even toward British missionary influences like Orange House, the circular debates over the essential character of prominent homes of the time—like those over the definition of elites—suggest a cultivated ambiguity. Composite forms of equivocal reference were a means of encouraging all members of society to see their identity and heritage reflected back in the architecture of a grand house. This was a way of helping everyone feel at home, thereby allowing homeowners to accumulate as much cultural capital and as many economic links in as many corners of society as possible.[92] The hybridity of the houses mirrored the lives of their inhabitants. A. W. Thomas, Taiwo Olowo, and J. A. Otunba Payne belonged to an elite class of opportunists in the best sense of the word, remaining loyal to their followers and kin while seizing the chance to serve as bàbá ìsàlẹ, to convert to Christianity, to take Yoruba or Christian names, to use colonial courts and auctions to serve their interests, and to construct lavish privately owned residences in the heart of town.

The facades and floor plans of Lagos homes exemplify the ambiguous nature of their architecture. Flower motifs and arches on house exteriors were nearly ubiquitous by the 1880s. The appeal and brilliance of these flourishes is that they could be read within a Brazilian, Yoruba, Islamic, or Victorian aesthetic. Early Brazilian houses like Fernandez House introduced floral imagery in the form of carved plaster cornices and wrought-iron window and door fittings. Craftsmen had transplanted these designs from Brazil at a time when Baroque revivalism was at its peak. Returnees and the local craftsmen they trained soon indigenized these designs, giving them the undulating and irregular proportions that characterize Yoruba architecture. Carved columns were commonplace in Yorubaland, a skill easily used on plaster.

The practice of dressing houses in patterned plaster was similar to the Yoruba custom of clothing one's kin and followers in matching fabric (aso ebi), styles popular among Saros returnees.[93] In oríkì poetry, cloth was often a metaphor for wealth: "I could take off my clothes and wrap myself in people."[94] At a time when real estate was beginning to rival people as the most valuable resource in town, it was fitting to "dress" one's house in patterns. Like cloth, the plastering of homes could change with trends in fashion, important in the fast-paced commercial city. The rough brickwork of elite homes gave craftsmen a surface on which to apply plaster that they could then mold into patterns. As architecture historian Nagel Shaw writes, "As a new motif became popular, such as the flower in the center of the window frame, the double volute leaf and flower in the spandrel, or a six-pointed star on the portico, it could be added by simply replastering, and applying the design to the west surface."[95]

Floral and geometric patterns transcended Afro-Brazilian aesthetics, appealing also to Christian-Victorian and Islamic-inspired tastes. Arriving from Brazil, Oyo (a major city in northern Yorubaland), and Sierra

Leone, Muslims were established in Lagos by the 1850s. Christians from Brazil, Sierra Leone, and European missions were not far behind. By the 1880s, immigration and local conversions resulted in 8,422 residents identifying as Muslim and 3,970 as Christian.[96] For the Muslim community, the formal balance of Lagos-style geometric patterns (including the six-pointed "seal of Solomon" star)[97] was appealing. Symmetrical arched windows, balusters, and columns covered with proportional patterns were incorporated into Muslim-owned houses like Elias House, Savage House, and Fred Williams House, as well as the architectural wonder, Shitta Bey Mosque, which was completed in 1894. Taiwo, who attended Anglican Church every Sunday, had his tomb created by the same builder who created Shitta Bey Mosque in a nearly identical style, suggesting his commercial ties and admiration of the Islamic community in Lagos. Founded in 1852 by Reverend Gollmer and rebuilt in 1880, St. Paul's Breadfruit Church was covered in the flamboyant exterior accretions of the era.[98]

Those who gravitated to Victorian Christian ideals found aesthetic expressions in floral facades. Flowers, representing purity and romanticism, were the visual symbol of choice for Victorian culture. Botanical gardens, codes written in floral enigmas, and people posing for pictures while holding bouquets symbolized Victorian taste.[99] Houses draped in floral designs appealed to aficionados of Victorian culture and might have signaled affiliation with flower societies in Lagos.[100] Floral patterns in England may have been introduced from Byzantine architecture, while much of Portuguese and Brazilian architecture also reflected Islamic (Moorish) influences. When these Islamic-inspired forms were incorporated into Lagos they joined up with another arm of Islamic architectural influence introduced by Muslims from northern Yorubaland and Hausa regions with trans-Saharan ties to North Africa and the Middle East. This confluence of three wings of Islamic influence in Lagos represents a fascinating rejoining after centuries of indigenization and deserves further research.

The interiors of grand homes were recognizable to many visitors in Lagos. The floor plans of most Lagos houses drew from several elements to create hybrid spaces that were both functional and accessible. A central hallway on the second floor is the feature most clearly borrowed from Brazilian homes. Long, narrow upstairs passageways became commonplace in Lagos houses by the twentieth century and made them easily convertible into rented apartments due to their streamlined arrangement, which allowed individuals to access their rooms without intruding on others. This privacy also appealed to African residents as rooms in Yoruba compounds fanned out from a central courtyard which made the rooms accessible while limiting foot traffic through them. Like Yoruba compounds, the upstairs consisted of small rooms to accommodate extended family, friends, and visitors. In contrast, the ground floor, with its parlor, verandas, workrooms, and shop, was similar to the Yoruba courtyard—a central meeting space, easily accessible to all residents of the house. This was where social, political, productive, and commercial activities were conducted.

The Rising Burden of Housing

The flipside to grand Lagos-style houses was the rise of housing—similarly because of its value and scarcity—as a form of social and political control. This contributed to a widespread sense of anxiety in Lagos over new opportunities and pitfalls as residents scrambled to navigate new uses of houses. Landlords backed by British courts had increased social power over their tenants as the gatekeepers to a coveted resource. British administrators began to recognize their political power to control the population of Lagos through housing regulations and the fines and foreclosures on noncompliant residents. British housing rules disproportionately affected small non-elite landlords at first, but by the end of the century the colony's governors began utilizing housing to consolidate political power on a wider scale. Over the course of the second half of the nineteenth century, the radically new understanding of private property rights, established by British ordinances and courts in Lagos, greatly enlarged the power that individuals could hold over physical space. The grand houses of Lagos were the most noticeable manifestations of these shifts, but the rise of private property brought less-celebrated changes to the city's sociopolitical landscape.

Though important in terms of distinguishing Lagos's elite class and setting trends for the rest of the city, the homes represented by the names on Lawson's map were the notable exceptions in the 1880s. Most residents lived in tight temporary quarters. Figures from the era suggest that the number of houses in Lagos rose from approximately 4,000 in 1871 to 6,500 only a decade later.[101] All but 108 of the city's houses in 1871 were made of clay: 3,789 "mud," 103 brick, 3 wood, 2 iron. While the number of brick and wood houses increased every year (there were 131 brickmakers in the city by 1891), most residents of the city still lived in earthen structures throughout the nineteenth century.[102] Many of these smaller houses were miniature versions of the city's more stately homes, plastered with floral patterns and containing mixed-use floor plans (see figs. 2.10 and 2.11).[103] Inside, first floors of small homes contained long parlors or hallways, like the upstairs hallways in larger homes, with private rooms for dependents or renters budding off each side. Smaller houses were fronted by commercial spaces and often hosted small vendors selling cloth or food goods in their front rooms or windows. The monetization of land meant greater incentive to sell off parts of family plots, leading to a fragmentation of the city and smaller subdivided plots. Traditional compounds constructed around courtyards were impractical on narrow plots, and much of the new construction moved cooking and washing to the backyard where the property abutted other yards, allowing greater ventilation and creating a shared courtyard-like space for the entire block.[104]

A detailed British map from 1891 shows how most buildings were arranged on plots in this pattern (map 1.3). Small single-story houses lined the bustling streets of late nineteenth-century Lagos, springing up

MAP 1.3. An 1891 cadastral map of Lagos showing the location and configuration of structures (in pink) in Central Lagos.

wherever a sliver of land could be found. The census figures for the era suggest an average of 7 people lived per house in 1871 and 5.8 per house in 1881 as a construction boom created more habitable structures.[105] Density was high, and sometimes even corners of rooms were even being rented.[106] As housing became scarcer, finding and keeping a decent living space in Lagos became more difficult for most residents. The challenge was exacerbated under an expanding British legal-regulatory system that began to privilege wealthy and connected landlords.

Property disputes were the most common form of litigation in the colony as the restructuring of the city's housing arrangements did not happen without significant contestation. Cole notes that "three-quarters of all civil litigation in Lagos were land cases."[107] Court cases involved trespass, damages, inheritance disputes, evictions, disagreements over terms of sale, and the seizure of property for debts. A key to winning a case, and itself the object of many cases, was of a Crown grant and thus private (fee simple title) rights to the piece of real estate.[108] So desirable were Crown grants that, as Mann describes, slaves and individual family members began applying for them behind the backs of their families or overlords or even stealing the documents. The ability to obtain and keep a Crown grant, from titling to litigation, favored wealthy men. The language of the ordinance requiring residents to obtain Crown grants was gendered male ("Donor, Mortgagor, Lessor or other person conveying, transferring, mortgaging, charging or demising the Land, or by some person authorized by *him* to acknowledge the same").[109] Of course, older men prevailed in taking out Crown grants for the property their family lived on because women and younger men could not afford the registration fee, even though according to Yoruba custom they had collective rights over their homes and property. Legal challenges proved too costly, foreign, baffling, and time consuming for all but the most affluent, and even being taken to court by a powerful man was enough to ostracize dependents and marginal household members.[110] It was not uncommon for people who had taken out Crown grants on behalf of their family to covertly claim individual ownership in order to sell or mortgage a property, since by the 1880s courts had ruled that family property could not be mortgaged or sold without the consent of the entire family.[111] This was a major reversal in British attempts to establish the principle of fee simple title in Lagos.

By 1900, British administrators had issued three thousand Crown grants on Lagos Island and four thousand for the Colony of Lagos to those who could prove a legal claim to the land for which they were seeking a grant.[112] Those who held Crown grants also held expanded powers and control over those who lived on their land. As Mann describes, this turned "housing into an instrument of control."[113] Extended family, slaves, and other dependents had long depended on overlords (or patrons) for a place to live in exchange for labor and allegiance, a practice that under British law became known as service tenure.[114] As property became scarcer and more valuable, the provision of living space became a more significant favor, allowing landlords to demand more labor and stricter behavior from "service tenure" tenants or for them to face paying back rent with wages they did not have. The evolving legal norms of "service tenure" became akin to domestic slavery over the second half of the nineteenth century, yet British courts repeatedly upheld landlords' rights to eject or evict tenants when "such a tenant deliberately applied himself to injure or annoy his chief or [the chief's] family."[115] Whether living under service tenure or as renters, tenants had very few rights when they lived on Crown grant land and could be evicted for perceived infractions such as failure to show "respect."[116] In this environment, acquiring titled property and defending it in court offered an unparalleled opportunity for the underclass to alter their lot, as some indeed did.[117]

As legal confrontations escalated, so did conflicts outside of the courtroom. Landlords became increasingly aware of the activities, such as being seen with a surveyor, of their family members and dependents that could be interpreted as prerequisites to obtaining Crown grants. Overlords used physical coercion, threats of eviction, and sorcery to prevent losing property and to keep dependents within their orbit, sending a message that severing ties by trying to establish one's own house would not be tolerated.

It was not uncommon for feuding residents to resort to arson, adding to the problem of fires in the crowded city.[118] In 1877 over one thousand houses burned down, including parts of Ọba Dosunmu's palace, in one of the forty major fires between 1861 and 1886.[119] Theft became more common in the 1880s as finding shelter and provisions in the city proved difficult for those without housing, those unwilling to enter into service tenure, or those unable to pay rent.[120] Some dependents, including former slaves, did find ways to acquire Crown grants or to buy property despite the dangers of doing so.[121] But once they owned property, they had to contend with British regulations.

The fires that destroyed hundreds if not thousands of houses annually in the crowded city were the most frequent target of British planning ordinances. In 1863, Governor Glover passed an ordinance banning any kind of flammable roofing material on the river side of Broad Street and allowing only "not easily inflamed" material in the rest of the town, which left bamboo "Calabar" mats as the only possible replacement for thatch and palm fronds. The penalty for failing to meet these requirements was a fine of up to £50 (property on the prime commercial location of Broad Street was sold for £100) or three months in prison. The purpose of this ordinance was to force the construction of a corrugated iron buffer zone around the small European district, even though the colony continued to enforce a tariff on corrugated iron until after a massive fire in 1877.[122] Most residents of the city could not afford to replace their roofs with either iron or Calabar mats, and the burden of meeting the requirement proved so enormous that even Church Mission Society officials considered once again moving the two-story mission in order to avoid paying to reroof it.[123] Led by powerful local men such as Taiwo, protesters succeeded in having the Calabar mat section of the ordinance repealed two years after it was passed.[124] As part of the 1863 efforts to reduce the incidence of fire, Glover also proposed widening and straightening the roads of Old Town (the Yoruba part of the city around Oba Dosunmu's palace), but backed down after Dosunmu vigorously protested.[125] As fires worsened in the later years of the nineteenth century when the city grew more crowded, the colonial government passed additional ordinances, such as one in 1887 that punished the residents of a home in which a fire started even if it was lit by arsonists or thieves.[126]

Another post-fire policy enacted under the colonial administration was to obligate the sale of burnt property to the government, which meant the British state could acquire land without having to pay for the value of the incinerated buildings.[127] Other regulations also aided the government's ability to seize property. Swamps ranked just behind fires as the bane of colonial officials, and an 1869 ordinance required property holders and Crown grant applicants to fill in swamps and remove "rubbish, ordure, or filth" or risk having the land sold at public auction.[128]

Bar   71

From the 1860s through the 1880s, the government threatened to and at times actually did auction off land on the waterfront and in the heart of the city that it deemed not to have made improvements.[129]

Europeans repeatedly blamed Africans' houses for outbreaks of disease and fire, yet there is evidence that the architectural features of native houses not only limited the spread of fires but also reduced the prevalence of mosquitoes. The much-maligned thatch that covered the nonflammable clay of most buildings offered dual protection against fire. The first was that the thatch burned so quickly that fires often burned themselves out before spreading to neighboring structures, leaving most of the original home roofless but intact. The second advantage of thatch was that if one building caught fire, teams could run ahead and quickly strip the roofs off nearby houses.[130] Likewise, the swamps fissuring the island that Europeans sought to fill in order to reduce the "poor air" thought to be connected to malaria were in fact excellent fire breaks.[131] Similarly misunderstood, the smoke from the small fires kept burning inside the rooms of African compounds (that Europeans blamed for fires) may have deterred mosquitoes, thereby reducing the spread of malaria.[132]

Yoruba residents could not understand how the homes that had protected one's family for generations posed a danger to the city or could be the exclusive property of a sole individual. This feeling of dislocation was part of a sense of confusion that swept through Yorubaland in the nineteenth century. J. D. Y. Peel masterfully describes this confusion in *Religious Encounter and the Making of the Yoruba*.[133] Upheaval touched every aspect of life from naming ceremonies to burial customs, as missionaries, warlords, explorers, and merchants introduced new ideas at a time when old institutions (slavery, political offices, and compounds) were under pressure. For native residents of Lagos it was almost impossible to surmise with certainty the terms of the new system when colonial administers came and went, passed and repealed regulations, and arbitrarily enforced the law. Added to this confusion were questions of jurisprudence over the rights conferred by new forms of land and property grants. The friend of a man who killed himself after losing his home to debt, only to see the colonial evictor buy that home at auction, lamented that Europeans kept their plans "secret from Black men in Black men's Country."[134] While ambiguity was likely born of the incompetence and inconsistency of inexperienced young officers, officials like the one who purchased the house at auction found that uncertainty among African residents benefited colonial authority and their personal wealth.[135] This pattern was observable from as early as 1867 when Governor Glover reminded a landowner who hesitated in ceding riverfront land to the government that no ordinance required embankment, "but I can make one."[136]

Peel writes how Yoruba speakers coped with uncertainty by clinging to their "'familiar names,' the *oriki orile* which defined their community of origin, 'tribal marks' (*ila*) cut into the face, food taboos (*ewo*) associated with lineage or cult membership, and often, the sense of a protective personal destiny (*ori*)."[137] In Lagos, Yoruba people continued to find their "safest refuge in the extended family, [their] second in the head of the compound, and the third in the tribal chief of the quarter."[138] But by the 1880s these groupings were under stress as chiefs, descent group heads, and eldest heirs secretly sold land for which they alone held the title without the permission of kin and, to do so, often evicted non-kin members of the household for a growing number of real or perceived offenses. Those who managed to purchase property to establish their own household found themselves under the constant threat of government intrusion over failure to comply with burdensome regulations. The result was that homes and households, the base of support to which people turned in troubling times, became unstable as housing became a form of social and political control.

Dredging the Bar

By the 1890s the sense that the ground was shifting beneath their feet was something even the most powerful class of non-European Lagosians knew. The depression of the 1880s spurred European merchants, initially with the support of African merchants, to push for British expansion into the interior where warfare was blamed for trade fluctuations.[139] A series of treaties and "pacifying" punitive expeditions in the late 1880s and 1890s created the Protectorate of Southern Nigeria in 1900. These events brought greater numbers of Europeans to Lagos, the hub and terminus of transportation projects like the dredging of the bar and the construction of a railway. Improvements in the treatment of malaria brought more than five hundred British civil servants to Lagos by 1905, many of whom arrived with their families.[140] Hardening lines of racial theories of colonial rule made it possible for European administrators and merchants to exclude non-Europeans from government jobs and trading opportunities. Local elites soon realized that the consolidation they had once insisted upon was pushing them out, as race, not grand houses on freehold property, became the basis for the acquisition of power and wealth. By 1900, all of the government positions Payne, Lawson, and Willoughby had held were occupied by Europeans.[141] In trade, European merchants based in Lagos showed a growing preference for other European merchants who were establishing their own trading outposts throughout the interior.[142]

Lawson's 1885 map hints at racial discrimination and the consolidation of British control over the city's landscape. The difference between the initial 1883 sketch, which included a large inscription for the ọba's palace, and its final form in 1887, which makes no mention of the ọba, suggests that Lawson may have been directed to remove the palace following consultations during the 1886 Colonial and Indian Exhibition in London.[143] Small dots—some black, some hollow—speckle Lawson's map. The symbols are for wells (hollow) and lamps (black) sunk and put up by the government as labeled on the map's legend. Most are distributed in the southern half of Lagos Island, the area around the European occupied marina. Toward the end of the 1880s, Lagosians noticed that despite large budget surpluses, the government was not investing in public works for the city. In fact, London had capped the funds earmarked for public improvements at £10,000 while larger sums were being transferred annually from Lagos to London.[144]

By the mid-1890s, exclusion based on race was impossible to ignore and organized African resistance had begun. Nonetheless, by 1900 the cultural and economic structures of Lagos had changed. It was a rocky period but the direction was clear, and by 1903 the Lagos Chamber of Commerce had excluded African members and the number of wealthy African merchants was greatly diminished.[145] In a colony already short on capital, credit further dried up, hindering their ability to repay their loans, which meant many were unable to keep their heavily mortgaged houses in their family after retirement or death.[146]

This is an under-analyzed aspect of the demise of the dominant African class of the late nineteenth and early twentieth century.[147] The merchants who remained in business did so by taking risks, often desperate ones, by venturing into cocoa or ivory; production rather than trade became the new road to wealth. This switch was due to the British decision to organize production in the colony and protectorate indirectly through native authorities.

Gradually, the colonial government relegitimized native institutions and practices by establishing a Native Advisory Board of chiefs. Many of these chiefs, particularly the *idéjọ* chiefs, became more aggressive in litigating claims to landownership under customary law as trustees of their families and communities. These chiefs, many of whom had resisted taking out Crown grants, saw that it was more strategic to have property holdings validated under native customs in British courts, since in that case land could never be alienated through debt or secret sales. At the same time, the benefits of social control over dependents (tenants) and rental income were persevered in perpetuity.

The next two chapters explain that the British were willing to tolerate the rise of landed chiefs, partly to control the organization of labor and housing. But the British did not want chiefs to amass too much power; governors wanted to acquire property at will for political control. They used housing as a colonial tool at each turn of occupation, segregation, surveillance, and intimidation. Going forward, the tension between native and British authorities along with the reality that private property rights were already established (though they would be gradually revoked from former slaves) created overlapping claims and new conflicts, but the colonial architecture, both imperial building forms and the institutions they contained, left no doubt as to who was in power.

The 1896 construction of a new Government House was symbolic of Britain's concentrated assertion of racial superiority and the creation of a ruling class in Lagos. The house was by far the largest and grandest structure in the city, eclipsing all of the mansions built by Lagos elites in the 1880s or 1890s, and raising the Union Jack high (fig. 1.9 and see fig. 2.15). Approximately nine thousand square feet, its massive two-winged, two-floor design contained twenty rooms, including a palaver hall and a billiard room. It was also unambiguously British colonial in design, with cold and rigid pitched roofs, verandas, and shutters, and none of the rhythmic playfulness of the Lagos style.

To create the new Government House, builders tore down the surveyor's house where Lawson had once worked to create the 1885 map

Bar

FIGURE 1.9. A skeletal Government House on a clear-cut field, ca. 1896. *Source:* The National Archives, Kew, UK.

of Lagos showing the names of the city's elites. The new Government House overlooked the water where the sandbar would be dredged to allow the entry of heavy ships into the harbor: an opening of the channel but a closing of opportunities for the cosmopolitan class and those who aspired to rise to their heights through a privately owned Lagos-style home.

2

Canal

Trenches in Land, Labor, and Sanitation Struggles: Imperial Lagos

Going from the Lagos mainland to Ikoyi on a Saturday night
was like going from a bazaar to a funeral. And the vast Lagos
cemetery which separated the two places helped to deepen
this feeling. For all its luxurious bungalows and flats and
its extensive greenery, Ikoyi was like a graveyard. It had no
corporate life—At any rate for those Africans who lived
there. They had not always lived there, of course. It was
once a European reserve. But things had changed, and some
Africans in "European posts" had been given houses in Ikoyi.
Obi Okonkwo, for example lived there, and as he drove from
Lagos to his flat he was struck again by these two cities in
one. It always reminded him of twin kernels separated by
a thin wall in a palm-nut shell. Sometimes one kernel was
shiny black and alive, the other powdery white and dead.

—Chinua Achebe, *No Longer at Ease*

Today it is easy to slip by car between Ikoyi and Lagos Island on
backstreets from Obalende to Onikan or over the E1 expressway from
Osborne Road into the sunken streets of Popo Aguda. Google Maps
renders the two boroughs as a contiguous landmass, such is the extent
to which they have merged over time. Only those paying close attention
might notice the remnants of a muddy, now garbage-filled canal cutting
between the island and its wealthier eastward extension, Ikoyi. But for

Canal

77

decades, beginning in the early twentieth century, this trench, known as MacGregor Canal, was the highly visible barrier between White and Black homes in Lagos, a gash in the soil structuring the movement and residential spaces of generations under colonial rule. Forgotten and barely visible today, the canal's effects are still felt. Ikoyi remains the most expensive and coveted property in the city, with home prices running into the millions of dollars, while Lagos Island continues to be a flyover for international corporations and expats.

Writing of coeval furrows in the earth, Italian political philosopher Antonio Gramsci compared the clusters of ideas and behaviors in society to World War I trenches and argued that each dictated the battle lines and terms of engagement in society and war, respectively. In MacGregor Canal the two sides of Gramsci's metaphor converge: the canal as a product of the ideas on race and cityscapes popular in British imperial thought of the time and its manifestation as a literal trench helped to create the spatial and societal positions in which Lagos residents would engage for years to come.[1] The ideas symbolized by the canal were entwined with its physical presence to have profound implications for the households of Lagos, particularly in the growing disparity in terms of race and access to land as the city changed from an experimental entrepôt into the administrative and economic nerve center of the imperial behemoth of Nigeria.

By the end of the nineteenth century, long-ossifying British fantasies of dominating and exploiting Africa's Black landscapes became more viable with arrival of new forms of technology and administration.[2] This chapter and the next cover this turn, reading housing as a central concern and strategy (a symbolic and pragmatic instrument) in early Nigerian struggles over land, labor, and sanitation, all of which were involved in the creation of the canal, and all of which came together—in a serendipitous coup d'état for the British administration—in its eventual use to segregate the city. What these chapters show is that *how* urban landscapes were envisioned through the intersection of aesthetic discourses and technologies of representation shaped these struggles and their outcomes—including house forms—in profound ways.[3] In particular, the increased state circulation of maps and photographs produced and affirmed British views of Black landscapes and of the progress of urban planning, while alliances of Lagosians pointed to maps and images of expropriated settlements and extravagant European houses as signs of rising injustice that cut to the very heart of Africans' livelihood: their homes.

The MacGregor Canal, three thousand feet long and twenty-five feet wide, encapsulates the break in the flow of history in Lagos and much of the world in the early twentieth century. In Europe, mechanized weapons were fired from foxholes, and radical changes in industrialized transportation and communication networks, professionalized urban planning practices, and nationalist and workers' revolutions accelerated change and altered the continent, its cities, and its colonial empires.

Many of the same forces were at work in the remaking of Lagos and its homes. A 1908 photograph from the British National Archives shows MacGregor Canal calmly flowing between two steep sandbanks and shrub-covered plains (fig. 2.1). The canal is a long slit in the ground between Lagos Island and Ikoyi—an opening between the nineteenth century, in which such colonial undertakings directed by the state in West Africa were less common, and the twentieth, in which such concerted upheavals of earth and urban centers became routine. Between the mid-1890s and 1911, railway tracks were extended 711 miles from Lagos to Kano, and total annual ship tonnage entering Lagos Harbor more than doubled from four hundred thousand tons to over eight hundred thousand (1905).[4] It was Lagos's role to perform the alchemy between earth and water. Dredging, draining, wharfing, bridging, and tarring were the elixirs. A fourfold increase in the total value of imports and exports passing through Lagos (1892–1910) was the *rubedo* result.[5]

Coordinating these complex and interconnected efforts were European surveyors, engineers, and inspectors with specialized training and specific tasks. Urban planning crystallized as a profession at the turn of

FIGURE 2.1. MacGregor's Canal, ca. 1908–12. *Source:* The National Archives, Kew, UK.

Canal

the century. Its prevailing vision, and raison d'être, was the redesign of the city for economic ends. At home, urban planning aligned with liberal reform movements to improve metropolitan living conditions, but in the colonies it could be employed for the ends of what observers like J. A. Hobson (1902) were beginning to defame with the newly popularized term "imperialism": "'aggressive,' 'cut-throat,' 'calculating, greedy,' and 'cynical,' [rule] egged on by industrialists and financiers cloaked in talk of a 'mission to civilize.'"[6] The British officials brought to Lagos to realize these "cynical" or "civilizing" ambitions needed to be sheltered and kept alive in order to execute their duties, and a large part of the Garden City model of planning popularized by the famous utopian Ebenezer Howard was providing suitable housing for workers. European bungalows, like the one just barely visible in the far distance of figure 2.1, soon became common colonial houses in Lagos. Government quarters like these were built to precise specifications and features depending on the position and rank of the colonial employees. Yet, despite the swelling of European ranks, Lagos was still overwhelmingly a city of Africans (one hundred Africans to every European as late as 1911), many of whom were migrants from the interior in search of work.[7]

Bent at the waist, two muscular African men look up from their labor on the far side of the canal toward the colonial photographer. Shirtless, they are schlepping buckets of silt into a canoe, widening and deepening the waterway. Once the canoe is full, they will steer it to the western end of Lagos Island where the silt will be used to fill Alakoro Swamp. Canoes like the long dugout in the image had been *the* crucial transport vessels of Lagos for centuries, moving enslaved people, palm, warriors, refugees, and cotton through riverine networks and out to seafaring vessels across the shallow lagoon channel.[8] In the context of the iron tramways, heavy steamers, and railways operating by the time of the photograph on Lagos Island and Iddo Wharf, the canoe seems almost anachronistic in the way horses dragging howitzers appear in World War I photographs. Despite iron rails and steam-powered engines, it was the flesh and sweat of African bodies that transformed Lagos into a colonial capital designed primarily to cater to the export of raw materials and the comfort, status, and health of the Europeans who directed the operations. Like the men toiling with canoes instead of steam power, British planning left African homes without the newly arrived gas streetlamps, piped water, and refuse collection services, in time reifying derogatory images of Black landscapes.

For the two men in the photograph, their route to decent and dependable lodging in the first decades of the twentieth century would have been difficult. For the British, both at home and abroad, the trend was for housing to be tied to one's labor (e.g., "working-class housing"), and increasingly regulated by the state.[9] But this bargain did not extend to most African workers. Rather, the British saw African homes in terms of disease and disorder, as health threats to the professional European labor force. Administrators were interested in African houses largely in terms of monitoring and surveilling them for pathogens and removing them to facilitate the unimpeded transport of exports. The provision of housing for African workers was left to chiefs and household heads, lowering labor costs by externalizing the expense of shelter and the cooking and caretaking associated with a home.

In the African quarters of Lagos, due to the continuation of contradictory legal rulings and maneuvers that upheld the claims of powerful families to the inalienability of their land and their broad rights over it, holdings of housing and land were the basis of power closed off to those unfortunate enough not to inherit it. This situation left men like the canal diggers beholden to landlords for small rental spaces or at the mercy of powerful African patrons. The colonial administration tended to empower landowners, organizing the control and sheltering of mass labor through them, but African elites and British administrators also clashed as the British sought to commandeer lands like Ikoyi in order to contain the city's boundaries and economic trajectory, controlling who entered the city and how it would expand. In this struggle over the future of Lagos, "it was land that cemented the coalition" of chiefs and landowning African elites who, together, founded the first protonationalist movements.[10] In 1912, Herbert Macaulay, the father of Nigerian nationalism, delivered a powerful speech on "The Lagos Land Question" at the foot of Government House. Despite Macaulay's efforts on behalf of African opposition, seven years later the land east of MacGregor Canal was sealed off as a European reserve.

There is a sense of possibility in the canal photograph, of new shores and verdant Edens, but there is also desolation, an unsettling reminder of nineteenth-century slavery as well as the looming knowledge

Canal

81

of the violence and death—fever, flu, and plague would soon envelop Lagos—waiting in the coming century. At exposure, it is a sunny morning, but, once developed, the monochromatic image reveals itself as a shadowy Styx. In the spatial alchemy that was Lagos, the canal would be the hermetic seal.[11]

Elevating an Image of an Imperial Capital

Ironically, MacGregor Canal was not originally a symbol of racial exclusion. It was Governor William MacGregor's attempt to literally lift Lagos and all its inhabitants from the island's mosquito-infested foundation as an alternative to quarantining them by race. Construction began in 1903 as part of a public works project to drain and fill wetlands, especially the Kokomaiko Swamp that squeezed the eastern end of the island like the fingers of a corpse (see map 1.1). As MacGregor described it, Lagos was "perfectly flat for miles inland from the seas ... geologically a combination of lagoon, swamp, and low-lying sand."[12] In other words, it was perfect for mosquitoes.[13] Several years earlier, Sir Ronald Ross had discovered malarial parasites in the gut of mosquitoes while stationed in the British colonial service at Secunderbad, India. Mosquitoes transmit malaria—a fact with drastic implications for colonial planning and housing schemes. At the time, malarial fever was the primary ailment behind West Africa's reputation as the "white man's grave" with annual death rates for Europeans averaging fifty-four per thousand (1881–97) and total rates at forty per thousand annually in Lagos, which was by 1900 a city with a population of more than forty thousand, with thirty thousand people in the surrounding areas.[14] But as historian Abosede George points out, by the turn of the century Lagos was the "burial place of black babies," with a 42 percent infant mortality rate; in 1899, 864 African infants died. MacGregor mentioned these figures in his lectures on malaria.[15]

Ross's discovery inspired MacGregor, himself a physician and correspondent of Ross, to clear Lagos of mosquito habitats and educate the town on prophylactic measures. He outfitted Government House with screens and nets and authorized the Lagos Ladies League, a group of "educated ladies of Lagos," to undertake home visits to persuade Africans to take quinine.[16]

To the chagrin of the Colonial Office, these tactics flew in the face of the emerging conventional practice of creating separate European enclaves away from African areas. This segregationist policy was promoted by British physicians at the Liverpool School of Tropical Medicine (founded 1898) based on India's model of cantonments.[17] In British West Africa, European reserves existed, or soon would, in major centers such as Freetown, Accra, Bathurst, and Ibadan, and in French West Africa at Conakry, Dakar, and Abidjan.[18]

This model of residential segregation stemmed from deeply held racist discourses of African difference combined with the institutionalization of more recent "scientific" Darwinist theories. Both ideas alleged that "fallen" Africans inhabited substandard and insanitary homes, which bred mosquitoes and disease. MacGregor knew this was unscientific nonsense. He showed that mosquito counts were actually lower in African neighborhoods in Lagos and ridiculed the prospect of European officials greeting native chiefs and choirboys from behind "a glass case or wire cage."[19] His proposal was to improve the environs of both natives and Europeans on Lagos Island and thereby raise the health and well-being of all. Such was the logic behind his plan "to advance ourselves, and take the natives along with us."[20] As his statement suggests, MacGregor's investments still focused first and foremost on Europeans' health, but he resisted segregation and recognized that standing water was the enemy, not African lodgings.[21]

His successors did not share his inclusive vision, balking at the cost of improving the entire city and opting for heavy-handed tactics and European reserves, eventually blaming native "huts" and African children for disease and making MacGregor Canal the cordon sanitaire between White and Black homes. While MacGregor's racial views were an anomaly, his broader campaign to reimagine and remake Lagos at a macrolevel proved enduring.

With MacGregor's arrival in 1899, a push to apply new ideas about city planning to Lagos gained momentum and continued under his successors, Governor Sir Walter Egerton (1903–12) and Lord Frederick Lugard (1912–19). Measures to elevate Lagos into a condition fit for the primary port of the Gulf of Guinea and the capital of the Colony and Protectorate of Southern Nigeria (joined in 1906) included the construction of a tramway (1902) around the island to collect "night soil," a railway line that would eventually reach Ibadan and Kano (1911), a series of streetlamps, a barrier to break the ocean's current and deepen the port,

Canal

a network of street drains, a pipeline for water from north of the city, a new embankment of the marina, and, of course, MacGregor Canal to empty Kokomaiko Swamp.[22] After years of op-eds and criticism by local newspapers, the government of Lagos was investing in improvements, albeit unevenly, throughout the city.[23] All these projects were linked. The harbor moles required tons of stone brought by rail from Aro Quarry; the officials overseeing this construction needed clean water and waste disposal; and all these undertakings were for naught if the eroding marina proved inadequate to meet the needs of the export companies that lined it. Planning in Lagos adhered to what Lugard would later declare: "The material development of Africa may be summed up in one word—transport."[24] The conception of a city as an interdependent space that could be planned with intentional motives to fit a specific end had been developing for centuries through experiments in British settlements from the American colonies to the British Raj; it was finally realized in the early twentieth century.[25] Again, Liverpool, Lagos's shipping link to the metropole, was central to distilling and disseminating these theories. A stone's throw from the Liverpool School of Tropical Medicine, the Liverpool School of Architecture was the first institution to offer coursework in urban planning through its Department of Civic Design and Town Planning, established in 1909. That department, like the School of Tropical Medicine, was endowed by W. H. Lever, who had made his fortune mass-producing soap from West African palm oil.[26]

Like Lever's business pursuits, the Department of Civic Design's vision for cities stressed comprehensive, integrated, and meticulous but paternalistic organization. The school was unequivocal on this point: "Like the School of Architecture, our School of Town Planning has a distinct point of view. It believes and teaches that a well-organized society expresses its existence only in a well-directed and well-planned way. A dignified city must have formal planning at its core."[27] Similar principles would make Unilever, Lever Brothers' successor, into Britain's largest company by market value.[28] These principles drove colonial city planning into a new era leading to anxious reorganization for imperial cities around the globe in a quest to become "dignified," which in Africa meant sanitizing Black landscapes (as Egerton wrote, "to let in the light")[29] or, if that was not possible, identifying them and keeping them from contaminating other areas.

Documenting, classifying, inspecting, charting, standardizing, labeling, and ranking were all part of a "trench" in modern British epistemology.[30] The principle of a proper order, or at least the appearance of it, dug deep into the collective mind of a nation. Out of this rut or bulwark, depending on how one views it, sprang racial taxonomies, professionalized bureaucracies, and a world empire built upon the combination of the two.[31] Moral virtue was attached to order, especially *visual* order, and schools like Liverpool's Civic Design stressed ideals of beautiful cities abloom with manicured gardens where everything had its place and everything could be scrutinized in a sweeping glance.[32] Emerging from industrial landscapes, homegrown "Garden City" or imported American "City Beautiful" visions for urban spaces merged a nostalgia for nature with a reverence for the industrial efficiency of disciplined grids and the monumental production capacities of iron and stone that had churned out Britain's unsurpassed might in consumer goods and naval vessels.[33]

In this era, in which the mass circulation of facsimiles first became possible, image was everything. Between two hundred and three hundred billion postcards were sent between 1885 and 1920 as the reproduction and sending of photographs (and maps) became easier than ever before.[34] The colonial state readily employed new technologies of representation across Africa, filling Colonial Office dispatches with photo books and maps. Images and the colonial bureaucracy's role in their production and distribution were a critical medium for defining, as Deborah Poole writes, race-based "feelings of community and sameness among metropolitan bourgeoisie, aspiring provincial merchants, and upper- and middle-class colonialists scattered around the globe."[35] Exterior surfaces were equated with moral essence, and to fall outside of what Europeans perceived as aesthetic ideals further pushed colonized spaces into "exteriority" (otherness) against which Europeans continued to codify an "interior," "superior" racial identity.[36] Black and brown skin as evidence of fallen races was the most pernicious manifestation of this way of seeing.[37] For many without MacGregor's devotion to the face-to-face process of negotiating pragmatic on-the-ground results like Ladies League efforts or the Native Council (through which he solicited the opinions of local elites), surfaces were taken as representations of reality, as face-value reflections of virtue.

During MacGregor's tenure at Lagos, the Malaria Committee of the Royal Society paid a visit to evaluate the progress being made by his

Canal 85

strategy of drainage, education, and quinine. The resulting report, written by Drs. J. W. Stephens and S. R. Christophers, reads like the words of men with their minds already made up to recommend segregation. Undeterred neither by the drop in malarial parasites found in the population nor by their inability to locate anopheles (the genus of mosquito that transmits malaria), they submitted that the disorder of native settlements was concealing the mosquitoes they failed in finding, writing that mosquitoes

> are more numerous in towns than would appear from a carefully made "spot map," for they are easily overlooked in native enclosures and other sites difficult to access. . . . Mere observation of breeding places has led to totally erroneous ideas as to the real distribution of anopheles at this time. . . . *The real distribution of anopheles would be indicated by a spot map showing the native huts of a district.* . . . In nearly every hut anopheles can be found by one practised in detecting them [then why did they not find them?]: feeding at night on the inmates, and secreted by day in the dirty thatch. . . . To stamp out native malaria is at present chimerical, and every effort should rather be turned to the protection of Europeans.[38]

The "spot map" they produced (yet which they sought to undermine, thereby undermining their own competence) testified to the progress MacGregor had made in shrinking anopheles to several small pockets on Lagos Island (map 2.1).[39] Elsewhere in the report, Stephens and Christophers analogized native dwellings and children to the livestock that acted as incubators for sleeping sickness, the disease (trypanosomiasis) transmitted by tsetse flies. They noted how in other regions of Africa the destruction of cattle had eradicated the disease, implying the removal of "dirty" African dwellings or the removal of Europeans from their vicinity would have similar results in rendering "malaria a comparatively rare disease."[40] In their statements, Stephens and Christophers were tacitly scapegoating the lack of legibility in the African landscape and what they perceived as the unsanitary quality of the native town for their inability to provide scientific evidence supporting segregation. Their criticisms of native neighborhoods drew on solidifying British ideals for what colonial cities should look like: wide, unobstructed streets, open squares, and standard, well-delineated plot sizes.[41]

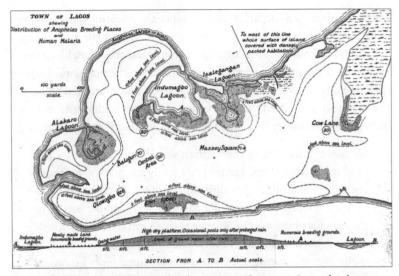

MAP 2.1. Stephens and Christophers's spot map showing a Lagos landscape mostly free from mosquitoes despite their claims otherwise. Source: "Reports, &c., From Drs. Stephens and Christophers, West Coast of Africa," in *Reports to the Malaria Committee of the Royal Society*, third series (London: Harrison and Sons, St. Martin's Lane, 1900), plate 2.

Realizing these ideals was a challenging task in Lagos, where officials wrestled with a low-lying landscape, hundreds of years of built-up settlements, vigorous claims to land rights, and a coiling entrenched road system. The Yoruba phrase for a "town planner" (*atun lu to*), meaning "he who *reorganizes* the town," gestures to the speciousness of the English assumptions behind the term.[42] In fact, the discussion of the "birth" of town planning and model cities in the early twentieth century is ironic in a Yoruba setting where authorities had spatially and architecturally designed cities based on a "grand model" of their own (the holy city of Ilé-Ifẹ) with an eye toward sanitation for hundreds of years.[43] On more than one occasion British officials considered planning from the ground up by building a new capital at Calabar (Egerton in 1905), or moving the capital to the mainland of Lagos (Lugard in 1913).[44] Yet despite the challenge, Lagos's islands were already the predominant port for Nigeria, and "order" would have to be instilled. Governor Egerton, taking over from MacGregor in 1903, applied thinking along the lines of Stephens and Christophers, seeking segregation and suspiciously viewing native settlements in terms of obstructions and disease incubators. Eventually, as Lagos historian Abosede George describes, "the climate of racial antagonism that Governor Egerton built up" killed the Ladies League as residents began to fear its members as "spies who came to inspect the houses in order to report the unhygienic conditions to the government."[45] Unable to institute segregation immediately as land expropriations on which to construct European reserves stalled in court, Egerton was forced to not entirely abandon native quarters, yet it was clear that he was, as George writes, "uninterested in the physical and material welfare of colonial subjects."[46] Through tactics of surveillance and intimidation, he was determined to impose legibility and his idea of order on Lagos. Given the pivot away from the successful programs MacGregor had instituted, it is clear that Egerton's motivations were as much visual as medical.

Over the opening decades of the century, colonial photographers and cartographers began to leave a more thorough visual recording of the many public works projects underway in and around Lagos. Photographs and maps were taken as "empirical" proof of progress, as unbiased imprints of observable improvements in installing the desired sanitized order.[47] A flurry of activity is captured in colonial photo albums from the era (figs. 2.2–2.3). In them, earth is moved, rivers superseded, ocean currents broken, and rains thwarted at a manic pace. The ideas for

FIGURE 2.2. House construction by African laborers overseen by colonial officers, ca. 1900. *Source:* The National Archives, Kew, UK.

FIGURE 2.3. Embankment of the marina at Lagos, ca. 1900. *Source:* The National Archives, Kew, UK.

transformative transport projects in Lagos, simmering for decades but always squashed by swamps and budgets, were now unleashed as materials, funding, manpower, and machines arrived. Egerton fought hard for funding for these projects, buying into the school of thought that "government cannot do the mining and agriculture, but it can make it profitable for others to embark on such speculations."[48]

Accompanying the photograph of MacGregor Canal in a series from 1908 to 1912, during the height of Egerton's rule, are a dozen before-and-after images of the reclamation of Alakoro Swamp. Lawson's 1885 map depicted the Alakoro area as a small, encircled islet within western Lagos Island surrounded by Balogun Street, Kosch Street, and Offin Lane (map 1.1). Initially, in the February 1908 pre-reclamation photographs, the streets are churned mud traversed by large stepping stones and crisscrossing boards (fig. 2.4). The photos show the crowding of Lagos and the sprawl of settlements to the edge of swamplands. One can imagine a certain familiar rhythm of hops, skips, and jumps to pass such a lane well known by residents. But to outsiders these streets appeared to be obstacles, slowing transport and inspections, and breeding mosquitoes; placing any objects in the road was outlawed.[49] By the June and July post-reclamation images, the building's walls are straightened, and the streets are packed, flattened, and dry in the height of the rainy season no less, with parallel cement drains channeling the runoff into the lagoon (fig. 2.5). This was the picture of success sent to the Colonial Office. Mission accomplished, the responsibility and cost of keeping up the newly graded and drained streets was passed to the residents whose homes bordered the streets.[50] Another 1908 photograph in the collection shows a swamp completely filled with refuse and sand brought from MacGregor Canal; Lagos was literally being enlarged and elevated after years of overflowing with people and water. By 1911, colonial maps show the area of Alakoro Swamp completely subsumed within the solid ground of the rest of the island (map 2.2), made legible and accessible to inspectors.[51]

Egerton and Lugard's interest in remaking the landscape of Lagos to facilitate their overarching schemes of order and more efficient transport extended at times to African houses, such as in the case of Alakoro. However, expediting transportation was an act of conquering terrain, and African houses mattered only insofar as they held back plans for

MAP 2.2. Map of Lagos showing the areas where thatch roofing was prohibited (in green), which included Alakoro, 1911. *Source:* The National Archives, Kew, UK.

FIGURE 2.4. Standing water traversed by stones and boards in pre-reclamation Alakoro, February 1908. *Source:* The National Archives, Kew, UK.

FIGURE 2.5. Filled, packed, and leveled streets in Alakoro, July 1908. *Source:* The National Archives, Kew, UK.

visually, materially, and epidemiologically oiling the landscape for the movement of goods.[52] Egerton, Lugard, and many other British officials at Lagos were imbued to varying degrees with what Maynard W. Swanson famously described as "the sanitation syndrome," a way of perceiving the colonial cityscape through "the imagery of infection and epidemic disease" and connecting blackness to blightedness and, to take Swanson further, moral decay.[53] Ross feared that British agents in West Africa were submitting to the "monstrous" nature of Black landscapes, with all its associations of amorality, writing, "Even in Lagos and Accra the houses can be described only as second-rate. In Freetown they are simply execrable; and it is monstrous that Englishmen, much more ladies, should be compelled to live in them. It should be remembered that many of these West African hovels are built by the Government."[54] At Lagos, colonial officials in the early nineteenth century sought to reverse this perceived downward drift, indeed seeing Black homes as medical and moral contagions, and finding culprits in features like the "dirty thatch" of Yoruba architecture, as Stephens and Christophers did, and in the "badly planned" windowless spaces of Afro-Brazilian homes. The Alakoro images show a number of traditional thatch and bamboo homes that still dominated much of the northern half of the city. A photograph from the Alakoro series shows a dense residential area on the edge of the swamp reclamation, a backdrop of rectangular buildings of several sizes (fig. 2.6). These structures on Lagos Island were similar to those found from the same era in towns near Lagos like Ebute Ero and Epe (fig. 2.7). The structures seem to almost spring out of the landscape but were the product of years of accumulated knowledge on the part of

FIGURE 2.6. Alakoro thatch and clay structures, which dominated the Lagos landscape into the early twentieth century, 1908. *Source:* The National Archives, Kew, UK.

Canal

FIGURE 2.7. Native houses (and canoes) east of Lagos at Epe, ca. 1900. *Source:* The National Archives, Kew, UK.

Yoruba builders. As the homes careened with the seasons, winds, and rain like the pre-reclamation Alakoro streets, families would maintain and reinvest in their homes, repairing and adjusting them over time.[55] Like the city's natural environs, British planners saw them as necessary yet frustrating to tame. Ordinances continued to regulate construction materials, and iron roofing can be seen in a number of images as Alakoro was located south of the section of the city granted relief to continue using thatch (map 2.2). The remaining thatched houses would have been in violation and at risk of being fined or torn down. Despite the open disdain for and scapegoating of African dwellings by British agents, contemporaneous photographs uncover that the colonial administration found natural materials sufficient for building officer quarters in the interior, and even covered standard-issue tents with thatch canopies for additional shelter (figs. 2.8–2.9).[56] What these photos of colonial bungalows constructed of palm, earth, and bamboo illustrate is the adaptability, durability, availability, and thus affordability of local materials and building techniques that had been developed over centuries. Deep technology existed in the houses that visitors and officials in Lagos dismissed as "dirty" huts.

FIGURES 2.8 AND 2.9. British officers' quarters in the interior of Lagos made of thatch and other natural materials, early 1900s. *Source:* The National Archives, Kew, UK.

Contempt did not stop with indigenous dwellings. Officials also targeted newer brick and plaster row houses. Colonial Office photographs accompanying a sanitary report from 1908 show a street of modest Afro-Brazilian-style homes with the caption "badly planned house showing good frontage" (fig. 2.10). In British eyes, the brick facades set back from the street were an improvement from what they saw as the helter-skelter bamboo and clay walls of Alakoro, yet on the following document was a floor plan of the home from the previous photograph, again with the handwritten comment "showing badly lighted + badly ventilated rooms" (fig. 2.11). Light and ventilation were British dogma for houses in the tropics endorsed by institutions like the School of Tropical Medicine—Ross wrote, "It is absolutely essential in the tropics to have good roofs and large airy rooms"[57]—but had never been a priority in Yoruba homes where the cool shade of thick solid walls was privileged over windows, which let in mosquitoes and rain and reduced

FIGURE 2.10. Afro-Brazilian-style house in Lagos, 1908. The caption of a sanitary report critique reads: "Badly planned house showing good frontage." *Source:* The National Archives, Kew, UK.

FIGURE 2.11. Ground plan of premises "showing badly lighted and badly ventilated rooms," Lagos, 1908. *Source:* The National Archives, Kew, UK.

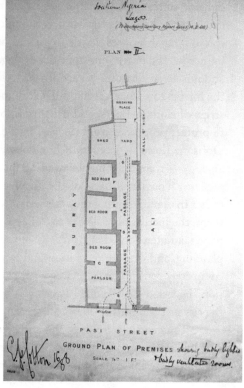

privacy.[58] By stressing light and ventilation, British inspectors showed their concern with visibility and miasma (bad air thought to cause disease prior to the discovery of germs) over mosquitoes and temperature.[59]

An emphasis on different priorities in urban morphology and aesthetics underscored tensions over the push to remake Lagos where officials preferred legibility, uniformity, and permanence in their effort to channel raw materials out of Lagos with as few obstacles as possible. These preferences differed, and even countered, what art historians point to as Yoruba aesthetic appreciations of natural beauty, harmony, functionality, utility, and an emphasis on inner qualities that may not meet the eye.[60] Yoruba visual landscapes, like those around Alakoro, embodied and communicated treasured cultural values, unappreciated by Europeans due to the fact that, as Herbert Macaulay, originally a surveyor, pointedly noted, "the European does not thoroughly understand the character of the native or he has no desire to study it."[61] An example from MacGregor shows that even the most sympathetic administrators did not comprehend African aesthetics and privileged the European urban form; he wrote that "in returning from the remoter parts [of the colony], fetish houses, fetish trees, and other 'Jujus' become strikingly numerous the nearer one approaches Lagos—the centre of civilization and missionary labour."[62] Part of what MacGregor likely observed was the increase in what Yoruba call ààlè, bundles of everyday objects (e.g., strips of cloth, peppers, and nails) positioned as "warning signs, meant to protect properties from thieves," in the words of art historian David Doris.[63] These objects, which symbolize—through metaphor and analogy—"the punishments awaiting those who disregard their warning," were "powerful parts of the Yoruba visual landscape."[64] In reality, rather than representing the antithesis of civilization as MacGregor saw them, the increase in ààlè closer to Lagos hinted at the disruption, suspicion, and tensions that British systems of property ownership, urban planning, and dispute resolution had caused in the city. Ironically, and completely contrary to MacGregor's way of seeing them, their proliferation suggested that colonial Lagos was perceived by Yoruba arrivals to the city as the opposite of a good, ideal, or moral place.

Ultimately, it is unlikely the author of the 1908 sanitation report was able to compel any changes to the Afro-Brazilian house in the photograph. Officials issued thousands of summonses for property owners

Canal

found to have violated building codes, but in 1910 alone, two thousand had to be canceled because the courts could not handle the volume.[65] African homes, both vernacular and hybrid, were a British nuisance, inspected and lamented, but in the early 1900s British officials did not yet have the means to completely remake native houses without causing a backlash or a massive housing shortage.

While African houses were at first passively corralled through inspections and fines, British planners made a more concentrated effort to remake European residences in Lagos. A series of map overlays made as part of a British Sanitary Report from 1913 spatially illustrates the town planning schemes and interventions sweeping early twentieth-century Lagos. One overlay in thick red shows the areas where thatch roofs were prohibited (map 2.2); another shows the borders of sanitary and inspection districts in blue and crimson; a third and fourth show the locations of colonial latrines, waste collections, dustbins, and additional drainage schemes; and a fifth shows areas of yellow fever quarantines from the 1913 outbreak. Planners had split up the city into crisscrossing tracts to keep tabs on African houses and activities through the sanitary inspectors whom the city's African residents had come to loathe (and whom they called *woléwolé*—a compound of *wo* and *ilé* repeated, meaning "looks at house").[66] The 1911 map produced by the Southern Nigerian Cadastral Branch over which these planning measures are plotted includes detailed contour lines, recording the elevation of each area of the city, as well as small roman numerals giving the number of structures contained within each city block. Compared to Lawson's quaint 1885 map—interested primarily in where local luminaries lived—the 1911 map and 1913 overlays look more like the detailed diagrams of an industrial machine broken down into thousands of individual components and symbols.

The Egerton and Lugard regimes recast the city as an impersonal series of mechanisms, a mode of planning that would only solidify in the coming decades within the rise of the modernist movement. In addition to the increase in trade, the result of the efforts captured in the overlays and other projects was a reduction in the annual mortality rate from near forty deaths per thousand to less than thirty per thousand despite the population quickening its increase.[67] However, these successes were not evenly distributed. Infant mortality rates remained high for Africans.[68] The fact was that planning measures themselves were not evenly distributed. For example, the tramway cut the island in half, collecting waste from only the predominantly European southern part of the island.[69] This division created two sides of the "tracks," enclosing African housing to the northern part of the island, a striking division still visible in aerial photographs from the 1970s (see chapter 5). Drainage schemes, electric lamps, embankments, piped water, and government services all predominately served the southern half of the island, where the European community lined the marina prior to codified segregation.

With the creation of new divisions like the Sanitary Department, the Municipal Board of Health, and the Public Works Department came an influx of British officials, many of whom, encouraged by anti-malarial strides, brought their families. Between 1904 and 1911 the total number of Europeans in Lagos rose from 250 to nearly 700.[70] Houses were needed to host these swelling ranks, and as was the trend at home in Britain, this could not be left to laissez-faire whims but had to be accounted for and ensured within a city beginning to adhere to organizational principles of a planned colonial city. In Britain the concept of "housing" as a social obligation was solidifying in the early twentieth century as shelter was increasingly connected to labor. In the first decade of the century, Parliament passed a series of housing acts, instituting housing standards for working-class neighborhoods in addition to the nineteenth-century Master and Servant Laws that required certain categories of employers to provide adequate housing to laborers.[71] Housing acts were part of a growing realization that the housing of the working class was connected to the health of cities and thus the productivity of the manufacturing-based economy. This marked the start of a long-term trend tying housing to labor and creating a conception of shelter as a worker's right.[72] In Lagos, where the concern was for the administration of a racially organized export economy rather than a class-based manufacturing economy, the social obligation of housing extended only to White British employees.[73] The Colonial Office and the Public Works Department developed an intricate catalog of housing models designated for the different positions occupied by White male British employees in the colonies. British photographs from the turn of the century show the quarters of Lagos officials from the surveyor's quarters (fig. 2.13) to the inspector's quarters (who, ironically, was afforded a tall wall around the property for privacy and protection). Each photograph included a label of the position of the person who occupied the house. Specific residential

Canal 97

spaces for specific professions went hand in hand with the standardization and professionalization of roles.[74] The designs of British quarters show an emphasis on upstairs ventilation, sunshades, and raised living quarters. Again, as historians have noted, like the unscientific priorities Stephens and Christophers pushed in the policing of native homes, "mosquito theory and, indeed, the germ theory of disease had failed to penetrate the ingrained beliefs of the administrators in the dangers of miasma."[75] While the era's hasty push to reorganize had been kicked off by legitimate scientific breakthroughs in epidemiology and management, it is clear that much of its implementation was shaped by much older images and fears of African landscapes that pervaded institutions like those in Liverpool. How far administrators were willing to push this vision and how hard Africans could push back would come to a head in "The Land Question"—with all its implications for occupation and dwelling—on which African livelihoods in Lagos and official segregation depended.

"The Land Question":
African Organization of Housing versus a Janus-Faced State

In the predominantly African parts of town—the northern side of Lagos Island and the expanding mainland suburbs lining the railway—living situations varied depending on underlying forms of land tenure. Systems of land tenure reached peak inconsistency in the first decades of the twentieth century, even pivoting between opposing trajectories within a single case as it worked through appeals (*Lewis v. Bankole*, 1909).[76]

The houses in the photos from Alakoro (fig. 2.6) and the "badly planned" row house "showing good frontage" (figs. 2.10–2.11) illustrate three archetypes of African housing in Lagos in the early twentieth century. These three housing models corresponded to the three prevailing, if often in flux, systems of land tenure.

Awori-style housing on family property. The Alakoro image shows two ends of the spectrum. In the foreground, the thatched houses represented the living situation of many Lagosians: closely clustered homes made of readily available materials built on often untitled family property held in equal shares by a lineage and administered by the head of family; in other words, the family essentially shared usufructuary rights (a right to use and derive income from the property indefinitely despite not having radical or final title, which was at the time interpreted to be held by the British Sovereign, while ìdéjọ chiefs were understood to have seigneurial—overseer and tributary—rights to all Lagos lands, including family lands, they had not sold outright).[77] The family either occupied the plot themselves or, as may have been the case on the marginal Alakoro land, had granted it indefinitely to dependents (migrants or former slaves) in exchange for combination of tributes, rents, labor, and allegiance (in turn, the granting family likely gave nominal annual tribute to an ìdéjọ chief in recognition of the property falling within his chieftaincy lands). At a time when most Africans in Lagos earned little income, working as petty traders, farmers, or casual laborers, these benefits derived from granting out land for housing were the greatest source of wealth for African families.[78] The grantees legally owned any structures they put up on the property, and if the granting family reclaimed the land in the case they agreed to sell it or were forced to by the court, the family would have to pay compensation to occupants for those structures. Most African residents of the city still had little cash for imported materials nor access to credit to acquire building materials or to increase trading operations. Of the 9,374 houses in Lagos in 1916, 8,265 had thatch roofs.[79]

Lagos-style mansions on titled land. In the background of the Alakoro photograph, a multistory house looms behind the palm trees (fig. 2.12), a remnant of the grand nineteenth-century Lagos homes individually titled through Crown grants (see chapter 1). Original owners had sold off many of these houses as debts mounted in the 1890s, but a minority hung on, figuring out niches within Egerton and Lugard's racist economic structures.

FIGURE 2.12 (EXCERPT OF FIGURE 2.6). A barely visible multistory "Lagos-style" house hides behind a palm tree in Alakoro, 1908. *Source:* The National Archives, Kew, UK.

Canal

Shotgun houses on once titled land. The row house photographs (figs. 2.10–2.11) depict a middle ground, a plot that was likely titled at some point—which had served as the security for loans to acquire (through trading enterprises) the imported materials to build the structure—but was either in the process of reverting to family property at the death of the title holder or had already done so, meaning all direct descendants of the original owner claimed a share and say in the small property.[80] The row house was likely crowded as units of the extended family occupied single rooms or rented them out to wage laborers for cash.

By 1917 a Committee on Tenure of Land in the West African Colonies and Protectorates observed that "much of the land (in Lagos) originally vested in some individual native by grant from the Crown appears to have relapsed into the condition of family land."[81] This did not happen by accident. Dismayed by the rate of fee simple title land sales and foreclosures, families and British administrators sought to stem the tide and keep land in the hands of local African authorities. Witnessing neighbors lose their family's land permanently, chiefs and families realized that they were better served deriving rents, status, and shelter indefinitely from their lands rather than selling it for a one-off payout. Excluded from the colonial economy, which itself involved little development of industry within Lagos other than transport, a stake in a piece of property and the rental income that could be derived through it were the only chance most Africans had for fiscal security. Realizing this, those who believed they could substantiate a claim to land under customary law or British law vigorously pursued so in court. Europeans scoffed when Africans spent more on litigation than the going value of the land in question, not appreciating that the fight was over maintaining the land in perpetuity, over which time the property value was limitless.

An early twentieth-century series of court rulings slowly expanded the rights of chiefs and autochthonous families to claim unalienable communal rights over land and to curb the land rights of former slaves. In *Oloto v. Dawuda* (1902), a split court ruled that even when an ìdéjọ chief had deeded property to a dependent via a conveyance, the chief still retained reversionary rights to the property (the ability to reclaim in the case of the death or misdeeds of an occupant) based on the inexistence of absolute alienation under native custom.[82] In *Sanusi Alaka v. Jinadu Alaka* (1904), the court ruled that a former slave who received a Crown grant from his previous master must split ownership of the property with all the entire household, thus weakening the rights of former slaves to claim individual ownership.[83] By 1910 the court had upheld the principle of "family property" under native custom, declaring that any disposal (sale, lease) of land required permission from each family member.[84] This doctrine made it nearly impossible to sell land in Lagos or to purchase land with an assurance of title, since distant family members often appeared after sales claiming they had not been consulted. Powerful chiefs and families were beginning to turn the tide in establishing the inalienability of family land and in securing reversionary rights to land they had granted out or even conveyed at one time. Still, those who had taken out or purchased Crown grants sought to confirm their exclusive and indefinite freehold rights, leading to a situation in which "those who obtained Crown grants for their holdings now considered themselves free from all obligations to their former landlords and free also from all rights of reversion [while granters still claimed tribute and rights of reversion]. This led to a great deal of litigation."[85] To fall outside of those with any substantive claim to property—whether under native custom or freehold principles— dimmed one's prospects in Lagos, reinvigorating one's dependency on a patron (a *baálẹ* or influential family) for shelter, connections, and protection at a time when slavery was ostensibly being stamped out.[86] In return for shelter, African landholders wielded powerful leverage to extract rents, tribute, favors, and labor from clients.

In need of a deeper labor pool for infrastructure projects, and shaken by a Lagos labor strike in 1897, the colonial administration was more than willing, to a degree, to go along with the push by local authorities and families for greater control of property and the people on it.[87] It was through powerful patron-chiefs and families with their networks of clients who depended on them for shelter that the government was able to organize labor inexpensively while simultaneously creating allies with local power brokers. MacGregor saw this and excelled in forging a strong working relationship with the ìdéjọ chiefs whose lineages claimed perpetual shared rights over all land underlying Lagos, and all of whom sat on his Native Council, which he consulted about any legislation, enhancing the ìdéjọ's prestige.[88] To build MacGregor Canal and drain Kokomaiko Swamp, MacGregor contracted chiefs to supply the workforce.[89]

Canal

In 1904 he asserted the strong desire of the Yoruba "to manage their own internal affairs in their own way.... As a class the chiefs have an exalted idea of their own position and dignity; and they certainly possess high administrative capacity.... Under such a system a great chief is a very valuable possession; his authority is an instrument of the greatest public utility, which it is most desirable to retain in full force."[90] In the light of these insights, MacGregor had the good sense to recognize that "in dealing with the native one must never touch their right in lands.... If one wished to stir up trouble ... all one would have to do would be to suggest that the land of the native is about to be taken away from them."[91] As historian Anthony Hopkins summarized: "The principal aim of British policy was to create the political conditions most favourable to the development of an export economy; there was no desire to see the Pax Britannica inaugurate a social revolution. Thus, the Lagos administration sought to delay the emergence of a free labour market because it was afraid that the abolition of slavery [or other forms of asymmetrical structures of dependency or servitude] would dislocate production."[92] Like the outright abolition of slavery, which did not occur Nigeria-wide until 1916, the weakening of native claims to the inalienability of land risked causing mass displacement and labor disruption. Starting in the late 1890s, the government began discontinuing issuing Crown grants, switching to a policy of "agreement permits" and "land grants," essentially leases of ninety-nine years, which still required yearly payments to the family or chief leasing the land.[93] This policy of long-term leases rather than sales via conveyance would not be fully enacted until 1908.

MacGregor acknowledged that "the soil remains the undisputed property of the natives" and argued that the government should pursue leases rather than outright transfers of land for projects like the railroad.[94] While Egerton was content to continue outsourcing housing and the corralling of labor to local chiefs, he sought greater control over the emerging morphology of the city as it spilled beyond Lagos Island. Ultimately, Egerton and Lugard wanted to administer the city and colony through landed chiefs but wanted to retain the right to remove them from their land when it suited the government's purposes. Over the next thirty years, Africans and British agents waged a battle over the fundamental organization of Lagos, a protracted conflict brewing since 1861. Trenches were dug around "the Land Question." At stake were how land would be owned and allocated, the power of local authorities, if the city would be segregated or not, the degree to which chiefs and families would be compensated for their land, and even the legality of British presence in Lagos. On one side, Egerton and Lugard's administrations sought to appropriate land through landed chiefs, arguing that ìdéjọ enjoyed only seigneurial rights (as "trustees," overseers and managers, of the land for the people) and were therefore only entitled to either lesser compensation based on tributes lost rather than land value or to no compensation if they had not asserted their reversionary rights or utilized the land in question.[95] On the other, non-Europeans, including the ọba, landlords and dependents alike banded together like never before around a vision of the city in which ìdéjọ chiefs were the undisputed and absolute owners (holding proprietary rights) of all land in Lagos under native custom. As Mann notes, these claims became widely popular by both furthering the material interests of ìdéjọ chiefs (and their followers) in a long-standing Èkó power struggle while also serving a broader ideological basis for challenging the sovereignty of the colonial government.[96] Intellectuals, though, pushed out of work by racist policies, developed this anticolonial ideology in response to the rising prejudice in British ranks, and they connected the uneven acceptance of African land claims to the overall pattern of the dehumanization of Africans.[97] This ìdéjọ-centric interpretation offered the legal fodder to ingeniously make the trifold claim that (1) the cession treaty of 1861 was illegitimate from the outset (having been signed by the ọba and not the ìdéjọ) and thus void, (2) or, if not null and void, then voidable because the land had been granted under the pretense of suppressing the slave trade in and around Lagos, and, as the land was no longer being used for that purpose, the slave trade having ended, the land would revert from the British to the ìdéjọ chiefs, or, (3) at the very least that the ìdéjọ should receive full compensation for any land confiscated by the government under the understanding that they retained full proprietary rights.[98] Despite the bold first two claims, the reality was the British were entrenched in Lagos for the time being, and the crux of the debate quickly came to center on compensation for chiefs.

As the amalgamation of Nigeria became imminent in 1914, the space for housing a vast number of bureaucrats became a driving force behind land acquisitions. In 1907, under the 1903 Public Lands

Canal

Ordinance, Egerton sought to acquire seven acres around the racecourse to build a segregated colonial settlement (under the auspices of a "public park"),[99] asserting that it was for a "public purpose" on "barren, destitute and unfenced" (unoccupied and therefore uncompensated) land.[100] The scheme displaced three hundred people but then stalled under litigation, and eventually Egerton's government sold off some of the land.[101] Yet the situation was so upsetting that, as one observer reported, Africans were "openly talking of stopping trade in order to make the Governor feel how much they resent it." The report went on to note:

> Several mass meetings have been held in Lagos, and the crowd went so far as to throw stones at the houses along the [water] front, and in one case pulled a European merchant off his bicycle; . . . it is not only the Government officers who are involved, but every White Man in the colony. . . . *The natives begin to see that it is [Europeans] who are finding money to build all these fine palaces; . . . the people look at their own poor little huts alongside the palatial buildings of the European and wonder how long and how far this thing is to go.* . . . They see these Government officers coming out for twelve months at a time, and then go away for six months on full pay; they see a pension list annually being added to; they see jinrickshas and servants, horses and stable boys, addition to the salaries of these officials. . . . The extravagance of the Government is becoming more than the people can stand. It is particularly visible in the luxuries of official Lagos life.[102]

Implementation of structural racial exclusion from industry and an ambiguous land tenure situation had impoverished the houses of many Africans. Galvanized behind the symbol of African families losing their land—and thus their remaining source of wealth—only to see Europeans then building extravagant houses on the land, Lagos residents began to rally behind men who articulated their plight, men such as the founder of Nigerian nationalism, Herbert Macaulay. Yet, unperturbed by an official petition and street protests, the government had its sights set on much bigger targets than the encampments around the racecourse. A year's passing brought the Ikoyi Lands Ordinance of 1908. This act "effectively dispossessed the Onikoyi [the ìdéjọ chief with claims to Ikoyi] of most of his land" by requiring him to produce nonexistent titles (since he had never applied for them) or forfeit all "of Lagos Island, East of the MacGregor Canal, generally known as Ikoyi," to the Crown.[103] Egerton had set a pincer movement in motion, claiming the lands east, west, and south of Lagos Island for government projects, and enclosing African land to the northern part of Lagos Island. All three ìdéjọ challenged the colonial government in court between 1911 and 1912, with mixed results.[104] For much of the land they received nominal or no compensation. In losing Ikoyi, residents of Lagos Island lost an escape from the city, the open plains and meadows that had actually long served as a public park for Sunday picnics and other outings.[105] The court defeats and the fact that it was revealed that Chief Oniru's land would be used by private European companies incensed Lagosians.[106] In a famous speech on the steps of Government House, Herbert Macaulay laid bare the cynicism of Britain's dual mandate[107] for indirect rule. He recounted how Egerton had claimed the goal behind his lease policies were to prevent "chiefs who perhaps unthinkingly are willing to give away land . . . which they only hold in trust for their town, village or tribe, for inadequate consideration and so leave future generations landless," only to turn around and pay pathetically inadequate amounts to chiefs for land around Lagos. Macaulay stated: "With regard to the Land Question, it is our humble opinion that the Commissioner of Lands is the chief source of trouble—It is he that troubleth Israel. His Department offers always inadequate compensation for lands acquired by the Government."[108] Macaulay exposed the dual mandate as a cost-saving mechanism dressed up in a theory of development and non-interference. Years earlier, Ross had called the bluff, writing, "Do not talk to me of lack of funds. There are plenty of funds, but they are thrown away on military expeditions; on the salaries of useless legal officials."[109] Egerton's overriding concern for Lagos was for transport, and Macaulay fumed that the only real priority was "to get at the Tin Mines far away yonder."[110] Unfortunately for Macaulay, the architect of indirect rule was on his way to relieve Egerton and join southern Nigeria to the tin mines of northern Nigeria. Still, Macaulay wondered what the colonial regime could possibly want with lands "so full of mosquitos, and . . . swamps which are natural hot-beds for mosquito-larvae?" His fateful last words in the quote were, "Nothing whatever I am sure."[111]

Canal

Segregating a City and Elevating a Ruling Class

With Ikoyi, Apapa, and Victoria Island in hand, Lugard did not have to wait long for an idea of what to do with the swampland. Yellow fever broke out in 1913. Through a series of confidential dispatches to the Colonial Office, Lugard floated the idea of a much larger segregated housing development, pitching Victoria Island or Yaba.[112] Nothing came of either of these schemes, but the idea lay in wait as a 1915 colonial report attests: "Considerable attention was given to the important question of segregation of the European population at many of the more important political and commercial centres. Definite areas were arranged, and, although immediate results cannot be obtained in all instances, progress is gradually being made as opportunity arises and means become available."[113] With another outbreak of disease, this time the flu pandemic of 1919, an opportunity arose to enact plans to barricade European houses behind MacGregor Canal under the pretext of medical quarantine.[114] Lugard had prepared for this moment with his 1915 Town Council Ordinance and his 1917 Township Ordinance, declaring Lagos a "first class township," in other words a European enclave, paving the way for the establishment of an exclusively European quarter once World War I ended and funds became available.[115] The cynicism of Lugard's dual mandate was complete. By asserting that the native community had "no desire for municipal improvement ... nor desires clean water, sanitation, or good roads or streets," he had withheld equal development and created the conditions for an epidemic. Flu allowed him then to decree a European reserve for a public health purpose.[116] This cynical cycle of racist exclusion and expropriation (and eventually demolition) would repeat itself with even larger consequences in the 1920s and after World War II. In 1919, building the colonial reserve east of the canal allowed the administration to provide housing for Europeans away from "diseased" parts of the city and thereby occupy the expropriated land for a "public purpose" (sanitation) as required by law.

The practice of building foreboding structures and separating colonial officers in reserves was part of the process of establishing imperial rule and elevating the authority of the men tasked with implementing that rule. Colonial housing estates formed a chokehold on the city—straddling Central Lagos to the east in Ikoyi, to the south in Victoria Island, and to the west in Ebute Metta and Apapa. While MacGregor had sought to raise all of Lagos from its soggy foundation, Lugard sought to give colonial officers the high ground, second-floor verandas and windows from which to survey the city. At the time, British Nigeria run out of Lagos was still a weak imperial state—Britain's most populous colony (16 million people with nearly 100,000 in Lagos) after India with still less than three thousand Europeans in the entire 335,700 square miles[117]— with British night terrors of native uprisings, which, if coordinated, could crumble Lugard's regime.[118] European homes and their locations in the early twentieth century became more than simple shelter from rain and mosquitoes; they become strategic instruments of empire.[119] MacGregor Canal and the houses behind it made the "thin white line" a little thicker.

This process was gradual as colonial agents clumsily refined British imperial architecture and planning to produce the proper awe and distance from the subjects of their gaze. In *Verandahs of Power: Colonialism and Space in Urban Africa*, Garth Myers uses Timothy Mitchell's term "enframing" to describe how colonial administrations created a "fixed distinction between inside and outside in domestic architecture and urban design, thereby codifying neighborhood, family, and gender relations in a manner distinct from African systems of domestic order."[120] Government House (discussed in the conclusion of chapter 1) was a major step in this process. Its enormity and solidness signaled that it was not built for a temporary British stay in Nigeria. It was a fortress where Europeans holed up during fear of insurrection in 1912. The Public Works Department prior to Lugard had already begun positioning Europeans behind walls and on shuttered second floors. The model of the colonial bungalow was a piece of technology for preserving proper living quarters by rising above mud and miasma, but it was also developing into a symbol of European elevation. The Lagos surveyor's quarters included two mimeses (perhaps used as bird roosts) of European bungalows literally placed on pedestals in front of the house (fig. 2.13). In the railway estate at Ebute Metta, European residences like Jaekel House (1898) included 360-degree covered veranda on the second floor, long written about in term of ensuring a breeze, but it also functioned in terms of fostering a "panopticon" feeling of observation in the surrounding grounds (fig. 2.14).[121] Another form of "enframing" was the electric bulbs that lit up European bungalows at night in contrast to unwired African quarters, reifying European images of the continent.

In this context, the stumpy but growing skyline of Lagos became inscribed with symbols of technological advancement, wealth, and power.

Canal

FIGURE 2.13. British colonial quarters at Lagos designed and allotted by rank and role, ca. 1900. *Source:* The National Archives, Kew, UK.

FIGURE 2.14. The Jaekel House (1898) created a panopticon feeling. Seen here in 2017 after renovation by Legacy 1996. Author's photograph.

This "verticalization," seen earlier to a degree in the ọba's palace and in the indigenized sobrado model of Brazilian hierarchy in the nineteenth century, represented a shift in architectural expressions of authority away from a spatial conception of power rooted in centrality. Vernacular Yoruba palaces obtained architectural status by being located at the heart of a city, but with new materials and ideas of racial imperialism, architectonic ideas of power began to shift from being surrounded by people to being above them.[122] The few twentieth-century Afro-Brazilian houses still being built by wealthy Black Lagosians reflected this idea. The pinnacle of the Afro-Brazilian style was Ebun House (1913), four stories of coiffured plaster and grandeur (see fig. 1.6).

Another symbol of authority beginning to appear in colonial residences at Lagos in the early twentieth century was the luxury of open space surrounding the home. These hedged lawns functioned as private cordons sanitaires and included African "mosquito catchers" running around squashing any bug that moved.[123] Even before official segregation, colonial homes were becoming segregated citadels encircled by lawns

FIGURE 2.15. Government House surrounded by manicured lawns. *Source:* The National Archives, Kew, UK.

FIGURE 2.16. Sir Egerton and his wife taking tea in the gardens of Government House juxtaposed, in a Colonial Office photo book, with naked children standing in the grassless yard of an African house, early twentieth century. *Source:* The National Archives, Kew, UK.

and fences (figs. 2.15–2.16). Lawns likewise represented the shift from people as the basis of power to a conception of power based on property and the ability to see past people to stand alone as a "great" man, a "self-made" man, an island not dependent on others. The governor perched in Government House (fig. 2.16) encircled by manicured lawns personified this mythos, as did planners and architects as solitary diviners of cities. In African quarters where families and chiefs had won rights to land, the landholders typically granted or rented extra space, as had long been the case, to kin and immigrants to settle on. In European estates, extra land was now for leisure and sport, mini garden-cities. There was perhaps no sharper symbol of the contrast between colonial and African sociopolitical systems. Colonial photographers juxtaposed these images in their album of Lagos (fig. 2.16), illustrating to the Colonial Office the ways in which British homes had conquered the Black landscapes of Africa.

Great lawns required space, and Ikoyi provided acreage for hundreds of stand-alone homes. The lots plotted in the blueprints for Ikoyi

Canal

FIGURE 2.17. Mushrooming cement block bungalows in Ikoyi, 1923. *Source:* The National Archives, Kew, UK.

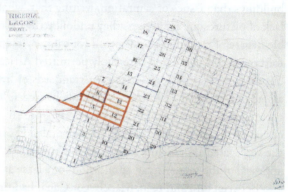

MAP 2.3. The three-hundred- by two-hundred-feet plots for British officers in Ikoyi, 1919. *Source:* The National Archives, Kew, UK.

granted ample land for such homes (map 2.3) in a grid pattern with broad streets and standard plot sizes of three hundred feet by two hundred feet (essentially the size of a football field). The houses only took up 1,800 of the 60,000 total square feet allotted. Administrators worked to make sure there was a "sufficiency of open spaces at Ikoyi."[124] The Ikoyi Government Reservation Area estates, built in the 1920s, were mushroom concrete-block bungalows (fig. 2.17), more bunkers than the earlier breezy brick or wood bric-a-brac shelters of the island or railway compound. The Public Works Department gave these homes names like SPTI, T2, T17A, more evocative of tank or airplane models in an occupying force than homey residences.[125]

Almost as soon as Lugard launched his scheme for Ikoyi, segregation fell out of fashion with the medical establishment. The Medical Department of the Colonial Office finally acknowledged that, in terms of health, the Ikoyi reserve was poorly conceived even under its under rationale of sanitary quarantine. From the start, Europeans in Ikoyi had continued to share space with African servants ("boys quarters" were provided for in the Ikoyi blueprints), and Europeans living in Ikoyi still had to travel to Central Lagos for work.[126] Yet the development of a European enclave at Ikoyi marched on even with the arrival of a governor who had spent his career in staunch opposition to the Colonial Office's push for segregation. Governor Hugh Clifford agreed to continue the project against his own misgivings, including his observation of the injustice of Africans paying the majority of taxes, which were then spent on European settlements.[127] Earlier in his career, Clifford had made the astute observation that his Colonial Office colleagues were much more concerned with the aesthetics of what they perceived to be "ugly" African buildings than issues of sanitation, writing that "what [African houses] lack of picturesque attractions they undoubtedly make up for by a notable degree of cleanliness and regard for sanitary requirements."[128] Clifford reversed Lugard and ostensibly permitted Africans to live at Ikoyi, but de facto segregation—based on "standards of living" criteria—was already entrenched.[129] European officials had been looking forward to occupying their new estates in Ikoyi away from the dangers they perceived on the island, and through the colonial old boys' club (centered at the segregated Ikoyi Club, known as the "gin tank")[130] they delayed the approval of the first African application for a lease at Ikoyi until 1950.[131]

Between 1919 and 1950, MacGregor Canal had time to cause intractable damage, structuring the division and disparity between White and Black Lagos. To return to the terminology of the previous chapter, by 1919 Lagos no longer had what was in retrospect a nineteenth-century phantasmagoric "dominant class." By World War I a ruling class had established itself at Lagos, dominating the city not through elevated culture and capital but through occupation and enclosure based on bureaucratically codified racial categories. Elite houses were no longer holds of impressive status to which all could aspire, but were a distant ring of fortress garrisons, constant reminders of the hegemony of the Crown. Shortly after Ikoyi opened, Europeans there would stir from their ensconcement in golf courses and gin and soon turn their eye across the canal toward an offensive on African settlements. With a major African legal victory in land compensation and an outbreak of a medieval disease in the 1920s, colonial planners would pivot on Central Lagos and envision a solution like the Haussmanization of Paris. Housing would again be at the center of visions and struggles over land, labor, and sanitation.

3

Swamp

Foci in Land, Labor, and Sanitation Struggles: Interwar Years

Slums are the swamps of cityscapes, and the inverse is true of landscapes. Loathsome low-lying places for serpents. Where scum settles and stays. Or so deep connotations go. As historian Liora Bigon points out, "slum" comes from "slump," which means "to fall or sink in a swamp or muddy place."[1] Both are shunned spaces, looked down upon out of a fear of sinking into sin and filth, and thus places to be eradicated. Lagos is often portrayed as the worst of both worlds: where slums sprout out of swamps, and all is consumed by two-sided squalor, primordial and human-made. This confluence of ills is the ultimate dystopia set and has drawn a perverse Western interest in recent decades. Rem Koolhaas and his troubled "Project on the City"[2] became the figurehead (and strawman) for an entire genre devoted to the "apocalyptic aura" of Lagos. Descending on the city have been documentary crews, reality television Brits, cowboy journalists, and, of course, a helicopter flying Koolhaas. Big, slum-ridden, and waterlogged was the frame for their productions.[3] One of the most memorable moments of the 2010 documentary *This Is Lagos* is the footage of a man building his house atop a foundation of trash poured into brackish water.[4] Innumerable articles have been

FIGURE 3.1. The iconic blue roof of the Makoko floating school, 2014. Author's photograph.

written about another architect and former Koolhaas employee, Kunlé Adeyemi, who built a floating slum school in Lagos (fig. 3.1).[5] Fascination exists where slums, swamps, and all their associated evils collide. Even more so when the combination "works," as Koolhaas has theorized and the floating school symbolized.[6] The twin depths of dark water and poverty canceling each other out has proved an appealing narrative.

The "Koolhaas effect" has generated considerable hot air, at times leading to an overblown backlash, but the core point of the critiques against slum-diving interlopers is important.[7] Urbanist Matthew Gandy and historian Laurent Fourchard forcefully argue that what parachuters into contemporary Lagos miss is the historical processes of how the city's current state arose (and therefore can be changed through a series of processes) not through "self-organizing" inertia, as Koolhaas fancied from his helicopter tour of the city, but through local politics and world imbalances of power.[8] These forces and the actors behind them explain how, through decades of decisions, Lagos housing conditions have taken the form of so-called slums sharing a bed with swampland—and how this history is deeply and paradoxically entangled with attempts to rid the city of swamps and slums.

This chapter, beginning in the 1920s, covers several crucial decades in this story, an era when the first aerial photographs of Lagos appear in British archives, flattening the city like Koolhaas's helicopter-scapes and reinforcing British perceptions of African "slums" as impediments to the structured order of the export economy (figs. 3.2–3.3).⁹ Airborne imagery swiveled surface readings of Lagos in the direction of horizontal forms of abstraction, contributing to a sense that amorphous African settlements, like swamps, were visual anomalies—like inkblots on maps—in need of rationalization.¹⁰ At the same time, the British and their allies were accumulating greater bureaucratic means of "slum clearance" to expand the logic of the swamp drainage campaigns described in chapter 2. These programs coincided with an influx of young male migrants—many untethered from traditional authorities—to Lagos Island, adding further stress to three major discourses underpinning the city's politics since the turn of the century: land, labor, and sanitation. Shelter continued to be a locus interlocking these issues, and, as pressure intensified, "housing" as a discrete social concern began to be articulated and politicized by both colonial administrators and opposition parties. In the course of

FIGURE 3.2. Koolhaas's "heli-scape" of Makoko. *Source: Lagos Wide and Close: An Interactive Journey into an Exploding City*, directed by Bregtje van der Haak (Netherlands: Submarine, 2006).

FIGURE 3.3. One of the first aerial views of Lagos's landscape, 1929. *Source:* The National Archives, Kew, UK.

this development, Nigeria's ascending spokesman, Herbert Macaulay, and his supporters became more steadfast in their desire for a hands-off approach that left the organization of housing and social welfare to local chiefs and families. Meanwhile, the two primary concerns of British planners in terms of housing converged: seeing African houses and settlements in relation to sanitation (like swamps), and linking housing to labor, a concern that administrators expanded to more African workers whose numbers and importance in the colonial economy continued to grow. Beginning several decades earlier, "insanitary" swamps had been filled to create more habitable land; now, increasingly after World War I, colonial agents followed a similar "two-birds" strategy of demolishing "insanitary" residences to make way for "worker" estates made up of detached utilitarian shelters. Displacement of longtime residents and dislocation of many workers to estates at Yaba and other parts of Ebute Metta set the groundwork for Lagos housing to be characterized in large part by disparity in living conditions sprawling away from the city center.

In this process, a small number of African workers began to obtain what anthropologist James Ferguson describes as a "slice" of the emerging British social system—the bureaucratic security nets and structural solutions that located societies' ills in the arrangements of family and intimate life rather than in the moral failings of individuals or races, as had previously been the diagnosis.[11] The provision of certain types of dwellings—detached government-built barracks and bungalows—was an obvious, if costly, way to establish new forms of sociality geared toward a model of a male worker supporting and supported by a "detached" (fiscally self-contained) family unit. Yet the cost-conscious colonial administration continued to outsource most housing and social care to the African community—intervening only to demolish or criminalize forms of social life deemed "unsuitable" for modern urban society. This "production of ambivalence," as AbdouMaliq Simone calls it, meant the colonial administration wanted a semblance of a welfare state with a stable workforce in some areas of the city while at the same time seeking self-sufficient yet subservient African settlements in other areas.[12] Those left outside either system, particularly migrants, experienced new forms of poverty and were the source of much political debate and finger pointing. Solidifying by the 1920s, loyalist African voices encouraged an extension of the colonial social state while anti-British parties like Macaulay's

Swamp

Nigerian National Democratic Party (NNDP) championed a retraction of the state to allow native society literally more room to govern.

With Lugard gone, a crack opened in Lagos' political scene in the 1920s, and all sides had to adjust immediately to new opportunities and constraints as a landmark court decision came down, plague broke out, and depression struck. The umbrella of ambivalence was punctured by lightning bolts of action. The creation of the Lagos Executive Development Board (LEDB) in 1928, with its power to declare, seize land for, and clear "town planning schemes," swung power back to the colonial state and collaborating anti-*eléèkó* party, thereby expanding insecurity not just to poor Africans but to all non-collaborators. Those outside the redevelopment schemes were left with their homes as legally uncertain assets or forced to create self-built slums further into the marshes and shadowlands surrounding Lagos. These were the seeds of an "apocalyptic" vista perceived by Koolhaas and others.

Several overlooked documents guide this chapter's exploration of a changing city in the 1920s, 1930s, and early 1940s, a prologue to the massive modernization schemes and independence transitions of the 1950s and 1960s. Much of the literature on the LEDB highlights the role of plague in its inceptions and then jumps to the board's role in the controversial "revitalization" via mass razing schemes of the 1950s. The intervening decades are swamp years of starts and stops and, seemingly, stagnation, passed over by scholars of the built environment in search of more fertile ground.[13] In contrast, this chapter looks at the LEDB's founding documents and first years of operation, drawing on legislative ordinances along with maps and photographs of early schemes and plans, and subsequent petitions and reports regarding opposition to its operations. This was an important period of hard-fought African aspirations and resistance as post–World War I prosperity followed by economic slowdown drove migrants to the city in search of work and shelter. In this span, Lagos's population more than doubled, from 100,000 to over 230,000.[14] The question once again, as it has been so often in Lagos's history, was, Where and in what form would the city absorb the influx? Who would decide? What would a "house" become? As administrators and African politicians were realizing, the way the city accommodated its people would be vital to its social structure, and by extension to urban political power.

Land, Plague, Labor, and the LEDB

Before the plague and rising colonial anxieties over labor and juvenile delinquents, slum clearance and the making of modern Lagos must be understood in terms of the struggle for land. The previous two chapters have charted the rising importance of the control of property in the form of land and houses in the increasingly congested city and the perennial question of ownership rights summarized from the perspective of most Lagosians in Macaulay's 1912 speech on "the Land Question." While the beginning of the century saw property disputes among Africans, with chiefs and well-off families shoring up their rights at the expense of dependents, the fight had soon turned also to an entrenched battle between ìdéjọ chiefs and the colonial state. The first decades of the twentieth century had been an era of African anxiety as amalgamators like Egerton and Lugard had sought to acquire land by compulsion at low prices, and courts and committees considered voiding native chiefs' evolving interpretations of their rights. Chiefs and their supporters argued that the 1861 Treaty of Cession preserved their inalienable and absolute ownership of land despite British agents' attempts to deny or argue limitations to those claims in order to expand the colony and colonial holdings while simultaneously needing the chiefs to run the city. Patrick Cole writes that by 1912 "almost fifty per cent of all the land of the Lagos Chiefs had been expropriated by the government for negligible sums."[15] This loss and the court fees spent fighting expropriations hit traditional elites hard at a time when land had become native chiefs' most valuable resource. Even London was taken aback at the blatant colonial-sponsored land grabbing in Lagos. Colonial Secretary Winston Churchill wrote to the governor of Lagos that the Nigerian colonial government was "not a monopolist landlord entitled to make what profits it could out of its monopoly."[16] Alarm and suspicion had united opposition among African traditional and immigrant elites against the colonial government. Segregation imposed on taken lands in Ikoyi and infrastructure exclusion on the island had been painful losses for African resisters who had lost court battles early in the century (chapter 2), but in the 1920s the stakes were arguably much higher as the city center was reaching peak capacity.

Density nearing five thousand people per square mile on the island in the 1920s meant Lagos had to expand; so began a power tussle over issues a Lagos newspaper described as "momentous and far reaching

Swamp

in their effects."[17] The short-lived postwar economic boom of 1918–20 witnessed the young men of Abeokuta, Ijebu, Oyo, and farther afield making their way down the rails and lorry-plied motor roads toward the lure of the "Liverpool of Africa." With wartime price restrictions lifted and European firms pushing to return to prewar production levels, the value of palm, cocoa, groundnut, and cotton exports from Lagos nearly doubled between 1918 and 1920.[18] The city enticed migrants with greater opportunities for wage labor than anywhere else in the colony, even if many newcomers ended up working piecemeal and part-time as little more than porters.[19] The arrival of scores of hopeful laborers and traders placed renewed pressure on the port city's confined space.

Comparing the cartographic record of the Oko Awo area of Lagos Island from an 1891 map of Lagos to a 1926 map illustrates how built up the city center had become as residents erected new structures in what had been yards or swamps (maps 1.3 and 3.1). The capacity of houses was squeezed to their limits with as many as fifteen people living in nine-by-ten foot rooms.[20] In this market, rents soared, and colonial rent controls

MAP 3.1. A 1926 map of Lagos showing the buildup of Oko Awo. *Source:* The National Archives, Kew, UK.

introduced in 1920 only protected already well-off and high-earning men.[21] The loss of Ikoyi, the obvious area of expansion for Lagos that instead had become the low-density segregated European reserve, as four ìdéjọ protested, had "disappointed the sanguine expectations of the native community who are thus compelled to huddle themselves together under insanitary conditions and are faced with the perplexing problem of discovering some other outlet for expansion" (see map 3.2).[22] Something had to give, and by the early 1920s it was becoming clear the city would spill into the mainland across Carter Bridge and up the railroad lines (map 3.2). Who would control the land there, and thus the form housing and society took, were other questions.

The answers to these questions were already playing out in what might have been the most significant Lagos court case of the century: *Amodu Tijani v. Secretary, Southern Provinces*. The colonial state was bent on developing Apapa, prime harbor real estate abutting the railway terminus on the mainland (map 3.2), and in 1913 had seized it from the ìdéjọ (white-capped chiefs) Chief Oluwa (Tijani), eventually offering £500 in compensation.[23] The meager payment was based on the British contention that Oluwa was not entitled to the full value of the land because he, as a white-capped chief, was the overseer or trustee of the land and therefore was only eligible for lost nominal tributes based on the legal principle of seigneurial rights.

Over the next decade, Chief Oluwa and his legal counsel, none other than the leader of opposition politics, Herbert Macaulay, challenged the terms of the seizure, appealing all the way to the Privy Council in London. There, in a 1921 decision celebrated throughout West Africa, Oluwa won full compensation with ìdéjọ chiefs being recognized as the holders of "communal usufruct rights," in other words, full legal rights of occupation and use on behalf of the people, a fact ruled to be unaltered by the Treaty of Cession.[24] Compensation for Tijani was raised to £22,500, though it was to be distributed among all descendants of the Oluwa chieftaincy.[25] Upon return to Lagos, Macaulay and Oluwa were greeted as heroes by ten thousand people waiting quayside. Lagosians had finally won relief in the fight over land. The government would have to pay full value for appropriations, a serious setback for colonial land grabs.

The events in London brought to a head the ambivalence of the Colonial Office toward native institutions. With the arrival of the less

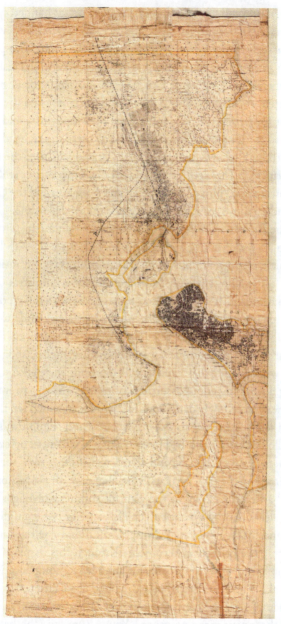

MAP 3.2. A 1932 map of Lagos showing the city's expansion up the railroad line in the mainland and a government reserve southwest of Lagos Island in Apapa. *Source:* Federal Survey Department of Nigeria.

racist Governor Hugh Clifford in 1919, Lugard's heavy-handed system of might-makes-right despite glaring contradictions was out, and Macaulay acted to reassert the bounds of native authority. In addition to pursuing legal action in London, Macaulay had represented the ọba Eshugbayi, known as the eléèkó ("owner of Èkó," the Yoruba name for Lagos). In a press conference with the *Daily Mail*, Macaulay lambasted the colonial government for letting the ọba's *igá* (palace), fall into decay and implied (according to the Colonial Office) that the ọba was the rightful ruler of Nigeria (although what Macaulay actually stated was that the ọba was the titular ruler).[26] The eléèkó downplayed the remarks, but still the administration stripped him of recognition and both him and the Oluwa of their stipends, a move seen as retaliation for the *Apapa* ruling.

Like the British attitude to chiefs' control of lands, the Crown had wanted the power of native institutions to go both ways—to have the ọba and chiefs empowered but to be able to snub their authority when expedient. In the labor strike of 1920, the colonial administration relied on the eléèkó and white-capped chiefs to negotiate with rail workers and eventually to escort them back to the Ebute Metta rail yards to resume duties, apologizing on their behalf.[27] The 1921 land decision was a blow to government's ability to continue governing and organizing labor through white caps while seizing their land at will; deposing the eléèkó was a way of shutting down indigenous assertions of power.[28] Such a move against the eléèkó was exceedingly dangerous in a climate in which ten thousand people had just turned out to cheer Macaulay and the Oluwa's return, but the Colonial Office had begun to make new alliances by exploiting local disputes between Jama'at and Lemonu Muslims over the Islamic titles conferred by the ọba. Jama'ats, who aligned with professionals like Macaulay, backed the eléèkó as the rightful authority of Lagos.[29] Lemonus, anti-eléèkó led by breakaway chiefs like Alli Balogun, distrusted Macaulay and his legal fees and saw opportunities for self-advancement by supporting the colonial government. Through this fissure, Clifford's government found ways to circumvent the revised compensation rates for land, making no efforts to standardize land acquisitions.[30]

For example, for the construction of a worker estate at Yaba in the mainland, the government prevented Yesufu Omidiji (the heir of the Oloto ìdéjọ chieftaincy) from hiring lawyers and surveyors to contest the land acquisition by reminding him that he needed the government's

Swamp

nomination to become the Oloto since the ọba had been stripped of office.[31] Other noncompliant white caps, like the Oluwa, lost their stipends, diminishing their financial ability to challenge land seizures. Still, without the eléèkó, as the lieutenant governor put it in 1921, "the whole machinery of relations of the Chiefs with the Government has been put completely out of gear."[32] By 1923, Macaulay had unified opposition by founding the NNDP and had compiled a "monster petition" of seventeen thousand signatures demanding the reinstatement of the eléèkó.[33] He was beginning to muster the support to strike back.

Then in 1924, in the midst of the "eléèkó Affair," bubonic plague broke out. The epidemic had only been a matter of time; the West African ports in the Gambia and Gold Coast had already been infected. For several years the Lagos medical officers had made frantic warnings about a potential epidemic. In 1922, white caps and African professionals had asked the governor for part of Ikoyi to reduce population pressure on the island. They were turned down.[34] The same year, in an annual report, the medical officer described what he considered a breeding ground for plague, writing, "eight, ten, or twelve and in at least one known case, fifteen persons sleep in a room measuring usually ten feet square or less."[35]

When these fears were realized two years later, the city was thrown into a panic with the town engineer throwing up barriers of iron sheeting along Oroyinyin, Docemo, Pedro, and Oreofe Streets in a futile attempt to contain the spread.[36] Infected rats had no difficulty skirting these obstacles and widening the disease's radius. The government removed 278 people from the epicenter, Oko Awo, the most densely populated area of the city. Over the next two years, 599 cases were reported, of which 501 were deaths.

Even before the outbreak, the colonial government had connected the possibility of plague to unsanitary and crowded conditions, a view reaffirmed when Oko Awo was identified as the hot zone. Yet there is evidence that this could have stemmed from its Muslim Hausa residents' roles in the kola nut trade, the suspected source of plague-carrying rats from the Gold Coast.[37] Nonetheless, the assumption of unsanitary conditions stuck, and, in response to the continuing annual outbreaks of plague, the colonial government created the LEDB in 1928 to "rid Lagos of the filth and unsanitary conditions,"[38] meaning swamps and slums, the two targets of LEDB schemes. Oko Awo would be among the first sites demolished and redeveloped by the LEDB. But first the land would have to be acquired.

The 1928 Lagos Town Planning Ordinance "to Make Provision for the Re-planning, Improvement, and Development of Lagos" centralized sanitary inspections and demolitions, swamp drainage, and other aspects of molding Lagos into a (re)planned city. The LEDB was charged with oversight of these functions and granted absolute power to acquire land for redevelopment schemes with the rate for compulsorily acquired lands left to the court to decide at fair market value without consideration of lost rents or leases.[39] Importantly, the LEDB also was the authority to manage acquired lands in perpetuity, leasing the land back to landlords or families.[40] This was a reversal of earlier practices encouraged by Governor MacGregor of leasing land from chiefs for government purposes.[41] The board's other option was to resell property postdevelopment to original or new owners at a profit, meaning the LEDB could acquire any land in Lagos, clear it and resell (or lease) it to net colonial state revenue.

In a latter inquiry into the board's activities, investigators acknowledged that the board had operated as a "quasi-commercial organization."[42] With the creation of the LEDB, state politics and large-scale property ownership and development were formally entwined. Five members initially made up the board: the commissioner of lands, the deputy director of sanitary service, the assistant director of public works, and two members appointed by the governor—who could appoint more members as he saw fit. As longtime Lagos architects John Godwin and Gillian Hopwood write, the LEDB and other 1930s and 1940s planning bodies "operating within the area of the municipality, produced no concerted action and could not be controlled through democratic processes."[43] While Clifford's government had granted an element of elective representation to African Lagosians in 1923, the resulting Lagos Town Council would have no say over LEDB activities.[44] With Macaulay's party and petition, there was British fear of Africans utilizing democratic processes to retake a larger say in the city, a fear similar to those in Natal of electoral "swamping" as the colony approached self-government in the 1890s.[45] As historian Maynard Swanson points out in regard to an earlier plague outbreak in Cape Colony, "Epidemics do not create abnormal situations' but rather sharpen existing behavior patterns which 'betray deeply rooted and continuing

Swamp

social imbalances."[46] In Lagos, bubonic plague had allowed for a recon-centration of spatial—and thus ultimate, in the contested city—power in the colonial government.

The primary power vested in the LEDB was the authority to ac-quire and redevelop property on a micro and macro level: to decree any individual building unsanitary and to declare any swath of land a town planning scheme to be redeveloped. The LEDB would then raze the building or area in question and replan it based on principles published in the Town Planning Ordinance. The guidelines aligned with standard "garden city" doctrines of the time, including an emphasis on the creation of "open spaces public and private and of parks, parkways and pleasure or recreation grounds," and a provision to "regulate the density of building for the purpose of securing amenity or proper hygienic conditions."[47] Full power was given to the board to "remove, pull down, or alter any building or other work in the area included in the scheme which is such as to contravene the scheme."[48] The LEDB was vested with expansive executive power to seize land and redevelop it under the broad defi-nition of sanitary interests. It was widely acknowledged in Lagos that there was a need for more attention to the health and growth of the city once plague broke out; however, as the LEDB was formulated, its truly novel function was as a financial mechanism (rather than a planning body), as an unchecked acquirer and leaser or seller of land, to fund the long-desired demolitions of swamps and African settlements.

As early as the 1860s, explorer Richard Burton had envisioned the "straightening, widening, draining and cleaning" of the city.[49] More re-cently, Governor Carter reported that "'the native portion of the town can only be described as a huge cess-pit,' about which nothing could be done short of complete reconstruction of the town."[50] Shortly there-after, Royal Society agents Christophers and Stephens had fantasized about an eradication of "dirty" native huts in the fashion of the extermi-nation of cattle to contain sleeping sickness in other parts of Africa.[51] The ability of the LEDB to acquire and then lease or sell land created the funding scheme to realize these dreams. Between 1929 and 1945 the LEDB would record a revenue-to-expenditure ratio of over two to one, providing the initial financing for the demolition of "old" Lagos.[52]

The initial board projects were a direct response to plague and tar-geted areas of outbreak like Oko Awo. In 1928 the board declared the

MAP 3.3. Town planning scheme just north of Oko Awo showing plans for new roads and road widening and a limit of twenty houses per acre, ca. 1928. *Source:* National Archives of Nigeria.

entire area west of MacGregor Canal on Lagos Island a "Town Planning Area," asserting it suffered from overcrowding and poor sanitation and was therefore in need of widespread inspections and demolitions (map 3.3). Next, the board launched a plan to ameliorate plague conditions through the "demolition of insanitary buildings in the worst areas surrounding [unregulated native] markets" alongside more sweeping town planning schemes for Oko Awo (1928 and 1930), Idumagbo (1931–32), and Isalegangan (1933). All three areas were on Lagos Island, and among them the LEDB acquired 26.8 acres by compulsion.[53]

Condemnations of the conditions in these areas echoed earlier invectives against swamps, the very reclaimed spots upon which some of

Swamp 125

the most blighted neighborhoods such as Oko Awo now sat. The Sanitary Service described all of Isale Eko around the eléèkó's ìgá (which Macaulay accused the colonial government of allowing to fall into disrepair) as "a rabbit warren of shanties . . . awash with mud and garbage."[54] An editorial in the pro-British *Nigerian Pioneer* remarked that "the virility of the African is generally conceded, but no where has the ability to exist anywhere and anyhow apparently impervious to bad surroundings been demonstrated by our people than the denizens of this most unhealthy and pestiferous district. . . . Such a place as Oko-Awo should not be allowed to continue in the middle of the Municipal Area of Lagos to the danger of lives in surrounding areas and the detriment of trade."[55] As land was seized and houses started to come down with the help of the town engineer and Medical Services Departments, protests flared. As historian Ayodeji Olukoju describes, "Matters reached a point that the [eléèkó] . . . Sanusi Olusi, and his chiefs petitioned the government in 1930 about the 'rampant' demolition of houses 'under the pretence of anti-plague measures' which had rendered 'many souls homeless.'" Petitioners argued that "houses were demolished even after having been deratted simply because they looked old." By 1933, on sanitary grounds, "400 houses and shacks had been demolished and about 30 new houses built."[56]

After sanitation, the second directive for the board was the provision of housing for workers. A 1929 labor ordinance had combined these two concerns by creating "Labour Health Areas" wherever large and dense numbers of African workers were employed, in order to "ensure adequate housing and sanitary conditions and allow for medical and administrative inspection."[57] While the provision and status of homes for European civil servants had been a government preoccupation since the turn of the century, concern for sheltering and thereby monitoring and organizing African labor came into focus in the aftermath of the plague outbreak as well as the 1920 railroad strike and other labor disturbances such as the disappearance of migrant workers once they earned enough money to return home with a bride-price in hand.[58] The LEDB's founding ordinance made the rehousing of "persons of the poorer and laboring classes who are displaced by schemes" a priority once slums had been cleared.[59] Still, despite the rise of interest in African housing, in 1926 Governor Thomson renewed the push for the segregation of

European workers' housing from African quarters of the city with the establishment of a "free zone" between Ikoyi and Lagos Island.[60]

The newfound concern for African housing was reflected in the inclusion of a new section on "Housing" in Nigerian annual reports beginning in 1931. "Housing" as a social concern connected to labor was becoming a colonial priority. The 1931 annual report admitted that the colonial government had given "little attention to [housing] architecture until recently." In a surprising statement that would rarely be repeated or practiced over the final three decades of colonial rule, the report continued, "An endeavor has been made to design in harmony with local conditions and native styles of building." It is likely this policy was inspired less by an appreciation for native architecture than by the reality of budget shortfalls for state-built housing in most of the colony. However, the report acknowledged that Lagos was "exceptional" in being "at present in transition from a town on the native African to one on the European plan." There, the report argued for the need to "abolish" traditional "sordid" compounds, as the "parochial habit is a great obstacle to progress," to put up "wholly detached houses and tenements of moderate size" (described in the report as "labour lines") to house wage earners in "houses of a European type . . . of cement with corrugated iron roofs." Regulations required houses in Lagos to be "totally detached and upon dwellings covering not more than fifty *per cent.* of the total size of the property."[61]

An example of such "line" housing comes from plans for homes built at Oko Awo as part of town planning scheme no. 2 (fig. 3.4). All three blueprints show long, slim, single-story, stand-alone structures made up of four rooms plus a semi-separate kitchen and pantry spaces. The designs moved communal outdoor space from the center of the house (courtyards) to the rear of the house to prevent these spaces from being counted against the amount of property the house could take up on the plot. The houses are little more than "barracks"—barebones structures for putting a roof over the bodies of laborers with no space for privacy, wives, or children. These structures could be easily inspected and sanitized as needed. The design is reminiscent of the Afro-Brazilian row houses on Lagos Island—seen in 1909 Colonial Office photographs— noted by inspectors to be "badly lighted + badly ventilated" (see figs. 2.10 and 2.11).[62] The new plans preserve the basic Afro-Brazilian floor

Swamp

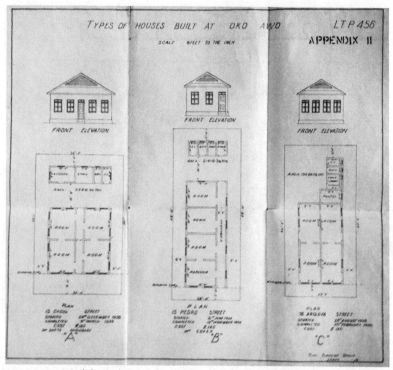

FIGURE 3.4. Model row houses for the Lagos Executive Development Board's town planning scheme at Oko Awo. *Source:* National Archives of Nigeria.

plans while rectifying the perceived deficiencies by adding numerous windows to all sides of the detached structures. The cost of encircling the houses with windows was a 50 percent reduction in the number of homes that could fit into Oko Awo. This reduction in housing stock is reflected in a comparison of a 1926 map to a 1942 map of Oko Awo (see maps 3.1 and 3.4).

Africans who benefited from the LEDB's redevelopment schemes were landlords who could afford to (re)acquire, by lease or purchase, the plots at the new LEDB valuation. These lucky few, often high-ranking African clerical staff or well-connected chiefs, were able to rent out the new properties to as many wage laborers as they could pack in—in Yaba developers added second and third floors to row houses similar to the ones at Oko Awo. Their economic incentive aligned with colonial desires for easy-to-inspect "line" houses in which units of male labor

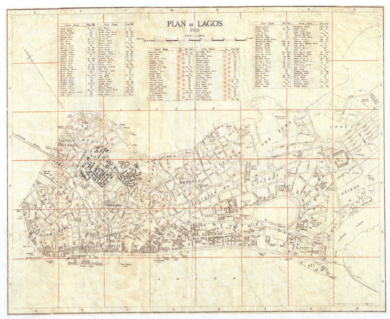

MAP 3.4. The reduction in density and housing stock at Oko Awo between 1926 and 1942. *Source:* Federal Survey Department, Lagos.

could be packed so long as they had access to a window. The 1933 annual report noted that "there have been cases where landlords obtained as much per annum by way of rent as the dwelling was worth."[63] These individuals were said to have received a "golden egg" from the British.[64] They had benefited from an extension of the British social state. The government had intervened in African housing for the laboring classes but had done so largely through and to the benefit of well-off local intermediaries willing to cooperate by ceding their land to LEDB schemes. From these landlords wage laborers rented shared rooms with four or more other single men; married laborers rented single rooms with their wife and children.[65] As historian Lisa Lindsay has shown, low government wages that did not provide family allowances for Africans, coupled with high costs of living, including rent, created a fiscal situation for laborers that clashed with both Yoruba expectations of husbands providing shelter and British ideals of male breadwinners.[66] This tension set the stage for a crisis of social reproduction, culminating in the 1945 Nigerian General Strike.[67]

Swamp 129

Those displaced by redevelopment schemes or unable to pay cash rents for housing in them—the vast majority of the city—were forced into precarious reliance on a patron, support from hometown networks, or places to squat and self-build on the margins of the city.[68] Now-famous Lagos "slums" like Maroko begin to appear on maps on the peripheries of state-sponsored housing redevelopments where occupants found work as drivers, gatemen, and houseboys and housegirls (map 3.2).

Even government agents recognized the "extreme hardships" endured by those who lost their homes in the demolitions.[69] Historian John Iliffe writes that in colonial Africa, "towns pioneered the transition in the nature of poverty," as "new forms of poverty—proletarianisation, unemployment, prostitution, delinquency—supplemented older forms of incapacitation, servitude, and hunger."[70] These forms of poverty had begun to show themselves decades earlier in Lagos with the rise of the racist export state but now intensified as slum clearance brought colonial logic into African communities. With these shifts underway, the global depression of the late 1920s and 1930s hit Lagos hard and only worsened conditions in Lagos. The price of cocoa plummeted in 1928, and by 1929 Macaulay's NNDP sent a memorandum to the government asserting that twenty-seven thousand African traders were unemployed in Lagos.[71] The Public Works Department, railway, and foreign firms sacked thousands of African workers.[72] Slum clearance could not have begun at a more inopportune time: depression set in as demolitions finished, leaving the displaced without the promised resettlement areas completed due to the drying up of funding for the African developers given contracts to rebuild. By 1932 only 174 homes of a planned 700 had been built in the Yaba worker's estate.[73] Stalling LEDB projects and widespread unemployment meant that by the 1930s the city was full of Africans sleeping on the streets, under Carter Bridge, along the marina, in public buildings, and even in graveyards.[74]

The eléèkó and chiefs petitioned against demolitions and deportations on behalf of the "many souls homeless," but the colonial state chose to criminalize poverty rather than extend social support further into the population. In 1930, as Olukoju describes, Administrator of the Colony F. M. Baddeley "acknowledged that there was an unemployment problem but did not believe there was any 'real destitution' since many of the unemployed were sustained by friends and relations. Hence, he argued that there was no need to establish a machinery to provide local relief for that 'would only create a problem which does not at present exist.' He recommended instead that unemployed migrants be repatriated to their hinterland homes under the provisions of the Township Ordinance."[75] Over the next few years the government removed thousands of people from the city. Many simply found their way back to Lagos.

Several social historians have shown how the interwar colonial state steered Lagosians to new forms of sociality by introducing, or "inventing," and policing novel, often vague bureaucratic categories of people such as "juvenile delinquents," "junior" and "senior" children, "vagrants," "prostitutes," and the "insane."[76] At the time, Lagos was a very young city with 40 percent of its population under age fifteen and 58 percent of denizens having been born elsewhere.[77] New forms of urban poverty drove many of these young migrants, once hopeful of earning a wage, into petty crime and other socially unacceptable ways of finding shelter and food. The state extended a modicum of social support to some children by establishing homes, hostels, or reform schools, but many more were imprisoned, fined, or deported.[78] By 1930 there were as many as ten thousand itinerant hawkers in Lagos, many of whom slept in the streets.[79]

In response, the colonial state outlawed hawking in many residential areas, and through boys' and girls' clubs promoted the idea that a woman's proper place was in the home and that streets were "potentially criminal spaces" rather than the extensions of the house they had been in Yoruba communities.[80] Streets were being visibly demarcated to overcome what the colonial state saw as the "disorder" of the "African family," the bounds of which the colonial state could not categorize. Despite extending social nets into some areas of African life, the colonial state reacted by painting any failure to comply as a personal moral failing despite the fact that colonial wages for African men were insufficient to support a lifestyle in which wives and children could reside within the home without additional income from hawking.

Living away from home, young, unemployed, and unable to support a family, many young men in Lagos turned to the rebellious and ruggedly individualist forms of "youth culture" emerging in the port city, which rejected Yoruba and European notions of a "proper" household. "Youth" was defined not so much by age but by the fact that even men in their twenties and thirties could not establish a household on government wages,

Swamp

preventing them from reaching "adulthood" in Yoruba culture. Long the wild western frontier town of Nigeria, by 1930 Lagos was growing into what P. E. H. Hair called the "El Dorado of Nigerian youth."[81] Cowboy culture was popular—it was originally inspired by American cinema and was then spread by railway workers across the colony until young boys in Kano and Enugu were singing Yoruba songs, joining cowboy societies, and dreaming of the legend of Lagos. In the famed city, cowboys formed youth groups with names like Alikali Boys, Jaguda Boys, and Boma Boys, which were at times affiliated with the "house" (sometimes a brothel) or "street" they occupied.[82] Others set up homes in graveyards or the swamplands around Yaba and Ikoyi. These group alliances and housing situations were driven not only by rising rates of unemployment but also by a countercultural protest to "disappearing" into the house of an African or European "master" as a houseboy or housegirl where they would have no recourse if they were abused.[83]

During the 1930s, pro-British Lagosians lobbied the colonial state to expand social programs to greater numbers of Africans while Macaulay's NNDP looked to empower native organizations to create their own social welfare programs. Kitoye Ajasa, the Anglophile founder of the conservative newspaper the *Nigerian Pioneer*, and Macaulay's rival, Henry Carr, advocated for full European institutions (education, health, legal, and infrastructure) across Lagos. For Ajasa, this included direct taxation to fund an expansion of the state. Collaborating white caps stumped for the tax plan, although Cole suggests that they harbored hopes of using the tax benefits to implement and lead native institutions, displacing anti-British eléèkó-supporters.[84] With the onset of economic depression and the evaporation of colonial reserves, Governor Cameron (who had served under Egerton) sought to relegitimize native authorities to run the colony after a decade of British administrators rolling back the power of the ọba and chiefs.

In an interesting turn, this entailed a return to a system that resembled Lugard's dual mandate of focusing on transportation infrastructure while governing through native authorities, though for decidedly different ideological ideas of "greater freedom and independence for the [colonial] states they had helped to evolve," with no reference to Lugard's terminology or authoritarian tenets.[85] Cameron allowed the eléèkó to return from his exile in Oyo and created the Native Administration

Ordinance, winning popularity with the masses and criticism from previous supporters like Carr and the anti-eléèkó crowd.[86] Macaulay and the NNDP wasted little time filling the administrative opportunity, working to formalize and incorporate youth clubs and social groups from the city's quarters into "cells" of the NNDP.[87] The Nigerian Ladies League reemerged at this time to help reform children as a native administration doing the work of the state.[88] Now that the NNDP was the de facto collaborating party, the city's youth pushed for more revolutionary politics, forming the Lagos Youth Movement, which superseded the NNDP as the country's most powerful political organization once it became the Nigerian Youth Movement with staunch nationalist Nnamdi Azikiwe onboard.[89] As funding again became available in the 1940s, the government revisited slum clearance against an opposition momentarily united behind the Lagos Youth Movement.

Pushback: Strikes, Petitions, and Housing as a Proxy

A remarkable file from the British National Archives reveals the opposing positions of prominent Lagosians and the colonial government over the LEDB's second round of land acquisition and slum clearance.[90] The file was created in 1947 by the government in response to a petition submitted by dozens of chiefs and heads-of-societies who feared the return of land grabs and displacement. It was sealed until 1997. The context for the file was a period of post–World War II strife and uncertainty as migrants filled the city and British envoys reexamined land policies. The Pullen Scheme (1941) and West African Produce Board had set food-price controls intended to halt wartime inflation but had ended up decreasing agricultural production and driving more farmhands into the city in search of work.[91] Then, beginning in 1939, Sir Mervyn Tew, a British judge who had once suggested sweeping "away the whole system of native land tenure," had been assigned to reopen the question of land rights at Lagos and to make recommendations for legislation.[92] While Tew's report awaited publishing approval, another British report "on the Planning and Development of Greater Lagos" called for the LEDB to sweep away huge swaths of Lagos "slums" while filling in surrounding swamps in a quick and concerted effort. The report was written in anticipation of resistance and urged "an intensive propaganda campaign [to acquaint the public with its] existence and the probable early approval

Swamp 133

of the plan."[93] Acting on the Planning and Development report in 1946, the governor legislated a new Lagos Town Planning Ordinance to amend the original 1928 LEDB Ordinance to enact redevelopment plans. These reports and ordinances were compiled as the Lagos Town Council announced that Lagos was almost full and could not keep up with construction (1944),[94] and as the country's African civil servants and railway workers had declared a general strike (1945) largely to improve their poor standard of living.[95] The strikers won cost-of-living pay increases and some family allowances as the government decided to push for the "modernization" of the labor force toward a nuclear family model, which would entail the restructuring of worker estates from line houses to greater numbers of government-leased single-family homes. Momentum was building toward a drastic spatial-legal-familial restructuring of Lagos. In this climate, the 1947 petitioners were understandably agitated, fearful, as landowning chiefs and other community leaders, of losing their lands and livelihoods in the LEDB's rush to redevelop the city.

The 1947 petition was submitted by ọba Falola (who replaced the deceased eléèkó in 1932), all the white-capped chiefs, and many other influential Lagosians on behalf of the "welfare and interest of over 200,000 African inhabitants of Lagos Island." It asked the Chief Secretary to the Government to "withhold his Royal assent to the new Town Plan for 'Greater Lagos' and to the Amending Ordinance to Lagos Town Planning Ordinance of 1928."[96] The petitioners argued that the new town plan was proceeding too quickly without consultation of the African community "for the pure purpose of converting Lagos lands into Crown lands for the benefits of the Europeans ultimately. The more so is this conviction when it is realised that Government land policy in Lagos is obscure and is causing a great deal of anxiety and embarrassment to the community." The petition then connects the new plan to a long tradition going back to the Treaty of Cession, in which "gradually, but very systematically, the small Island of Lagos, Ikoyi, and Apapa and all Lagos environs are being converted into Crown lands by right of acquisition." A map attached to the petition powerfully illustrated their point (map 3.5). With dark red ink, it shows the encircling of Lagos Island by Crown-owned lands: 4,350 acres of Crown lands to 720 left in the hands of Africans, despite an African population of 200,000 and a European population of only 5,000. At this point in the petition, the argument against the scheme shifts from the decades-old strategies of chiefs and the ọba asserting ownership rights based on native custom and history to a claim based on the welfare of the city's poor who lived in the areas affected by the schemes. They asserted that poor families would lose their homes, land, and ability to support themselves if the schemes came to pass. Any claims that these families were actually well-off because of the high rents they collected were refuted by arguing that they only charged high rents in order to cover the government taxes. Having witnessed the slum clearance of the late 1920s, the petitioners argued that rather than improving living conditions in Lagos, the state would actually create more slums by displacing the poor and forcing them to find shelter elsewhere. The core disputation of the petition rested on an argument for general welfare of the people and families of Lagos.

The British administration forcefully responded point by point to the petition's claims. "The memorial [petition] comprises a mass of vague and groundless supposition, misapprehension and what I can only regard as deliberately misleading statements and I can only deal with it adequately by commenting upon it paragraph by paragraph." The government's first rebuttal was that the petition was signed by not "a single member either of the poorer classes who make up the bulk of the population or of the stranger native element that constitutes a large proportion of the tenant class." Rather, the majority of the signatories were asserted to be landlords and/or moneylenders. After disputing the petition's land and population statistics, the administration argued that the state was actually the one looking out for the welfare of the city's people. It insisted that most properties were owned by well-off chiefs, families, and speculators who exploited tenants by "exacting the most exorbitant rents for insanitary shacks, many of which have virtually no roofs, and several inches of water on the mud floor in the rainy seasons. No attempt whatever has been made to render these shacks habitable, nor will any be made except under Government pressure." It continued, "The tragedy of the present position is that the majority of the poor have no security for either their houses or their lands and are liable at any moment to be ruthlessly evicted by the moneylenders and others who make their living out of the purchase of property at low prices for re-sale at a handsome profit." The administration claimed

MAP 3.5. Map of Lagos showing (in pink) the areas taken by the British government—a powerful illustration of the constriction of African settlements, 1946. *Source*: The National Archives, Kew, UK.

that the proposed LEDB schemes were designed for the benefit of the poorer classes and would improve conditions for them through swamp reclamation and by replacing one story buildings with two- to three-story buildings of an improved quality. The British concluded the poor "will still be tenants but in very much better buildings," and "will have everything to gain."

The ọba's petition and the government's response paint diametrically opposed pictures of the housing situation on Lagos Island. The former portrays a system of small plots personally held and rented out by destitute families crushed under the burden of government taxes; the latter describes devious slumlords squeezing every penny out of their neglected tenements. Both sides claimed to represent the interests of the city's poor. Conspicuously absent are the voices of poor tenants themselves. The historical evidence for the makeup of the landlords of Lagos Island is murky and varies by the neighborhood or block in question, but both sides—petitioners and the British respondents—likely had some legitimacy, as there remained two overlapping and entangled systems of land tenure on the island. The presence of both freehold and family property systems meant that there were two classes of landlords: landlords who had final claims to the land in question (via freehold titles from Crown grants or via communal usufructuary rights as the customary overseers of the land), and intermediary landlords who shared rents as part of an extended family and owed loyalty and tributes to higher-up granters of the land.[97] Still, 60 percent to 70 percent of occupants in areas like Central Lagos were renters with no claims—intermediary or otherwise—to the property they lived on.[98] With the interwar rise of the socially concerned state, arguments between African elites and the British over the control of land had shifted from legal claims over customary prerogatives to a proxy over the social welfare of "the people."

The actual outcome of the aftermath of the 1946 petition was arguably a win for everyone in the file except the poor. After a six-year delay, Sir Mervyn Tew's report was finally released and made into law in 1947.[99] The "Tew Ordinances" proved an unexpected boon for "chiefs"[100] and their customary claims to land rights. The ordinances declared that freehold interpretations of Crown grants had been inconsistent with "native law and custom" and therefore put "all land subject to Crown grants back into their pristine state," giving chiefs reversionary rights

Swamp

to any of their lands that had subsequently been registered as Crown grants by other families or individuals (grantees or buyers). The laws stripped *arota* (former slaves or dependents) of any freehold titles they or their forefathers had once enjoyed from Crown grants.[101] The legislation was the final extinguishing of claims to freehold land tenure in Lagos, placing most land under the usufructuary dictums of family property, thereby empowering white caps and other "chiefs" to more forcefully begin collecting tributes from the occupants of the tracts of Lagos they claimed, creating a dual system in which the legal purchase or contractual lease of land did not preclude the continual payment of tributes to traditional authorities.[102] In the aftermath of these ordinances, another British envoy on land matters, Stanhope Simpson, would write that the arota legislation was "an extraordinary little ordinance" that was an "example of sovereign or administrative rights which have got translated into proprietary rights," thereby causing hardships that "are really feudal burdens."[103] Unless one had a customary claim to land, there would be no avenue for escaping overlords when it came to property ownership in Lagos, setting up a system of tiers of patronage that would undergird the city henceforth. Meanwhile, government plans for the razing of Central Lagos and the reclamation of swamps went ahead in the 1950s—by then with the ọba and white caps' blessing—culminating in the displacement and dislocation of thousands of poor families and tenants from their communities and from their spatially dependent economic livelihoods, as the next chapter details. Despite the "profound" concern for the "poorer classes" in the rhetoric of elites and the administration, their needs often came in last across the coming decades.

Swampland

Thinking about swamps and slums and their historical overlaps calls to mind the Yoruba locution known as *òwe*. Oyekan Owomoyela writes that in Yoruba, òwe "is a speech form that likens one thing or situation to another, highlighting the essential similarities that the two share."[104] In imperial eyes, African slums shared many essential qualities with swamps. Both were scum-filled places blamed for disease and seen as blots of disorder, and therefore as a discredit to colonial Nigeria's capital. The process for destroying them was similar as well. Both involved passing responsibility to landowners and, when that stalled, initiating massive public works projects to "re-claim" and "re-plan" the city, frequently with lopsided benefits.

But òwe often have a deeper or double meaning. All of the five-thousand-plus òwe published by Owomoyela include a literal translation and a parenthetical explanation of further connotations. For instance, *o ti yoo mu miran si isalẹ ninu ẹrẹ gbọdọ duro ninu ẹrẹ lati pa fun u* means "he who holds another person in the swamp (or mud) must stay in the swamp to do so," but, of course, it also implies dirty practices or politics, like those British agents employed to prevent certain individuals and classes from controlling valuable land in Lagos. Likewise, swamp and slum similarities go deeper than was contended by British planners. After all, as Alan Mayne points out, the English word *slum* is a "fundamentally deceitful construct," perpetuated, like any pejorative term, to flatten historical and empathetic understandings of subaltern processes and injustices.[105] Swamps and their housing counterparts are vital in their own ways to natural and urban ecosystems. Long thought to be health hazards, wetlands filter toxins from the environment, prevent erosion, and produce rich soil deposits, not to mention the benefits of the biodiversity they host. "Slums" (like Oko Awo, Makoko, and Maroko) were in fact thriving communities with deep layers for African residents in Lagos who had built and maintained businesses, connections, and shelters despite decades of colonial exclusion from infrastructure and development programs. These spaces were the homes of the people ignored by the colonial state who nevertheless served the needs and demands of the colonial economy by working as laborers, hawkers, caretakers, recyclers, creditors, importers, and distributors. The consequences of conflating African communities with swamps and treating them as such were devastating. Not only were homes erased but both the visual evidence of colonial neglect and the history of African urbanism were sunk into the depths of the resulting rubble, occluded in the blindered scurry forward as seen in the next chapter.

4

Lagoon

Hidden Depths across Independence

In her 2014 science fiction novel, Nnedi Okorafor pushes back against—in fact she *submerges*—shallow portrayals of Lagos and Nigerians. She has the reader dive into an urban archipelago of female scientists, dreamers, and military men all caught up in a strange race to alert the world to the arrival of intergalactic marine creatures (who likewise may be more complex and compassionate than assumed). We are swept up in a space where time is short, water overwhelms land, and people are real and resourceful. Okorafor's title for her fantastic story is simply *Lagoon*. A place of depth, unexpected encounters, and informational lacuna. *This is Lagos.*

Lagos Lagoon looms large over Nigeria's largest city, a brackish body hung above the city's central islands and Lagosians' urban imagination. Since Iddo Island was first inhabited, the lagoon has always been the lifeblood of its redundant namesake. A moat for early Awori-Yoruba settlers, Portuguese smugglers, and dodgers of all sorts. A treasure chest of fish, crustaceans, and valuable vegetation. A clot amid twenty-four hundred miles of littoral arteries awash with commerce originally connecting the Bight of Benin kingdoms (Dahomey, Ijebu, Benin) to one another, and later Nigeria and West Africa to Europe, the Americas, and beyond. Lagos simply would not exist without Lagos Lagoon. In Okorafor's adventure as well as in Yoruba mythology, the lagoon is a living entity capable of anger and hunger, personified in the form of a woman, a shapeshifter named Ayodele (joy has come home)[1] in *Lagoon*, and Olosa, a goddess of abundance and prosperity, in Ifá traditions.[2] Today, petroleum, rubbish, and sand mining have taken a devastating toll on Lagos Lagoon, souring her mood and appearance, but in 1960 Olosa was buoyant and teeming with life.

In the years around independence, Lagos became a city unimaginably different from the place the Portuguese had centuries before (re)named after its defining "lake." From raffia palm homes and burned-out canoes, it had become a city of cement and automobiles in the space of a single lifespan.[3] Lagos's shallow channel, swamps, and then lagoon had been tamed by dredges, retaining walls, drainage canals, and, as seen in a 1952 photograph of Ikoyi, a "bank between the lagoon and the swamp [that] excludes high-tide flooding" (fig. 4.1).[4] Yet the lagoon was still a critical part of the city's identity and economy. Fishing fed and supported many households; timber logs and other goods were floated into the lagoon marketplace from the Osun and Ogun Rivers; and

FIGURE 4.1. Aerial photograph of ditch to prevent Lagos Lagoon from flooding the flat plains of Ikoyi. *Source:* Francis Uher, "Aerial Views of Lagos," *Nigeria* 38 (1952): 121.

Lagoon 141

regattas during Eyo Festivals reminded residents of their heritage. The era itself was lagoon-like, a time of much continuity sailing across the colonial and then independent capital, as well as a time of abundance and possibility stretching to the horizon. But like the endless view of Lagos Lagoon from the shore, boundaries hid beyond the sightline and harsh currents churned beneath, constricting the city and thwarting its jubilant ambitions.

Opportunity and uplifting turnover are often the theme for independence studies, but as this chapter shows, continuity prevailed in the realm of urban planning and housing frameworks in Lagos. The Lagos Executive Development Board (LEDB)—the city's urban planning body founded in the 1920s to seize and raze neighborhoods afflicted with bubonic plague—changed hands but only increased slum clearance schemes despite widespread opposition. Nigerian executives and civil servants moved into former European estates, maintaining housing hierarchies based on three tiers of labor: expansive enclaves for elite managers, cube-like boxes for the families with a male wage earner, and unregistered and thus legally insecure sprawl for everyone else (the marginally employed, unemployed, and supposedly unemployable). Tropical Modernism, the climatically concerned style of modern architecture associated with Africa's independence era, was not simply an articulation of a bold new "African" vision but had in fact been developed by Europeans in the 1940s for imperial purposes. It brought with it not a clean slate as claimed but prejudiced and economically calculated thinking. Modernist buildings and settlements were part of a program of "modernization" built around colonial claims to universalist conceptions of social progress and economic development aimed to extend colonialism's reach in response to postwar fiscal and political challenges. The postwar colonial project revolved around the reentrenchment of British power after the destabilization of war and the rise of anticolonial activism. In the face of these challenges, the Colonial Office turned to technocrats who were unconcerned with historical or local context in order to reestablish European political and cultural hegemony. The foremost historian of African decolonization, Frederick Cooper, describes this as a situation in which "new leaders—before and after independence and in dialogue with 'experts' of the 'developed world'—came to define social policy around an imported future more than the extension of an observed present, around a package of institutions . . . rather than around the complex, category-crossing social processes that had been going on around them."[5]

In other words, as this chapter describes, Tropical Modernism and its agents—initially architects and technocrats from Europe—were what Okorafor fights against in *Lagoon*, a surface-deep approach by outsiders to Lagos and West Africa. In housing interventions and the broader colonial social program of the time, the past was painted as darkness—stale, jumbled, and unimportant—whereas the future was presented as bright and full of the promise of development, just beyond the present pain of reorganization via vivisection—brutal slum clearance and socially incongruous rehousing situations in the case of Lagos. This was an era of continual historical erasure in the pursuit of the possibility of the future—the dangled justification for continued colonial power structures.

By looking at the writings of its founders, their rhetoric, and the designs of modernist projects for houses and housing estates, this chapter offers an analysis of Tropical Modernism's historical myopia to counter the celebratory and defensive tone found in strands of recent literature on the subject. It argues that the devaluation of history and of local conditions was central to Tropical Modernism from the outset and across independence in a postwar environment driven by profit. Colonialism had moved from a "civilizing mission" in which Africa had no past ("a continent without history") to a modernizing raison d'être, in which there was no time for the past and no value in premodern society to a modern industrial society. Any unsettling understandings of the realities of African urban conditions caused by decades of colonial racism and misrule were overlooked by modernists, as were any local networks, institutions, or living arrangements Africans had created to cope with and survive within these biased conditions. Any plight found in African neighborhoods was the consequence of the stubborn persistence of "tribal life" that had to be eradicated by breaking up the "cobwebs" of the old African quarters and realigning them into neat, detached or semi-detached homes to host industrial, industrious, reliable, and predictable units of labor. The postwar British anxiety around the "labor question" had quickly expanded to include keen

Lagoon

attention to a housing problem and the recruitment of modernist designers. Lagosians unable or unwilling to find a home in the new mold were left to eke out a living through increasingly strained appeals to familial, ethnic, and hometown connections. Single-family homes were seen as the basis of urban prosperity that would lubricate revenue and attract investment—a formula drilled into the managers and leaders promoted to colonial posts and given the keys at independence. Of course, an array of Lagosians challenged, subverted, altered, and cracked these plans at every turn because their lives did not "fit" into the boxes assigned to them.[6]

In the end, in a process largely overlooked by historians, the rationale behind postwar colonial policy was an astonishing act of flimflam: the visible evidence of colonialism's half century of marginalization and impoverishment of urban Africans was contorted into the justification for continued and expanded colonial rule by blaming the visually "jumbled" state of cities like Lagos not on a decidedly racist imperial legacy but on African society's persistent "tribalism" and "bush" mentality and then closing the door to any investigation into this claim by placing all focus on the future. Racism had not disappeared. Rather it had pivoted and deflected attention by pitting "modern" urban life against "tribal" rural life. Racist temporal notions of Africans' lack of "evolution" became spatialized as a lack of "development."[7] Skylines replaced skin tone as the acceptable visual cues of civilization. An entire myth of a wholly and eternally rural continent was invented, and the remnants of any contradictions were razed in "slum" clearance and pushed aside in the race forward. This was not a mass conspiracy but the product of a toxic late-colonial climate of anxious capitalism, architectural egotism, and imperial decline. The final section of this chapter draws parallels between Tropical Modernist schemes and the now infamous archival erasures of decolonization that they foreshadowed. Despite some pushback and several designers who experimented with local history and knowledge, by the time the Nigerian Federal Survey Department published a 1968 map of Lagos (map 4.1) privileging the locations of international corporations, modernist ideas and housing schemes had fulfilled their role in perpetuating colonial relationships and imbalances and in holding back the momentous change hoped for in the lead-up to 1960.

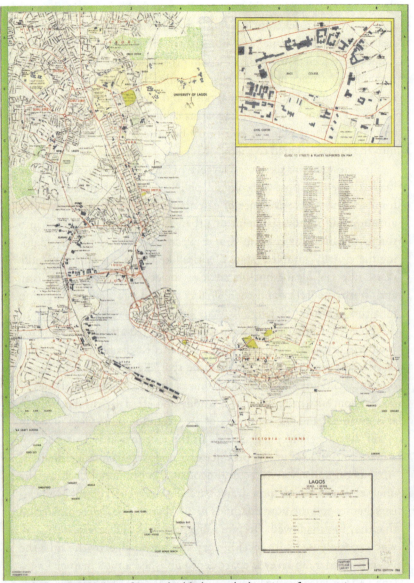

MAP 4.1. A 1968 map of Lagos highlighting the location of corporations.
Source: Federal Survey Department of Nigeria.

Lagoon   145

The Limits of Enlightened Rule:
Tropical Modernism—When the Light Only Shines Forward

> [The house's] functions are aspects of family life of which we have
> all had experience, and the means of fulfilling them, though simple,
> have a large degree of universality; once [one] understand[s] the
> problems of the house much else becomes clear.
>
> —Maxwell Fry and Jane Drew, *Tropical Architecture*
> *in the Dry and Humid Zones*

In the midst of World War II, the British Colonial Office realized it had
a problem. Production in the colonies was erratic, labor was fickle, and
leaders like Nigeria's Nnamdi Azikiwe and the Gold Coast's Kwame
Nkrumah were making a powerful case for greater self-rule, staging successful protests and gaining international support. Instead of attempting
further austerity measures (the previous staple of imperial policy), in
1940 and then again in 1945 Parliament passed Colonial Development
and Welfare Acts, infusing funding into the colonies and creating the
British Colonial Research Committee and the Colonial Social Science
Research Council to investigate socioeconomic issues. The hope was that
by increasing infrastructure and the number of trained African workers
and by appeasing calls for greater attention to the social welfare of colonial subjects, production could be increased through greater efficiency
and savings in labor costs once European salaries were replaced with
lower African wages. This was an investment intended to eventually finance the repayment of Britain's wartime debt.[8] In the architecture and
urban design that followed, the Colonial Office attempted a corresponding approach of modern construction based on scientific principles and
industrial minimalism rather than the blunt intimidation and exclusive
grandeur of past imperial designs.[9] British politicians presented the Development and Welfare Acts and the construction projects they funded
as a new beginning—a "reset" of colonial relations. However, after nearly
a century of occupation, it was not that simple.

Modernist architecture and urban planning originated in the early
1920s in Europe. Its founders asserted that it was a radically new form
of architecture intentionally free from references to the past or politics.
Reinvention, purism, and positivism reigned in the post–World War

I work of Le Corbusier and Walter Gropius, two of the iconic founders of the movement who partnered with and inspired a generation of architects working in the tropics. Desiring an architecture with a force in and of itself unbound from the post–World War I disappointments of nationalistic styles, their foundational ideas were *une machine-à-habiter* (machines for living in), as Le Corbusier famously stated, and the creation of "the purely organic building, boldly emanating its inner laws, free of untruths or ornamentation" in the words of Gropius. Le Corbusier's Villa Savoye (1929), outside Paris, and Gropius's residence near Boston, Gropius House (1938), are essential prototypes of modernist homes: white, minimally adorned rectangular forms built with industrial materials and fixtures on a cleared plot (fig. 4.2). The houses were intended to be pristine and functional against their wooded surroundings. Yet underneath their veneers are historically situated assumptions about society and empire. Both were elite homes equipped

FIGURE 4.2. The white rectangular facade of Gropius House (1938) set above a green yard and against a wooded backdrop. Author's photograph.

Lagoon

with servants' quarters to support a small nuclear family and to perform the constant cleaning required to keep the open and always visible "free" floor plans presentable. During the time of the construction of Villa Savoye, thousands of domestic servants were working in France from its colonies.[10] Many of the industrial materials for the homes, such as rubber, concrete, and chemicals, came from French and American colonies, where modernism would soon be employed to quicken extraction.

The veneer itself—the white facades and interiors that define residential modernism—was a statement linking rational supremacy to the color white. Later, in the tropics, intense sunlight would be used to justify white paint (despite the intensive upkeep required), but in northern France and New England a darker hue would have warmed the homes the majority of the year. Seen from their driveways, the white geometric structures stand in contrast to their forested local landscapes, pale monuments to human-imposed order and human conquest. Before fleeing Nazi Germany for London and then the United States, Gropius had helped popularize Bauhaus-style white walls in exhibition spaces with the intention of creating, in the words of art historian Charlotte Klonk, "a perfect space for argumentation and discussion, such as that which forms in the mind on reading the pages of a book."[11] In the 1930s Hitler embraced this "white cube" museum aesthetic as a symbol of purity, of man's domination over his environment, and of the Reich's power to purge anything or anyone thought to be a blemish.[12] A perversion of purism espoused by Le Corbusier's L'Esprit Nouveau or not, there is no way to avoid the fact that whitewashed walls and empirical functionalism had deep symbolic ties to interwar theories of racial hierarchy and imperial hegemony.[13]

Maxwell Fry, the most influential British architect behind Tropical Modernism in Africa, worked with both Le Corbusier and Gropius. He headed a firm with Gropius in London from 1934 to 1937 and, with his later design partner and wife, Jane Drew, worked on Le Corbusier's 1950s master plan for Chandigarh, a new administrative capital for the Punjab Region of India. Fry grew up in Liverpool and was trained in the 1920s at the Liverpool School of Architecture, where he won the Lever second prize.[14] During the 1930s, Fry became a leading figure in the emerging modernist movement in London through his work with Gropius and his energetic participation in the Design and Industries

Association and the Modern Architecture Research Group, the British chapter of Corbusier's Congrès International d'Architecture Moderne. The outbreak of World War II meant the state became the most dependable place for architects to find employment, and after a short stint with the War Office, Fry found himself posted to Accra where he soon became the town planning adviser for all of West Africa. Becoming well regarded in modernist circles in her own right, Drew joined Fry in Accra shortly after. Between 1942 and the 1970s, Fry and Drew designed dozens of buildings in British West Africa, first for the Colonial Office and then as a private firm with offices in Accra, Lagos, and London. The architectural ideas they developed during these years were foundational for the Department of Tropical Studies (1955)[15] at the Architectural Association in London, where Drew had trained, and the Colonial Office's West African Building Research Station in Accra (1952)—two institutions with fingerprints on a generation of tropical structures.[16]

Throughout this time, Fry and Drew's style adapted standard modernist frames to tropical climates, as did much of the work of their peers, including Otto Koenigsberger and James Cubitt, with whom they worked to establish the Architectural Association Department of Tropical Studies.[17] The majority of municipal and private homes in Lagos during the 1950s and 1960s were built in some variation of the Tropical Modern style, either by European architects or by draftsmen who had trained in European institutions like the Architectural Association or who had worked for firms like Fry and Drew. Climatic control, empiricism, and economy of building costs were the critical considerations. Techniques to reduce internal temperatures of buildings included screens, sunshades and louvers, large awnings and overhangs, perforated facades elevated and angled to catch the cross breeze, and, of course, brilliantly white exteriors. Fry, Drew, and Partners' House at Ikoyi was a white cube—like Kensington House, Fry had designed with Gropius in the UK—but altered to mitigate sunlight and insects (fig. 4.3).

Large, recessed windows welcomed a continuous waft of air, and a thick roof and raised foundation insulated the living space and removed it from mosquitoes. Of course these tactics were not as novel as architects of the era liked to claim; as far back as the middle of the eighteenth century in West Africa, colonial builders had sought to out-design the dual nuisances of sun and stinging insects with raised bungalows

FIGURE 4.3. A brilliantly white elevated concrete cube. Fry, Drew, and Partners' House at Ikoyi, 1940s. *Source:* Maxwell E. Fry and Jane Drew, *Tropical Architecture in the Dry and Humid Zones* (London: B. T. Batsford, 1964).

and breezy verandas that simultaneously elevated the status and gaze of their colonial occupants.[18] Like the London School of Hygiene & Tropical Medicine and the School of Tropical Medicine in Liverpool, the Department of Tropical Studies prioritized sanitary considerations and emphasized the establishment of boundaries between spaces to overcome the perils of the surrounding landscape.[19] What differentiated Tropical Modernist houses from earlier colonial plans were two elements: the dogmatic emphasis on the primacy of technical calculations to overcome ecological challenges—Fry's, Drew's, and Koenigsberger's widely read manuals and books were full of technical drawings showing sun angles and thermal properties—and the stripping away of any kind of nonfunctional ornamentation, which was part of the purity of an adherence to the frill-lessness of rational scientific calculations (and reducing costs).[20] Fry and Drew's House at Ikoyi, like their contemporary Edward Mills's Residences at Ikoyi, were Public Works Department bungalows reduced to their essential shape and purpose.

In stressing empiricism, the work of Fry, Drew, and other Tropical Modernists was part of the Colonial Office's postwar turn to "experts"

150   WATERHOUSES

to transform broad sociopolitical issues into narrow technocratic problems.[21] Through this strategy, the colonial state maintained its position
as the "gatekeeper" between colonies and the outside world, deciding the
frame of inquiry into the challenges of the day and what theories or
concepts would be applied.[22]

Empirical building science and the ostensible removal of symbolic
references intentionally distanced Fry and Drew's designs from historical context, as did their writings and lectures. Although there have been
several analyses of their work in recent years ranging from nostalgic to
apologist to critical, Tropical Modernism's diminishment of the past
and the consequences of Fry and Drew's ahistorical approach in perpetuating racial stereotypes and colonial justifications have not been
adequately addressed.[23] Writing in their widely read manual, *Tropical
Architecture in the Dry and Humid Zones*,[24] Fry and Drew do not mince
words in their evaluation of the state of West Africa when they first arrived, describing the people as having "slumbered on for centuries" while
being "sunk in agricultural apathy" in a setting of "extreme disorder."[25]
In a 1946 speech describing his visits to West African cities and his prescriptions for them, Fry repeatedly praised their timeless natural beauty
and latent potential but lamented their neglect (in the passive voice),
recommending the clearance of African sections of towns.[26] In the same
speech, Fry acknowledged "the problems of Nigeria are extremely difficult" but did not explore the origins or complexity of those problems and
how to avoid repeating them; instead, he simply tossed off suggestions
for the creation of more open spaces and a business center for Lagos. In
1950, the head building liaison officer for British colonial housing policy,
George Anthony Atkinson, erroneously suggested that Lagos did not
exist before Europeans arrived. He noted that no comparative studies
of traditional African housing had been conducted and, although he
thought this should be rectified, he was not held back from laying out
remedies to the African housing problem that throughout his time at
the helm would focus primarily on finding climatically suitable materials and inexpensive designs.[27] As architectural historians Ian Jackson
and Jessica Holland describe, Fry and Drew presented themselves as
"trailblazers, inventing a new architecture for the continent," which had
no historical precedents other than "raw, ruinous, primitivism."[28] Hubris
is found in Fry's repeated claims of having no precedents to follow in

Lagoon 151

either Africa or in earlier forms of European architecture. More virulent racism is found in Fry and Drew's boasting of the power of their cooling systems and rigid concrete forms to "awaken" and "inscribe order" on the "slumbering" minds of Africans.[29] For Fry and Drew, "primitive" African housing did not rise to the level of "Architecture" and had nothing to offer. Drew would only cite the African landscape as influencing her work, being careful not to give any credit to African architecture for her "original" designs: "In some cases, particularly in blocks and balcony details, an attempt has been made to design in a way which without in any sense copying African detail, gives a response which is African; the sunshine and moisture and heavy overcast sky and feeling of oppressive lethargy seem to call forth moulded forms which are rhythmical and strong, not spiky and elegant, but bold and sculptural."[30]

This perception of Africa as primitive, rural, and responsible for its own "lethargic" development was representative of the wider late-colonial view and widespread among even liberal colonial reformers. Elspeth Huxley—a press officer and then widely read commentator on the future of the British Empire whom conservatives viewed as dangerous—saw the need for breakage from "colonialism" and heavy-handed "rule" toward a "commonwealth" based "partnership." Yet in her 1954 travel memoir she wrote that the "sad and silent landscape" around Lagos, "among these gentle, sleepy-seeming people, might have been a thousand miles and several centuries away."[31] This view of African society as stagnantly anachronistic was celebrated in a British society profoundly affected by war and industrial schedules, and scholars turned wistfully to the continent to study the "pristine state of man." Most of the nascent historical and anthropological studies of the era examined tribes in the countryside, whereas urban studies were left to sociologists to gauge how Africans were adapting to city life.[32] Cooper writes that the majority of studies of Africans in cities echoed "a quest colonial bureaucrats had begun on their own: to separate the modern from the traditional."[33] A sociological study from the era described Isale Eko—the heart of Lagos Island—as "a traditional Yoruba town ... untouched by modernity, virtually frozen in time, waiting for the thaw."[34] But at least some contemporaries took a different view, casting European ways of building as frozen in form and presentism. In 1960 the well-known Yoruba expert Ulli Beier critiqued the ubiquitous patterned walls that

Fry and Drew became well known for as "rigid and frozen" in comparison to their Yoruba counterparts:

> The artistic life in Nigeria is being powerfully influenced by European architects who at the present time build all-important public buildings. Much of this architecture seems ill-adapted to its surroundings both from an aesthetic and from a practical point of view. Fry, Drew and partners, who built the University College, Ibadan, are among those who tried to get "the feel of the place" and adjust their buildings to the climate. One of the principal features of the university buildings—the broken wall patterns—is also found in traditional Yoruba mud architecture. The university buildings are here juxtaposed with traditional mosques from Ilorin. Compared with the swinging rhythm of the traditional mud buildings, the modern concrete architecture seems rigid and frozen.[35]

While working to design housing in the Gold Coast, Fry and Drew considered anthropological experts like Beier, in the words of architectural historian Viviana d'Auria, "blind to the urgency of modernising colonial territories in need of proper urban planning and housing design."[36] This attitude was part of what Cooper means when he writes that "what is remarkable about postwar era reform was that it demanded little actual info about the complexities of African life in cities or nuances of labor."[37]

The full throttle to modernize Africa and the lack of perceived guiding precedents created a titillating sense of freedom for architects like Fry and Drew. For them and other modernizers there was a feeling of wide-open experimentation without the fear of repeating historical failures because, in their minds, they were working ground up from immemorial squalor—they presumed they could only go higher. Their evaluation ignored or was ignorant to the history of places like Lagos, where, rather than stasis, immense changes had taken place in the previous 150 years. In that span, Lagos had moved from a small trading post to a regional slave market to a cosmopolitan boomtown to a segregated city—with one side squashed and rumbling with discontent and the other recessed in large lawns catered to by servants.[38] Yet in the same book in which she described the "sleepy-seeming people around Lagos,"

Lagoon   153

Huxley ignored what was in front of her to state that "Nigeria has no
style or tradition either to inspire or constrain. The architects had a
true *carte blanche*."[39] Fry and Drew likewise wrote, "How invigorating
it has been for us as architects working in England to shake free from
the crippling mental state brought about by too great a reverence for
habits and customs which have outlasted their time."[40] Fry was based
primarily in London beginning in the mid-1940s and worked also on
British commissions there. Africa became his playground, a space where
he could work ideas out, where he could build projects that would not
be accepted in Britain. As one architect working in Nigeria wrote:
"Under the pretext of 'adaptation to climatic considerations,' architects
have let fly with all the clichés, gambits and stylistic treatments which
restrictions and considerations of public taste would not allow them
to do in Europe."[41] The burden to actually live in the spaces fell to the
Africans who moved in. By the time Fry, Drew, and other modernists
began to have second thoughts about their approach as independence
neared, their economical and minimal aesthetic was standard issue in
British colonial designs.

Modernizing the Capital: The LEDB Carrying the Torch

"You've never seen a place like it," the one who had touched
and smelled London would begin; a London-inspired half
smile would etch itself in his face.... "Everywhere you look,
as far as your eyes can go, all you see is concrete. There's no
patch of grass in London. In fact, you can't see any sprout of
grass."

That picture of an infinitely paved landscape struck me. It
cast a spell over me, stayed branded on my mind for years,
even past the time when it dawned on me, finally that it was
a false, concocted portrait....

For sure, in those days, grass and trees were part of our
shame. They accused us as inhabitants of accursed Africa.
They spelled our lives as "bush" people. They connoted the
absence of "civilization," meant that we were "native" and
backward. Grass and trees marked us as primitives who
lived in a state of nature. To me and, doubtless, to many of
my classmates, a landscape that was grassless and treeless,
covered in concrete, was the epitome of civilized glory.

—Okey Ndibe, describing his childhood in 1960s Nigeria[42]

When it came to modernization schemes in Nigeria's capital, the Lagos Executive Development Board became the torchbearer. The board had existed since 1928 but had languished from a lack of funding and political will during the 1930s. The British colonial government had seized the opportunity of an outbreak of bubonic plague to establish the board and instill in it the power to declare, seize land for, clear, and manage town planning schemes, providing the government a pivotal tool in the struggle to control land rights in the increasingly constricted coastal city.[43] Bolstered by renewed funding and interest in redeveloping Central Lagos, the board would become the Tropical Modernists' vehicle for removing "the village" from Lagos.

In the mid-1940s, serving as the town planning adviser for West Africa, Fry described in Lagos "a rush not only of Africans wanting houses but also Government departments [wanting houses for employees]." To his frustration, however, in his condescending words, "These were the last people who wanted to plan." Entrepreneurs, pioneers, and developers were scrambling to claim large chunks of the city, and the local town planner, according to Fry, "was doing anything else but town planning."[44] In response to the melee, at the recommendation of a report by the commissioner of the colony, T. Hoskyns-Abrahall, the LEDB was revamped as the "one authority responsible for all aspects of [Lagos's] development."[45] By 1946, the board had immense power to restructure who lived where and in what type of accommodations as it undertook plans for extensive slum clearance and new housing schemes. To direct these efforts, the board expanded from a handful of employees to over one hundred (ninety-five Nigerians and eighteen expats by 1957–58) with positions ranging from architects to public relations officers. By the 1950s the board was overseeing at least a dozen schemes covering hundreds of acres and affecting hundreds of thousands of people in every area of the city from the mainland to Victoria Island. The Central Lagos clearance scheme alone covered seventy acres and affected two hundred thousand people (map 4.2).

In what is otherwise the best architectural writing on Lagos's independence era, which explores how the state utilized modernism and how Lagosians resisted these state-directed schemes, Daniel Immerwahr's work errs in wholly differentiating LEDB housing projects from Tropical Modernism.[46] In purely formalist readings of each's designs there are small

Lagoon

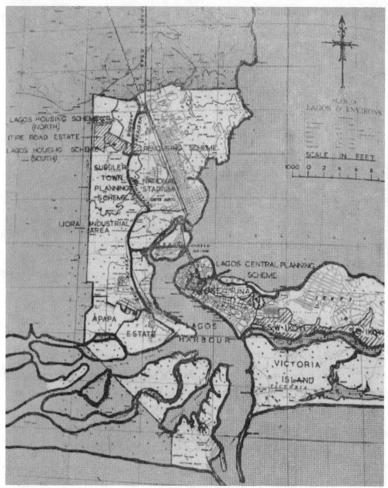

MAP 4.2. The Lagos Executive Development Board's schemes spanned the city by 1958. *Source: Lagos Executive Board Annual Report and Accounts* (Lagos: Lagos Executive Development Board, 1957–58), 8.

differences, such as the LEDB's more traditionally sized floor plans and windows, although ventilation was emphasized in LEDB housing designs. But taking a step back from the minutiae of window frames, the LEDB's body of work falls fundamentally in line with Tropical Modernism.

The board's slum clearance and rehousing schemes were animated by the same doxological trinity as the plans of Fry, Drew, and their Department of Tropical Studies peers: economic asceticism, environmental

FIGURE 4.4. A concrete Lagos Executive Development Board house in the Tropical Modernist style. *Source: Lagos Executive Board Annual Report and Accounts* (Lagos: Lagos Executive Development Board, 1957–58), 25.

subjugation, and a (theoretical) deference to empirical decision-making processes. These principles translated into a rubrical form of housing estates constructed on cleared plots intended to negate ecological conditions without input from occupants or the past. Like Tropical Modernists, the LEDB promoted its plans as a fresh start, a new beginning for the city. Any understanding of how Central Lagos was organized and operated or what had caused its "ramshackle" appearance were written off as a product of Lagos being fundamentally "a Yoruba village with a village mentality."[47] Hoskyns-Abrahall suggested that past maldevelopment was due to a lack of "self respect" on the part of Lagosians and that any "future development of Lagos on satisfactory lines depend[ed] primarily on inculcating into the people, the common people, a sense of self respect and civic pride."[48] This story served as a simple (myopic) explanation for Lagos's housing conditions that exonerated colonialism and claimed that Africans did not know how to live in cities unless they were taught how to do so properly.

Operating from this perspective, the LEDB's two primary objectives were to clear out areas where "slum minds" proliferated and to create "respectable" housing estates that instructed workers on how to live in the city with the intention of making them more productive and quantifiable. Rehousing those displaced by slum clearance was an annoying side

Lagoon

project. Hoskyns-Abrahall sighed: "There is little to be said in favour of supplying this temporary shelter [for those displaced], except that it is an unfortunate necessity, unavoidable unless slum clearing is delayed indefinitely."[49] In constructing houses, colonial agents gave more attention to housing, and thus molding, the "new professional class." In her social history of Nigerian railway workers, Lisa Lindsay describes how in the 1950s the government extended housing to greater numbers of African staff as part of a strategy to "keep workers healthy and contented so as to raise labor productivity and quell discontent."[50] Having fought for improved wages and living conditions for years, African workers jumped at the chance to live in the estate residences, especially when the plots were offered freehold.[51] Allotment of estate homes went to residents of Lagos who had lived in the city for ten years and had been continuously employed for five years.[52] New estates like Surulere and expanded old Government Reserve Areas like Apapa and Ikoyi (finally open to African families)[53] provided thousands of units of low-density rows of standardized cubical housing. In LEDB annual reports from the 1950s, photographs of the new houses in the rehousing estates were printed in each issue adjacent to photographs of dense multigenerational and multifamily homes in Central Lagos (figs. 4.5 and 4.6).

FIGURES 4.5 AND 4.6. The "disorder" and village mentality of Central Lagos contrasted to the "order" and modernity of a Lagos Executive Development Board estate. Source: *Lagos Executive Board Annual Report and Accounts* (Lagos: Lagos Executive Development Board, 1957–58), 10.

For those like Hoskyns-Abrahall and Fry, these photographs visually juxtaposed disorder of the "slum mind" to the order of the industrial working class. Architects like Adeokun Adeyemi (who as a student in London had inspired the founding of the Department of Tropical Studies) and engineers working for the LEDB had trained with European Tropical Modernists and clearly brought away an appreciation for the stark simplicity and economy of the endeavor, which they reproduced on a massive scale in the whitewashed concrete-block structures of LEDB rehousing estates. Peter Marris, an urban sociologist working in Lagos at the time who left a remarkable firsthand account, wrote, "Everything about the scheme suggested that both its conception and its execution followed British housing policy. The squalor of the slum area was condemned without regard to the quality of its community life, and the new housing estate assumed that husband, wife and children constituted the proper pattern of a household. Shops replaced markets and the new residential area was segregated from industry."[54]

The small single-family structures were intended to "modernize," which meant detribalize and decommunalize, African families into sizes that colonial wages could support while also restricting the extent of workers' family obligations, which might otherwise interfere with their official duties.[55] The irony, as Lindsay explains, was that the low-density suburbs allowed families to bring their relatives and kin from their hometowns to live with them as they sought to straddle ideas of what it meant to be "modern" bureaucrats with "traditional" familial and community obligations. Throughout this period, higher wages consistently correlated with larger families.[56]

The other, more politicized half of the LEDB's objective, slum clearance, lagged behind the progress of new housing estates as the country's political system underwent changes in the late 1940s. The old guard, famous Lagosian Herbert Macaulay's Nigerian National Democratic Party (NNDP) and the Nigerian Youth Movement, handed over power to up-and-coming parties like ọba Adele's (the traditional ruler of Lagos) Action Group (AG) and Azikiwe's new National Council of Nigeria and the Cameroons (NCNC). In 1950 Lagos held its first democratic elections for a fully elective Town Council. In that election, the NCNC in its first year on the ballot won every seat in six of Lagos's eight wards, whereas the AG won the seats in the other two wards.

Lagoon

MAP 4.3. A 1955 newspaper showing the Lagos Executive Development Board's Central Lagos Slum Clearance Scheme located in the heart of the two wards that voted against the National Council of Nigeria and the Cameroons.
Source: "Slums: The New Look and the Old," *Evening Times*, October 8, 1955.

At this point, Azikiwe began to break away from his former alliance with the NNDP, which had deep ties to "old Lagos," transforming the NCNC into a party representing the interests of migrants to the city, mostly from the east. The 1950 election brought the lopsided political power needed for NCNC councillors to unleash the LEDB to carry out extensive slum demolitions.[57] In 1951 the LEDB initiated the Central Lagos Slum Clearance Scheme (map 4.3) to raze "old" Lagos. It did so under the rhetoric of public health and modernizing the capital.

The location of the scheme was the two wards that had voted against the NCNC.[58] The clearance scheme would displace many of these voters, opening avenues for further NCNC gains, a fact not lost on protesters. Opposition newspaper articles from the era asserted that "the NCNC government decided to force [the scheme] down the throat of an unwilling people."[59] A 1955 *Daily Service* article wrote, "One wonders why the NCNC controlled Council of Ministers is bent on carrying out the slum clearance scheme with suspicious haste. If you go round central Lagos today you will find out that all the people affected by the scheme are not only bitterly against it but are prepared to go to any length in their opposition."[60] Another article from the same issue asked "if Lagos is being cleared for the indigenous natives or for foreigners?" Its verdict: that "it is the intention of the British Government in Nigeria with the aid of some Nigerian Minions and Uncle Toms to turn Lagos Island into a citadel for foreigners whilst the natives will be made to live in the mainland."[61] Even London newspapers mocked the scheme with the headline "Facade by Lagos Lagoon" and presented the planners' goals as a scramble to make the city presentable for the queen's 1956 visit, a narrative that has endured.[62] Facing eviction from their homes and markets, and after delaying protests until after the queen's visit, twenty thousand women marched against the scheme, citing the homelessness caused by the 1929 demolitions and calling on AG representatives and the ọba to steadfastly oppose clearance. In response, AG leaders proclaimed having no part in the scheme and that it would proceed "over their dead bodies." However, eventually AG leadership's opposition weakened, and the AG head of the LEDB in the late 1950s ended up with a large, stylish home in one of the schemes. Meanwhile, Azikiwe's *West African Pilot* consistently promoted the scheme under a banner of "National Pride" and public health. Quoting Muhammadu Ribadu, the powerful Northern People's Congress's federal minister of land, mines, and power, the paper argued that the schemes were necessary "to make Lagos a capital of which all would be proud."[63] With police and security forces surrounding work teams, demolitions commenced, and authorities forcibly removed residents to rehousing estates in Surulere where Public Works Department workers strew their belongings on the ground and sprayed them with chemicals to rid the new area of any pests.[64] Demolitions and protests would continue for several more years.

In his classic 1950s study of Lagos, Marris described the familial, financial, and medical consequences for those uprooted by the LEDB's schemes.[65] To understand this process and what it meant for the people affected, he conducted a granular survey of 110 households across 150 rooms in Central Lagos. This unique record offers a rich description,

Lagoon

not of a blighted city center tethered hopelessly to village life or the past, but of a dynamic and evolving urban community. A constant theme in Central Lagos's history up to this point had been its increasing density. By the 1950s its core had grown into a honeycomb of old, new, metallic, wooden, permanent, and temporary structures. Family lineages had long since outgrown their original compounds and splintered across the neighborhood. When heads of households died, their children had often continued to inherit the home collectively, a custom upheld by colonial courts, and heirs worked out numerous arrangements to break up the family property into smaller dwellings of two to six rooms, to sell one's shares, and to occupy some rooms and rent out others. Many properties in Central Lagos were family-owned and family-managed, and at least partially family-occupied. Repairs and upgrades fell behind under the logistics of shared ownership in an environment where building regulations required materials and dimensions beyond the means of cash-strapped individuals who preferred to invest in the education and pursuits of their kin. In addition, after plans were set for the clearance of Central Lagos, the LEDB banned new work that would increase property and thus compensation value, despite the actual implementation of the scheme taking over a decade from its start in the mid-1950s to its abandonment in the mid-1960s.

Due to the prevalence of renters (60–70 percent) and the outgrowth of extended families from their family property, Marris found that "the household had displaced the compound [lineage] as the predominant unit of residence." Most households were small and made up of myriad combinations of kin—both immediate and distant, by marriage and by blood—living far from their hometowns, reliant on each other in an unfamiliar city. For older Lagos families, despite not being grouped within the walls of a compound, individuals' and households' connections to a lineage remained important in terms of economic support and one's identity in the community. Dispersed throughout the neighborhood, lineages (as many as one hundred kinsfolk) began gathering in external outdoor spaces like streets, alleyways, and front stoops for meetings and social events—activities that had once been centered on a communal courtyard within a compound. Compensating for the lack of constant interface, extended families increasingly outlined and formalized mutual obligations through weekly or monthly conventions when they came together to maintain ties, adjudicate disputes, and to raise funds for property repairs, for younger relatives' education, and for needy relations. Migrants, meanwhile, were developing new organizations to serve similar functions as extended families, creating "mutual aid" societies based on hometown affiliations and religion.[66]

The economy of Central Lagos was built on these social and familial bonds. Trade was the profession of 87 percent of women (26 percent of men), and trust was the capital through which sales were made and stocks replenished. Access to cash for Nigerian traders and households was limited at independence, and personal relationships based on years of living and working alongside one another in Central Lagos created the fragile webs of credit among importers, middlemen, hawkers, and customers. Traders bought merchandise on credit and quickly dispersed into their web of connections, turning it over as quickly as possible in order to repay creditors. There was little accumulation of capital, because traders invested any profits in larger orders and in supporting one's household and lineage. Rent was actually lower than many other areas of the city, because tenants and landlords had known each other for years and established a rate that worked for both parties. Trust and accountability were a product of years of shared experiences in close proximity.[67]

The other critical element of Central Lagos was its spatial niche in the city, which residents exploited to make a living. Familial ties and social groups were enmeshed in a complicated but thriving community centered at the crossroads of Lagos Island, between Ikoyi and the mainland, between the sea and the lagoon. Location in addition to relationships was key to the economy of Central Lagos households, the majority of which made their rent and put food on the table by selling goods to the foot and automobile traffic passing through the neighborhood. It can be argued that at the time the seventy acres cleared by the LEDB was at the economic heart of Nigeria in terms of the distribution of imported goods that average Nigerians consumed. In reflecting on his study several years later, Marris wrote:

> At the outset, I was preoccupied with the disruption of family ties by slum clearance. . . . But in Lagos the economic disruption turned out to be an even stronger objection. Craftsmen and traders who worked for themselves lost their contacts when they moved to the rehousing estate, and they seemed

Lagoon 163

unable to establish new ones. A delicate informal network of personal relationships was pulled apart. In part, they lost their livelihood because they could not afford to commute between the suburbs and the centre, and their old customers could not afford the time or trouble to trace them to their new homes.[68]

The buildings of Central Lagos were in need of fresh paint and new roofs and infrastructure, but rents were manageable, and the location was ideal for the kinds of economic pursuits open to the majority of Lagosians who found themselves unqualified for government or corporate posts.

This was why demolition and displacement were so devastating to the households of Central Lagos. Those lucky enough to secure one of the four thousand units of rehousing in the new Surulere estate (which means "patience is rewarded") found that its location on the fringe of the city cut them off from their customers, and because commerce within the estate was banned, the commute to town added to their expenses. This distance frayed traders' networks of credit and also frayed lineages as kin were forced to spread out around the city to find new accommodations. Many elders lost the support upon which they depended. Although Surulere was intended to epitomize modern urban life, its residents ironically described it as the "bush" and bristled at the fact that rents were higher there than they had been in Central Lagos. The dislocation from family, other households, and trading opportunities weighed heavily on residents of the rehousing estate. Marris found that in this environment health problems were actually more common than they had been in the "insanitary" Central Lagos "slum." In addition to the anxiety and loneliness residents felt, mosquitoes proliferated in the lawns of the estate and many residents reported having malaria for the first time in their lives. Most families were never able to return to Central Lagos as they had been promised by the LEDB.[69]

The irony of the LEDB's embrace and expansion of modernist designs to large swaths of Lagos housing in the mid-1950s was that by that time European modernists were beginning to question their repudiation of local architectural idioms and were seeking to incorporate vernacular uses of space. The reasons behind this change of heart had largely to do with growing discontentment among residents of new model towns and flats (in both Europe and colonies) who saw architects as, in the words of sociologist Nathan Glazer, "arrogant, unresponsive to what ordinary

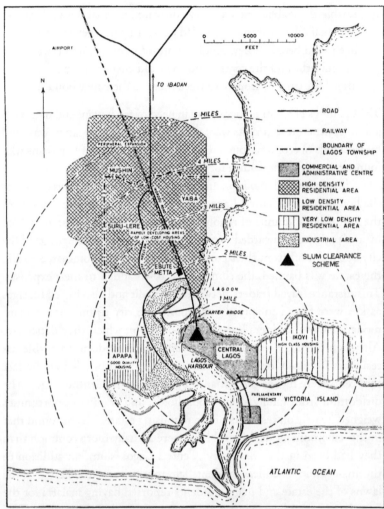

MAP 4.4. The enduring imprint of colonial density patterns. *Source:* C. Abrams, S. Kobe, O. Koenigsberge, M. Shapiro, and M. Wheeler, "Metropolitan Lagos [an edited selection of the Report Metropolitan Lagos (UN Department of Economic and Social Affairs, 1964)]" *Habitat International* 5 (1980): 59.

people wanted, indifferent to their interest." He continues, "[Modernism] had broken free from its origins and moorings, drifted away from the world of everyday life, which it had hoped to improve, into a world of its own."[70] By the late 1950s Fry and Drew had done a complete about-face and were labeling their own approach "anthropological" and were

Lagoon

openly turning to the African compounds they had once disparaged as "unsanitary" for inspiration in a Gold Coast housing scheme.[71] In West Africa, by 1960, Atkinson was finally getting around to intensively studying indigenous African homes, pointing to the value of a courtyard in tropical climates and working to incorporate them into colonial designs.[72] The Department of Tropical Studies cofounder Koenigsberger proclaimed that "social patterns in tropical countries differ widely from those in the West and unless the planner is aware of the differences he cannot hope to render useful service," going on to emphasize that this was particularly true in the "unit of the household."[73]

Yet the LEDB continued full-bore with its rubric of family-in-a-box-on-a-plot housing projects and slum clearance into the 1960s. Nigerian politicians and bureaucrats had inherited what Cooper calls the "gatekeeper" state, deciding, through their control over powerful institutions like the LEDB, who had access to land, housing, construction contracts, licenses, and other state-distributed privileges. The LEDB became the fiefdom of Kofo Abayomi, who exercised tremendous power in the city.[74] In her study of midcentury Lagos politics, Pauline Baker writes, "All plans had to receive [Abayomi's] personal approval; only he could authorize evictions or issue notices requiring individuals to forfeit property, only he could call meetings. Although not authorized to do so, he handpicked all chairmen of the LEDB's committees."[75] Opposition parties like the newly reborn NNDP (made up of disaffected AG members and some former NCNC members) strategized that "top officials of the [LEDB] Board should be bought over by the NNDP so that they can cooperate with the party in its aim to check the desire of the Ibos to own as much landed property in Lagos as possible. The NNDP should also use its influence with the Minister to make the Minister accept its nominee to replace any member who has completed his own term of office."[76]

This kind of pressure put LEDB bureaucrats under tremendous stress to accept kickbacks in exchange for construction contracts and for the distribution of plots of land. Many succumbed, as a later inquiry found.[77] These individuals found themselves at the gate between a nascent Nigerian state trying to prove its "modernity" and the realities of how people—including themselves—actually survived through community connections and family groups.

By the late 1950s, the driving factor behind the LEDB's schemes was no longer the creation of pods to mold a stable workforce but the merger of desires for personal economic gains and for the creation of a capital city with a "modern" aesthetic that would attract the praise and investment of international executives and diplomats. As it became obvious in the mid-1950s that independence was around the corner, Lagos officials described the city as "a humiliation to any person with a sense of national pride" and "a disgrace to the capital of Nigeria."[78] Clearing Central Lagos was intended to symbolize Nigeria's modernity to international visitors, its willingness to leave behind old ways in the dogged pursuit of progress even if that leap required displacing tens of thousands and tearing down some of the city's few architectural ties to the past. Determined to showcase Lagos's modernity to the world, the city invited Walter Gropius to design the Nigerian Houses of Parliament, although the project did not proceed beyond that.[79]

Another round of European "experts," which included Koenigsberger, eventually arrived, this time from the UN, and chastised the LEDB's scheme in a 1964 report. They found the audacity to write, "Government departments and local authorities have alienated land for specific projects without sufficient study of the consequences for the rest of the metropolis."[80] The report omitted any mention of British planners' role in designing the schemes. It flipped the script on slum clearance and argued that slums should be "aided in rehabilitation" rather than demolished, and went on to sing the praises of "the traditional Lagos courtyard house" as being high density—"convenient for families with many friends and relations of various degrees of dependency and are easy to protect against incursion by animals or human beings."[81] The knowledge–power dynamic of European technocratic "experts" over local voices continued across the threshold of independence. This change of heart and residents' continual opposition to the schemes finally drove clearance to a halt in the mid-1960s. Between 1967 and 1972 the Lagos Executive Development Board was replaced by the Lagos State Development and Property Corporation (LSDPC).

Other Western observers were more sanguine on the outcome of the LEDB's slum clearance. Donald W. Griffin, a UCLA professor, presented the scheme as a necessary part of "urbanization" and remarked that although the scheme had failed to provide sufficient housing for the

Lagoon

city, "benefits have resulted from the project and *the skyline of the area has been strikingly altered.* [Fig. 4.7] illustrates part of the office complex now found on Martin Street. Nearby, the Bristol Hotel and small-scale commercial developments have emerged. *Sections of Broad Street could pass for any metropolitan area in the United States.*"[82]

FIGURE 4.7. The "strikingly altered" skyline of Lagos, which "could pass for any metropolitan area in the United States." *Source:* Donald W. Griffin, "Urban Development in Africa: The Case of Lagos," *California Geographer* 8 (1967): 44.

For Griffin and many other producers of "modernization theory," skylines were definitive steps toward civilization. As Marris reflected in 1967, "The evolution of modern African civilization dramatizes our own ideological dilemmas."[83] By the 1960s, Central Lagos was occupied by wealthy investor and international corporations like British Petroleum, which engaged firms like Fry and Drew's to design concrete skyscrapers. For many, this was what progress looked like. For others, as Nigerian newspapers in the 1950s had warned, the LEDB had succeeded in turning Lagos into "a citadel for foreign commercial interests."[84] In 1968 the Lagos Survey Department published a map of the city highlighting first and foremost the location of corporations and businesses (map 4.1). It was a cartographic illustration of how Lagos had been "postcolonized" into what Nkrumah called a "neocolonial regime" that catered to the interests of its former colonizer. Anthropologist Brian Larkin likewise describes how "colonial urbanism provided public buildings and streets that created the skeleton of colonial and postcolonial urban life."[85] By diminishing the past in the technocratic chase for the "modern" future, late-colonial authorities had in reality dimmed prospects for a genuine Nigerian independence by neglecting local histories and knowledge. Their schemes ultimately produced new pains—in particular for those displaced from their homes—while failing to reckon with past injustices. It is ironic that this consequence would have been predictable to Yoruba Lagosians, many of whom lived, as Wole Soyinka writes, "a cyclic reality . . . which denies periodicity to the existences of the dead, the living and the unborn." They knew the past and the future as inseparable and alive in the present.[86]

History's *Place* in Decolonization

> Aiye li Okun, enia li Osaa, aki imo iwe ki ako aiye ja.
> The world is an ocean; mankind is the Lagoon Ossa. However well a person swims, he cannot cross the world (It is presumptuous for man to attempt to compass the whole world).
>
> —Samuel Crowther, *A Vocabulary of the Yoruba language*, 1852[87]

Some of the most provocative and consequential work in African studies over the past several decades has been historical revisions of decolonization. Engaging with the "historical turn" in the humanities, Africanists have revisited the colonial archive with a more skeptical eye, treating it as a "subject" of inquiry instead of simply as a "source" to be

Lagoon 169

plumbed.[88] Questions of where and how late-colonial archives were produced has led to the uncovering of silences, erasures, and falsifications. As Caroline Elkins writes after years of fighting to find Mau Mau records in British archives, "We now know with some certainty the scale of archival erasure on the eve of decolonization in Kenya, and we can reasonably assume a similar scale of erasure throughout the empire at the time of British colonial retreat."[89] Revelations of colonial violence and abuses have emerged through locating and creating new kinds of oral and pictorial archives, although the built environment has not yet been documented in the same fashion.[90] Within the field, these revisionist histories have changed our understanding of the colonial state, decolonization processes, and postcolonial conditions. Moreover, they have altered theories of political power and have led to litigation and other forms of claims-making for reparations and acknowledgments of colonial atrocities.

Going forward, Elkins suggests, "we must consider interrogating the ways in which the production of the British colonial archive reflected the nature of the colonial state itself."[91] How did records come to be destroyed, misplaced, and hidden as Britain decamped in the late 1950s? Here, the creeds that Fry, Drew, and other Tropical Modernists brought to the colonies in the early 1940s during colonialism's "turn to technocrats" offers insight into the path toward archival destruction at decolonization. As this chapter has argued, Tropical Modernists' work devalued critical history, especially local histories, in favor of techno-universal building and clearance schemes based on claims of empirical rationality. Their programs flattened local landscapes and, in doing so, destroyed remnants of past colonial abuses like the conditions in Central Lagos that decades of segregation and neglect had contributed to. It is not surprising, then, that an era that ideologically devalued history led to an era that actively erased history. Modernists' grail of timeless ("anti-ideological") universal principles helped create a culture and permission structure that eventually enabled more concerted efforts by archivists and administrators to actively cleanse the past into a narrow and sanitized version of history. Guilt and culpability were motivating factors, but late-colonial archivists also felt empowered as technocrats to monopolize claims to the past and to how it should be preserved and stored. Like modernists' plans to sanitize cities to make way for the future, archivists sanitized the past for the future of Britain. This was the last-gasp of the centuries-old imperial fantasy of conquering all of the world and mastering all knowledge.[92]

Beyond modernists' influence, even deeper epistemological foundations existed in colonialism's history of elevating visual images to truth. Facades were acceptable, for they were empirical in their visuality.[93] The stunning size, endless rows of documents, and complicated labeling systems at the British National Archives at Kew are a symbol of historiographic authority and bureaucratic integrity. Only recently has it been revealed that the British Archives for decades hid (secretly "migrated") thousands of documents from thirty-seven former colonies (including Nigeria) through a program called "Operation Legacy."[94] Scholars suggest that British agents first drew up this scheme in the Gold Coast in 1956 before "institutionalizing" it in London and sending directives to other colonies preparing to hand over power.[95] Even more documents were destroyed as part of Operation Legacy as British administrators and archivists took it upon themselves to burn records "to save Britain's honour and to protect its collaborators."[96] We do not know what records were destroyed from Nigeria and do not know what accepted narratives they might have overturned, allowing unknown gaps to creep in—like how we might still think of Central Lagos as a desultory slum deserving demolition without the work of Marris and others to recover the voices and stories of households before it was razed. Still-standing historic homes and historical maps and photographs of houses and of the built environment can continue to shed light on some of what has been left out of the colonial archive and out of the narrative established by those committed to a particular myopic ideology of progress and order.

There are depths to the epistemologies beneath how the colonial state decolonized through a process of digging up the heart of cities like Lagos. Treating and documenting the built environment of colonial landscapes as an archive may help continue to uncover these connections and the ways of seeing, thinking, and ruling embedded in colonial practices of governing. In his work on what he calls "imperialism modernism," Mark Crinson describes how part of the British response to the Mau Mau "emergency" was the villagization of pastoralist rebels. This strategy mobilized modernization theory's view of people progressing along a "civilizing timeline" from nomads to villages to industrial cities.

Crinson writes that villagization "in response to revolt in Kenya and Malaya was infused with the sense that it was in ordinary rural buildings that crises could be dealt with . . . could reform the land and do away with violent opposition. The new villages, as their name conceals, were actually a brutal intervention into the domestic and the locally particular, and an enforcement of new patterns of settlement." Crinson quotes a British observer "writing on 'Kenya landscape' in 1960": "It has become common knowledge that whilst we in Europe over the past few centuries have become preoccupied to a large extent with the technical aspects of architecture, the natives of tropical Africa have been content with either their wattle and mud huts or their caves or tents."[97] There is a connection deserving continued exploration between this way of seeing and the process of creating an archive that found it acceptable to expunge atrocities against resistant Mau Mau.

We must continue to probe the fact that slum clearance and villagization schemes were both architectures, like later colonial archives, that deemed African perspectives and certain aspects of the past irrelevant, and thus omittable. Like archives' ongoing relevance in postcolonial politics, the housing schemes of decolonization have continued to structure and influence ways of thinking, living, and governing in postcolonial spaces—the past and the future continue to be inseparable and alive in the present.

5

Atlantic

Gatekeepers of Wealth and Power: The Oil Years

The Kodachrome cover of the 1975 *Guide to Lagos* sets the city and its harbor against the lustrous horizon of the Atlantic Ocean (fig. 5.1). This is unusual; tourist guides tend to portray coastal cities from the perspective of the water, the skyline rising at the ocean's edge, a dramatic announcement of land as a sea-weary traveler would first encounter it. Produced by the government, the Lagos guidebook's counterintuitive photograph appears a purposeful reversal of this formula. It reflected the outward orientation of Nigeria's capital, awash by the mid-1970s in oil money and highlife music, as it looked forth onto the world with boundless aspirations and welcomed it all in. The cover, like the rest of the book, represented Lagos not as a solitary cluster of buildings on the African shore but as a worldly place of old and new wonders, as open as the Atlantic. Lagos had long been part of the "Atlantic World," exchanging cultures and commodities with those circulating in its waters, but with its newfound prosperity in the 1970s, the city became accessible and exciting like never before. Filling its hotels and restaurants listed in the guide were foreign leaders, Afrobeat enthusiasts, Ghanaians on visas from the newly formed Economic Community of West African

Atlantic

FIGURE 5.1. "Old" and "new" Lagos (bottom to top) looking out at the Atlantic. *Source:* E. Seriki and E. Pullybank, *Visitors Guide to Lagos* (Lagos: published by West African Book Publishers; Lagos: printed by Academy Press, 1975), front and back cover.

States, and celebrities like Paul McCartney and Arthur Ashe. Available to many for the first time were imported consumer goods like those sold in the department stores the guide advertised. Receiving these imports and people, the port and airport were packed, and automobiles idled everywhere in go-slows. As the guide boasted, "[Lagos's] growth in recent years, both economical [*sic*] and social, has surpassed all expectations."[1]

All the while, behind the festivities and the cover's frame, Lagos tentacled into mainland areas like Mushin and Shomulu where problems of housing maldistribution, shortage, and disparity deepened as fast as the price of petroleum skyrocketed. This chapter covers the late 1960s through the crash of the oil boom and the end of Lagos's status as the federal capital. By the 1970s, Nigeria's postcolonial state had proven itself willing to reproduce colonial patterns of vampire capitalism, leeching commodity profits and determining in whose deep pockets these fruits and the favors they made possible ended up.

Political scientist Richard Joseph described Nigerian politics of the era as a form of "prebendalism," a term customarily associated with feudal states, but which in the Nigerian context meant politically empowered persons (patrons) exchanging income-generating "offices" (property, titles, jobs, and contracts) to supplicants (clients) who in return aggregated and delivered votes or other forms of political support from their followers to whom they passed on pieces of state resources. Joseph showed how these relationships were increasingly structured along regional ethnic lines as people sought security through shared bonds within a nation-state with weak legal guarantees.

The first section of this chapter "spatializes" Joseph's theory of how the Nigerian petro-state functioned in the capital city by reading it in tandem with the neighborhood-level ethnography of Sandra Barnes and other local sources.[2] In Lagos, where federal power was centralized in the 1970s, houses served as a critical spatial link in the state's operation of patron-client networks, acting as an axis mundi between the abstract and outward-facing world of the Supreme Military Council and the everyday ethnic, familial, and religious relationships that structured and sustained communities. Houses were part of the glue connecting what the guidebook misleadingly frames as "old" and "new" Lagos (a false geotemporal dichotomy it asserts on the cover: rusty roofs overshadowed by skyscrapers). Housing illustrates the ways these two sides of the city were anything but static or self-contained realms, as the state was in "old" residential areas through land registrations and political representatives, and ethnofamilial affiliations were in the "new" state offices in the form of prebendal favors and backing.

To acquire a house was to acquire a hinge in the gate of goodies and political support in the boundary crossing patron-client relationships at the heart of Nigerian politics. By the nature of how housing was organized and distributed in 1970s Nigeria, owning a house meant one had both patrons and tenants or dependents. The hinge that housing offered was a step in joining—to return to the terminology of chapter 1—the "dominant class" of the city and country. But, because of its value in these relationships, housing stock, like anything profitable in a gatekeeper state, was itself a commodity controlled by the state, making

Atlantic

it increasingly harder for those outside the ruling class's inner circle to own securely. Additionally, like oil, real estate became a fetishized commodity, its value no longer pragmatically attached to use or even exchange value, but to purely representational value, resulting in garish palaces of the nouveau riche. As Lagos rode the musical notes of high-life to new heights as the largest city in sub-Saharan Africa, its leaders constricted housing opportunities, widening disparity into an epidemic, especially after state patronage dried up in the structural adjustment programs of the 1980s.

After years of civil war ended in the 1970s, Nigerians were ready for an extroverted outlook again. Once oil started flowing, everyone wanted a drop, but Yakubu Gowon's victorious military regime was in the best position. As shown on the cover of the tourist guide, parastatal towers stood between the city and the sea, a symbol of the state's power over who came and went, who ended up with import and export rights, and who had a place to stay in the federal capital.

God, King, and Country: Oil, Real Estate, and Power in 1970s Lagos

Oil uncorked an ocean of wealth with all its opportunities for opulence and treachery under military (1966–79) and quasi-democratic (The Second Republic, 1979–83) rule. In his book on Nigeria's staging of FESTAC '77 celebrations—arguably the pinnacle of Nigeria's petro-fueled bonanza—Andrew Apter captures the heady days of the oil miracle that brought prosperity to state-connected actors but also suspicion and anxiety to those unsure where the wealth was coming from and how to keep the oil flowing.[3] The catalyst was the worldwide peak in oil production in the late 1960s, followed by the 1973 OPEC embargo that limited the oil supply and set prices on a ten-year surge, at its height bringing Nigeria, as the *New York Times* wrote at the time, "eighty million dollars' worth of wealth every 24 hours, $55,555 a minute."[4] Petroleum fees accounted for more than 80 percent of government revenues.[5]

According to Apter, this unexpected growth quickly created a "vampire" economy lacking the utilization or long-term cultivation of domestic production and labor.[6] It became a system in which capital was controlled by the state's collection of licensing fees but distributed through private patronage networks via a ballooning and leaking bureaucracy. By 1980 Nigeria's public expenditure was 1.5 times the country's entire 1964 GDP.[7] Petroleum became the nation's lifeblood, fetishized and feared for its mystical powers, pumping through the body politic in what economists describe as a "circulation economy," in which petro-cash (dollars and naira) skimmed from the privatization of national resources flowed from the highest office holders all the way to street hawkers, the product of prebendalism.[8]

Joseph's evocation of the antiquated term conveys how, as the fountainhead of oil wealth, the Nigerian polity became "a magnet for all facets of political and economic life, consuming the attention of traders, contractors, builders, farmers, traditional rulers, teachers, as much as that of politicians," all of whom struggled "to control and exploit the *offices* of the state" for personal benefit.[9] The primary avenue through which individuals gained access to state resources was through the cultivation of patron-client relationships, which Joseph calls the "sustaining framework for prebendal politics."[10]

In this environment, the Nigerian state attempted to conjure spectacular displays of culture and development, straddling an image of itself as a modern state capable of global diplomacy and deals with international oil companies through the construction of stadiums, airports, highways, and hotels, and as a bastion of Black culture through patronage for the arts that supported a sanitized "African" culture and destiny. Apter writes that this show of culture "made ideological sense, masking divisive ethnic cleavages and the absence of indigenous production through the production of Indigenous Culture."[11] During FESTAC, the state became the unifier and conjurer of the productive energies it portrayed as embedded in Nigeria's pan-African precolonial culture. Describing the elaborate and expensive regattas and durbars and the state's sale of souvenirs of African art reproductions, Apter illustrates how FESTAC presented indigenous African cultures as the bedrock of Nigeria from which its otherwise mystifying prosperity had sprung.

The exhibition of cutting-edge and ostensibly traditional cultural landscapes is seen in the 1975 guidebook produced in preparation for Lagos's hosting of FESTAC. Its introduction describes a city where "the old and new mingle together: Large commercial complexes next to small trading stands; mini skirts and traditional robes."[12] This proximity and "the sights, sounds, and smells" gave "evidence of the vibrance of the city," according to the guide. The book's central section, laying out walking

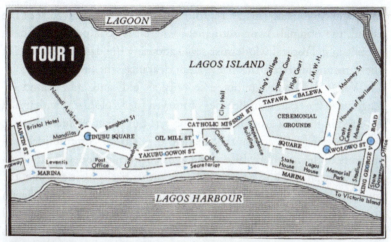

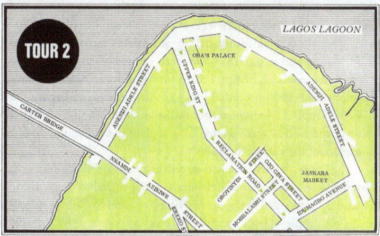

MAPS 5.1 AND 5.2. Curating a dual image of Lagos: walking tours of "modern/new" Lagos (tour 1) and "old" Lagos (tour 2). *Source:* E. Seriki and E. Pullybank, *Visitors Guide to Lagos* (Lagos: West African Book Publishers, printed by Academy Press, 1975), 51 and 66.

tours of the city, helped curate a spatial experience of a cityscape spanning "Modern Lagos" (tour 1) and "Old Lagos" (tour 2) to its readers in Lagos and elsewhere.[13] The map for tour 1 shows the southern part of the island along the harbor with stops at Kingsway (department) Stores, City Stadium, Lagos State Governor's Office, Lagos State High Court, the Federal Supreme Court, Bristol Hotel, and the Federal Ministry of

Works and Housing (map 5.1). Tour 2 covers the northern lobe of the island, the original Awori settlement where the ọba's palace had been rebuilt in a Tropical Modernist style, adopting the design aesthetic of the surrounding reclamation and slum clearance schemes (map 5.2).

What the book attempted to reify as "old" and "new"/"modern" Lagos was the residue of decades of uneven (neo)colonial rule that had invested in the area around the marina, the European business district, while severing and attempting to raze the African communities and markets to the north. By bisecting Lagos between a modern and developing African city and an original and "authentically" African one, the guidebook, like FESTAC, perpetuated an image of Lagos and Nigeria that, as Apter writes, "indigeniz[ed], and thus nationaliz[ed], colonial culture" by treating what was very much a product of colonial rule as the untouched "old" hearth of the city, "thereby absorbing the 'imprint' of colonialism under the sign of its erasure."[14] The guidebook took the visual legacy of a colonial bifurcated city and made it into a representation of the nation and its capital—a modern outward-facing eagle (i.e., on Nigeria's national coat of arms) rising from its African nest with the end of colonialism. The primordial image of African areas of Lagos echoed those of Tropical Modernists, but in the guidebook and FESTAC the value of these areas was inverted from a place to be demolished to the birthplace of the nation's prosperity.

The cover's spatial distinction did not reflect the complementary, competing, entwined, and ambiguous sociopolitical systems through which Lagos operated in the 1970s. Nigeria's capital had all the trappings of the official "new" legal-rational state and corporate sector (which, as under colonialism, was a parastatal industry intimately tied to the state),[15] but much of the heavy lifting was done by "old" community networks not often recognized by the state except in sanitized "traditional" African forms like FESTAC. On one side were strong Yorùbá-Èkó obligations, values, relationships, and political structures, which had been sustained, reworked, and strengthened in the absence of colonial and early postcolonial state welfare programs; on the other were government regulations, representatives, roads, and other physical and legal infrastructure.

In an area like Mushin on the mainland, where Barnes conducted an intensive ethnography of political power in the 1970s, there was a complex network of local councillors, committee members, and several tiers of

Atlantic

chiefs all jostling to make decisions, allocate resources, and adjudicate disputes through formal and informal mediations. Each of Lagos State's four districts (of which Mushin was one) operated at the local government level through similar combinations of customary and municipal offices. Above district offices, regional politics played out at the state level following the 1967 military coup that restructured Nigeria into a federation of twelve states. Local governments received funds from state governments, which themselves received funds from the national government based on each state's population.[16] Between 1967 and 1979 the federal government consisted of a Supreme Military Council and federal agencies.

Complicating this three-tiered vertical system and the local arrangements between the chiefs and councillors was a series of coups, tensions between Lagos State (based in Ikeja after 1976) and the federal government (based in Lagos until 1991), as well as the ongoing confusion over interpretations of customary and British legal principles, the legitimacy of certain chieftaincy titles, and the gap between formal (permitted or meeting code) and informal (doctrinally illegal) economic ventures and settlements. What connected and incorporated old into new, modern and traditional, formal and informal, and other binary sides of Lagos was the land—whose widespread value is apparent in the density of the old parts of town and the height of the new.

While oil was a gift from heaven, real estate remained king in metropolitan Lagos. Houses were an *axis mundus*—a liminal space between the mundane and mystical, between daily life and the world of oil wealth, stitching the tiers of Nigeria's government and the patron-client networks that flowed across them. Homeowners were intermediaries in these relationships, able to serve as power brokers by funneling resources and political support through their residences by way of the socioeconomic standing and community connections that accompanied a piece of residential real estate. Barnes called this the "residential basis of leadership" in Lagos and described the accumulation of power in terms of initially "acquiring real estate" followed by "adding political content to the interactions that grew out of landlord-tenant relationships."[17] These relationships grew into patron-client bonds that Joseph argued were the "very channel through which one joins the [Nigerian] dominant class."[18] As had been the case since the end of the nineteenth century, when Lagos first became congested, land and housing were at the base of power and prosperity for those outside of the military government who made it in the city. What was novel about the situation into the 1970s was the ways in which the postcolonial state grafted local community leaders—whose power was based in their residences—into state distribution networks that ran through patrons and clients.

Since land first became scarce in Lagos in the nineteenth century, housing in the city had been key to becoming a patron and was at the center of relationships between patrons and their dependents. In the 1970s, as had traditionally been the case, land and a house allowed its owner to establish an *idile*, a house and household—a place to establish a lineage group and to display the largesse and self-reliance idealized in Yoruba-Awori and much of Nigerian national culture.[19] In the language of Barnes, a house became an "umbrella" under which the owner could grow his or her immediate family to sizes impossible in small and often shared rented rooms. It is also where one could shelter relatives, renters, family friends, orphans, and migrants from one's hometown (fig. 5.2).

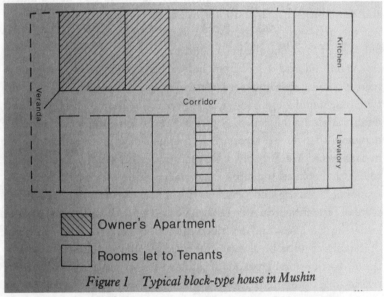

FIGURE 5.2. A house designed to host as many people as possible. *Source:* Sandra T. Barnes, *Patrons and Power: Creating a Political Community in Metropolitan Lagos* (Manchester: Manchester University Press, 1986), 59.

Atlantic

In his 1979 study of the Agege area of Lagos's mainland, Adrian Peace called homeowners "urban gatekeepers," observing how "entrepreneur-landlords act[ed] as hosts to young migrants from their home towns in search of wage-employment in Lagos."[20] Opening one's doors to others with generosity and hospitality opened one's own avenues in the community. Barnes found that homeowners were more likely than renters to be involved and elevated to positions of authority in civic organizations and social associations; 60 percent of owners but only 10 percent of renters belonged to two or more civic groups.[21]

A network of dependents also provided an array of benefits to landlords, not least of which was an abundance of eyes and ears in the community where information on trading opportunities, people's character, and government development schemes was crucial to acquiring profitable goods like land.[22] Becoming a landowner, homebuilder, and ultimately landlord generated rental revenue and commanded respect. Savvy landlords could quit their wage labor jobs to remain at home and live on their rents; this gave them the time to invest in social pursuits, expand their business ventures, and manage their dependents. These people, according to Barnes, were known as *ominira*, "one who has freedom."[23]

After an economic windfall from business pursuits, Nigerians in the 1970s usually invested their profits in conspicuous displays of wealth, like cars, clothes, and ceremonies, but quickly turned to longer-term investments in land and housing.[24] Real estate was the most sought-after long-term resource in Lagos. The freehold purchase of property was a tried-and-true strategy, a conspicuous display of one's stake and standing in the community. Barnes describes how residents viewed property as a foothold—in the words of one landowner, "a security in life"—in an ocean of rampant insecurity and scarcity in employment, housing, sanitation, and nutrition.[25] To own a home was to be somebody, while "where a man rents he considers himself small," in the words of Barnes's informant.[26]

Local clients received benefits from their relationship with a house-owning patron. Housing itself was one of these benefits, and the first patron whom many migrants to Lagos found was a relative or former resident of their hometown who offered shelter and protection in the city.[27] These relationships often grew into what a 1972 newspaper called "a protective jacket." The paper declared that "life without godfathers and long legs [influential patrons] can be and is usually terrible."[28]

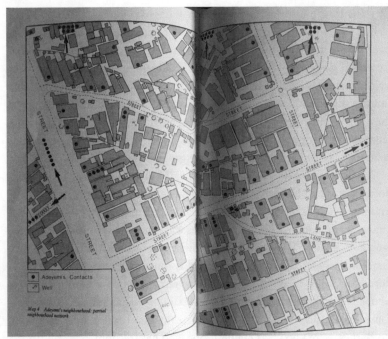

MAP 5.3. A patron's neighborhood network of clients in the 1970s. *Source:* Sandra T. Barnes, *Patrons and Power: Creating a Political Community in Metropolitan Lagos* (Manchester: Manchester University Press, 1986), 80–81.

One of Barnes's primary informants was a man named I. A. Adeyemi, who had built a network of clients over twenty years "primarily on the basis of residential familiarity." A map of his clients shows the density of Mushin and his network within it (map 5.3). His clients came to him for favors and to solve problems, such as settling disputes, navigating legal matters, and extending credit in tough times.[29]

As had long been the case in Lagos, property owners had sway in local politics. This influence went back centuries to when ìdéjọ were recognized as an Awori chieftaincy class vis-à-vis their control over fishing and land-use rights. This tradition had continued throughout colonialism as the state empowered landowners to manage African areas of the city. In the 1970s, Barnes found that landownership was a de facto requirement for anyone aspiring to become a chief or town councillor in Mushin. A permanent residence was an assurance of a leader's continued place and investment in the community, and community members

Atlantic

had a tacit understanding that chieftaincy titles should be held by landowners.[30] Likewise, houseowners were empowered to choose chiefs and councillors: the eldest members of an idile (household) were allowed to participate in selecting new chiefs, while members of landowners' associations united behind preferred candidates for councillor seats. Barnes describes how in this process, households were "in a fundamental sense, permanent representational units with 'constituencies,'" their head member representing the idile, family, and tenants.[31] Connection to local politics gave houseowners access to those with the power to hand out contracts, appoint committee members, settle legal disputes, and enact planning decisions.

Nigeria's Supreme Military Council replicated the two sides of the colonial state in Lagos: a ruling "state class," as Apter calls the military elites who lived in the former colonial reserves of Ikoyi and Apapa and in the new federal enclaves of Dodan Barracks and Ikeja; and the rest of the city's four local districts circumvented by federal highways and most of the state's modernist infrastructure projects. This reproduction of a bifurcated state occurred after a twenty-year interlude in which political parties like Obafemi Awolowo's Action Group, which controlled the Western Region of Nigeria during the 1960s, had built grassroots power through local landowner associations and chiefs' meetings. Through these contacts, Action Group representatives invited powerful local leaders to meetings, thereby cultivating party leaders who were tapped into large community networks.[32] The Action Group rewarded successful and loyal local leaders with resources and appointments to regional positions. When Gowon's military regime came to power in 1967, it initially imposed authority figures on the district level, issuing top-down directives. Yet its attention was directed first to the Nigerian Civil War and then to oil deals, leaving local districts to their own devices. During the late 1960s and early 1970s, Mushin had annual federal funding of $1.20 per resident, and Lagos newspapers complained that local governments were "starved" for qualified personnel.[33]

As oil wealth began to saturate the inner circle of the military government, factionalism developed along ethnic and regional lines as prominent members of the military regime fought over lucrative contracts and kickbacks. A strong client base became imperative for any "big man" who hoped to acquire and sustain government prebends. By

1975, patron-client networks distributing state resources in return for political support had reached the district level and the rich community networks already operating there. As the number of local government areas continually increased, creating new posts to be filled, federal officials made inroads in gaining district-level supporters by appointing local committee members with large client networks and by approving chieftaincy titles for loyal local chiefs who were able to muster large groups of followers in support of their case for official recognition. Chieftaincy titles became the most valuable political resource in Mushin, since titles were permanent and not subject to political winds. Loyal chiefs and committee members were rewarded with contracts, legal protection, and state-level appointments. These local patron-client networks continued to flow through housing but were attached increasingly to the state.

This grafting of the local onto the state occurred as the state was producing an image of modern Nigeria's prosperity emerging from traditional local cultures in the preparations for FESTAC. While this production of indigenous culture masked underlying divisions and a lack of domestic production, it also demonstrated that it was through the accumulation of support of traditional chiefs and community leaders that individuals actually shared in the mysterious oil wealth. In Lagos at least, power and access to oil wealth depended on housing—a base of clients built through ownership of residences—and as this became clear, real estate began to take on the fetishized and occult properties of oil. Acquiring and maintaining real estate became convoluted, as much about image as its use-value in collecting clients and rents, and as property became more sought after, it, like oil, became subsumed by the state.

Distribution: The Dynamics of a Cryptic and Increasingly Exclusive Housing Market

The population of Lagos doubled between 1965 and 1975 and then again between 1975 and 1985, growing from a city of less than one million people in 1965 to one approaching five million by 1985.[34] It took Lagos twenty years to grow by the same demographic parameters that it had taken London the entire nineteenth century. It took New York nearly the entire twentieth century to add a similar net number of people. In part, the explosive growth of Lagos was driven by policies that funneled

Atlantic

the country's economic prosperity into urban centers at the expense of its rural areas. Nigeria moved from a net exporter to a net importer of food as the central government implemented controls to stabilize the cost of food for urban residents.[35] Farmers were soon unable to compete on international markets because of the lack of revenue caused by the price controls. The bright lights of the city and stories of prosperity lured restless youth and struggling farmers into cities like Lagos where landed men were always looking to take more people under their umbrella even if the spaces they rented were already at capacity. By the late 1960s, federal officials noted that the "class of people faced with the most excruciating housing problem is the low-income group and this sector of the community."[36] Between 1960 and 1980 the shortfall in housing stock swelled from 100,000 units to 700,000.[37]

This section examines the allocation of the limited stock and explores how securely owned housing came to be clustered in the hands of a small, well-off, and well-connected elite. As housing became even scarcer, state-connected actors wielded their influence to undermine any interventions or attempts to use state mechanisms to increase the availability or improve access to housing. Instead the city's elite sought to redirect those programs to their own benefit.

The historical and political importance of housing coupled with explosive economic and demographic growth meant that demand and the value of housing were growing rapidly by the end of the Nigerian Civil War (1970). Between 1959 and 1978 the value of land in metropolitan Lagos rose 620 percent.[38] Plots were often sublet several times over as tenants sought to cash in on rising land values, adding another layer of confusion to Lagos's history of poorly documented ownership claims.[39] In this environment, the distribution of housing stock was governed by neither well-defined rules nor broader normative principles. Instead, and unsurprisingly given its position at the crossroads of state institutions and informal community traditions, the land used to build houses had to be acquired through a complicated and risky market involving official (statutory) and unofficial (customary) channels. Buying a plot and building a house required prolonged and repeated negotiations with numerous parties at each stage. Finding land that was legitimately for sale by the owner if it was held freehold, or by all the co-owners if it was family property, required working a large network of contacts to find trustworthy sellers and to confirm the number of people with a familial claim to the land. This was a monumental logistical challenge. Documents could have been lost, forged, or duplicated over the years as family property was sold off to individuals and then willed back into family property upon the death of the buyer, a common but bureaucratically convoluted cycle not always properly recorded. Even once money changed hands, seemingly straightforward transactions were frequently complicated by relatives coming out of the woodwork to claim they had not been consulted. This could result in the nullification of the purchase, the loss of any payments already made, time-consuming and expensive litigation, or further payments to be doled out in order to settle. Obtaining a bulletproof title only made ownership official in the courtroom and with the state records office.

In the older districts in the city, local ọmọ onilẹ ("children of the land holders" or "sons of the soil" chiefs, like ìdéjọ, who claimed ultimate rights to the land)[40] still demanded annual payment or a tribute, leveraging their power and position in the community, which had been legitimated by the Tew Legislation decades early. Buyers not in good standing with local landed chiefs could expect harassment during the construction phase and beyond. Those able to pull off each step and to defend the legality of their purchase of land tended to already own property or come from a family network of property owners. Once the hurdles of acquiring a plot of land and building a first house were surmounted by borrowing money through a combination of friends, family, or local moneylenders and credit associations, access to institutional forms of credit became possible for the purchase of additional properties by pledging the first as collateral.[41] Likewise, once one managed to cobble together the funds needed to build a house on a plot one had acquired, courts were more likely to recognize the legitimacy of the claim to the land.[42] Acquiring land and building the first house was the key, door, and welcome mat to additional real estate ownership. Inflation and the ever-widening expansion of the city also increased the speculative rewards of owning a piece of Lagos. A 1986 Shell Oil map of Lagos (available in the Harvard Map Library) illustrates the spatial growth of the city, a rippling out since the 1960s that could quickly turn a fringe plot of land into a desirable spot once Lagos rose to envelop it, as happened to early investors in Mushin.

Atlantic 187

Turning to legally dubious schemes to drink from the oil-wealth spigot was commonplace in the 1970s, and this ethos of getting a piece for oneself and not meddling with others doing the same extended deep into the real estate market in Lagos. Individuals from a lineage (or even outsiders posing as owners) would sell or mortgage property with forged freehold titles only to then have accomplices invalidate the sale based on the family property legal requirement of full approval of all members of a lineage for a sale to proceed. The sellers would then disappear with the cash. These schemes and others famously became known as "419s" after the section on fraud in the Nigerian criminal code. Fraud was blatant, at times violent, but more often rigged around complicated and ingenious cons. At times it was petty and carried out by brazen criminals but more often was conducted in concert with powerful officials and families preying on poor would-be buyers.[43] Aspiring homeowners were willing to assume a significant risk because of the immense rewards of owning a home.

The Nigerian federal and Lagos State governments did try to intervene sporadically throughout the oil years with lavish plans for low-income estates that would provide thousands of units annually to reduce the pressure for accommodations and give wage workers a chance to settle in Lagos without falling prey to abusive landlords or fraud. Unfortunately, many of these schemes sputtered as funds disappeared and those that were built more often ended up in the hands of political cronies.

In 1972 the LEDB along with the Epe and Ikeja planning bodies "metamorphosed" in its words into the LSDPC.[44] This Corporation was responsible for acquiring, developing, and managing housing estates in Lagos while the planning and development of the city became the responsibility of the Lagos State Ministry of Works and Planning. The ability to design and plan housing estates rather than just the houses on them did not fall within the purview of the LSDPC until 1978, handcuffing a more integrated approach to housing solutions. Indeed, bureaucratic disorder and hurdles became a common complaint against the LSDPC and other development organs beginning in the late 1960s. For all the critiques of Fry and Drew's form of high modernism, they had brought an emphasis on organization and specified roles to their undertakings. A 1970 letter from their firm (Fry, Drew, Akinson) to the Military Governor's Office deplores, in a careful hypothetical conditional tense, the lack of organization for developing Lagos:

> There would appear from their [NEDE Co.] investigations that there are a number of departments both Federal and Lagos State working on parts of Lagos planning.
>
> It would seem very necessary to have some kind of co-ordination which with the correct backing could solve so many problems like that of the proposed ringroad, water accesses, allocation of space for low cost housing, open spaces etc etc. This planning could be incorporated into a master plan with Government authority and become the document from which each area is individually developed.[45]

Five years later the same diagnosis was still being made for "the need to co-ordinate more closely the efforts of all the agencies concerned [with housing], public or private. This calls anew for the preparation of a master plan as a framework for bringing together and getting maximum contribution from the different agencies."[46]

A year after the LSDPC was created, the military government established the Federal Housing Authority and headquartered it in FESTAC Town (a satellite of Lagos built as a model settlement to host visitors for the 1977 festival), complicating a streamlined approach to the city's residential space problem.[47] After largely ignoring housing in the First National Development Plan (1962–68), the Second (1970) and Third (1975) National Development Plans gave serious attention to the development of thousands of low-cost units in Lagos.[48] However, rivalries led Lagos State to refuse to cede anything but remote land to the federal government for housing developments—land outside of the metropolitan area in places like Ipaja and what became FESTAC Town (twenty kilometers from Lagos Island), unappealing places far removed and disconnected from the city. Like so many other federal projects during the oil years, the grand schemes boasted about on paper and in the press became white elephants bogged down by regime change and contractor delays and kickbacks. Out of the 101,000 units planned in the Second National Development plan, only 19,000 were ever built.[49]

Meanwhile, the LSDPC was responsible for developing the inner-city housing projects where people actually wanted to live. During the

Third National Development Plan, the federal government granted the LSDPC 10 million naira to develop one thousand low-income housing units, but the majority of projects (157.7 million nairas worth) were left to the state to fund through "prepayment of ground rent, bank loans and internal resources."[50] These projects included Dolphin Estate, the development of housing estates for Victoria Island, South Surulere, Oshodi, Omole, Gbagada, Ogba, and Odofin.[51] Again, many of these units never came to fruition. Only 10 to 13 percent of the planned units for the Lagos metropolitan area were finished.[52] Those that were built catered to middle- and upper-class residents ("High Class Residential Flats" were budgeted for)[53] or were distributed to wealthy individuals through their government connections, despite the stated objective to "create conditions under which all home building programmes, whether public or private, will particularly serve the needs of low income groups."[54] Lotteries for plots in low- and middle-income housing estates were rigged to go to wealthier, well-connected buyers. Other middle-income developments became prohibitively expensive to the intended occupants when construction costs and inflation pushed purchase prices to 140,000 naira at a time when the average yearly income of Lagosians was 20,000 naira.[55]

A 1974 letter from Surulere Rehousing Estate's Residents' Association protesting the LSDPC reneging on LEDB promises that residents would be able to purchase their homes and general lack of LSDPC upkeep of Surulere revealed that the swampland in southwest Ikoyi promised to many people displaced from Central Lagos "was reclaimed quite alright, but contrary to the promise from high places persons displaced from Central Lagos were not given land there. Nearly all the 900 residential plots reclaimed in that area were shared among people in high places not affected by the Scheme."[56] This was all too familiar an experience for low-income Lagosians displaced from their homes or hoping to find a home in a government estate.

The LSDPC was operated similarly to how the British administration had used the LEDB to acquire valuable land for "public use" only to utilize it for projects conducive to government power and profits. The only difference was that these land grabs benefited connected landlords rather than British export schemes. Land and housing rights were only as secure as one's connections. Residents in Surulere knew this only too well. In a subsection titled "Our bitter experience as rent payers," the Residents' Association complained that

> one needs to witness one eviction in process to appreciate the crudeness of the method employed . . . the practice whereby doors were forced open during the night and tenants forcibly evicted and sometimes manhandled and personal belongings damaged in the process. The eviction time then was between 2 and 4 a.m. when everybody was in bed.

They feared that they would be evicted after eighteen years of paying rent so that the LSDPC could replace their homes with multistory blocks of flats that they would be unable to afford. They protested that

> as responsible citizens of Lagos State we fully appreciate the problems confronting our Government with regard to land shortage in the state. We realize the explosive nature of the situation. But we are also conscious of the fact that there is a limit to which we can conveniently stretch ourselves in order to accommodate all comers.

Another example of arbitrary evictions by the government reveals the widespread uncertainty and anxiety over property rights under military rule. In a 1977 *Sunday Times* feature titled "What Are Your Property Rights within the Law?" the harrowing, but not unusual, story of a military convoy showing up and kicking a middle-aged woman out of her house is recounted, and a lawyer weighed in as to whether she has any legal recourse:

> [Alhaja Ayinke Aberuagba's] house which she had built with all the sweat of her brow was forcibly taken over from her without previous notice and with indignity by armed soldiers who were apparently acting on orders from the executive branch of government. . . . It is perhaps of interest to mention that Wing Commander Osho who requisitioned the house now lives there with his family.[57]

The author offers a deep analysis of British common law precedents, the Nigerian Constitution, and various legislative decrees, including the 1967 Requisition and Other Powers Decree, which provided the executive with a nearly unlimited right of compulsory appropriation. However, the law still required a public purpose and prior notice if land was to be taken, neither of which the author considered satisfied by the "purely selfish purpose" of a military commander living in the property with his family. It is unclear what the outcome of Aberuagba's situation was, but the courts were unlikely to rule against the military. Emboldened, months later, the Lagos State government confiscated Kalakuta, the Lagos headquarters of the leader of rebels, rouser of zombies, Fela Kuta.[58] Resistance no longer had a home.[59]

One year later, the government would confiscate nearly all land in Nigeria, making compulsory acquisition no longer necessary. In 1978, Olusegun Obasanjo, who had come to power when General Murtala Muhammed was assassinated in 1976, decreed the Land Use Act, a radical piece of legislation that transferred all property to the government in an effort to streamline and simplify confusion over titles and registration, to reduce the conflict between customary and freehold tenure, and supposedly to increase the ease of access to land and housing for the poor.

Here oil comes back into the story. There is a strong argument that the driving factor behind the law was the government's desire to control and profit from any natural resources found in the country. Section 40(3) of the 1979 Constitution would go further, declaring all minerals, oil, natural gas, and natural resources found within the borders of Nigeria to be the legal property of the federal government.[60] The 1978 Land Use Act (enshrined in the 1979 Constitution) gave the governors of each state the privilege of approving "titles" (a statutory or customary Certificate of Occupancy) to land and for approving subsequent applications to let or mortgage the land. This approval process gave governors immense possibilities for self-enrichment and a reason to remain loyal to the federal regime. The resulting system was reminiscent of the aftermath of the British Treaty of Cession to acquire Lagos in 1861, which was accomplished under the premise of creating a more efficient and organized real estate market, but resulted in a scramble to claim titles from Governor Glover in a process that privileged the wealthy, educated, and those who curried favor with the government. Because of the bureaucratic costs and disorganization that accompanied the enforcement of the law, the 1978 law made it nearly impossible for poor landowners to reestablish a legal right to their property.[61] Ten years after the Land Use Act took effect, an expert on Lagos housing wrote that "the existence of a parallel system, loopholes in the law itself, and official connivance in breaking it have all led to the perpetuation of old practices, failure of reform, and the continuous deprivation of the urban poor in terms of access to land."[62]

Deepening Disparity in the Face of a Fizzling and Then Gutted Economy

Through the 1970s and into the 1980s, international attention to Lagos increased, not only for its spectacular oil wealth but also for its "spectacular" slumscapes. As Lagos became sub-Saharan Africa's largest city, academics hastened to investigate the expansion of the city's horizons, and especially the material conditions of the city's poor. Every scholar who visited was struck by the rampant insecurity. A standard way to guarantee publication in a peer-reviewed journal was to go into one of Lagos's many "shanties" and to conduct a simple survey of households (e.g., lack of running water, toilet facilities, electricity, and roads). The shocking findings were sufficient enough for acceptance.[63]

A 1977 article, "Living Conditions of the Poor in Lagos," charted the "filthy residential environment" in much of Maroko, Ajegunle, Mushin, Isale Eko, and Ojota. Most homes were found to lack pipe-borne water and wells and to be using pits and pails for waste disposal.[64] Another study of Lagos's four wards found that majority of the city's residents lived in single rooms (an average of nearly four people per room) and were cooking their meals over fires, filling their neighborhoods with thick fumes.[65] Researchers usually included brief commentary blaming the squalor on some combination of mass migration, the high price of construction materials, and the lack of financing for building. This reflected a continuation of the search begun at the end of British rule for a technocratic solution to the problem of mass housing. If only a new kind of domestic concrete could be created, or if only a breakthrough banking scheme could be dreamed up, then housing stock would roll off the belt and into the yards of waiting families. Rarely, if ever, were there pointed criticisms of the military government programs or of large-scale landlords. In reality, former colonial reserves continued to be airy, low-density spaces for government managers and military officers, while the densities of the island and the peripheries of the city climbed ever higher. The state was also pumping funds into new highways and

Atlantic

ring roads around the island, happy to import massive amounts of cement and other materials manufactured overseas (since this was a prime opportunity for kickbacks)[66] instead of investing in domestic production and training. Urbanist Giles Omezi has critically read the Lagos landscape produced by the military government in the 1970s:

> The ordering is clear in the instance of the Agege Motor Road/ Western Avenue, which in mimicking the colonial railway alignment up to the tough neighborhood of Mushin rises to avoid the Ojuelegba junction, skirting the National Stadium to the east, and climaxes at the intersection where the relic of the National Theatre nestles, as the expressway forks in a dizzying spaghetti of complex elevated intersections, ramps, and roundabouts leading to the Apapa Port and Eko Bridge. The marshlands of Ijora and Iganmu are avoided by the road system, despite holding the centre of national culture, built at the height of the petro dollar boom of the 1970s: the National Theatre. The building itself is a curious mimesis of the Palace of Culture and sports in Varna, Bulgaria, which somehow in its appropriated guise served to reinforce the projection of Nigerian nationalist aspirations. Concrete spokes radiating out skyward and suggestively converging the energies of the black world into its womb as the centrepiece of the 1977 Second Festival of Black Arts and Culture commonly referred to as FESTAC 77. The National Theatre's collision with the expressway system created an ambiguous space that combined high culture, industrial detritus and marshlands enclosed somewhat by the slender columns of the elevated expressways. The two-speed city shaped by concrete is present at its most extreme here. The German-engineered bridge piers and road deck shade an assortment of commercial activity in a somewhat unorthodox landscape of appropriation, which is as much a metaphor for the polarised economic realities as the juxtapositions of the rulers' will against that of the ruled, rural space versus urban space, tradition versus modernity. These binaries unwittingly burden Lagos with a complexity often read superficially as simply chaotic, rather than a work in progress

where the aspired modernity of post-colonial Nigeria is being resolved and reworked.[67]

Contrasting the scale and texture of National Theater and roadways is a researcher's early 1980s description of "Life in a Single Room House" in Mushin:

The following is a characteristic example of such a house: The number of occupants in this 8.64 sq.m. room (3.60m x 2.40m) was eight persons. The head of the household is Alhaji Karim, with his wife, mother-in-law, four children and one cousin of his wife. He was very happy to say that he usually had a few guests from his village. Since his wife is working in a school for handicapped children, her mother is in charge of the house-work. The wife usually comes back home around 3p.m. to help her mother at cooking. Alhaji works as a messenger in a private company; he usually gets home around 7p.m. By that time his dinner is ready at the table, and after having his meal he would go out to see his friends or sit on the verandah in front of the house and chat with his friends. He come[s] back into the room around 11p.m. to sleep. Children usually eat their food whenever they feel hungry; they carry their plates and eat wherever they like, usually not inside the room. Mother and grand-mother eat whenever they are hungry, usually not inside the room. They eat in the kitchen or corridor, where they chat with other housewives of the compound.

The furniture of the room consists of one twin bed which occupies one side of the room, two narrow benches on another side, with a table in front, two small cupboards on both sides of the entrance door and one T.V. set. Four shelves, hung at the far corner of the room are full of books, pictures and some important documents. Two big suitcases are under the bed, full of clothes. All the walls of the room are covered by pictures, photographs and calendars.

At night, table and benches will be shifted out, into the corridor to give enough sleeping space. Alhaji, his wife and the youngest child sleep on the bed and the rest of the family manage to sleep on the floor. Apart from grand-mother, who is

Atlantic 195

the last one to go to sleep at the door-step, the arrangement of sleeping space is not the same every night, depending on who will go to sleep first and at which corner. The grand-mother mentioned that sometimes, the number of people who sleep on the floor is as high as eight persons.

Spending evening time within a family circle is not common in Nigerian social life. Every member of the family organizes his own pleasure time separately. Father usually goes to see his friends or receives them on the verandah. Mother and grand-mother chat with the other housewives in the corridor or in the street, while children are hanging around, playing or watching T.V., making themselves busy.[68]

Despite the single-room density and the lack of basic amenities, a sense of community and fellowship is clear. But even that elemental bit of a "home" would be under stress by the 1980s.

In the early 1980s a trident of recession, federal relocation, and structural adjustment programs speared Lagos's economy and severed its patron-client supply lines, straining even the most basic ways in which marginalized areas of the city had cultivated a semblance of community. In 1981 construction began on Abuja (decreed in 1976 and inaugurated in 1991), a new centrally located federal capital, initiating a flood of people, power, and capital to the new city and, in the process, the desertion of Lagos and its ills (which, in part, had driven the desire for a new capital).[69] Also in 1981, a global recession sent oil prices plummeting and plunged Nigeria's economy into decline and the government into massive debt. This added to the abandonment of Lagos infrastructure projects, such as the ambitious master plan issued in 1980, as the government turned its attention to Abuja and the oil money dried up. Then in 1986, to combat the freefall, Nigeria adopted IMF-mandated structural adjustment programs (SAPs) to abolish import licenses and subsidies, to devalue the currency, and to eliminate marketing boards.[70] Nigerian writer Fidelis Balogun describes the consequences for Lagos:

The weird logic of this economic programme seemed to be that to restore life to the dying economy, every juice had first to be SAPed out of the under-privileged majority of the citizens. The middle class rapidly disappeared and the garbage heaps of the increasingly rich few became the food table of the multiplied population of abjectly poor. The brain drain to the oil-rich Arab countries and to the Western world became a flood.[71]

It is impossible to overstate the devastation that SAPs in combination with the recession and downgraded federal status wrought on Lagosians' homes. Not only did the government turn its back on Lagos in its march to Abuja and as international "experts" commanded that the Nigerian state not build housing,[72] but Lagosians began to turn on each other. There had always been extreme disparities of wealth in Nigeria's petro-economy, but there had been distribution channels that flowed down and through Lagos's poorest residential areas, communities where well-off landlords lived side by side with migrants and the lowliest city dwellers, offering assistance and a way up. The lack of tension between economic classes had originally flummoxed researchers in 1970s, who eventually found through ethnographic work that areas like Mushin and Apapa had functioning, if informal, social contracts even if Nigeria's macrolevel policies for housing and other services rarely delivered. Poor neighborhoods had been surprisingly heterogeneous and were governed by strong social codes with an emphasis on Big Men—landlords—showing generosity in gifts and assistance (patronage) to community members (clients). Those with control over urban spaces were expected to host and set up newcomers, and landlords' kin back in their hometowns were inquisitive as to whether they were fulfilling these obligations.[73] Gossip patrolled the promotion of the interests of the underprivileged.[74] Stinginess would expose landlords to "withering displays of antagonism and disrespect on the grounds that 'they [did] not follow custom.'"[75] Mobility was possible over time in this environment that stigmatized miserliness. And if migrants and the poor lived under abusive conditions or found themselves destitute, they could shuttle between rural areas and the city, a condition that Sara Berry documented.[76] SAPs changed all this.

The removal of subsidies decimated what remained of Nigeria's small-scale farming enterprises, closing off a return to rural areas for many migrants. Crime, particularly armed robbery, proliferated as patronage along with entrepreneurial opportunities evaporated and social bonds snapped. Homeowners soon began building walls around their compounds, adding barbed wire and broken-glass barriers against home invaders.[77]

FIGURE 5.3. An archaeology of violence: a Lagosian showing me the four additions he made to his compound's walls as crime escalated across the 1980s and 1990s. Author's photograph, 2014.

A photograph I took in 2014 shows the layers a resident of Lagos added over time to the wall around his compound as violence in the neighborhood intensified (fig. 5.3). Walls allowed the wealthy to insulate themselves and their possessions not just from crime but from community obligations as patronage from higher-ups slowed to a trickle. By the late 1970s, houses had started to become unmoored from their use-value of cultivating a client base and collecting rents. Apter describes how in the late 1970s a class of nouveau riche "grew up as quickly as the new houses and hotels [they] built" at a time when "signs became the basis of generating value rather than the media of its accumulation through exchange."[78] Fake diplomas and false credentials were easily obtainable, just as "real" as the growth the Nigerian economy was producing. It became a time of *"semiotic suspension, in which signs, stripped of their referential moorings, [were] almost literally up for grabs."*[79] Houses became facades. Residential structures were not valued because of the patron-client bonds fostered within them but because of their purely representational value—empty concrete monstrosities adorned with the "floating signifiers" of vaguely "modern" or "African" geometric symbols.

This "crisis of credibility" preceded the 1980s downturn when distrust started spiraling downward as walls went up, crime skyrocketed, and houses became about fortification above all else, hidden behind towering gates that continue to characterize the city's residential landscapes (fig. 5.4). People who could afford a plot and the construction of a large house no longer built utilitarian structures to host renters; instead they took refuge behind walled compounds, leaving poor areas of the city with decrepit buildings and self-built shanties. By the 1990s, Lagos would be declared by many "the world's most dangerous city."

FIGURE 5.4. "A city of walls." A staggering variety of gate and wall designs around Lagos, 2014–17. Author's photographs.

Conclusion

Flooding: Barometers of Human Security in a Fractured Global Landscape

At night, there are swathes of Lagos that are a gloomy grey from power cuts, lit only by a few generator-borne lights, and there are areas that are bright and glittering. And in both one sees the promise of this city: that you will find your kin, where you fit, that there is a space somewhere in Lagos for you.

—Chimamanda Ngozi Adichie, "Still Becoming"

Overnight on a recent weekend in August, it rained in Lagos like the ocean was falling from the heavens. Crocodiles swam through neighborhoods, cars stalled and were forsaken, and ground floors became feral swimming pools. I lay awake listening to the deluge, watching it creep into my room, certain my hosts would reconsider waking at 6 a.m. for church. But sure enough, the next morning, through the downpour and several feet of water in the streets, we began to make our way church-ward along with throngs of sputtering vehicles (fig. C.1). After a long journey of backtracking and alternate routes, I sat in the pew like a wet dog while somehow everyone else managed to look immaculate in slick suits and pressed dresses. I thought how, despite the storm, at that moment across the city in the Apostolic Church, the Cherubim and Seraphim Christian Church, the Mountain of Fire and Miracles Ministry, and hundreds of other houses of worship, Lagosians were praying, as they do every Sunday, emphatically for Nigeria, for Lagos, for their households, for deliverance, for redemption, for Jesus to return, and for

FIGURE C.1. A flooded-out road in Lekki with its abandoned victim, 2016. Author's photograph.

his Father to remember them. Biblically and across mythology, floods are bringers of change, of fresh beginnings wiping away the past and enabling a space for elevated ways of living. But in Lagos, floodwaters are stagnant, thick with toxic runoff, unfit for fertilizing the land or the city that has always had an intractable relationship with water—which, after years of rocky equilibrium, may finally be subsuming land. And yet, somehow, so far, Èkó ò ní bàjé o.[1]

The annually worsening flooding is a familiar feeling for a city where waves of potentially purgative surges often bring disappoint and new problems: independence followed by civil war; countless new regimes, resets, and reneged promises; master plans and development schemes that never materialized; structural adjustment programs that brought painful cutbacks rather than revitalization. Momentous events intended to wash out the old and unleash latent potential have more often stalled or heaped on additional trials, leaving a city thirsty for change soaked in undrinkable water.[2]

Still, Lagos is more than Sisyphean endurance. In spite of these setbacks, it has thrived as a center of arts, trade, and innovation into Africa's

Conclusion

megalopolis bar none. It is the continent's largest city, celebrated and broadcast across "Afropolitan" mediascapes, feared but also revered around the world, exerting more muscle and attracting greater global investment by the day. Lagos's GDP trails only six *countries* in Africa.[3] Nollywood now produces the second most films in the world.[4] Every young diasporan knows Lagos's landscapes and sounds from reading *Americanah*, listening to Wizkid and Burna Boy, and following the #EndSARS protests. Many—before the COVID pandemic and its economic fallout—had been moving back to seize what they saw as wide-open opportunities.[5]

Today, Lagos is desirable, stylish, and moneyed, and the wealthy are noticing, infusing the funding to build luxury villas, high-rises, and hotels downtown and along a soon-to-be-unrecognizable waterfront. But this glitzy success is pushing out all but the richest from the urban core and is conspiring with floods to once again heap newfangled crises on the city.

In Lagos, two global urban challenges are crashing into one another: a shortage of affordable housing and the reality of climate change. The city is spilling over as the water is rising up.

The final pages of this book outline these challenges that threaten to handcuff the city's future and consider the perspectives, possibilities, and policy ideas offered by 150 years of Lagos housing history.

"Lagos, a City of Shanty Towns and Millionaires"

The world is becoming increasingly urban with more people living in cities than not, and yet, for more than 330 million urban households worldwide, joining this trend has meant living in unsafe and inadequate shelter and facing severe financial stress.[6] This is particularly true in Lagos. Since 1960 Lagos has been city-exemplar of Africa's relentless urbanization rates, growing from less than a million residents to a megacity that some estimate has already crossed the 20 million mark (although more reliable estimates place the population closer to the 10–15 million range), and may well be the third-largest city in the world by 2040.[7] In 2014, a UN study in conjunction with the London School of Economics found that Lagos was adding 85 people per hour, making it the fastest-growing city on earth.[8] According to the McKinsey Global Institute, Lagos's "affordability gap," as defined by "the difference between the cost of an acceptable standard housing unit (which varies by location) and what households can afford for housing using no more than 30 percent of income," is among the worst in the world: over 90 percent of Lagos households cannot afford standard housing units at market rates even when McKinsey calculated that a "standard unit" in sub-Saharan Africa is only forty square meters (as compared to ninety square meters in North America).[9] Another study estimates that the housing deficit in Lagos is 2,949,912 units, more than double the estimated number of units that actually exist in the city (1,417,588).[10]

Where do the nearly three million households left out live? In massive sprawls of "informal"—unpermitted construction on untitled land—housing on the fringes of the city. In 2019 a United Nations special rapporteur, Leilana Fartha, was appalled after a ten-day visit to Lagos, stating, "Successive Governments have allowed economic inequality in Nigeria to reach extreme levels, a fact that is clearly evident in the housing sector."[11] Over 75 percent of Lagos households occupy one room, with an average of eight to ten people per room.[12] Some of the largest areas of informal housing, such as Ajegunle and Makoko, are built as much on water as land. Since these areas are informally settled, they often have little in the way of proper drainage systems, meaning the ground is becoming waterlogged and prone to floods that refuse to recede. Maps of Lagos's geographic expansion tell a remarkable tale of residents occupying land farther and farther from the city center in order to afford a place to call "home." This morphology did not happen randomly but is rather part of global trend of denizens being pushed out (through force and unaffordability) to make way for global capital.

The cities with the worst affordability gaps on McKinsey's list are predominantly large, internationally prominent cities like New York, London, Beijing, and Mumbai.[13] They are members of what are sometimes called "global cities" or "superstar cities," colossal concentrations of people who are materially and digitally connected to other megacities around the world, attracting and facilitating the flows of financing and knowledge that drive contemporary capitalism.[14] Being at the center of a megacity means gaining profitable proximity to these flows. With this incentive, the value of dense downtown real estate in cities like New York and London has escalated rapidly over the last decade, first as individuals and businesses placed a premium on it and then as financial speculators began turning inner-city housing into an investment vehicle in what has come to be known as the financialization of housing.[15]

Conclusion

Lagos is no exception to this trend. A study of the luxury housing market in Lagos found that 85 percent of buyers currently reside abroad, the majority of whom purchased properties in Lagos as an investment without plans to occupy it.[16] Almost all new developments in the center of Lagos—like the much-publicized ten square kilometers of the Eko Atlantic project dredged from the ocean—cater to these buyers, a process facilitated by the state. In a city where there has long been a premium on land and housing, the scramble has reached a fever pitch, driving prices for luxury properties to an average range of 80,000,000 to 1,300,000,000 naira (between $220,000 and $3,600,000). This in a city where less than 1 percent of people earn more than 800,000 naira ($2,216) per year with over 61 percent of the city earning less than 120,000 naira ($332) per year. The average price of a modest three-bedroom house is 48,000,000 naira ($132,000), in other words, at least 400 times the annual income of over 99 percent of Lagosians. The average annual rent for an agent-listed one-bedroom apartment is 440,500 naira ($1,200).[17] The numbers speak for themselves and explain why most of the city's property development, management, and construction companies cater to higher-end buyers and renters. The returns are so astronomically greater at the 1 percent end that builders and landowners are willing to wait out a big payday rather than take the risk of smaller returns on more affordable properties. Developers would literally have to build and rent hundreds or even thousands of units to middle- or low-income Lagosians to make the same profits they make by building and selling a single luxury unit to an international buyer. As one resident said, "The problem is not that there are no houses. If you look around, there are empty houses all over Lagos, some can even go a year without being rented out."[18]

The result has been that much of Lagos's prime real estate in areas like Ikoyi, Victoria Island, and Lekki has been converted to concrete monstrosities with little character or charm: every surface inside and out is raw and bone hard. But the point is not comfort or livability: rather, it is about converting cash to an appreciable asset, in which regards a durable slab of concrete surrounded by spiked walls guarantees structural longevity and minimal upkeep and oversight. Luxury Lagos houses are immovable and impenetrable claims to a chunk of urban space. Walking around some of the city's wealthiest gated estates is a ghostly experience with at least every third house unoccupied (fig. C.2). Capital—often

FIGURE C.2. One of many empty plots in an upscale Lagos neighborhood, 2016. Author's photograph.

from ill-gotten gains—haunts the most secure houses in Lagos while the least secure areas of the city are crammed with people desperate to establish a claim that might shield their tenancy from rival claims.

The seeds of Lagos's disparate mass and elite housing landscapes run deep and have grown remarkably strong roots over more than a century. Across each era of the city's colonial and postcolonial history, those in power or aspiring to power have recognized the strategic value of property, particularly housing stock with its social cachet and economic returns, in buttressing their position and sway over the city. They utilized every combination of racism, claims to scientific reason and customary rights, legislation, planning bodies, courts, and, at times, force to expand their holdings and their control over land and housing in Lagos. The resulting reality, as Tom Goodfellow and Olly Owens show in their recent ethnography of land tenure in Lagos, is that "everyone is deploying their mixed bag of social, legal, economic and political assets to lodge a stake in various domains and then leverage it."[19] In order "to secure themselves in place" in the city, middle-class Lagosians rely on multiple forms of cadastral evidence of their rightful tenancy, including

Conclusion

recently paid tax receipts, to "progressively thicken property claims."[20] This is necessary in Lagos's reality of "institutional layering" in which memories and remnants of each era's systems coexist and are seen as the legitimate arrangement in some quarters.[21] "Rights" in the conventional legal sense can hardly be said to exist for most residents in the city where laws conflict one another, are unevenly applied and enforced, and butt heads with popular legitimacy and with the facts and forceful acts on the grounds. Most Lagosians today live with a "radical sense of uncertainty, unpredictability and insecurity."[22]

In bending property systems in Lagos to their aims, whether Lagos's historical leaders and elites have used their control over property for the public good or for their personal enrichment and pursuits has been a central question in Lagos politics. Governments unaccountable to the denizens of Lagos, whether colonial or military regimes, have been particularly prone to capture land and housing for their own purposes at Lagosians' expense. Colonialism's cutting down of successful Africans at the end of the nineteenth century and its housing segregation schemes in the twentieth ran through land expropriation. Across the booms and busts of postcolonial Nigeria, government officials pumped their cut of petro-dollars into Lagos property as a tangible store of private wealth. Today, land purchases and real estate developments in Lagos are used to convert and disguise illicit financial gains and are the heart of the city's systems of organized crime and corruption.[23] More often than not, the state's enabling of large-scale land development has been for sheltering elites' capital, not people.

In this environment, the traditional landowning families, now known also as ọmọ onilẹ (children of the land holders), have more aggressively treated their current and former lands in terms of cash extraction, organizing offices to collect yearly payments and harassing those who fail to pay with militias.[24] In Lekki, Lagos's eastward flank, the Elegushi family (a white-capped chieftaincy) collaborated in 2016 and 2017 with Lagos State to use un-uniformed armed men to forcibly remove forty thousand longtime residents from the family's lands at Otondo Gbame to make way for high-end developments, despite a court injunction against the demolitions.[25] The cofounder of Justice and Empowerment Initiatives (a nonprofit that builds solidarity among informal settlement dwellers and advocates on their behalf), stated accurately that "the chieftaincy families' are reinventing their history and the nature of their historical control over land, with active support from the state government."[26] White-cap chiefs are continuing to shift their claims from guardians of community lands to proprietary owners of private property, a process begun with the Tew Legislation of 1947. At least eleven people died (shot and drowned) in the demolition mayhem, and seventeen more disappeared. Residents of Otondo Gbame lost their homes and many of their possessions as bulldozers crashed through the beachside settlement without warning while men fired guns into the air. These evictions are part of a widespread campaign by Lagos State and powerful families to flush out communities from prime real estate without compensation or resettlement plans. According to Amnesty International, between 2000 and 2009 "Nigerian authorities forcibly evicted over two million people" and have evicted tens of thousands more since.[27] Registering a new property requires the governor's consent and an 8 percent fee of the property's value be paid to the government, incentivizing the governor to clear out old properties and replace them with new luxury ones.[28]

Recent state programs to increase housing stock and affordability likewise have more often benefited the already well-off or have served as token enticements and appeasements. Entering a recent lottery for one of the few LSDPC properties available through the "home ownership mortgage scheme" required a steady income, a 30 percent deposit, and the ability to repay the rest over a ten-year mortgage. The online promotions for these homeownership schemes have all the pageantry of a sweepstakes (lavish celebrations for winners—who are inducted into the "homeowning" class) to keep Lagosians hopeful of one day having a permanent home even though the odds are an extreme long shot. The state is currently aiming to provide twenty thousand properties (again, there is an estimated 2.9-million-unit deficit) in the next few years, mostly catering to upper-middle-class buyers. Currently, there are several property developments with units available on the LSDPC website. They are selling for between 26,500,000 and 75,000,000 naira, far out of the reach of most Lagosians.[29] Lagos State falls into what political scientists Nicole Gurran and Peter Phibbs call the political strategy of "look busy but change little," putting up billboards and advertisements for big developments that promise to remake the city but rarely materialize.[30]

Conclusion 207

Together, market prices for property, a lack of state assistance, and mass evictions are pushing the city to the edge. For the overwhelming majority of Lagosians, the only option for finding shelter in the city is moving farther and farther to the periphery. Rings of peri-urban frontiers expand farther every year from the city's central islands. These settlements form what Lindsay Sawyer terms "plotted" urbanism to describe the piecemeal process through which houses are developed individually with their own water (borehole), electric (generator), sanitation, and even road infrastructure.[31] Lagos State has largely struggled to integrate these areas into the metropolitan area or to distribute tax income from luxury properties to geographically marginal communities.

The sprawl is running into the water and into low-lying areas, at times creating new flood-prone terrain. A 2013 study found that "a large chunk of the urban development (built-up) in the study area [Lagos State] within the study period [1984–2006] occurred mostly in areas where it displaced sensitive natural ecosystems consisting of wetlands, vegetation, and water bodies."[32] Between 1984 and 2006, built-up areas in the city increased from 49 to 283 square kilometers while mangroves and swamps decreased, respectively, from 88 to 20 square kilometers and from 345 to 165 square kilometers.[33] The wetlands around the city are increasingly being settled, exposing residents to the effects of rising seas and worsening storms caused by climate change while also impinging on the city's natural barriers to storm surges and flooding.[34] Annual rainfall has remained steady, but the number of rainy days per year has decreased, meaning the storms are more intense when they come.[35] Floods have become more frequent.[36] Rising sea levels threaten to erode the shoreline and seep deeper into the communities that line the city's waterfronts.[37] The contact between the city and water is inflaming disease and pollution: 50 percent of hospitalized Lagosians suffer waterborne diseases.[38] Lagos may already be losing over four billion dollars (4 percent of its GDP) per year to flooding.[39]

Architects have been at the center of proposals to solve Lagos's flooding troubles. Two projects of vastly different scales—the singular Makoko "floating school" (see chapter 3) and Eko Atlantic, an entirely new borough dredged from the ocean—continue to grab headlines and offer observers a way to end their publications on an optimistic note. Made of timber louvers and royal blue photovoltaic roofing, the A-frame school designed by Kunlé Adeyemi cut an iconic symbol of an amphibious future. It suggested the homes of Makoko's one hundred thousand denizens could be buoyed rather than demolished or washed away. In her eye-opening article, "Things Fall Apart," Allyn Gaestel chronicles the triumphant rise of Adeyemi's vision, which won the Venice Biennale's Silver Lion Award, and its tragic fall a week after the award when a storm splintered the school into pieces.[40] Even before the award and storm, while Adeyemi toured the world stoking glowing press reviews for the "school," the actual structure sat falling into disrepair, barely ever holding classes because toilets and blackboards were not included in the design and parents wisely feared the structure's violent swaying. As Gaestel uncovers, the $130,000 project propelled Adeyemi to international acclaim but never served the Makoko community.

What Gaestel calls the architecture world's weakness for "hypervisibility" over substance is also alive in the seductive renderings and models for Eko Atlantic. The project's promoters attracted billions of naira in investment, but, more than a decade into construction, their pitch has yet to yield much more than an expanse of soggy sand stretching precariously into the Atlantic. In a fate looking increasingly like that of the floating school, storm surges have begun breaching Eko Atlantic's design, casting doubt on investment returns.[41] Heralded by its engineers as impenetrable to the worst waves imaginable in a thousand years, "the great wall of Lagos" may also actually be worsening flooding in the areas adjacent to it.[42]

The Makoko floating school and Eko Atlantic highlight the shortfalls found in the popular idea that poverty and environmental crises are simply glitches in need of new technology and a disruptive "innovator." This paradigm centered on the "starchitect" (star architect) as a "a sort of secularized God"[43] has precursors in colonial midcentury planners. In the 1940s and 1950s, architects like Maxwell Fry and Jane Drew, narrowed inquiries into housing and environmental issues to technocratic concerns that lacked broader discussions of political structures and urban histories. Similar constriction is seen in much of the discourse around the housing crisis today, as Steffen Wetzstein shows, because "the spotlight has been put almost everywhere on questions of how to release more land, build more houses and apartments and reregulate mortgage and rental markets rather than to deal with the more contentious issue of how to help households to earn salaries and wages

Conclusion

in line with rising housing expenses."[44] The majority of fixes put forth involve the reduction of red tape and the creation of market-friendly financial instruments or construction techniques that will "unleash" new housing stock. Wetzstein argues that many of these prescriptions lack a fundamental understanding of how contemporary urban markets actually work and the ways that urban land and housing have become a very real, even central, form of capital—with houses "increasingly viewed as investment rather than a home"—that powerful developers and wealthy individuals are not likely to make more accessible or sell off anytime soon. If more urban land and housing stock becomes available, those who already own property are likely buy it up in a fashion similar to how corporations buy back their stock when given an infusion of cash rather than lowering prices for consumers or raising wages. This fundamental misunderstanding of housing and its place in the economy accounts for what Wetzstein calls the "policy-outcome" gap found where many market-friendly policy "innovations" have been introduced yet have failed to produce the expected increase in affordable housing. To begin bridging this gap, she "follows a recent call to urgently bring back political economy into housing questions."[45] These are exactly the considerations that observers and planners have avoided in trying to give expedient explanations for the roots of Lagos's housing crisis. The state of Lagos housing today was not the inevitable historical terminus for the city; it was the result of political decisions in each era that were shaped by perceptions of the city's landscapes, reigning cultural discourses, and the continual strategic importance of housing in the city.

Theorists of political economy like Manuel Aalbers and Brett Christophers are fundamentally reevaluating the place of land and housing in traditional economic models, arguing that "the issue of housing has not been granted an important role in post-war political economy.... In recent years, however, there has been a growing and broadly based recognition of the increasing centrality of housing to the political economy of advanced capitalist societies in much more than a production-related sense," and that land should be placed "at the very heart of [political-economic] theory, which, in an era of land grabbing, 'planetary urbanisation' and proliferating international housing crises, is clearly where it needs to be."[46] Much of the reason that fixing the housing crisis has ended up in the hands of singular starchitects and innovators in the first place is that economic and political theory has often pushed it to the periphery of academic and policy discussions (much the same can be said for approaches to climate change before recently). Houses have always been central to life in Lagos, and it makes sense that approaches to housing would recognize this fact in considering how the city can be made more secure and prosperous for all.

What Wetzstein, Christophers, and Aalbers are doing is re-asking, What is house? Revisiting this question is needed to begin to find policy fixes that actually address and, if necessary, reshape housing's place in the political-economic matrix. This is necessary in order to slow and reverse the fracturing of urban spaces into what are rapidly becoming zones of "secure" enclaves and "insecure" sprawl around the globe.[47] This question can also be approached and informed from other disciplinary angles as part of a broad examination of the meaning of a house. The final section of this project returns to the original question with which it began: What is a house in Lagos? Looking back at Lagos's history and working with the writings of Nomusa Makhubu, Achille Mbembe, and Robert Pogue Harrison, I reflect on this question and on what houses in Lagos could become.

What Is a House in Lagos and What Can It Be?

In Lagos, it is common to come upon houses with the hand-painted sign: "this house is not for sale." This arises because con artists frequently sell other people's homes to unsuspecting buyers. The notion of a home being sold off through a con echoes the discourse surrounding the flight of the country's oil resources, from which the majority of the citizens do not benefit. The "crisis" of the home is symbolic of the "crisis" of the nation. As a visual metaphor, the home or the house is correlated to deception, illusion, or the ruse through which the experience of place is inseparable from image and imagination.

—Nomusa Makhubu, "This House Is Not for Sale"[48]

The simple question of a house's definition is more elusive than it might appear at first pass, particularly in Lagos and many global cities today. There is palpable uncertainty around the home, its place in theoretical models, in society, and in the city. The home has become a symbol and manifestation of "crisis." This uncertainty runs across ideas and scales of "the house" and "housing." The latter, the contemporary "housing

Conclusion

landscape" in Lagos, is a refraction of Nigeria's particular articulation of global crises, involving oil, exclusion, layering of property claims, and climate change.[49] The barricaded gates, atomized plots, splintered floating school, painted "419" warnings, and banalized shelters—both concrete compounds and makeshift shanties—are visual symbols of contested claims, financialized urban space, and rising seas.

"The house" is likewise a site of uncertainty. In her article examining the homes found in Nollywood film sets and in Zina Saro-Wiwa's installation art, Nomusa Makhubu suggests that these domestic spaces "are a microcosm for the 'crisis' in social relations in contemporary Nigeria."[50] Alienation, marginalization, and dispossession are themes in Saro-Wiwo's depiction of her art video's title character, Phyllis, "a young woman who lives alone in Lagos and spends her days watching Nollywood films in her apartment and hawking colorful wigs in the city."[51] Home for her floats between an imagined space of escape, a place that does not exist, and a cramped apartment where her "experience in the home is based on *watching* rich women who are also mostly confined in domestic spaces on television, wearing fancy wigs."[52] Her own pink, blue, and tan wigs both confine and liberate her, like the stigma and freedom of being a single woman living alone in Nigeria. Makhubu writes, "In Nollywood video-film, the house is represented as masculine, but the home is depicted as feminine."[53] Rich men in many of these films that Phyllis watches own luxurious houses with "few or no women" and instead often have an occult shrine or corpse hidden in a secret part of the home: "The refusal of reproduction for magical creation of wealth and the sacrifice of the conjugal family constitute crises" on which the melodrama of many Nollywood films track.[54] In these films, relations, obligations, and traditions of "home" (often also represented by "the village") are *sacrificed* by ambitious men in order to accrue urban houses as repositories of material wealth and personal power that is not shared with the community. Occupying the otherwise empty male-dominated estates in Nollywood films are "imported leather couches, stuffed animals, green curtains, glass-topped coffee tables with metallic frames, chandeliers, alcohol bars, and large-screen televisions, as well as glass and porcelain sculptures that signify modern wealth."[55] Like the monstrous exteriors seen everywhere in moneyed Lagos, the warm, welcoming, and protective ambiance of a familial home is sacrificed to the cold shrines of commodified wealth in these interiors.

In another project, *Parlour*, Sara-Wiwo and collaborator Michalene Thomas reproduce these spaces in their installation of a replica Nigerian living room, evoking feelings of the uncanny—familiarity and strangeness—in the room's assemblage of universal fashionings and fake objects. Sara-Wiwo's artwork and Nollywood's sets, as Makhubu makes clear, "are indices of real concerns about spatial politics," illustrating how "the house" has become an uncertain and disorientating space in Lagos.[56]

In his philosophical history of tombs, burial, and the dead, Robert Pogue Harrison includes a chapter titled "What Is a House," in which he writes, "The question in my chapter title is intended reflectively. It does not sound like one, yet it may well be *the* philosophical question of our time—a time when traditional philosophy, or so we are told, has come to an end, leaving us confused about who or where we are, insofar as we are human."[57] This resonates in Lagos, where a central motif in Nollywood films is the metaphorical homelessness of society and where many millions of people across the city are quite literally homeless. Harrison wonders, "Is something like the housing of modern homelessness conceivable? What would such housing look like?"[58]

A house—to paraphrase Makhubu—is a confluence of *place, image, and fantasy*, which she calls "a multilayered profound space."[59] In her essay, she reads the "dialectic of depth and surface" between deep-seated socioeconomic trends and contemporary visual images to better understand "the home" in Nigerian art.[60] A similar approach has been at the center of this book's methodology: an examination of "surfaces" (maps and photographs of houses and the city) to reveal a dialectic between ways of seeing and seeking to shape the city's landscapes, and the changes to what a house is in Lagos.

Looking back and briefly outlining how images and dreams of houses in Lagos have shaped their place and changed in turn with the city's evolving landscapes may suggest different trajectories for what houses might become out of this moment of crisis.

The Place, Image, and Dream of a House in Lagos

Before the arrival of Europeans, houses in Lagos were the domain of the unliving. "The city of the dead antedates the city of the living," wrote Lewis Mumford, whom Harrison quotes in arguing that "human beings housed their dead before they housed themselves."[61] This was the

Conclusion

case in Lagos, where houses originated as places of sacred kinship and coeval bonds between the past and future. The original Awori settlers of Lagos, who, fleeing war, had abandoned their homelands and fled to the coast, eventually reconstituted their new dwellings and their sense of community on Iddo Island by burying their dead in the floors of their family compounds (see page 33). The buried ancestors substantiated claims to the land on Iddo Island through their presence. "The house," as Harrison muses, was "a place where two realms—one under and the other on the earth—interpenetrated each other . . . a place of insideness in the openness of nature where the dead, through the care of the living, perpetuate their afterlives and promote the interests of the unborn."[62] Fittingly, "house" (*ilé*) shares an etymology with the Yoruba word for earth or ground (*ilẹ̀*); the floor of a house is called *ilẹ̀-ilé*. Houses and the land on which they rested were the dwellings of the dead—and, quoting Harrison, "the dead's indwelling define[d] the human interiority which . . . houses buil[t] walls around and render[ed] inhabitable."[63] The house was where knowledge, objects, and legacies were passed down, where the "sacred fire" and the "vital heat" associated with the home's hearths and shrines were kept alight. History, in the most human sense, was bequeathed through the archive of the house in precolonial Lagos. Being outside of "a house" meant vulnerability not only in terms of physical security but also in terms of living an ahistorical existence.

The images of early houses in Lagos were associated with the reputations and power of the large extended families who occupied them. Their surfaces and their signs were legible to Awori residents who could discern their architectural distinctions connected to the rank and status of the lineage occupying it. For those without affiliation to a house, there was no greater dream than becoming a full-fledged member of a family compound and enjoying the rights and privileges it granted. The objective for many outsiders (migrants, enslaved people, and orphans) was to "move inside" a kinship group centered on an earthen compound. Houses were the poles—as well as the portals in the earth between the past and the future—around which Èkó's landscape was seen by early Awori denizens.

With the arrival of Europeans with imperial aims, houses began to become places catering to living bodies and earthly ambitions. Settlers brought with them what Harrison describes as "a singleminded effort undertaken by the West, in the last few centuries [for emancipation], by whatever means necessary, from . . . millennial bondage to the land and . . . servitude to the dead."[64] Visual mediums of landscape like detailed maps and photographs facilitated a reimagining of space and of the very possibility of restructuring cities and houses. This dream was evident in the early British observations and maps of Lagos that sketched plans to clear native houses and to deepen the port's shipping channel. In these gazes, the image of African houses was alien, ugly, and an obstacle. Europeans thus cast them and their residents as dirty and diseased, and as places that could be taken and through which reforms could be rapidly instituted. The pursued urban "reforms" were more often than not an aesthetic rather than a scientific project to eliminate what was seen as a blemish and to remake the city into a photographable British colonial capital. Colonial bungalows and segregation schemes were concerned primarily with keeping Europeans in positions of power over African subjects. An important fissure in the meaning of a house occurred when, in the late nineteenth century, the Britain banned in-home burials in Lagos and inspectors began searching houses for the deceased to move to cemeteries, severing many African families' sense of home. Great nineteenth-century men like Taiwo found ways to remain near their houses in the afterlife by building mausoleums next to their earthly abodes. Houses had become increasingly for the living, yet for the "Lagos-style" houses seen on Lawson's 1885 map, legacy was still an important part of building a grand house to establish a stake in the city that one's family could inherit collectively.

The twentieth century saw rapid, confusing, and profound changes to the place, image, and dream of houses in Lagos. Gradually, under colonial rule's reshaping of the city's economy and landscape, crowded rented rooms and barracks became more common as families chose or were forced to sell off or split up properties and to look to them for income as Africans were excluded from the racially organized colonial economy. "Home" for many migrants and workers living in these spaces was more often associated with "hometowns" in Nigeria's interior.

"Housing" as a social issue concerned with hosting living bodies was given intensified attention and funding after the Second World War. Colonial reports and dispatches defined housing in terms of holding and molding workers as dependable units of labor cut off from rural dependents who might burden their wages and distract from their productivity.

Conclusion

Fry and Drew's modernist designs obsessed over "the body"—sheltering it from the tropical elements and rousing it into productivity. Fry, Drew, and their modernist cohort and disciples (including the LEDB) dismissed history, especially histories contained within African houses, as irrelevant to the needs of the bodies inside their "new" housing plans. Yet, like their colonial predecessors whom they did not study, their structures were designed to realize an aesthetic project of dominant forms rather than actually adhering to rationalist plans and inquiry. Their planning model resulted in the razing of hundreds of African houses in the old heart of Lagos that did not fit this image and that held a different way of house-building.

In the precarity of postcolonial Lagos's boom-and-bust economy helmed by an underequipped government, houses became places that linked residents to the nation's oil wealth through the distribution channels their politically connected landlords offered access to. But houses themselves soon became places to park that wealth, pushing out people through increasingly coercive methods as landowning families, military officers, and anyone who had cash joined the rush to claim a piece of the city's real estate and ride its exponential financial appreciation. While already by the second half of the nineteenth century houses in Lagos had become vessels for storing and producing wealth through rental income and its use as collateral and speculative investments, in the twenty-first century these uses of houses have become primary functions in Lagos's real estate developments. Makhubu cites an increasingly relevant Yoruba proverb for contemporary Lagos housing, "The world is a market, the otherworld is home."[65]

The arc of the house in Lagos follows a familiar global historical pathway that Gilles Deleuze and Felix Guattari write of in *Anti-Oedipus: Capitalism and Schizophrenia*. The privileged dwellers in Lagos's houses have changed, like that of the social body credited by humankind for economic production, from "the ground" (and the ancestral spirits in the earth), to "the body," and finally to "capital."[66] Of course, there have been many local processes, dead ends, decisions, overlaps, and conflicts along this deterritorialization of housing. It is not a teleology, but rather a discrete end pursued vigilantly by colonial and postcolonial agents in Lagos (and around the world) for two centuries. It is a pathway that has led to crisis in Lagos as the place, image, and dream of houses have become subservient to the interests of capital.

While this process has had deleterious impacts on housing security for many, it is important to note that the initial separation of humanity and the house from "the ground" has meant liberation for many who were confined by "the house's" often exploitative bonds over reproduction and labor.[67] *Phyllis* is caught between this liberation and the contemporary crisis of capital's capture of the home. Surveying the landscape of Lagos's history—both its missteps and forms of oppression as well as its moments of alternative possibilities—may offer different pathways for what houses might become. This project's archive, to borrow from James Ferguson's description of looking at historical southern African societies to expand our political imagination, "may contain resources that might be of some use as we seek to find new ways both of understanding the present and of envisioning possible futures."[68]

House Places

What is the place of housing in a city, and who or what has a privileged place in a city's houses? In Lagos, houses have historically been cherished and valuable places in a coastal city short on habitable land. It is not surprising, then, that securing and holding onto land and housing has been a priority for so many in the city's history. Housing has been at the center of the city's modern political struggles. Some Lagosians have commented that the drive that began with the British to possess a piece of Lagos has been so strong that the city itself been "possessed" (i.e., controlled by the evil spirit of this energy).[69] The abstract object of possession, capital, now possesses much of the core city through its control over real estate. Lagos State's housing and construction schemes cater to Nigerian and international capital by green-lighting projects that push poorer Lagosians to the periphery in favor of luxury developments. To not facilitate the disembodying of the central city would risk incurring the wrath of international investment funds and the organizations that rank the "ease of doing business" in global cities.[70]

The contemporary place of houses in Lagos is paradigmatic of the modern emphasis on "habitation" (from *haber*—to have and thus to possess, control, and dominate a place)[71] in approaches to homemaking. Possess or be disposed. This has led to a deemphasis of ideas of dwelling (securely occupying, living in, and passing down) in housing research and praxis in Lagos and beyond. Dwelling is to have a rooted

Conclusion

connection to a place like the grounding buried ancestors provided in early Awori homes. Resurrecting some of the stability that these relationships nurtured does not require reinterring the deceased; rather, it can entail beginning to think differently about the place of houses and also defining and prioritizing houses differently in policy and legislation.

In place of houses being objects of possession unattached from the socioecological fabric of cities, Achille Mbembe suggests that the notion "custodianship" that he grew up with in Cameroon may be a mode of dwelling to bring us out of this moment of crisis:

> I grew up in Cameroon in the fear that I would die young, but with the deep conviction that I would never die abroad. In those years, to die abroad meant to die in a foreign land. It was understood that to die away from home was the biggest misfortune to befall any human being, the kind of misfortune one only wished to one's enemies. One thing was to die abroad, another was to be buried away from home. To be buried away from home meant to have been turned into a complete foreigner.
>
> I always thought I would be buried in my own country, so deeply convinced I was that Cameroon was my home. In truth, many of us in the world today no longer know where home is. We spend most of our lives silently mourning the home we either never had or never knew or the home we actually lost.
>
> We were taught that "home" is the land one belongs to and which, in turn, belongs to one. "Home affairs" were affairs of co-belonging and reciprocal ownership, which is not exactly the same thing as "private possession." In the narratives of autochthony I grew up listening to, to be the owner of the land meant to take care of that land and to care for all who inhabited it, humans and non-humans. Ownership had a double meaning. It was about caring and caretaking, taking care in memory of those who came before and on behalf of those who were still to come. *We were neither subjects nor citizens, but custodians.*
>
> *Ownership and belonging were not about private possession.* Priceless, incalculable and unquantifiable things could not be the object of private possession. They could only be the subject of care and *caretaking was the closest to ownership.* Home was the land or more precisely the piece of ground, the vital

envelope, the abode supposed to protect the body, the earth every fully constituted human person or being hoped to return to once his or her journey had reached its final destination, in a grand gesture of share (as opposed to appropriation) and cosmic reciprocity.[72]

Mbembe's stirring memories of what home meant in Cameroon may serve as the etchings of response to Harrison when he wonders how to make cities not "merely places to live [but also] places to die." In Mbembe's vision, ownership does not equate possession but rather a position of trusteeship and caretaking. For a house, city, or country to be a place to rest and to finish one's journey with a sense of being home, it must be a place that has been cared for in preparation for those who are still to come, the descendants who will carry the memories of those who came before. If this cannot occur, a crisis of social reproduction and deceitful images and dreams envelop a city.

Similar to Mbembe's experience, a sense of custodianship was perhaps the closest equivalent to the concept of private ownership in Awori systems of tenure in Lagos before the introduction of private property rights by the British in the middle of the nineteenth century. Landed chiefs were understood to be overseers and managers of the land for their lineages and for the humans and nonhumans living on it. Like capitalist cities to various degrees the world over, control over Lagos's spaces has become largely unmoored from a sense of trusteeship and caretaking today. In a world of housing shortages, climate refugees, and myriad other crises, the Yoruba concept of ilé may be a place to start reimagining what custodianship—making houses central places of caretaking for humans and nonhumans, living and unliving, arriving, staying, or leaving alike—might look like in cities like Lagos today.

House Images

Ilé literally means "a house" but can also mean "a community," "a city," or "a nation" in Yoruba. It is a powerful concept for imaging one's place and society's possibilities. It illustrates the scalability of imagining the image of housing as an organizing concept for sociopolitical change, which is what Mbembe and Harrison are gesturing toward in their writings on reimagining the house and the home. The word *ilé* evokes the shared

Conclusion 219

spaces, especially the communal courtyards, of historical Yoruba homes. These dwellings had connotations of security and continuity yet were also a site of creativity and improvisation and were open and hospitable to visitors. This is not to say that there were not rivalries, betrayals of the duty of custodianship, and disagreements, but the image carried a set of expectations—a social contract—for the families and baálẹ who oversaw these places. For centuries, as Akinwumi Ogundiran writes in his study of Yorùbá history, ilé "were the primary basis of Yorùbá social organization and the fulcrum of its social reproduction."[73] Members of an ilé shared rights and obligations to the house and initiated newcomers into the ilé when they could, inducting them into its social relations.[74] This ethos of receiving strangers and hosting kin and connections from a hometown or abroad is still common in Lagos. I have been the beneficiary of it many times. Even if there is a palpable sense of uncertainty, through all the expropriations, displacement, and demolishing of old houses, there is a warmth to many of the city's homes, in which there is always room for another person. These connections and networks help Lagosians remain in place and resist the forces that would dislodge them and occupy their land. These modes of dwelling are under immense pressure. Yet I suggest they are still the sediment and strongest force in Lagos, though they have been fractured and their supporters made suspicious of those outside their walls. If made more conspicuous and interwoven, they could perhaps push back with success against anti-caretaking modes of possession Lagos.

What would an image of ilé-centric urban landscape look like and how could this vision of more secure societal housing be depicted and mediated in ways that facilitate its realization and entrenchment? When the system of ilé reigned in Èkó, the architecture of the house was legible to residents. For those who know how to look at Lagos's landscapes there is much to delight in, and parts of the city—spots like Freedom Park, the New Afrika Shrine, and pockets of old and undemolished residential areas in Yaba and Ebute Metta—remain vibrant with creativity and uniquely Lagosian designs. Kevin Lynch, in his well-known 1960 book *The Image of the City*, argues that "legibility is crucial in the city setting" for inhabitants to feel secure and at home and avoid a sense of being "lost." Legibility has long been prioritized in Lagos by European planners and outside observers, who, as this book has described in detail, have been repeatedly mystified by their perceptions of African cities, dismissing them as disordered and ugly. In critiquing surface readings of Lagos, this book has illustrated the perils of urban planning paradigms intended primarily to materialize an aesthetic (the example today is the trend of "greening" cities in a way that substitutes a palette for structural reform). Rather, as has rarely been prioritized in Lagos, residents' ability to read and see themselves in urban signs is what planners should strive for rather than imposing schemes for imperial or state legibility or external prestige. Bringing ilé and their values of care to the surface and making them the prominent features in the landscape and representations of it—similar in ways to what Lawson created with his 1885 map of great Lagos houses—is a different project than empire building or policing Lagos's urban order. What such a city and its maps would look like is open-ended, but it will surely not result in the "Dubai" or "New York" of Africa.

Imagining and rendering a different Lagos housing landscape in ways that can create buy-in and support from residents and politicians will require talented artists, architects, cartographers, tour guides, preservationists, and city planners. Artists like Zina Saro-Wiwa are starting with the work of showing how Lagos housing faces crisis and needs reflection. In the face of this crisis, Harrison suggests we might move forward by *regrounding* the house as a human place by creating "a humic architecture . . . palpably haunted by the earth in which the existential and historical past ultimately come to rest."[75] Architects and planners will not solve Lagos's housing crisis alone, but imaginative designers who listen to Lagosians and draw on historical lessons and what security has looked like in the past can help us imagine what the city can be.

House Dreams

So much emphasis in architectural discourses continues to extol "newness": a new vision for housing or a "new urban agenda" generates buzz. Ironically, this kind of architectural talk is as old and as failed a trope as exists in Lagos. As the Sudanese architect Ola Hassanain and the "diasporic Afrarealist" Egbert Alejandro Martina write, any evocation of something "new" in architecture "repeats a prior erasure" in imagining that there could possibly be a tabula rasa "as if what came prior has ended or was never there."[76] Architecture in any landscape is a form

Conclusion

of iteration. Intentionally probing and recovering the past for inspiration and for the kind of regrounding Harrison describes are a path forward as we imagine housing as caretaking and plot the political and policy course to realize it. Hassanain and Martina, in a vein similar to Mbembe's, describe how humanity is rushing into irreversible climate catastrophe by assuming that we can continue along "modernity's linear time" forward with its fantasies of "newness" as apolitical fixes for crises. They tell us that Black livingness, which Europeans mistook for "Black as a void of historical movement," means living "in a folded temporal field—we are coeval with the dead."[77] In an age when paradigms of economic degrowth are gaining mainstream attention as modes of planetary caretaking, the attributes of a society of ilé that were perceived as "historical stillness" in landscapes like Yorubaland before and during colonialism take on a different light. Custodianship can look like ahistoricity to societies consumed with possession.

Any dream of reiterating elements of the past into a more secure future for Lagosians today will entail political struggles and radically reshaping the city's housing approaches and incentives. How can this begin?

For decades, housing policy has focused on market-based solutions or small-scale upgrading as planners and officials saw the problems that arose from the ambitious midcentury state-directed plans. As historian of Tanzanian socialism Priya Lal writes, "Many scholars ... have ... in universally condemning large-scale state-led development initiatives for adhering to a totalizing, simplifying 'developmentalist' logic, fallen victim to a tendency toward overgeneralization ... [and] reproduced ... a neoliberal narrative of the state as villain."[78] Recognition that alleviating the current housing crisis requires resources and the custodianship of empowered states is being revived in academic and policy literature.[79]

Lagos State's government has tremendous power to remake the city's housing conditions and broader housing ethos. A visionary leader and shrewd municipal government could leverage its authority over land provided by Nigeria's 1978 Land Use Act to prioritize tenure security and real estate developments that create affordable mass housing. Few cities have this head start of what their legal codes make possible. But currently the political will in Lagos is lacking, and a fear of spooking global capital is omnipresent.[80] The United Nations special rapporteur who evaluated the city in 2019 came away with the impression that

"Nigeria's housing sector is in a complete crisis. There is no current national housing action plan or strategy. Coordination and communication between federal and state governments seems lacking. . . . I was shocked to see that the communities most in need of protection and assistance by the state are instead persecuted, harassed, extorted and even arrested and jailed without having ever committed a crime."[81] Political organization—the kind of work that groups like Justice and Empowerment Initiatives are doing—is needed to advocate for these secure housing priorities and to hold politicians to account. Currently, political will to take housing and flooding seriously is missing.[82]

Motivated policymakers who seek to address Lagos's many colliding challenges might be wise to ground their overall strategic plan in housing. This would make policy sense in a city where houses have historically been the single most important strategic instruments. The planning literature is beginning to agree. In a well-received essay, "The Housing Theory of Everything," three experts on housing argue that societal issues as wide ranging as climate change, economic inequality, poor health outcomes, and financial instability are all loosely connected but made worse by housing shortages, insecurity, and long commutes.[83] Targeting ways to make housing more available and governed by principles of custodianship could bring back a dream of making a home for oneself and one's kin that has escaped so many over the last century in Lagos.

Lagos is nothing if not resilient and, as a century and a half of upheaval to its landscapes make clear, change is possible. Ultimately its health and endurance will be bound up in how it houses its people, for, as Lagos historian Margaret Peil once wrote, *the city is the people.*

Notes

Introduction

1. Bigon, "The Former Names of Lagos (Nigeria) in Historical Perspective."
2. See Daré, "Beaten, Raped and Forced to Work."
3. For a discussion of the discourses that often focus on Lagos's "dirtiness," see Newell, *Histories of Dirt*.
4. Mbembe and Nuttall, "Writing the World," 348.
5. As Mbembe and Nuttall note in "Writing the World," many observers of the urban development paradigm "approach the [African] city as a problem to be solved. . . . In the process, they underplay many other aspects of city life and city forms" (358).
6. The theorist Homi Bhabha and the geographer Edward Soja describe them as "third spaces" to capture how "real" and "imagined" spaces interact and enter into motion. For historians of urban centers, the dense theories of Henri Lefebvre that Soja was reinterpreting and applying in his writings on Los Angeles are an appealing theory of change. Bhabha and Soja provide a framework for thinking about how seemingly static spaces move and the processes through which they are "produced" over time. Lefebvre and Soja add an elusive yet vital synapse—a space of interchange—to traditional historical dialectics between material and social. See Soja, *Thirdspace*; and Bhabha, *Location of Culture*.
7. See, for example, Quayson, *Oxford Street*; De Boeck, "Inhabiting Ocular Ground"; Larkin, *Signal and Noise*; Melly, *Bottleneck*; and Emily Callaci, *Street Archives and City Life*. For a review of the themes, methods, and possibilities to come out of these studies of African cities, see Guyer, "Describing Urban 'No Man's Land' in Africa."
8. Mbembe and Nuttall, "Writing the World," 348.
9. Robinson, *Ordinary Cities*.
10. Agbiboa, "Stomach Infrastructure."
11. Olukoju, *Infrastructure Development and Urban Facilities in Lagos*.

224   Notes to Pages 7–16

12. Simone, "People as Infrastructure."
13. In "Describing Urban 'No Man's Land' in Africa," Guyer reminds us "of [Bronisław] Malinowski's admonition that we should study what 'looms paramount' in people's lives" (477).
14. See Duerksen, "Making Africa's Megalopolis."
15. The term *facade* is derived from the Latin *facere:* "to make."
16. Mbembe and Nuttall, introduction to *Johannesburg: The Elusive Metropolis;* all quotes in this paragraph from pp. 22 and 28.
17. Newell, *Histories of Dirt,* 3. Newell and Ademide Adelusi-Adeluyi have recently explored African Lagosians' cultural imaginaries of uncleanliness and urban geography respectively. See Newell, *Histories of Dirt;* and Adelusi-Adeluyi, "Africa for the Africans?"
18. Mbembe and Nuttall, 22, 28; Scott, "Colonialism, Landscape and the Subterranean."
19. Simone, *The Surrounds.*
20. Olinto, *The Water House.*
21. Ogundiran, *The Yorùbá,* 82; see also 47–52.
22. King, *The Bungalow,* 193.
23. For a summary of these discourses that imagined African landscapes as "natural" ("all that exists prior to civil society") in contrast to "civilized" European landscapes, see Comaroff and Comaroff, "Africa Observed: Discourses on Imperial Imagination," 1:86–125.
24. The journalist Nurith Aizenman writes, "It's important to be sensitive to the way Africa has been historically portrayed in the Western world, opined Dixon Chibanda, a psychiatrist from Zimbabwe. And too often, he said,'the word "hut" has been associated not only with poverty, but with an inferior type of lifestyle'" ("Is It Insulting to Call This a Hut?").
25. Sluyter, *Colonialism and Landscape.*
26. Geary, "Early Images from Benin at the National Museum of African Art," 46–48.
27. Importantly, however, this does not mean that housing landscapes and material conditions in African countries should be considered "equal" to elsewhere in the world either. As James Ferguson writes, "Local [African] discourses on modernity more often insist on seeing a continuing lack . . . a lack that is understood in terms not of a cultural inferiority but of a political-economic inequality. For this reason, the question of modernity is widely apprehended in Africa in relation to the concept of 'development' and the issue of social and economic standards of living" (*Global Shadows,* 33).
28. Schoenauer, *6,000 Years of Housing.*
29. As Tanis Hinchcliffe writes, "There is a difference between housing history and the history of houses. The first has to do with the production of houses and their occupation. The second is concerned primarily with

Notes to Pages 16–22   225

their physical presence, and the aim of the best studies is to unite the two" ("Pandora's Box: Forty Years of Housing History," 3).

30. Engels, *The Housing Question.*

31. Davis, *Planet of Slums,* 70–94.

32. Adekemi and Olugbenga, "Challenges of Housing Delivery in Metropolitan Lagos," 3, citing Oshodi, "Housing, Population and Development in Lagos, Nigeria." Estimates of Lagos's population are notoriously political, as Nigerian federal budgets are distributed based on the official census. The 2006 national census (parts of which were declared invalid in court) estimated a population of 9 million for Lagos, whereas Lagos State projected that the 2016 population reached over 23 million. In this context, the widely cited Lagos housing deficit of 5 million units deserves further scrutiny. For an estimate of a deficit of 2.9 million units, see Roland Igbinoba Real Foundation for Housing & Urban Development, *The State of Lagos Housing Market,* 2:85.

33. Wetzstein, "The Global Urban Housing Affordability Crisis."

34. Mbembe and Nuttall, introduction to *Johannesburg: The Elusive Metropolis,* 15.

35. Croese, Cirolia, and Graham, "Towards Habitat III."

36. Nikuze, Sliuzas, Flacke, van Maarseveen, "Livelihood Impacts of Displacement and Resettlement on Informal Households."

37. Robert Pogue Harrison interpreted Heiddeger's quote "The talk about the house of Being is no transfer of the image 'house' to Being. But one day we will, by thinking the essence of Being in a way appropriate to its matter, more readily be able to think what 'house' and 'to dwell' are" as meaning "It is by thinking the essence of a house that we will come to know what being is" (*Dominion of the Dead,* 37–38).

38. Johnson, *The History of the Yorubas from the Earliest Times to the Beginning of the British Protectorate,* 90.

39. As Strother writes, "[Frobenius] marveled at the 'gorgeous' coloration, the sculptural variety, the mixing of materials: 'The whole scene . . . was superbly impressive'" ("Breaking Juju," 21).

40. Frobenius, *The Voice of Africa,* 1:149–50, 153.

41. Frobenius, 1:326.

42. Frobenius, 1:324.

43. Frobenius, 1:348.

44. See Derricourt, *Inventing Africa,* 105–10.

45. Law, "The 'Hamitic Hypothesis' in Indigenous West African Historical Thought."

46. Gutkind, "African Urban Studies."

47. Wheatley, "The Significance of Traditional Yoruba Urbanism," 393.

48. Wheatley, 423. Yoruba and, more broadly, African urbanism continue to be described as resulting from outside forces. Historian Laurent Fourchard

writes, "From the perspective of economic history, trans-Saharan and trans-atlantic trade and Western capitalism are effectively seen as the determining forces of the urbanization process. Such a perspective tends to downplay the role of political leaders at the local, national, or regional levels in shaping multiple urban forms on the continent"; one of Fourchard's examples of this way of relegating African cities to secondary forces is the work of Anthony King ("Between World History and State Formation," 239).

49. The plans for the university were supported by British officials who had no idea of how to begin reading Yoruba landscapes. As architectural historian Tim Livsey describes, "metropolitan experts," examining the plot for the future University of Ibadan—"their eyes unattuned to West African agriculture"—saw land so uninhabited (a terra nullus redux) that one remarked, "In a few minutes you could be out of sight and sound of anything that reminded you of higher education or Western Civilisation." However, a local official with more experience pointed out that there were in fact "40 or 50 villages of two or three mud huts" on the land ("Suitable Lodgings for Students," 676).

50. Fathy, *Gourna: A Tale of Two Villages.*

51. Pyla, "Hassan Fathy Revisited."

52. Silverstein, "Of Rooting and Uprooting."

53. Bourdieu, "The Kabyle House or the World Reversed." In chapter 1, Bourdieu critiques his own early works, pioneering poststructuralist ways of tracing how human inhabit their worlds.

54. Ojo, "Traditional Yoruba Architecture," 17, emphasis added.

55. More recently, David T. Doris has written of how Yoruba-speaking landscapes are rich with objects that communicate discernible messages to those who know how to read them. See Doris, *Vigilant Things.*

56. Blier, "Vernacular Architecture."

57. Among several works of Lévi-Strauss discussing *sociétés à maisons,* see Lévi-Strauss, *The Way of the Masks.* For a discussion of Yoruba houses as sociétés à maisons, see Ogundiran, *The Yorùbá,* 47–52. Studies of African sociétés à maisons include Kus and Raharijaona, "Domestic Space and the Tenacity of Tradition among Some Betsileo of Madagascar," and Donley, "A Structuring Structure," both in *Domestic Architecture and the Use of Space*; Kuper, "The 'House' and Zulu Political Structure in the Nineteenth Century." For an overview of studies pertaining to "the household" in Africa, see Guyer, "Household and Community in African Studies."

58. Carsten and Hugh-Jones, introduction to *About the House,* 4.

59. Blier, *The Anatomy of Architecture,* 1.

60. Blier, 2.

61. Trevor H. J. Marchand pushed this thesis farther in his 2007 work on the clay structures several hundred miles north in Djenné, working alongside

Notes to Pages 26–32   227

masons to learn their trade and how they planned, created, and rejuvenated their buildings over time. See *The Masons of Djenné*.

62. Meier, *Swahili Port Cities*; Steven Nelson, *From Cameroon to Paris*.

63. Melly and De Boeck have recently drawn, respectively, on the stages of construction and reappropriated afterlife of buildings in their ethnographies of African urban housing. See Melly, *Bottleneck*; and De Boeck, "Inhabiting Ocular Ground."

64. Morton, *Age of Concrete: Housing and the Shape of Aspiration in the Capital of Mozambique*. Also see Miescher, *A Dam for Africa*; and Smith, *Nairobi in the Making*. Historians of the empire have more readily embraced architecture as a "textured" source, examining how buildings were part of the technologies European powers employed in the pursuit of colonial hegemony, reflective of imperial ideologies and tensions. For a recent overview of the field and its literature, see Bremner, ed., *Architecture and Urbanism in the British Empire*; for colonial architecture in an African context, see Demissie, ed., *Colonial Architecture and Urbanism in Africa*; and for the British Atlantic see Maudlin and Herman, eds., *Building the British Atlantic World*. Important histories of colonial housing in Africa with varying degrees of vernacular context include King, *The Bungalow*; Home, *Of Planning and Planting*; Miescher, "Building the City of the Future"; Bloch, "Statis and Slums"; and Myers, *Verandahs of Power*. Myers returned to the subject of his book and incorporated local context in Richard Harris and Garth Myers, "Hybrid Housing."

65. Morton, *Age of Concrete*, 9.

66. Morton, 11.

67. Mitchell, ed., *Landscape and Power*, 2, 5. For collections discussing African landscapes, see Beardsley, *Cultural Landscape Heritage in Sub-Saharan Africa*; and Ute Luig and Achim von Oppen, eds., "The Making of African Landscapes."

68. I return to Harrison's ideas in the conclusion, "Flooding."

69. Mitchell, *Landscape and Power*, 17. He elaborates, "These semiotic features of landscape [the protected, shaded spot of the viewer and its connection to feelings of hunting, war, and surveillance], and the historical narratives they generate, are tailor-made for the discourse of imperialism, which conceives itself precisely (and simultaneously) as an expansion of landscape understood as an inevitable, progressive development in history, an expansions of 'culture' and 'civilization' into a 'natural' space in a progress that is itself narrated as 'natural'" (17).

70. Bunn writes of how landscapes were "exported from metropolitan Britain to the imperial periphery" in "Our Wattled Cot" (127).

71. As Mann notes, there are few sources available for Lagos's early history compared to other West African coastal cities due to the fact that Lagos was relatively small and only regionally influential until the nineteenth

228   Notes to Pages 33–38

century; see Mann, *Slavery and the Birth of an African City*, 17. For accounts of Lagos's origins, see Mann, *Slavery and the Birth of an African City*, 23–50; Aderibigbe, "Early History of Lagos to about 1850"; Losi, *History of Lagos*; and Agiri and Barnes, "Lagos Before 1603." For architectural insights into Lagos's early history, see Agiri, "Architecture as a Source of History"; and Akinsemoyin and Vaughan-Richards, *Building Lagos*, 3–10.

72. Mann, *Slavery and the Birth of an African City*, 24.

73. Writing of in-home burial patterns among Yoruba people, Ogundiran writes, "Ancestral shrines anchored members of the *ilé* in place and reaffirmed the cohesion and permanence of the House" (*The Yorùbá*, 77).

74. Bigon, "The Former Names of Lagos," 229–40.

75. Law, "Trade and Politics behind the Slave Coast."

76. See Johnson, *The History of the Yorubas from the Earliest Times to the Beginning of the British Protectorate*, chap. 6.

77. Mann, *Slavery and the Birth of an African City*, 27–29, but as Patrick Cole writes, "The origins of the Obaship of Lagos are ancient, controversial and essentially obscure" (*Modern and Traditional Elites in the Politics of Lagos*, 15).

78. Cole, *Modern*, 11–14; Mann, *Slavery and the Birth of an African City*, 28.

79. Gbade Aladeojebi, *History of Yoruba Land*, 331. While the ìdéjọ are officially the "landed" chiefs of Lagos, at the time of the Treaty of Cession (1861), it was established that the other two grades of white-capped chiefs also had legitimate claims to land rights; the Treaty stated: "[The White Capped chiefs] are the rightful possessors of the land.... [The King] and War-men hold no rights unless by grant from the White Capped chiefs." Other scholars have understood white-capped chiefs to include ìdéjọ chiefs, leading to confusion regarding the now widely accepted claims to land by àkárígbéré and ògáládé chiefs.

80. Productive activities within the compound were organized by ilé temi. See Mann, *Slavery and the Birth of an African City*, 26.

81. Agiri, "Architecture as a Source"; Krapf-Askari, *Yoruba Towns and Cities*, 70–72.

82. Ogundiran, *The Yorùbá*, 47–48.

83. Iliffe, *The African Poor: A History*, 7; Mann, *Slavery and the Birth of an African City*, 26.

84. Mann, *Slavery and the Birth of an African City*, 43; Agiri, "Architecture," 345; Scala, *Memoirs of Giambattista Scala*; Smith, *The Lagos Consulate*.

85. For debates over the reasons behind the British bombardment and annexation of Lagos, see Mann, *Slavery and the Birth of an African City*, 84–85; Ajayi, "The British Occupation of Lagos, 1851–1861"; Smith, *The Lagos Consulate*, 33; and Hopkins, "Property Rights and Empire Building."

86. Glover's 1859 map notes that it is based in part on an 1846 survey of Lagos River and its surroundings.

Notes to Pages 38–44

87. Mann, *Slavery and the Birth of an African City*, 97.
88. Brown, "A History of the People of Lagos," 61.
89. Brown, 49.
90. George, *Making Modern Girls*, 24.
91. Quoted in Kirk-Greene, *Britain's Imperial Administrators*, 219.
92. The comment on the channel (added after 1877) states, "Caution. Several important changes have taken place at the entrance since Lt. Glover's Survey and the Spit off Bruce Pt. is reported to have extended about a ¼ of a mile. The channel in 1877 was marked by 3 buoys on its western side. H.M.S. Tourmaline. A Red light 47 feet high is said to be situated on the beach eastward of the Lagoon at Lagos."
93. Whitford, *Trading Life in Western and Central Africa*, 87.

Chapter 1: Bar

1. For a processual reading of peri-urban Lagos, see Lindsay Sawyer, "Piecemeal Urbanisation at the Peripheries of Lagos." For a description of the "mobile architecture" of classic Lagos buses, see Osinulu, "Painters, Blacksmiths and Wordsmiths." Osinulu suggests Molue buses got their name from their propensity to "mold together" human limbs in their frequent accidents. Emeka Udemba recently turned a Molue bus into a traveling art exhibit titled *Molue Mobile Museum of Contemporary Art*. See Obidike Okafor's interview with Emeka Udemba, "When Are You Coming Back to Our Street?"
2. Much of this chapter is informed by and in conversation with the work of these three authors.
3. Macdonald, *H Is for Hawk*, 116.
4. Burton, *Wanderings in West Africa from Liverpool to Fernando Po*, 2:204.
5. In the 1890s, detailed depth charts and specially outfitted heavy iron steamships with a depth of 6 feet made bar crossings safer but more expensive. In 1907 the British brought the steam dredger *Egerton* to Lagos to deepen the bar to 10.5 feet. Between 1908 and 1937, the bar was stabilized and deepened again to 27 feet through further dredging and the construction of three large stone moles, a plan proposed by Messrs. Coode and Partners in 1892. See Hopkins, "An Economic History of Lagos," 339–55; Mabogunje, *Urbanization in Nigeria*, 246–50; Akinsemoyin and Vaughan-Richards, *Building Lagos*, 40; and Godwin and Hopwood, *Sandbank City*, 61–63. The title of Godwin and Hopwood's excellent architectural book, *Sandbank City*, is a reference to the fact that, as Brown writes, "the island barely deserved its status [as an island]; for judging from its many permanent creeks, lagoons, and swamps, not to mention large flooded areas during the rains and/or high tides, sand bar would have been a more appropriate designation" ("A History of the People of Lagos," 3).

6. These decades were the time between the British bombardment of 1851 and the 1890s groundwork (including racist policies and punitive expeditions) for the infrastructural and administrative expansion of the colony. This term is inspired by Joanne Nagel Shaw's architectural description of "The Flower of Lagos Phase." "Historic Buildings of Lagos, Nigeria," 16–18.

7. Notable deaths that contributed to the turbulence of the 1880s and 1890s included Ọba Dosunmu (1885), beloved native king of Lagos since 1853; Madam Tinubu (1887), a wealthy local trader and powerbroker; John Hawley Glover (1885), respected administrator of the colony, 1863–72; and perhaps the most enduringly famous, Samuel Ajayi Crowther (1891), the first African bishop ordained in the Anglican Church and the original translator of the Bible into Yoruba. Litigation, especially around issues of property, was constant during this period.

8. There were fewer than 111 Europeans in the city of thirty thousand in the 1880s. Between 1872 and 1877, Lagos was governed from Freetown, Sierra Leone, and then from the Gold Coast. Most of the Europeans in Lagos were merchants while the thin British administrative presence was what Spencer H. Brown has described as "colonialism on the cheap" ("Colonialism on the Cheap," 551).

9. Gore, "Neils Walwin Holm"; Gbadegesin, "Picturing the Modern Self"; Gbadegesin, "Photographer Unknown."

10. Echeruo, *Victorian Lagos*; França, "Producing Intellectuals."

11. Sawada, "The Educated Elite and Associational Life in Early Lagos Newspapers," 92–125. See also Shaw, "Historic Buildings of Lagos, Nigeria," 16.

12. On average, two-thirds of Lagos's government revenue came from import duties on the more than one million gallons of liquor imported annually in the 1880s and the more than two million in the 1890s. For these figures and recorded descriptions of excess in Lagos, see Brown, "A History of the People of Lagos," 211–14, 292–95; and Heap, "A Bottle of Gin Is Dangled before the Nose of the Native"; Echeruo, *Victorian Lagos*, 32.

13. The architectural conservation group Legacy 1995 (http://legacy1995.org .ng/) continues to restore buildings, educate, and fight for the preservation of Lagos architecture in the face of much government indifference. For an overview of the work and history of Legacy 1995, see Godwin and Hopwood, *Sandbank City*, part 8; and Gaestel, "How Long Is Now?" I am grateful to several members of Legacy 1995 for taking me on tours and providing me with material on Lagos's historic buildings. The illegal but yet unprosecuted destruction of Lagos's architectural heritage was recently covered internationally by CNN and *The Economist*. See Jean-François and Giles, "Lagos' Afro-Brazilian Architecture" and "Bulldozing History."

Notes to Pages 47–50

14. The map is inscribed "*Plan of the Town of Lagos West Coast of Africa,* Prepared for the Lagos Executive Commissioners of the Col. And Indian Exhibition 1886 . . . , by W.T.C. Lawson, C. E., &c. (Native of West Africa), Asst. Colonial Surveyor—Lagos. 30 December 1885. Corrected to June 1887." "W.T.C. Lawson" is a misprint; it should read "W.T.G. Lawson": William Tevi George Lawson.

15. *Lagos Standard,* December 17, 1913.

16. Jones and Sebald, *An African Family Archive,* 155. See also Herskovits Kopytoff, *A Preface to Modern Nigeria,* 291–92; França, "Producing Intellectuals," 188–200.

17. *Lagos Observer,* May 24, 1883. The guests included the bride's uncle Samuel Crowther as well as R. A. Coker, C. B. Macaulay, J. J. Thomas, among others.

18. Scholars were establishing the field of African history at the same moment many African countries were becoming independent in the 1950s and 1960s. A major question of the day was the character and origin of the "elites" who were leading their countries to independence. For an overview of this literature, see Mann, *Marrying Well,* 1, 133–34; Mann, "A Social History of the New African Elite in Lagos Colony," 1–5; Sawada, "The Educated Elite," 17–20; and França, "Producing Intellectuals," 118–21.

19. As noted in the second paragraph of Lawson's obituary, *Lagos Standard,* December 17, 1913. Lawson's own home appears on his map in the southeasternmost edge of the city near the telegraph company and colonial hospital. It is interesting to speculate why he would have chosen to distance himself from the center of town when he was well connected through his daughter and her well-regarded family, the Crowthers. It is tempting to suggest that true to his profession, he preferred to observe the city from somewhat of a distance. His salary would not have put him in the dominant class, but he may have had family money.

20. Mann, *Marrying Well,* 2–5; Cole, *Modern and Traditional Elites,* 41. Mann more fully theorizes the differences between class and status and argues that those with elite status in Lagos distinguished themselves through their skills and culture rather than through their control over production or of the political process, though she acknowledges that status did help elites gain wealth and influence, which in turn helped them to maintain their status. I should note that Mann uses the term "elite" in reference to "elite theory" while I use it more broadly in relation to the dominant class, those at the top of society both in terms of economic and cultural power.

21. Cole, *Modern and Traditional Elites,* 41.

22. Mann, *Marrying Well,* 2.

23. Cole, *Modern and Traditional Elites,* 41.

24. Mann, *Marrying Well,* 2–4.

232 Notes to Pages 50–51

25. Mann, 5–6. Mann's methodology accounts for the importance of literacy and one's occupation in attaining elite status but is unable to account for Mann's own argument that how "the elite lived was as important for elite status as what it did" (*Marrying Well*, 4). As this chapter argues, not only *how* but *where* they lived offers a clue to who had attained the highest levels of elite status in nineteenth-century Lagos.

26. The historical depth of claims to "tradition" from the era are far from clear as the onset of colonialism sparked new claims to tradition over landownership, suzerainty, and decision-making rights. See Mann, *Slavery and the Birth of an African City*, 238–39; and Cole, *Modern and Traditional Elites*, 26. See also *Lewis v. Bankole* (1909) on unreliability of native "expert" witnesses in Irving, *A Collection of the Principal Enactments and Cases Related to Titles to Land in Nigeria*, 217–38.

27. Between 1880 and 1890, 80 and 90 percent of all exports from Lagos were palm products; Hopkins, "An Economic History of Lagos," 29. For debates over how the trade was organized in the interior, see Berry, *Cocoa, Custom and Socio-economic Change in Rural Western Nigeria*, 25–26; and Hopkins, "Economic Imperialism in West Africa: Lagos, 1880–1892."

28. On the prominence of chiefs, ọbas, and bàbá ìsàlẹ̀s, see Cole, *Modern and Traditional Elites*, 24–29; On moneylenders, see Hopkins, "An Economic History of Lagos," 200–201.

29. Examples of this crossover are numerous. Mann's list of the names of "educated" elites includes parenthetical Yoruba names for dozens of individuals, and Sawada provides examples from newspapers of local men announcing changing their names from English to Yoruba. Mann, *Marrying Well*, appendix, 128–32; Sawada, "The Educated Elite," 235.

30. Mann, *Marrying Well*, 4.

31. Bourdieu, *Distinction*, 114. See also Bourdieu, "The Forms of Capital," 241–58. Other types of "capital" were also in play in nineteenth-century Lagos political and social life. For a description of the cultivation of what Christopher Brown later called "moral capital," see Ajayi, *Christian Missions in Nigeria*.

32. Doris notes that the "Yoruba model of àṣà as a culturally limiting 'tradition' characterized by constant innovation (Yai 1994:113) is uncannily similar in its form and implication to sociologist Pierre Bourdieu's (1977) conception of habitus. For Bourdieu, habitus is a kind of 'cultural unconscious,' an internalized system of collectively held codes of thought, feeling, and behavior that allow a person to act with consistency within established fields of ordinary practice" (*Vigilant Things*, 41).

33. Olukoju, "Accumulation and Conspicuous Consumption," 209. Olukoju's chapter draws on Falola, *The Political Economy of a Pre-colonial African State*, 71.

Notes to Pages 51–54   233

34. Sawada, "The Educated Elite and Associational Life," 19–21.

35. As Cole describes, a local newspaper editor E. O. Macaulay wrote in 1883 how the top class of Lagos "absorbed by its influence all other 'societies'" (*Modern and Traditional Elites*, 47).

36. Since the publication of Cole (1975) and Mann (1985), many scholars, beginning with Paul Gilroy, developed a concept of the "hybridity" of the cosmopolitan cultures of the Black Atlantic (see Gilroy, *The Black Atlantic*). Blending cultures and straddling economies, nineteenth-century Lagos elites became what Radcliffe, Scott, and Werner call "true 'cosmopolitans,'" who, by employing a "politics of hybridity," leveraged their position in Lagos to enrich themselves and to accomplish "cultural mastery" (introduction to *Anywhere but Here*, 4, 9, 15). Lindsay describes hybridity in regard to Lagos Brazilians, writing, "Brazilians were able to mobilize their affiliations strategically, emphasizing their status as Brazilians, immigrants, Yorubas or Egbas when their social, political or economic positions would benefit" ("To Return to the Bosom of their Fatherland," 31).

37. See Herskovits Kopytoff, *A Preface to Modern Nigeria*, 299.

38. Sawada, "The Educated Elite," 224.

39. Sawada, 222–35; França, "Producing Intellectuals," 171–201. For a discussion of the role of Lawson's map in presenting Lagos as a harmonious and orderly colonial city (at the expense of geographic accuracy at times) during the exhibition, see Adelusi-Adeluyi, "Historical Tours of 'New' Lagos."

40. As Mann points out, within a Weberian economic concept of class "in commercial cities like Lagos credit often formed the basis of class stratification" (*Marrying Well*, 2).

41. I have culled this incomplete and undoubtedly imperfect list of houses, dates, and original owners from conversations with members of Legacy 1995; Shaw, "Historic Buildings of Lagos, Nigeria"; Akinsemoyin and Vaughan-Richards, *Building Lagos*; Godwin and Hopwood, interview at their residence in Cheltenham Spa (April 12, 2017); Godwin and Hopwood, *Sandbank City*; Alonge, "Afro-Brazilian Architecture in Lagos State"; Aradeon, "Planning Lagos"; Agiri, "Architecture as a Source of History," 347–48.

42. Cole, *Modern and Traditional Elites*, 1. In her later scholarship on the history of slavery in Lagos, Mann examines how fundamental changes to the organization of land and housing made real estate a critical battleground in the reorganization of society as slavery was slowly stamped out under British rule; see Mann, *Slavery and the Birth of an African City*.

43. The origin of the name "Fernandez" for the house is unclear. While most sources have claimed that Fernandez was a Brazilian slave merchant, Femke van Zeijl suggests that the name derives from a Spanish merchant named José Amoedo Fernandez who came to Lagos via Brazil and was

234 Notes to Pages 54–56

well established on the plot by the 1880s. This would mean that an individual named Fernandez lived in the house after the consulate government supposedly seized it and auctioned it. One intriguing hypothesis is that the Fernandez was able to return to Lagos and reclaim the house, reinventing himself as a Spanish "wine and spice" merchant rather than a Portuguese slave trader. Van Zeijl writes that the house then passed to a friend of José Fernandez, Napoleon Rey Couto, who lived in it until his death in 1918, at which point it was auctioned. Femke van Zeijl, "Telling New Stories of Ilojo Bar: An Invitation," Legacy, https://mcusercontent.com/f66694a4deeb825a673c0b934/files/bcd4119b-0055-b84a-aaf9-6addb6b998e6/telling_new_stories_of_ilojo_bar_an_invitation.pdf.

44. Alonge, "Afro-Brazilian Architecture in Lagos State," 263–64; Tigidam, "The Fernandez House in Lagos: Relic of an Afro-Brazilian Past."

45. Mann, *Marrying Well*, 84. The average sizes of Lagos estates were: £1,499 for merchants, £300 for professionals, and £34 for colonial servants (Mann, 33). Alonge claims Thomas resold the house to Alfred Omolona Olaiya, "Afro-Brazilian Architecture in Lagos State," 263. However, most sources suggest that Alfred Olaiya (godson of the original Fernandez and father of the famous highlife musician Victor Olaiya) did not buy the house until 1934 or 1933, a decade after Andrew W. Thomas had died; "FG Vows to Punish Collaborators in the Demolition of 'Ilojo Bar'—a National Monument in Lagos."

46. After a career as a clerk and registrar for Colonial Civil Service, Thomas made an enormous fortune as an auctioneer, "famously procuring the contract for [the] disposal of German assets after WW[I]" (Keazor, "The 100 Greatest Nigerians We Never Knew Pt 1"). See also Shaw, "Historic Buildings of Lagos, Nigeria," 22–24; Akinsemoyin and Vaughan-Richards, *Building Lagos*, 17; and Agiri, "Architecture as a Source of History," 348.

47. Mann, *Slavery and the Birth of an African City*, 247–49.

48. Mann, 251–53; Brown, "A History of the People of Lagos," 103–5.

49. Tony Godwin (son of John Godwin and Gillian Hopwood), "The Brazilian Influence on Buildings in Lagos," 4–5.

50. In which case collective or family rights were upheld. Mann, *Slavery and the Birth of an African City*, 255.

51. An earlier sketch of Lawson's 1885 map was "produced in 1883 in response to complaints about the lingering swamps in the city" (Adelusi-Adeluyi, "Africa for the Africans?").

52. Mann, *Slavery and the Birth of an African City*, 262–74.

53. Mann, 263–64. On indigenous forms of credit, see Falola, "Pawnship in Colonial Southwestern Nigeria."

54. Mann, "The Rise of Taiwo Olowo," 87.

Notes to Pages 57–58   235

55. For details of Taiwo's life, see Mann, "The Rise of Taiwo Olowo"; Mann, *Slavery and the Birth of an African City*; Olukoju, "Accumulation and Conspicuous Consumption"; Akinsemoyin and Vaughan-Richards, *Building Lagos*, 13, 21; Cole, *Modern and Traditional Elites*, chaps. 1–3; and Losi, *History of Lagos*.

56. Mann, "The Rise of Taiwo Olowo," 92; his origins are murky and other sources (perhaps at Taiwo's behest after he established himself) claim he descended from the *ọlọfin* of Isheri; Akinsemoyin and Vaughan-Richards, *Building Lagos*, 13.

57. Mann, "The Rise of Taiwo Olowo," 93, citing Losi, *History of Lagos*, 82–83. It is unclear if Taiwo purchased this land or was allowed to occupy it under native custom. Eventually he took out a Crown grant for the property (94).

58. Mann, "The Rise of Taiwo Olowo," 93. Once the British outlawed of slavery, acquiring a loyal following of laborers became crucial for powerful merchants. Mann describes how many domestic slaves (or former slaves) absconded or switched households by becoming a powerful man's *asáforíge* (boy) (*Slavery and the Birth of an African City*, 295). Taiwo's palace and numerous properties helped him in luring "boys" away from other Big Men with the promise of shelter and the ample trading opportunities he could provide in exchange for labor. For an example of Taiwo convincing "boys" to desert their overlords and pledge themselves to him, see Mann, *Slavery and the Birth of an African City*, 299–300 (although in this instance the boys had a change of heart once they risked paying cash back rent for disloyalty to their former overlords).

59. Mann, "The Rise of Taiwo Olowo," 93–94. Mann writes that "if G. L. Gaiser required that Taiwo pledge property to secure credit, the firm's agent did not register the agreement at the colonial land office. Gaiser may have given Taiwo credit on trust, thanks to Lieutenant-Governor Glover's introduction. In 1866 Taiwo traded for a short time with the Hamburg firm William O'Swald, which asked him to mortgage a property at the Marina in return for 'money and goods lent from time-to-time' (LLR, mortgage, Taiwo to Phillippi, 1866). In 1867, the agent for Regis Ainé, a French firm, lent Taiwo goods and money sufficient to buy 40,000 gallons of palm oil, and Taiwo guaranteed this large loan by mortgaging seventeen properties."

60. Mann, 94, 100.

61. Mann, 94, 100.

62. Mann, 96–97, 100; although, according to Mann, he "seems to have been as interested in disciplining people as he was in recovering land and capital."

63. For a sketch of the monument, see Akinsemoyin and Vaughan-Richards, *Building Lagos*, 21. For photographs, see 104–5. Mann writes that "his bones kept developers at bay during the real estate boom of the 1970s

and 1980s bespeaks his lasting importance in Lagos's history," "The Rise of Taiwo Olowo," 101.

64. Brown, "A History of the People of Lagos," 155–56; Hopkins, "An Economic History of Lagos," 59–60; Akinsemoyin and Vaughan-Richards, *Building Lagos*, 15–22. As Hopkins describes, by the 1880s large several-acre "factories" run by large firms had been replaced by smaller outfits run out of private houses, which contained shops and stores within them ("An Economic History of Lagos," 60). Akyeampong describes how the 1880s rise of steamship companies as separate entities from expatriate firms made possible the proliferation of smaller trading outfits in West Africa by allowing African traders "to trade directly with Europe, bypassing expatriate merchants on the West African Coast" ("Commerce, Credit, and Mobility," 252–53, 236–38). However, this development not only opened opportunities to African traders but also incorporated more oil producers from Asia into the market, resulting in a depression of prices just as many new West African traders were entering the market directly for the first time (Akyeampong, "Commerce, Credit, and Mobility," 241).

65. Mann, *Marrying Well*, 19.

66. *The Lagos Observer* and *Eagle and Lagos Critic* quoted in Brown, "A History of the People of Lagos," 155.

67. Godwin and Hopwood note that the plaster was made of lime, fine lagoon sand, and seashells to form a low strength "stucco" that needed to be replaced frequently but not as often as it would have in the cold and snow of northern Europe (*Sandbank City*, 141–42).

68. Brown, "A History of the People of Lagos," 118, 154; Hopkins, "An Economic History of Lagos," 78; Mann, *Marrying Well*, 31; Mann, *Slavery and the Birth of an African City*, 268–69.

69. Brown, "A History of the People of Lagos," 141–43.

70. Several scholars have commented on the high level of suspicion between segments of societies in West African ports. See Cole, *Traditional and Modern*, 47–50; and Akyeampong, "Commerce, Credit, and Mobility," 232–33.

71. Hopkins, "An Economic History of Lagos," 53.

72. Akinsemoyin and Vaughan-Richards, *Building Lagos*, 21; Gbadegesin, "Picturing the Modern Self," 81.

73. Cole, *Traditional and Modern*, 47.

74. *Lagos Weekly Record*, February 23, 1901, quoted by Olukoju, "Accumulation and Conspicuous Consumption," 211; Mann, "The Rise of Taiwo Olowo," 101. Karin Barber describes this Yoruba culture venerated in Taiwo's obituary: "No single quality—whether power, wealth, possessions or people—is desired *in itself*. Wealth in itself is no use—it has to be spent generously to attract followers and to buy the symbols like beads, cloth and horses which confirm and embellish high status. The totality of desired qualities

Notes to Pages 60–62

is conceived of in the abstract as *ọlá*. *Ọlá* is the state attained by a man of substance: a state of sufficiency, respect, esteem and 'honor.'" Barber, "Documenting Social and Ideological Change through Yoruba Oriki," 46.

75. Barber, "Documenting Social and Ideological Change," 44–45. For a history of Ibadan and the Yoruba Wars, see Falola, *The Political Economy of a Pre-colonial African State.*

76. Cole, *Modern and Traditional Elites,* 45.

77. In this way the "houses" of Lagos differed from the "houses" Onwuka Dike describes in the Niger Delta that were corporately organized and not tied to an individual's identity and wealth (*Trade and Politics in the Niger Delta*).

78. Agiri, "Architecture as a Source of History," 345.

79. Many have noted the chronology of brickmaking in Lagos. See, for example, Agiri, "Architecture as a Source of History," 345–46.

80. Shaw recounts how Esan da Rocha and his heirs over several decades "built [Water House] on the most fashionable street of the Brazilian Quarter as a duplicate of the house [da Rocha] owned in Bahia" ("Historic Buildings of Lagos, Nigeria," 14).

81. See, for example, Curtin, "Medical Knowledge and Urban Planning in Tropical Africa."

82. Akinsemoyin and Vaughan-Richards, *Building Lagos,* 38.

83. Agiri, "Architecture as a Source of History," 345–46, 348.

84. Akinsemoyin and Vaughan-Richards, *Building Lagos,* 17; Vlach, "The Brazilian House in Nigeria," 7, 9.

85. Laotan, "Brazilian Influence on Lagos"; Akinsemoyin and Vaughan-Richards, *Building Lagos,* 23. For a description of the master craftsmen of the era, see Agiri, "Architecture as a Source of History," 349.

86. Laotan notes that Isaac A. Cole "opened a technological institute to train Lagos youths in carpentry and cabinet making" ("Brazilian Influence on Lagos," 164); Agiri notes that J. P. L. Davies founded an Industrial Training Institution in 1861 ("Architecture as a Source of History," 348).

87. Many prominent homes were built during this era as attested by the timeline found in Alonge, "Afro-Brazilian Architecture in Lagos State," 177–81.

88. Da Cunha, *From Slave Quarters to Town Houses;* da Cunha, "Brasileiros Nagos em Lagos no peculo XIX"; Marafatto, *Nigerian Brazilian Houses.*

89. Da Cunha, *From Slave Quarters to Town House,* 110; Shaw, "Historic Buildings of Lagos, Nigeria," 13.

90. Alonge, "Afro-Brazilian Architecture in Lagos State," chap. 9. Jack agrees, taking an openly pejorative view of Yoruba architecture, writing, "On Lagos Island the original native hut has been supplanted by more permanent structures based on West European and Latin American styles" ("Old Houses of Lagos," 96).

91. Vlach, "The Brazilian House in Nigeria," 3.

238   Notes to Pages 64–68

92. Titilola Euba quotes an 1883 article in the *Anglo African* regarding the Lagos culture of "dropping in": "So too are we not over-particular as to when we make a call, especially if it be on business, so that we do not arouse a man at midnight; and many of us are all the more pleased if a visitor calls at dinner time, for then we ask him to take a chair and be welcome, and if our neighbours are well behaved and respectable we don't usually make them feel that we esteem ourselves their superiors" ("Dress and Status in 19th Century Lagos," 155).

93. Euba cites examples of Saros adopting native dress, including a wedding registry of R. B. Blaize's niece that listed native cloth, and R. B. Blaize's daughters wearing "an unusual combination of *adire* 'tie dye' wrapper and differently patterned European prints as *buba*-like overblouse, headtie, and shawl" ("Dress and Status in 19th Century Lagos," 154, 160). In *The Liverpool of West Africa*, Olukoju writes that aso ebi did not come to Lagos until after 1920 but that *aso egbe* (dressing as members of same club or organization) did exist in Lagos earlier (133).

94. Barber, "Documenting Social and Ideological Change through Yoruba Oriki," 46.

95. Shaw, "Historic Buildings of Lagos, Nigeria," 25.

96. Cole, *Modern and Traditional Elites*, 45. Brazilians tended to be Catholic while Saros were typically Protestant. In the census, 14,797 Lagosians were identified as worshippers of Yoruba *orisha*.

97. A symbol that frequently appears on mosques in the Islamic world and eventually appeared on Nigerian currency. See Shaw, "Historic Buildings of Lagos, Nigeria," 22–23.

98. For photographs of Shitta Bey Mosque, Elias House, Fred Williams House, St. Paul's Breadfruit Church, and Taiwo's tomb, see Shaw, "Historic Buildings of Lagos, Nigeria."

99. See Seaton, *The Language of Flowers*.

100. Shaw, "Historic Buildings of Lagos, Nigeria," 16.

101. Brown, "A History of the People of Lagos," 112; Hopkins, "An Economic History of Lagos," 21.

102. Brown, "A History of the People of Lagos," 25, 112, 142. Over this period, clay became more difficult to find and had to be dredged from the lagoon or brought from Iddo Island and Ebute Metta.

103. Shaw, "Historic Buildings of Lagos, Nigeria," 24–26; Akinsemoyin and Vaughan-Richards, *Building Lagos*, 19, 21.

104. In this way, city blocks became almost extended compounds in themselves—a series of individual plots and private rooms clustered around a sheltered congregating space for working and socializing.

105. Brown, "A History of the People of Lagos," 112; Hopkins, "An Economic History of Lagos," 21.

Notes to Pages 68–70

106. Mann, *Slavery and the Birth of an African City*, 261, 267.

107. Cole, *Modern and Traditional Elites*, 90.

108. In cases not involving Crown grants, long-term occupancy was often a deciding factor. Cases involving a Crown grant were required to be heard in British courts (rather than native land tribunals), where judges interpreted Crown grants as conferring fee simple title. See Mann, *Slavery and the Birth of an African City*, 261.

109. Ordinance No. 8, 1883, in Stallard and Richards, *Ordinances and Orders*, 425, emphasis added; Mann, *Slavery and the Birth of an African City*, 253.

110. Mann, 272.

111. Mann, 256, 265.

112. Mann, 253.

113. Mann, 295.

114. For a discussion of service tenure, see Mann, *Slavery and the Birth of an African City*, 271–74. "Dependents" or "clients," commonly known as *allagbaso*—"one who has somebody to plead one's case" (Mann, "Interpreting Cases," 198)—were a broad category ranging from slaves or former slaves (*arota*, "slaves born in their owners' households," and *eru*, "those bought in interior markets" [Mann, *Slavery and the Birth of an African City*, 170, 228]) to women and children (Mann, 285–95; Mann, *Marrying Well*, 36–40) and to "boys" (*asaforige*, which literally means "one who hurries to tote [loads] with the head" [a slang word for "porter"] [Mann, "Interpreting Cases, Disentangling Disputes," 200]). See also Mann, "Owners, Slaves and the Struggle for Labour in the Commercial Transaction at Lagos."

115. Previously overlords could not throw out dependents under customary understanding of tenure if the tenant had done nothing wrong; Mann, *Slavery and the Birth of an African City*, 242.

116. Mann, *Slavery and the Birth of an African City*, 273.

117. Mann, 258–62.

118. Brown (*Observer*, January 7, 1888) cites evidence that 80 percent of fires were thought to be intentionally set ("A History of the People of Lagos," 374); C. Onyeke Nwanunobi writes, "Incendiarism thus recommended itself as '. . . a ready means of revenge for those who believed themselves wronged' and who then 'proceeded to revenge a wrong, real or imaginary, [without] regard whatsoever for innocent lives'" ("Incendiarism and Other Fires in Nineteenth-Century Lagos," 113).

119. Brown, "A History of the People of Lagos," 373–81.

120. Brown, 381–90.

121. Mann, *Slavery and the Birth of an African City*, 258–62.

122. Nwanunobi, "Incendiarism and Other Fires in Nineteenth-Century Lagos," 112; Brown, "A History of the People of Lagos," 378.

240   Notes to Pages 70–73

123. Brown, 376.

124. Brown, 375.

125. Brown, 33.

126. Brown, 374.

127. Brown, 107.

128. Mann, *Slavery and the Birth of an African City*, 249; Brown, "A History of the People of Lagos," 107.

129. Brown, 108.

130. Brown, 22–23.

131. Brown, 78.

132. See Brown, 113.

133. Peel writes that "the experience of confusion—of communities racked by internal conflict or destroyed altogether, of families broken up, of large-scale displacement, of radical changes in personal circumstances, of the norms of social life challenged or overthrown—was fundamental to Yoruba lives in the nineteenth century" (*Religious Encounter and the Making of the Yoruba*, 50).

134. J. P. L. Davies quoted in Brown, "A History of the People of Lagos," 225.

135. Olasupo Shasore writes, "In order to maintain imperial control of the Colony of Lagos matters of law, fairness and justice suffered dubious standards and inconsistent application. The courts and judicial personnel we have seen were sometimes inadequate in number and qualification for a government that ought to honor the rights of the local natives, the Lagos Africa. The highest instrument of judicial power for the colony was the Judicial Committee at the House of Lords; its emergence was itself an acceptance of the random nature of the justice dispensed by the colonial machinery" (*Possessed*, 268).

136. Glover quoted in Brown, "A History of the People of Lagos," 108.

137. Peel, *Religious Encounter and the Making of the Yoruba*, 50.

138. Brown, "A History of the People of Lagos," 172.

139. See Cole, *Modern and Traditional Elites*, 53–56; and Mann, *Marrying Well*, 22.

140. Mann, *Marrying Well*, 23.

141. Cole, *Modern and Traditional Elites*, 75.

142. Hopkins, "An Economic History of Lagos," 392–95.

143. The map states that it was revised based on recommendations made in London.

144. Hopkins, "An Economic History of Lagos," 128; Brown, "A History of the People of Lagos," 330.

145. Mann, *Marrying Well*, 24; Hopkins, "An Economic History of Lagos," 278–79.

146. Kopytoff, *A Preface to Modern Nigeria*, 174. For an account of European banks' systematic rejection of African mortgage recipients in the early

Notes to Pages 73–79   241

nineteenth century, see Uche, "Foreign Banks, Africans, and Credit in Colonial Nigeria, c. 1890–1912."

147. Other scholars like Ayodeji Olukoju (following Anthony Hopkins) have examined cultural reasons for why nineteenth-century Nigerian entrepreneurs did not prosper into the twentieth century, arguing that a "capitalist class capable of competing successfully with expatriate firms" did not develop because wealthy Yoruba men maintained a socially expected "grandiose style of living" (conspicuous consumption) rather than cultivating institutions (corporate firms) that could remain productive and profitable after their death ("Accumulation and Conspicuous Consumption," 208). While recognizing the restraints colonial rule placed on African businessmen, Olukoju sees their demise as a case in which "economic rationality succumbed to social pressure even in the face of global distress" (228). This account seems to underestimate the monetary returns that late nineteenth-century men like Taiwo made by cultivating social status in the commercial city and the devastation that racist foreclosures had on African merchants' ability to cultivate (and host) followers and to thereby create commercial links.

Chapter 2: Canal

1. Gramsci, *Selections from the Prison Notebooks*, 235.
2. By "Black landscapes" I mean the ways in which, since the eighteenth century, much of European discourse had constructed an image of Africa as a place of raw natural settings governed by "dark" primal instincts where "humanity gave way to animality" in the form of the Black Africans (Comaroff and Comaroff, *Of Revelation and Revolution*, 1:99) and where "superstition, death, and ugliness always lay close by" (Mbembe, *Critique of Black Reason*, 49). In this "savage" landscape, "the West set up a mirror in which it might find a tangible, if inverted, self-image" (Comaroff and Comaroff, 98).
3. There have been several important studies of the medical and legal discourses behind sanitation and segregation in West Africa. Yet none of these studies examine the visual records from the era and the ways colonial administrators were photographing and mapping African landscapes as they imagined schemes to transform them.
4. Hopkins, "An Economic History of Lagos," 317, 351.
5. Hopkins, 27, 380. *Rubedo* (Latin for "redness") is the fourth and final step in an alchemist's creation of gold.
6. Hobson, *Imperialism*, quoted in Jasanoff, *The Dawn Watch*, 258.
7. Census, southern Nigeria, 1911.
8. See Robert Smith, "The Canoe in West African History"; and Mabogunje, *Urbanization in Nigeria*, 246.

242   Notes to Pages 80–82

9. Which allowed employers and the state to reap the benefits of a healthier and happier work force.

10. Cole, *Modern and Traditional Elites in the Politics of Lagos*, 75.

11. The term *hermetic* is derived from the Greek god Hermes, via the vocabulary of alchemy. The alchemists invented a process for making an airtight glass tube, which they used for distillation. The process used a secret seal, whose invention was attributed to the legendary inspiration of alchemy, Hermes Trismegistus (Wikipedia). Of course, the canal was hardly "hermetic," but it did aid in the push toward British hegemony.

12. MacGregor, "A Lecture on Malaria."

13. Njoh recounts the legend of how Nigeria's government at independence considered making a mosquito part of the national flag, *Planning Power*, 72.

14. Dumett, "The Campaign against Malaria," 156; Mabogunje, *Urbanization in Nigeria*, 259.

15. George, *Making Modern Girls*, 37; MacGregor, "A Lecture on Malaria," 1890.

16. Cell, "Anglo-Indian Medical Theory and the Origins of Segregation in West Africa"; George, *Making Modern Girls*, 39. The luxury of Government House was part of what convinced MacGregor to take the governorship of Lagos after initially trying to find a better post; see Joyce, *Sir William MacGregor*, chap. 10.

17. Cell, "Anglo-Indian Medical Theory and the Origins of Segregation in West Africa," points out that cantonments originally served a military purpose in India, while they were adopted in Africa, at Ross's behest, as a form of medical quarantine. See also Curtin, "Medical Knowledge and Urban Planning in Tropical Africa"; Goerg, "From Hill Station (Freetown) to Downtown Conakry (First Ward)"; Gale, "Ségrégation in British West Africa"; Spitzer, "The Mosquito and Segregation in Sierra Leone"; and Dumett, "The Campaign against Malaria."

18. Goerg, "From Hill Station (Freetown) to Downtown Conakry (First Ward)," 26.

19. MacGregor, "A Discussion on Malaria and Its Prevention," 682; MacGregor, "A Lecture on Malaria," 1902.

20. MacGregor, "A Lecture on Malaria," 1902.

21. However, MacGregor did seek to quarantine the dead from the landscapes of the living, a rigid demarcation not recognized in Yoruba religion. In the early twentieth century, the majority of the city continued to identify as practitioners of Yoruba orisha worship. As part of an effort to sanitize the city, the administrators of Lagos banned the widespread practice of burying the dead within a family's compound. Home burials often meant bodies avoided postmortems by a colonial doctor, precluding accurate statistics on disease. An 1888 ordinance not only banned in-home burials

Notes to Pages 83–84 243

but allowed courts to prohibit the inhabitation of any house where people were interred and gave inspectors the power to enter homes to search for fresh corpses (since decoy coffins could easily be buried in graveyards). Maps from the era show the construction of new cemeteries beyond MacGregor Canal. For Lagosians who practiced home burial, perceptions of "home" were tied to the presence of ancestors who protected the dwelling and its residents and legitimized claims by descendants to the space; see Ojo, "Making Markets with the Dead: Residential Burial among the Yoruba." Graveyard burial for the Ga in Accra was "akin to being cast unburied into the bush" (Parker, "The Cultural Politics of Death and Burial in Early Colonial Accra," 214).

22. For specifics and an overview of this flurry of projects, see Mabogunje, *Urbanization in Nigeria*, chap. 10; Bigon, *A History of Urban Planning in Two West African Colonial Capitals*, part 1, chap. 2, and part 2, chap. 2; Olukoju, *Infrastructure Development and Urban Facilities in Lagos*; and Hopkins, "An Economic History of Lagos," chap. 5.

23. For a discussion of these late nineteenth-century newspaper editorials in Lagos, see Brown, "A History of the People of Lagos," 329; and Bigon, *A History of Urban Planning*, 134–38.

24. Quoted in Olukoju, *Infrastructure Development and Urban Facilities in Lagos*, 14.

25. On the co-constituted origins of modern urban planning, see Home, *Of Planting and Planning*; Bremner, ed., *Architecture and Urbanism in the British Empire*; Demissie, ed., *Colonial Architecture and Urbanism in Africa*; and Maudlin and Herman, eds., *Building the British Atlantic World*.

26. Home, *Of Planting and Planning*, 49. W. H. Lever's companies included Lever Brothers (which became Unilever in 1929) and the United African Company. While Lever Brothers prioritized decent housing in building factory-cities like Port Sunlight, these considerations did not extend to the African end of the supply chain. For Lever's abysmal labor practices in the Congo, see Marchal, *Lord Leverhulme's Ghosts*.

27. Adshead, "The School of Civic Design at the Liverpool University," 108.

28. Waters, "Review of *So Clean*."

29. Egerton wanted to build "good, broad straight roads" in order "to be able to let in the light." Quoted in Nicolson, *The Administration of Nigeria*, 100.

30. Mbembe shows race to be the "foundational category"—"the nuclear powerplant"—of the modern European episteme centered on categorization, *Critique of Black Reason*, 1–2, 16–17; Foucault, *The Order of Things*, chap. 5.

31. Citing Arendt, *The Origins of Totalitarianism*, chap. 7, 185; Mbembe writes, "Two new devices for political organization and rule over foreign peoples were discovered during the first decades of imperialism. One was race as a principle of the body politic, and the other was bureaucracy as a principle

244   Notes to Pages 84–88

of foreign domination." Mbembe argues that "racism and bureaucracy were conceived of and developed separately, [but] it was in Africa that they first revealed themselves to be tightly linked" (*Critique of Black Reason*, 56).

32. For an overview of the Garden City and City Beautiful movements, see Stern, Fishman, and Tilove, *Paradise Planned*, chaps. 3 and 7; Peterson, *The Birth of City Planning in the United States, 1840–1917*.

33. Crouch, *Design Culture in Liverpool, 1880–1914*, chap. 7. Standish Meacham describes how a vision of Anglo-Saxon (White) "Englishness" was embedded in the Garden City movement (introduction to *Regaining Paradise*, 10).

34. Rogan, "An Entangled Object."

35. Poole, *Vision, Race, and Modernity*, 112.

36. On the genealogy of this way of seeing surfaces as evidence of interior truth and "moral cores," see Comaroff and Comaroff, "Africa Observed."

37. As Mbembe writes, "Racism is a site of reality and truth—the truth of appearances" (*Critique of Black Reason*, 32).

38. "Reports, &c., From Drs. Stephens and Christophers, West Coast of Africa," 15, emphasis added.

39. "Reports, &c., From Drs. Stephens and Christophers, West Coast of Africa," plate 2.

40. The implied rest of the sentence is, of course, "for Europeans."

41. Home, *Of Planting and Planning*, 9.

42. Conversation with Prof. Modupe Omirin, Faculty in the Department of Estate Management, University of Lagos, August 24, 2016.

43. Indigenous quarters of Lagos had long practiced annual communal cleanups, and in 1900 chiefs were contracted to organize the scavenging of refuse from streets as their program produced better results than the various Inspectors of Nuisances who were widely seen as incompetent and lazy; see Brown, "A History of the People of Lagos," 339–40. For histories and analysis of Yoruba urbanism, see Mabogunje, *Yoruba Towns*; Ojo, *Yoruba Palaces*; Ojo, *Yoruba Cultures*; Smith, *Kingdoms of the Yoruba*.

44. For Lugard's desire to move the capital to Zungeru, see Cole, *Modern and Traditional Elites*, 124.

45. George, *Making Modern Girls*, 45, quoting Awe's sources in *Nigerian Women in Historical Perspective*, 111.

46. George, *Making Modern Girls*, 44. On Egerton's snubbing of Lagosians with whom MacGregor had forged relationships, see Cole, *Modern and Traditional Elites*, chap. 3.

47. On this point, see Landau, "Empires of the Visual"; Schneider, "Portrait Photography," 38.

48. John M. Carland, "Public Expenditure and Development in a Crown Colony," 372. See also Lawal, "The Politics of Revenue Allocation in Nigeria."

Notes to Pages 88–94

49. Ordinance No. 10 of 1878, "Towns Police and Public Health Ordinance." In the case of insurrection (a serious fear at the time), wide uncluttered streets prevented barricades from being put up—barricades which could shelter trenches and the entrenchment of ideas opposed to colonial sovereignty. It is telling that policing and public health overlapped in Ordinance No. 10 of 1878; in Stallard and Richards, *Ordinances and Orders*.

50. Ordinance No. 2 of 1864, "Road by and Shores of Lagoon," in Stallard and Richards, *Ordinances and Orders*.

51. Interestingly, it appears reclamation may have made matters worse. A 1911 map showing where thatch roofing was permitted on the island shades the entire area around Alakoro as swamp, whereas Lawson's map only shaded a very small swamp near the Alakoro inlet. It may be possible that by filling in the water ring around Alakoro, British planners interfered with drainage patterns to the lagoon and caused the area to become even more waterlogged over time.

52. At times this was not metaphorical; officials coated bodies of water with petroleum and Paris green to kill mosquito larvae. See Mabogunje, *Urbanization in Nigeria*, 258; and Gandy, *The Fabric of Space*.

53. Swanson, "The Sanitation Syndrome," 387.

54. Ronald Ross, "Sanitary Affairs in West Africa," 159.

55. On the sociopolitical strategies found in impermanent African architecture, see Strother, "Architecture against the State."

56. For a description of a similar double standard of how the Lagos Public Works Department erected bamboo and thatched "Bush Houses" in Ikoyi for European occupation that were approved by the director of medical and sanitary services as well as the governor of the colony, see Newell, *Histories of Dirt*, 30.

57. Ross, "Sanitary Affairs in West Africa," 159.

58. Newell quotes interviewees in Lagos in 2014 and 2016 who recalled traditional Yoruba dwellings fondly, with one woman stating: "But those days they build their house with mud. Even if the weather is hot, you feel the cold, you will be comfortable in the house. And if is very cold out there, you feel the warmth within. That is the level of what they use build the house, the mud, the clay, it helps. But now we use blocks, anything that is outside we feel it immediately, so that is the influence of the Western culture. Even our building it has affected" (*Histories of Dirt*, 179).

59. Curtin notes that despite the development of mosquito and germ theory, British administrators continued to show concern with miasma in submitting their opinions on staff housing in the tropics to the Colonial Office, "Medical Knowledge and Urban Planning in Tropical Africa," 604.

60. See Hallen, *The Good, the Bad, and the Beautiful*, chap. 5; Lawal, "Some Aspects of Yoruba Aesthetics"; Doris, *Vigilant Things*.

246 Notes to Pages 94–97

61. Deputation from the Lagos Auxiliary of the Anti-Slavery and Aborigines Protection Society to His Excellency F. Seton James, Esq., C.M.G. Acting Governor and Commander-in-Chief of Southern Nigeria, "The Lagos Land Question," speech delivered on the occasion by Mr. Herbert Macaulay, C. E. at Government House, Lagos, June 13, 1912, Schomburg Center for Research in Black Culture.

62. PRO, CO 879/62, Lagos: Report of Two Journeys in the Lagos Protectorate by Governor Sir Wm. MacGregor, June 19–24, 1900, quoted in Bigon, *A History of Urban Planning*, 66.

63. Doris, *Vigilant Things*, 5.

64. Doris, 5, 17.

65. Seun, "Malaria and Sanitation in Colonial Lagos," 68–69. For a description of how Lagos townspeople were "perfectly aware" of the impossibility of the British enforcing all ordinances in Lagos until the 1920s, see Newell, *Histories of Dirt*, 24.

66. Táíwò, "Headedness and the Structure of Yorùbá Compound Word," 45–46.

67. Dumett, "The Campaign Against Malaria," 184 and 186. Meanwhile the mortality rate of Europeans in S. Nigeria dropped below twenty per thousand.

68. Down only from 439 to 357 per thousand. Dumett, "The Campaign against Malaria," 184–85.

69. See Bigon, *A History of Urban Planning*, 80–81; Bigon, "Tracking Ethnocultural Differences"; and Miller, *Lagos Steam Tramway*. Map 3.4 shows the steam-tramway's route, which coincided with the areas of the city where "night soil" was collected by the tramway.

70. MacGregor, "Lagos, Abeokuta and the Alaka," 464.

71. See, for example, the Housing and Town Planning Act of 1909. For an example of how Master and Servant Laws were not applied in Africa, see Anderson, "Master and Servant in Colonial Kenya."

72. Today, this notion still dominates the discussion of housing as a right of the formal working class, tying a universal need to only one segment of the population.

73. The British did provide the Hausa police force at Lagos with housing in the form of land east of MacGregor Canal and funding to construct barracks due to the increasing cost of land in Lagos and the need for the foreign Hausa force to find shelter. See Hausa Lands Ord. 13 (1906), in *Colonial Reports—Annual, 1906*.

74. For a discussion of the professionalization of urban planning through the creation of organizations like the Town and Country Planning Association (1899), see Home, *Of Planting and Planning*, chap. 6.

75. Curtin describes how, in 1906, the Colonial Office had sought input from West African governors in designing colonial residences, many of whom

Notes to Pages 97–99 247

responded stressing the need for ventilation, "Medical Knowledge and Urban Planning in Tropical Africa," 604.

76. In the case's initial judgment, acting Chief Justice of Nigeria, Sir Edwin Speed, declared, "The institution of communal ownership has been dead for many years and the institution of family ownership is a dying institution, and it is idle to expect the court at this time to make use of a power which was given to it in order to avoid or mitigate the individual hardship and injustice which would necessarily be incidental to the abolition of a primitive native system and the immediate substitution of modern methods in order to perpetuate or bolster up what is at the best an interesting relic of the past." Yet the full court reversed Speed and went on to lay down, as G. B. A. Coker writes, "The most explicit and imperishable exposition of native law and custom with respect to family property [see footnote 77]." *Family Property among the Yorubas*, 15–16.

77. "The legal tenets of Family Property laid out in *Lewis v. Bankole* (1909) are as follows: (i) When the founder of a family dies, the eldest surviving son called the 'Dawodu,' succeeds to the headship of the family with all that that implies, including residence and the giving of orders in his father's house or compound; (ii) On the death of the eldest surviving son, the next eldest surviving child of the founder, whether male or female, is the proper person to succeed as head of the family; (iii) If there is going to be any important dealing with family property all branches of the family must be consulted, and representation on the family council is also *per stirpes* according as there are wives with children. (iv) The division is into equal shares between the respective branches, regard being had to any property already received by any of the founder's children during his life-time. (v) The founder's grandchildren only succeed to such rights as their immediate parents had in the family property. (vi) The founder's compound or house is usually regarded as the 'family house' which must be preserved for posterity." Quoted in Elias, *Nigerian Land Law and Custom*, 230.

78. In 1911, by far the largest occupation in Lagos remained petty trading (45.9 percent of working population); see Hopkins, *An Economic History of Lagos*, 418. See also the petition sent to Andrew Bonar Law from Prince Eshugbayi Eleko, May 30, 1916, 3 (Macaulay, "The Lagos Land Question"), which claims, as part of an argument against paying the proposed water rate, that "in the absence of any kind of properly established industry, there is no real wealth within the Colony of Nigeria."

79. Statistic cited in petition sent to Andrew Bonar Law from Prince Eshugbayi Eleko, May 30, 1916, 3.

80. As the West African Lands Committee noted, "Lineage lands had become so partitioned that Crown grants rarely covered areas more than

one-eighth of an acre." Quoted in Meek, *Land Tenure and Land Administration in Nigeria and the Cameroons*, 63.

81. Quoted in Simpson, *A Report on the Registration of Title to Land in the Federal Territory of Lagos*, 23.

82. Irving, *A Collection of the Principal Enactments and Cases*, 207.

83. Irving, 205.

84. See, for example, *Lewis v. Bankole* (1909); Irving, *A Collection of the Principal Enactments and Cases*, 217–38.

85. Meek, *Land Tenure and Land Administration in Nigeria and the Cameroons*, 63.

86. Barnes, *Patrons and Power*, 31; Mann, "Interpreting Cases."

87. Hopkins, "The Lagos Strike of 1897."

88. Cole, *Modern and Traditional Elites*, 82–84.

89. Animashaun, "A Historical Study of the Development and Growth of Medical and Health Services in Lagos," 55.

90. MacGregor, "Lagos, Abeokuta and the Alaka," 467.

91. Quoted by Herbert Macaulay in his pamphlet, *An Antithesis on the Public Lands Acquisition (Amendment) Ordinance* (Lagos, 1945, 8), quoted in Cole, *Modern and Traditional Elites*, 89.

92. Hopkins, "The Lagos Strike of 1897," 144. The Colonial Office's view at the time was that "trading in slaves, which means raiding for them, must of course be put a stop to with a strong hand but domestic slavery is quite another matter." Denton to Chamberlain (1897) quoted by Hopkins, 145.

93. Meek, *Land Tenure*, 62. The colony's administrators attempted to switch to leases in 1897, but African pushback forced a continuation of sales until 1908. This legislation only applied to transactions involving Africans granting land to foreigners; land sales continued between African parties. See Rayner, "Land Tenure in West Africa," 3.

94. MacGregor, "Lagos, Abeokuta and the Alaka," 468.

95. See Cole, *Modern and Traditional Elites*, 92–93; and Elias, *Nigerian Land Law and Custom*, 12.

96. Mann, "African and European Initiatives in the Transformation of Land Tenure in Colonial Lagos," 226.

97. These early twentieth-century Lagos alliances challenge Gramsci's notion of "false consciousness," as intellectuals and dependents—whose material interests were not necessarily immediately served by customary land tenure—banded together behind chiefs in what became a form of anticolonial protest.

98. For a summary of these lines of argument see Mann, "African and European Initiatives"; Mann, *Slavery and the Birth of an African City*, chap. 7; and Macaulay, "The Lagos Land Question."

99. Cole, *Modern and Traditional Elites*, 93.

Notes to Pages 103–106   249

100. Curtin, "Medical Knowledge and Urban Planning in Tropical Africa," 603; Cole, *Modern and Traditional Elites*, 93.

101. Cole, *Modern and Traditional Elites*, 93; Bigon, *A History of Urban Planning in Two West African Colonial Capitals*, 150.

102. *African Mail*, January 31, 1908, quoted in Coleman, *Nigeria: Background to Nationalism*, 179, emphasis added.

103. Irving, *A Collection of the Principal Enactments*, 165; and Cole, *Modern and Traditional Elites*, 93.

104. See Cole, *Modern and Traditional Elites*, 93–94.

105. For descriptions of the leisurely Sundays and holidays in the presegregation Ikoyi plains, see Olinto, *The Water House*, 99; Laotan, "Brazilian Influence on Lagos," 165; Macaulay, "The Lagos Land Question," 16.

106. Cole, *Modern and Traditional Elites*, 94–95.

107. Put down on paper in 1922 but operating in practice long before, Lord Lugard's *Dual Mandate in British Tropical Africa* put forth the imperial principles of making a profit for the metropole while protecting the interests and well-being of Africans—which Macaulay contested as a cynical tool of the first principle.

108. Macaulay, "The Lagos Land Question," 17, 18.

109. Ronald Ross, "Sanitary Affairs in West Africa," 165. However, contrary to what has been written in recent publications, it should be noted that Ross, unlike his friend MacGregor, was in favor of sanitary segregation in West Africa; see Ross, "Sanitary Affairs," 160.

110. Macaulay, "The Lagos Land Question," 17. On the 1903 expansion of land appropriations for "public purpose" to include minerals "for exclusive government use," see Cole, *Modern and Traditional Elites*, 232n135.

111. Macaulay, "The Lagos Land Question," 16.

112. Bigon, *A History of Urban Planning*, 154.

113. *Colonial Reports—Annual*, 1915, 21.

114. Oluwasegun, "Managing Epidemic," 416.

115. See Bigon, *A History of Urban Planning*, 156–57; Curtin, "Medical Knowledge and Urban Planning," 606; Gale, "Ségrégation in British West Africa," 503.

116. Lugard to Law, August 16, 1915, quoted in Gale, "Ségrégation in British West Africa," 502. From 1917 through 1920, the colony had positive revenue to expense ratios, so budgets were not the issue; *Colonial Reports—Annual*, 1921.

117. *Colonial Reports—Annual*, 1921. Lagos's population density doubled between 1901 and 1921; Baker, *Urbanization and Political Change*, 35.

118. Macaulay mentions an episode in which "some ill-disposed person or persons manufactured an information of some sort which somehow or other got to the hearing of His Excellency the Governor who imagined that on

250 Notes to Pages 106–111

the night of the 10th of August the whole of the natives of Lagos were going to rise and kill every European in the town of Lagos" ("The Land Question," 18–19).

119. King, *The Bungalow*, 195.

120. Myers, *Verandahs of Power*, 9.

121. See Legacy 1995's restoration of Jaekel House, https://legacy1995.org.ng/.

122. See Ojo, *Yoruba Palaces*; Smith, *Kingdoms of the Yoruba*, 6.

123. MacGregor encouraged the use of mosquito catchers, "A Lecture on Malaria," 1901–2.

124. Acting Surveyor-General, Lagos to the Director of Medical and Sanitary Services, "Confidential Despatch [*sic*]" of March 28, 1923.

125. Akinsemoyin and Vaughan-Richards, *Building Lagos*, 50.

126. Gale, "Ségrégation in British West Africa," 503.

127. Gale, 500.

128. Quoted in Newell, *Histories of Dirt*, 30.

129. Fourchard, "Lagos and the Invention of Juvenile Delinquency in Nigeria," 120; Olukoju describes how clauses were included in Ikoyi and Apapa leases that forbade letting or subleasing to Africans ("The Segregation of Europeans and Africans in Colonial Nigeria," 279).

130. Kaye Whiteman writes that Africans were not even permitted to dine as guests of Ikoyi Club members until after the infamous 1947 incident at Bristol Hotel (*Lagos: A Cultural History*, 63, 149–50).

131. Olukoju, "The Segregation of Europeans," 279–83; Seun, "Malaria and Sanitation in Colonial Lagos," 67. For an excellent history of how race, state, and space were contested and renegotiated in Ikoyi between 1935 and 1955, see Livsey, "State, Urban Space, Race," 178–96.

Chapter 3: Swamp

1. Bigon, *A History of Urban Planning in Two West African Colonial Capitals*, 171; see also Mayne, *Slums: The History of a Global Injustice*, chap. 2.

2. According to Koolhaas, the Harvard Project on the City (begun in 1995) was an opportunity for Koolhaas and his team of Harvard Design School students to replace "painfully inadequate" architectural discourses that "perpetuate an image of the city which is essentially Western, and subconsciously insist that all cities, wherever they are, be interpreted in that image." Koolhaas and van der Haak, "A Discussion on Koolhaas's research with the Harvard Project on the City on Lagos, Nigeria." When the Harvard Project on the City turned to Lagos in 1999, it sought to understand the city's "continued existence and productivity in spite of a near-complete absence of those infrastructures, systems, organizations, and amenities that define the word 'city' in terms of western planning methodology"; Koolhaas and Harvard Project on the City, *Mutations*, 652.

Notes to Pages 111–115

3. See, for example, Kaplan, "The Coming Anarchy"; Packer, "The Megacity"; Marsh, "Overpopulated and Underfed: Countries Near a Breaking Point."

4. BBC, *Welcome to Lagos*, episode 2, April 2010.

5. See, for example, Collins, "Makoko Floating School"; and Kimmelman, "School at Sea."

6. Koolhaas would famously proclaim that "Lagos, as an icon of West African urbanity, inverts every essential characteristic of the so-called modern city. Yet, it is still—for lack of a better word—a city; and one that works" (Koolhaas and Harvard Project on the City, *Mutations*, 652). The floating school was written about as a "beacon of hope" for architecture's ability to make water-bound settlements work, but in 2017, despite claims that it was "invulnerable to flooding and storm surges," flooding destroyed the school. See Frearson, "Kunlé Adeyemi's Floating School Suffers 'Abrupt Collapse.'"

7. Duerksen, "The Koolhaas Effect."

8. Fourchard, "Lagos, Koolhaas and Partisan Politics in Nigeria"; and Gandy, "Learning from Lagos"; see also Godlewski, who in "Alien and Distant" writes that Koolhaas presented Lagos as "mute, abject, and 'otherworldly' and *beyond comparison*" (16).

9. In his article on Koolhaas's use of helicopter photographs, Tim Hecker discusses the history of airborne photography and notes how architectural modernists such as Le Corbusier used aerial views as an indictment of cities, calling for the radical destruction and rebuilding of the irrationality they perceived. He argues that, conversely, Koolhaas presents a "de facto celebration of poverty via a laissez-faire aesthetics of the status quo, an aesthetic realism emptied of any substantial social critique," which he describes as an "aesthetics of immensity and the apocalyptic sublime." While their planning visions diverge, both the views of Corbusier and Koolhaas flatten understandings of street-level lives and historic processes; Hecker, "The Slum Pastoral."

10. James C. Scott writes that "by virtue of its great distance, an aerial view resolved what might have seemed ground-level confusion into an apparently vaster order and symmetry. It would be hard to exaggerate the importance of the airplane for modernist thought and planning. By offering a perspective that flattened the topography as if it were a canvas, flight encouraged new aspirations to 'synoptic vision, rational control, planning, and spatial order'" (*Seeing Like a State*, 58).

11. Ferguson, *Give a Man a Fish*, chap. 2.

12. Simone, *For the City Yet to Come*, 138.

13. Ayodeji Olukoju, an economic and maritime historian, is one scholar who has looked deeply at the interwar years. His scholarship guides much of this chapter.

14. Between 1920 and 1950; Mabogunje, *Urbanization in Nigeria*, 257.

15. Cole, *Modern and Traditional Elites in the Politics of Lagos*, 118, citing the West African Land Committee Report of 1912–14.

16. Quoted in Okpala, "The Potentials and Perils of Public Urban Land Ownership and Management," 82.

17. *Lagos Weekly Record*, July 23, 1921, quoted in Adewoye, "The Tijani Land Case," 28. Density figures from Olukoju, *Infrastructure Development and Urban Facilities in Lagos*, 10.

18. Olukoju, *The Liverpool of West Africa*, 131–32.

19. See Olukoju, "The Travails of Migrant and Wage Labour in the Lagos Metropolitan Area in the Inter-war Years," for more on the lives of migrants and what drove them to Lagos and the disappointments they found once there. Fourchard, "Lagos and the Invention of Juvenile Delinquency in Nigeria, 1920–60," 117.

20. Nigerian National Archives at Ibadan (hereafter NAI), CSO 26 06276 Vol. I, Annual Report, 1922, p. 7, quoted in Olukoju, "Population Pressure, Housing and Sanitation in West Africa's Premier Port-City," 95.

21. Olukoju, "The Travails of Migrant and Wage Labour," 54–55.

22. Quoted in Olukoju, "Population Pressure," 96.

23. Cole, *Modern and Traditional Elites*, 118.

24. The Privy Council stated: "The radical title is now in the British Sovereign [via the Treaty of Cession]. But that title is throughout qualified by the usufructuary rights of communities, rights which, as the outcome of deliberate policy, have been respected and recognized.... That title, as they have pointed out, is *prima facie* based, not on such individual ownership as English law has made familiar, but on a communal usufructuary occupation, which may be so complete as to reduce any radical right in the Sovereign to one which only extends to comparatively limited rights of administrative interference." See Elias, *Nigerian Land Law and Custom*, 18–20.

25. It is unclear when or if the compensation was ever actually distributed throughout the family, however Macaulay was paid £5000 for his services; see Cole, *Modern and Traditional Elites*, 118; Adewoye, "The Tijani Land Case," 30.

26. Cole, *Modern and Traditional Elites*, 126–27.

27. Olukoju, *The Liverpool of West Africa*, 138; Olukoju, "The Travails of Migrant and Wage Labour," 55–56.

28. Cole, *Modern and Traditional Elites*, 119.

29. Cole, 101–4 and chap. 5.

30. Other strategies included bribery, assertions that the land in question was unoccupied, legal technicalities, and complicit engineer valuations; see Cole, *Modern and Traditional Elites*, 94; and Okpala, "The Potentials and Perils," chaps. 4 and 5.

Notes to Pages 121–125 253

31. Cole, *Modern and Traditional Elites*, 234n144, 252n51.

32. Lieutenant Governor Moorhouse, quoted in Cole, *Modern and Traditional Elites*, 131.

33. Sklar, *Nigerian Political Parties*, 46–47; Cole, *Modern and Traditional Elites*, 132–33.

34. Olukoju, "Population Pressure," 96.

35. NAI, CSO 26 06276 Vol. I, Annual Report, 1922, p. 7, quoted in Olukoju, "Population Pressure, Housing and Sanitation in West Africa's Premier Port-City," 95.

36. Bigon, "Bubonic Plague, Colonial Ideologies, and Urban Planning Policies," 213.

37. Bigon, *A History of Urban Planning*, 162.

38. Okpala, "The Potentials and Perils," 95.

39. PRO, CO 583, 163/9, "An Ordinance to Make Provision for the Re-Planning, Improvement and Development of Lagos," 1928, 19, 21–22, British National Archives at Kew.

40. Elias, *Nigerian Land Law and Custom*, 284.

41. See p. 101 in this book.

42. *Report of the Tribunal of Inquiry into the Affairs of the Lagos Executive Development Board.*

43. Godwin and Hopwood, *Sandbank City*, 120.

44. Cole, *Modern and Traditional Elites*, 137.

45. Swanson, "The Sanitation Syndrome," 391.

46. Swanson, 389, quoting McGrew, *Russia and the Cholera.*

47. PRO, CO 583, 163/9, "An Ordinance," 8–9.

48. PRO, CO 583, 163/9, "An Ordinance," 13–14.

49. Burton, 1860s, quoted in Bigon, *A History of Urban Planning*, 77.

50. Carter, 1897, quoted in Brown, "A History of the People of Lagos," 333.

51. See chapter 2.

52. Okpala, "The Potentials and Perils," 131. The initial surge of funding came primarily via a government block grant with the belief that LEDB would then turn a profit. This did not end up happening due to economic depression, mismanagement, and litigation.

53. Okpala, "The Potentials and Perils," 166.

54. Bigon, *A History of Urban Planning*, 171.

55. *Nigerian Pioneer*, August 29, 1919, quoted in Olukoju, "Population Pressure," 94.

56. Olukoju, "Population Pressure," 98–99.

57. *Colonial Reports—Annual*, 1931, 17–18.

58. See Olukoju, "The Travails of Migrant and Wage Labour," 55–57; and Lindsay, "No Need . . . to Think of Home?," 447.

59. PRO, CO 583, 163/9, "An Ordinance," 15.

60. Cole, *Modern and Traditional Elites*, 258n111.

61. *Colonial Reports—Annual, 1931*, 17–18.

62. The bamboo and thatch houses from the Alakoro photographs in chap. 2 of this volume were outlawed by the 1930s. *Colonial Reports—Annual, 1933*, 25.

63. *Colonial Reports—Annual, 1933*, 30.

64. Okpala, "The Potentials and Perils," 180.

65. The 1932 colonial annual report for Nigeria describes the housing situation for wage laborers at Lagos: "In Lagos wages have fallen considerably during the past two years. Until lately the standard labourer's wage has been a shilling per day, but retrenchment and lack of employment has made labor at eightpence per day available, if the employer provides free housing, and ninepence if the labourer has to house himself. Causal labourers if unmarried or apart from their wives usually live in communities, four or more of them sharing a living room at a cost to each of from a shilling to two shilling per month. A large number of men sharing a dilapidated house and its yard will pay the rent by contributing each as little as sixpence a month. There is no such thing as lodgings in the English sense of the word. The landlord lets an empty tenement at from two to ten shillings per month and the number of his tenants does not concern him. They provide what little furniture they require and their own food, which they either cook themselves or buy already prepared from street vendors. Threepence per day is the minimum cost of food for a man performing hard manual labour Married labourers often live in single rooms at an average monthly rental of from two to four shillings, but the whole cost being borne by one man. In the majority of cases the wives of wage earners and those on low salaries are petty traders and their profits are sufficient to pay for their own food and that of their children." *Colonial Reports—Annual, 1932*, 50.

66. Lindsay, "No Need . . . to Think of Home." British administrators had long debated family allowances, eventually deciding that Yoruba women could provide income to make up the deficit through petty trading but then curbed women's ability to trade by outlawing hawking and demolishing several markets.

67. Lindsay, "Domesticity and Difference."

68. As late as 1950, only 13 percent of Lagos earned wages; Lindsay, "No Need . . . to Think of Home," 442.

69. Olukoju, "Population Pressure," 99.

70. Iliffe, *The African Poor*, 164.

71. NAI, Comcol I, 894, memorandum on trade depression, unemployment and income tax collection prepared by the NNDP, n.d., quoted in Fourchard, "Lagos and the Invention of Juvenile Delinquency in Nigeria, 1920–60," 119.

Notes to Pages 129–136

72. Fourchard, "Lagos and the Invention of Juvenile Delinquency," 120; Olukoju, *The Liverpool of West Africa*, 194–95.

73. Olukoju, "Population Pressure," 99.

74. Heap, "Their Days Are Spent Gambling and Loafing."

75. Olukoju, "The Travails of Migrant and Wage Labour," 60.

76. See Fourchard, "Lagos and the Invention of Juvenile Delinquency;" Heap, "Their Days Are Spent Gambling and Loafing"; and George, *Making Modern Girls*.

77. George, *Making Modern Girls*, 92–93.

78. Fourchard, "Lagos and the Invention of Juvenile Delinquency," 126–27.

79. Olukoju, *The Liverpool of West Africa*, 160.

80. For a discussion the criminalization of hawking and squatting, see Bigon, "Between Local and Colonial Perceptions"; and Fourchard, "Lagos and the Invention of Juvenile Delinquency," 131.

81. Hair, "The Cowboys," 89.

82. Fourchard, "Lagos and the Invention of Juvenile Delinquency"; Heap, "Their Days Are Spent Gambling and Loafing."

83. Bigon, "Between Local and Colonial Perceptions," 63–65; George, *Making Modern Girls*, 93.

84. Cole, *Modern and Traditional Elites*, 141–42.

85. Nicolson, *The Administration of Nigeria*, 239. Cameron explicitly rejected the philosophy of "indirect rule," describing his system as "local native administration" or "local government" (Nicolson, 244).

86. Cole, *Modern and Traditional Elites*, 177.

87. Cole, 137, 142–43.

88. George, *Making Modern Girls*, 102.

89. Cole, *Modern and Traditional Elites*, 179.

90. CO 583/295/5, "Development of Lagos Representations by Oba Chiefs," 1947, British National Archives at Kew.

91. George, *Making Modern Girls*, 92–93.

92. Okpala, "The Potentials and Perils," 51–52. Also Cole, *Modern and Traditional Elites*, 95, 235n153.

93. *Report of the Lagos Town Planning Commission*, 8.

94. Lagos Town Council report, 1944.

95. Lindsay, "Domesticity and Difference."

96. CO 583/295/5, "Development of Lagos Representations."

97. See Meek, *Land Tenure and Land Administration in Nigeria and the Cameroons*, 57–76.

98. Marris, *Family and Social Change in an Africa City*, 20.

99. Tew, *Report on Titles to Land in Lagos*.

100. The definition of a "chief" as having "customary" claims to land had gradually become less clear as powerful families began to assert independent

256   Notes to Pages 137–140

control over their lands. In addition to the ìdéjọ class of chiefs who had long maintained their customary prerogative to overseeing and granting out all the land in Lagos, other powerful families began to claim ultimate rights over land as the "first settlers" on it. These families are known as *omo onile* and have come to include non-Yoruba ethnicities such as Igbo. See Akinyele, "Contesting for Space in an Urban Centre"; and Mann, "African and European Initiatives in the Transformation of Land Tenure in Colonial Lagos," 225–28.

101. See Elias, *Nigerian Land Law and Custom*, 23–26; Coker, *Family Property among the Yorubas*, 225–31; and Mann, *Slavery and the Birth of an African City*, 274–76.

102. Akinyele, "Contesting for Space in an Urban Centre"; Okpala, "The Potentials and Perils," 53.

103. Simpson, *A Report on the Registration of Title to Land in the Federal Territory of Lagos*, 39. As many scholars, including Jack Goody, have pointed out, precolonial African political systems were not analogous to European feudalism. In Europe, the feudal system exploited the facts that land was scarce and peasants were indebted to landowners, paying rents for the right to farm their overlord's land, whereas in Lagos, dependents who had been granted land by chiefs gave only nominal tributes of respect to their granters. Simpson's point was prescient, as chiefs and landowning families increased and formalized the rents they collected, eventually developing a system of patronage on which the postcolonial city operated (see chap. 5 in this volume).

104. Owomoyela, "The Good Person."

105. Mayne, *Slums*, 8–9; he argues: "The time has come to ban this deceitful word from today's reform agendas as well as from rigorous research" although "can be used legitimately in a historical sense" (12).

Chapter 4: Lagoon

1. Ayodele and her extraterrestrial crew use their powers to miraculously rejuvenate and supernaturally strengthen the creatures living in Lagos Lagoon and the lagoon herself.

2. For reporting on Olosa's recent stirrings, see Ogbeche, "Lagos Lagoon Hungry."

3. For early histories of Lagos from the perspective of the built environment, see Agiri, "Architecture as a Source of History"; and Akinsemoyin and Vaughan-Richards, *Building Lagos*, 3–10. For accounts of Lagos's origins, see Mann, *Slavery and the Birth of an African City*, 23–50; Aderibigbe, "Early History of Lagos to about 1850"; Losi, *History of Lagos*; and Agiri and Barnes, "Lagos before 1603." For more recent debates on Lagos urbanism and history, see Duerksen, "The Koolhaas Effect."

Notes to Pages 140–148

4. Uher, "Aerial Views of Lagos," 121.

5. Cooper, *Decolonization and African Society*.

6. For a classic description of the strain on Nigerian civil servants in Lagos during independence, see Chinua Achebe's sequel to *Things Fall Apart*, *No Longer at Ease*.

7. As Lévi-Strauss observed, American scholarship from the era "tends *to spread out in space* those forms of civilizations which had been imagined as *spread out in time*" (*Race and History*, 337, emphasis in the original). Similar epistemologies were clearly visible in British thought by the 1940s. Cooper writes that the "constructs of 'African society' or 'African culture' or 'traditional society'—often used interchangeably—enabled colonial officials in the 1940s and 1950s to make an argument about culture with the same structure as one they were no longer willing to articulate publicly about race: African culture and African societies were now portrayed as obstacles to the progress toward which all races could now aspire. To get there, however, Africans would have to give up everything that was distinctly Africa" (*Decolonization and African Society*, 17).

8. Cooper, *Africa since 1940*, 36.

9. It is important to note, as Livsey does in "Suitable Lodgings for Students," that architects were not always "part of a seamless colonial establishment that consciously used progressive associations of modernist architecture to conceal a hegemonic agenda" (675). For studies of earlier imperial architectures in Africa, see King, *The Bungalow*; Myers, *Verandahs of Power*; and Demissie, ed., *Colonial Architecture and Urbanism in Africa*.

10. As depicted in the classic film *La Noire de . . .* [The Black Girl of . . .] by Ousmane Sembène (1966).

11. Klonk, "Myth and Reality of the White Cube," 70.

12. Klonk, 73–75.

13. For a summary of recent books pointing to the fascist elements in Le Corbusier's thought and practice, see Rachel Donadio, "Le Corbusier's Architecture and His Politics Are Revisited." However, the "neutrality," and thus malleability, of modernism also appealed and opened doors to aspiring architects, like Minnette de Silva, in British colonies who even saw it as a form of anticolonial expression; see Crinson, "Imperial Modernism," 201–3.

14. Jackson and Holland, *The Architecture of Edwin Maxwell Fry and Jane Drew*, 1–8.

15. Originally the "Course in Tropical Studies."

16. See Godwin and Hopwood, "View from Lagos, Nigeria"; and Uduku, "Modernist Architecture and 'the Tropical' in West Africa," 3.

17. For a discussion of the connections between European architects working in the tropics, see Hannah Le Roux, "The Networks of Tropical Architecture"; and Chang, *A Genealogy of Tropical Architecture*.

258   Notes to Pages 149–152

18. See Curtin, *The Image of Africa*, 1:177–97.

19. Le Roux, "Building on the Boundary"; Fry was the head of the Department of Tropical Studies from 1954 to 1956.

20. Fry and Drew, *Tropical Architecture in the Dry and Humid Zones*; Koenigsberger, *Manual of Tropical Housing and Design*.

21. Chang, *A Genealogy of Tropical Architecture*, 175.

22. Cooper, *Africa since 1940*, 5.

23. For example, a claim that "both Fry and Drew admired traditional African society and culture, but without either the condescendingly romantic or racist attitudes that had generally characterized British colonialism," see Liscombe, "Modernism in Late Imperial British West Africa"; for a nostalgic perspective, see Uduku, "Modernist Architecture and 'the Tropical' in West Africa."

24. An early version of the manual was published in 1956 as *Tropical Architecture in the Humid Zone* (London: B. T. Batsford, 1956).

25. Fry and Drew, *Tropical Architecture in the Dry and Humid Zones*, 6–7.

26. Fry, "Town Planning in West Africa." This echoed Fry's earlier proclamations for British "slums," which he saw as "a fixed and hard-crusted mass" needing to be wiped away completely rather than dealt with "piecemeal"; see Fry, *Fine Building*, 3.

27. Atkinson, "African Housing," 228–37. This view was encouraged by contemporary publications on African architectural history such as a 1955 article by W. Murray Jack, "Old Houses of Lagos," which argued that precolonial Lagos had "no prevalent building tradition of its own," besides "huts," 96.

28. Jackson and Holland, *The Architecture of Edwin Maxwell Fry and Jane Drew*, 156.

29. Fry and Drew, *Tropical Architecture in the Dry and Humid Zones*, 6.

30. Hitchins, *Fry, Drew, Knight, Creamer Architecture*.

31. Huxley, *Four Guineas*, 190. For details of Huxley's political leanings, see Liscombe, "Modernism in Late Imperial British West Africa," 207–8.

32. For an early critique of this division in studies of West Africa, see Peel, "Urbanization and Urban History in West Africa"; for a broader, more recent overview, see Anderson and Rathbone, eds., *Africa's Urban Past*, 10–12.

33. Cooper, *Decolonization and African Society*, 19.

34. Baker, *Urbanization and Political Change*, quoted and critiqued in Peel, "Urbanization and Urban History in West Africa," 274.

35. Beier, *Art in Nigeria*, 55–56.

36. D'Auria, "In the Laboratory and in the Field," 337. She continues, "More directly than her husband, Drew would dryly assert the uselessness of Fortes' sociological advice for their town planning efforts. In their views

Notes to Pages 152–154

the main focus of anthropology appeared problematic to a modern architect striving for social change and who was confident architecture had a role to play in such improvement. . . . As Fry would recount, 'Anthropologists are always warning people such as ourselves who must make decisions that we know nothing, with the inference that the more we know the less we will care to act. In a country emerging from tribalism with involved and compelling family systems, the anthropologist is to be respected as an observer, especially when he is alive to change.'"

37. Cooper, *Decolonization and African Society*, 16.

38. For this historical context on the tensions and protests caused by decades of British land appropriation and segregation, which had reduced the "African" section of the central city to only Lagos Island, see Olukoju, "Population Pressure, Housing and Sanitation in West Africa's Pressure, Housing and Sanitation in West Africa's Premier Port-City"; Olukoju, "The Segregation of Europeans and Africans in Colonial Nigeria"; and Bigon, *A History of Urban Planning in Two West African Colonial Capitals*.

39. Huxley, *Four Guineas*, 198.

40. Fry and Drew, *Tropical Architecture in the Dry and Humid Zones*, 18.

41. Percy, "Thoughts on Building in Tropical Africa," quoted in Immerwahr, "The Politics of Architecture and Urbanism in Postcolonial Lagos," 170.

42. Ndibe, *Never Look an American in the Eye*, 6–7.

43. It was widely acknowledged in Lagos that there was a need for more attention to the health and growth of the city once plague broke out; however, the way the LEDB was formulated, its truly novel function was as a financial mechanism (rather than a planning body)—as an unchecked acquirer and leaser or seller of land—in order to fund the long-desired demolitions of swamps and African settlements. For a history of how the LEDB was set up and structured, see Okpala, "The Potentials and Perils of Public Urban Land Ownership and Management," 82. For an introduction to the extensive literature on the importance of land and changes to systems of landownership in Lagos's history, see Mann, "African and European Initiatives in the Transformation of Land Tenure in Colonial Lagos," 226.

44. Fry, "Town Planning in West Africa," 200–201.

45. *Report with Recommendations on the Planning and Development of Greater Lagos*, 3.

46. Immerwahr places LEDB schemes within the "British New Town" style of architecture and writes that "when it came to the sorts of buildings that *might* be of importance to non-elite Lagosians—housing estates and apartment complexes—Tropical Modernists had conspicuously little to say" ("The Politics of Architecture and Urbanism in Postcolonial Lagos," 6). This is not true. Fry and Drew designed several housing schemes for West Africa and were integral in the development of "New Town" models

and slum clearance schemes in the UK. See, for example, Fry, "Slum Clearance in the Town," in which Fry argued for massive, coordinated slum clearance programs, "not on the basis of recording black spots so that they may be neatly cut out for everyone to see how easily we cure slums, but rather surveying the whole machinery of a town to see how the vital work of slum clearance can be brought to the reorganisation of the structure upon which the health of the town rests" (9). See also Drew, Fry, and Humphries, *Village Housing in the Tropics.*

47. *Report with Recommendations on the Planning and Development of Greater Lagos,* 38.

48. *Report with Recommendations on the Planning and Development of Greater Lagos,* 38. These comments echo what Fry wrote about English slum dwellers two years earlier: "The jerry-built house is a good idea of the confusion of [the slum-dweller's] mind" (*Fine Building,* 11).

49. *Report with Recommendations on the Planning and Development of Greater Lagos,* 30. An estimated twenty thousand Lagosians were displaced by the schemes. Only 8 percent of an estimated four thousand rehousing units built went to low-income residents; see Peil, *Lagos,* 167–70.

50. Lindsay, *Working with Gender,* 146.

51. Lindsay notes that there were four thousand applicants for one thousand units (*Working with Gender*).

52. Henderson, "Housing in Lagos, Nigeria."

53. Olukoju, "The Segregation of Europeans," 279–83; Seun, "Malaria and Sanitation in Colonial Lagos," 67.

54. Marris, "Motives and Methods: Reflections on a Study in Lagos," 41.

55. Lindsay, *Working with Gender,* 161.

56. Lindsay, 150.

57. On these political developments, see Baker, *Urbanization and Political Change;* Sklar, *Nigerian Political Parties;* and Coleman, *Nigeria: Background to Nationalism.*

58. Determined from data in Baker, *Urbanization and Political Change,* 156. Wards A and B continually voted for the AG over the NCNC in the 1950s. These were the two wards most affected by the Central Lagos Slum Clearance Scheme.

59. "Dual Responsibility."

60. "They Oppose Clearance: Postpone the Scheme."

61. "Lagos Slum Scheme?"

62. Dunn, "Facade by Lagos Lagoon." In 1997, Nigerian urbanists Agbola and Jinadu wrote, "The pre-independence demolition . . . resulted in the celebrated Isale-Eko clearance to give the visiting Queen of England a pleasing view of the area" ("Forced Eviction and Forced Relocation in Nigeria," 272).

Notes to Pages 160–166

63. "Lagos Slums Must Be Cleared."

64. "Removing to the New Homes."

65. Marris, *Family and Social Change in an Africa City*.

66. Marris, chaps. 2–3.

67. Marris, chap. 6. On the continued importance (and fragility) of trust in Nigerian urban economies, see Guyer, Denzer, and Agbaje, eds., *Money Struggles and City Life*.

68. Marris, "Motives and Methods," 46.

69. Although the LEDB had assured Central Lagosians that they would be able to repurchase a plot in the vicinity of their old land, this ultimately proved to be virtually impossible for displaced residents for several reasons. The first obstacle was that in order to reacquire land in Central Lagos, residents were required to pay 20 percent on top of their original compensation price—and this was just to buy the land back. Reconstruction of buildings was left up to residents to finance. After the financial hit taken while living in Surulere or elsewhere (due to paying higher rent in addition to the loss of rents from tenants and the loss of trade income) most people did not have money saved to rebuild. Many residents had been evicted from Surulere because, between the higher rent and trade hardships, they had little income. In addition, new zoning requirements in Central Lagos for the construction of multistory foundations and the limiting of ground floor to commercial businesses further handcuffed returnees. The result, as Marris observed, was that "scarcely of the owners possessed such capital sums [to repurchase and rebuild], or were in a position to borrow it" (*Family and Social Change in an Africa City*, 87).

70. Glazer, *From a Cause to a Style*, 2.

71. Jackson and Holland, *The Architecture of Edwin Maxwell Fry and Jane Drew*, 202, 204. The double irony was that Gold Coast residents then rejected their designs, instead asking for the cubical houses they had been for so long told were "modern."

72. Atkinson, "Mass Housing in Rapidly Developing Tropical Areas."

73. Proceedings of a conference on Tropical Architecture, March 1953, quoted in Marris, *Family and Social Change in an Africa City*, 127.

74. Baker, *Urbanization and Political Change*, 185.

75. Baker, 185.

76. "Constitution of the Nigerian National Democratic Party," quoted in Baker, *Urbanization and Political Change*, 130–31.

77. *Report of the Tribunal of Inquiry into the Affairs of the Lagos Executive Development Board*.

78. Minister of Lagos Affairs, quoted in Marris, *Family and Social Change in an Africa City*, 119.

79. Akinsemoyin and Vaughan-Richards, *Building Lagos*, 55.

262   Notes to Pages 166–175

80. Abrams et al., "Metropolitan Lagos," 57.
81. Abrams et al., 79.
82. Griffin, "Urban Development in Africa," 44–45, emphasis added.
83. Marris, "Motives and Methods," 39.
84. "Lagos Slum Scheme?"
85. Larkin, *Signal and Noise*, 148, quoted in George, *Making Modern Girls*, 231.
86. Soyinka, *Myth, Literature and the African World*, 10.
87. Crowther, *A Vocabulary of the Yoruba Language*, 19.
88. Stoler, "Colonial Archives and the Arts of Governance." See also Drayton, "Where Does the World Historian Write From?"
89. Elkins, "Looking beyond Mau Mau."
90. For examples of histories retrieved through spoken and photographic archives, see Stoler, "Colonial Archives," notes 8, 9. More recent studies of decolonization through images include Faulkner and Ramamurthy, eds., *Visual Culture and Decolonisation in Britain*; and Feldman, *From a Nation Torn*.
91. Elkins, "Looking beyond Mau Mau."
92. See Richards, *The Imperial Archive*.
93. Articles such as Dunn's "Facade by Lagos Lagoon" called out this ruse once again being set into motion as the queen was scheduled to arrive in Lagos.
94. See Sato, "Operation Legacy."
95. Sato, 699–704.
96. Sato, 697.
97. Quoted in Crinson, "Imperial Modernism," 225–26.

Chapter 5: Atlantic

1. Seriki and Pullybank, *Visitors Guide to Lagos*, 10.
2. Barnes and Joseph published within a year of each other: Barnes, *Patrons and Power*; and Joseph, *Democracy and Prebendal Politics in Nigeria*.
3. Apter, *The Pan-African Nation*.
4. Equivalent to approximately $240,000,000 per day in today's value (Cowell, "Lagos, Oil Boom Fading").
5. Joseph, *Democracy and Prebendal Politics*, 56.
6. Apter borrows the imagery from Ken Saro-Wiwa's description of Nigeria "sitting over the Ogoni and expropriating their oil to finance a corrupt and wasteful regime," writing, "We can map its blood-draining logic more precisely onto the accumulation and distribution of oil royalties and rents, not only in terms of the enormous wealth that was mysteriously conjured and publicly invested, but more specifically in terms of the hidden costs exacted by the concurrent privatization of the public sphere—the kickbacks, prebends, and wholesale diversion of public funds into private accounts and personal fiefdoms" (*Pan-African Nation*, 267, 269).

Notes to Pages 176–184

7. Schatz, *Nigerian Capitalism*, 2.
8. See Watts, "The Shock of Modernity."
9. Joseph, *Democracy and Prebendal Politics*, 1.
10. Joseph, 8.
11. Joseph, 8–9.
12. Seriki and Pullybank, *Visitors Guide to Lagos*.
13. Seriki and Pullybank, 50–67.
14. Apter, *The Pan-African Nation*, 279.
15. See Joseph, *Democracy and Prebendal Politics*, 82.
16. This has instigated a long debate over the politicization of censuses in Nigerian history and questions about the size of the population of Lagos. For a summary of this history, see Okolo, "The Nigerian Census."
17. Barnes, *Patrons and Power*, 70.
18. Joseph, *Democracy and Prebendal Politics*, 55.
19. While men more often bought land and established houses, Barnes found that one in six houses in Mushin was owned by a woman (*Patrons and Power*, 67).
20. Peace, "Prestige Power and Legitimacy in a Modern Nigerian Town," 36.
21. Barnes, *Patrons and Power*, 66.
22. On the scarcity of reliable information in 1970s Lagos and "people's dependence on word-of-mouth transmissions for what knowledge they did have," see Barnes, *Patrons and Power*, 77–78.
23. Barnes, 68.
24. Biersteker, *Multinationals, the State, and Control of the Nigerian Economy*, 148.
25. Barnes, *Patrons and Power*, 49.
26. Barnes, 69.
27. On the importance of hometown networks in establishing oneself in Mushin, see Barnes, *Patrons and Power*, 73.
28. Barnes, 78.
29. See Barnes, 82–85 for a timeline of disputes and interventions (from marriage disputes to questions over chieftaincy succession rules) that I. A. Adeyemi was involved in over a ten-week period.
30. Older community members try to restrict these requirements by arguing that only descendants of original owners (sons of the soil) could hold chieftaincy titles, while settlers argued that autochthonous families had forfeited that right by selling land. See Barnes, *Patrons and Power*, 100.
31. Barnes, 110.
32. Barnes, 104, 132.
33. *Daily Times*, January 25, 1973, quoted in Barnes *Patrons and Power*, 157.
34. Ahonsi, "Nigeria: Glimpses and Interpretations from an Informed Lagosian," 133.

Notes to Pages 185–189

35. See Taylor, ed., *Urban Development in Nigeria.*
36. Lagos State Records and Archives Bureau, LGS34, Federal Ministry of Works and Housing, "Summary of 'Progress Report' to the Permanent Secretary/Director General, Federal Ministry of Works and Housing, concerning efforts to secure staff for planning activities in Lagos, through the United Nations," April 31, 1967.
37. Ahonsi, "Nigeria," 133.
38. Tade Akin Aina, "Petty Landlords and Poor Tenants in a Low-Income Settlement in Metropolitan Lagos," 93.
39. Barnes writes that in Mushin, "land transfers had been carried out publicly, verbally and with the use of witnesses. In keeping with the past, initial sales by Mushin's descent groups often were informal, with verbal agreements or rudimentary receipts serving to verify those transactions. But due to the large number of sales and the wide cross-section of participants, such verbal agreements were forgotten and witnesses moved away" (*Patrons and Power*, 54).
40. Akinyele, "Contesting for Space in an Urban Centre," 109–34.
41. Barnes, *Patrons and Power*, 59.
42. Barnes, 55.
43. For examples of more elaborate schemes, see Apter, *The Pan-African Nation*, chap. 7.
44. "Historical background," LSDPC official website, online, accessed July 11, 2018, http://www.lsdpc.gov.ng/his.php.
45. Lagos State Records and Archives Bureau, LGS34, Federal Ministry of Work and Housing, Letter from J. R. Atkinson to Adeyemi Bero, December 4, 1970.
46. Lagos State Records and Archives Bureau, 3rd National Development Plan, 1975–80, Lagos State Programs, chap. 19, "Housing."
47. Conversation with Prof. Modupe Omirin, Faculty in the Department of Estate Management, University of Lagos. August 24, 2016.
48. Conversation with Prof. Omirin, August 24, 2016.
49. Conversation with Prof. Omirin, August 24, 2016.
50. Lagos State Records and Archives Bureau, 3rd National Development Plan, 1975–80, Lagos State Programs, chap. 19, "Housing."
51. Lagos State Records and Archives Bureau, 3rd National Development Plan, 1975–80, Lagos State Programs, chap. 19, "Housing."
52. Ahonsi, "Nigeria," 133.
53. Lagos State Records and Archives Bureau, 3rd National Development Plan, 1975–80, Lagos State Programs, chap. 19, "Housing."
54. Lagos State Records and Archives Bureau, 3rd National Development Plan, 1975–80, Lagos State Programs, chap. 19, "Housing."
55. Peil, *Lagos*, 167–70.

Notes to Pages 189–197

56. Lagos State Records and Archives Bureau, LGS/268, Olowogbowo Rehousing Scheme, letter from Surulere Rehousing Estate Residents' Association, The Officially Recognized Representative Organ of the People Displaced from Lagos under the L.E.D.B. Slum Clearance Scheme, to Brigadier Mobolaji Johnson, Military Governor, Lagos State, et al., January 4, 1974.

57. Onagoruwa, "What Are Your Property Rights within the Law?"

58. Okutubo, "Kalakuta Acquired."

59. These evictions peaked in 1990, when Lagos State displaced over three hundred thousand people from Maroko, a poor but habitable community, which was "later parceled out to high-ranking military officers and private developers," while "less than 5 percent of former Maroko residents were resettled" (Ahonsi, "Nigeria," 133). For a summary of the dozens of uncompensated mass evictions in Lagos in the 1970s and 1980s, see Agbola and Jinadu, "Forced Eviction and Forced Relocation in Nigeria."

60. See Okonta and Douglas, *Where Vultures Feast.*

61. Mabogunje, "Land Reform in Nigeria."

62. Aina, "The Construction of Housing for the Urban Poor of Lagos," 37.

63. See, for example, Sule, "The Deterioration of the Nigerian Environment"; Abiodun, "Problems in Nigerian Cities"; and Nwafor, "Physical Environment, Decision-Making and Land Use Development in Metropolitan Lagos."

64. Ayeni, "Living Conditions of the Poor in Lagos."

65. Sada and Adefolalu, "Urbanisation and Problems of Urban Development."

66. This reached the point of national crisis during the 1976 cement scandal. See Soyinka, *The Open Sore of a Continent,* 79–81.

67. Omezi, "Lagos: City of Concrete."

68. Aboutorabi, "Problems of Housing in Lagos," 236–37.

69. See Elleh, *Architecture and Politics in Nigeria.*

70. Braimoh and Onishi, "Spatial Determinants of Urban Land Use Change in Lagos," 506.

71. Balogun, *Adjusted Lives,* 80, quoted in Davis, *Planet of Slums,* 152.

72. For the history of this non-interventionalist ideology that celebrated the "praxis of the poor," saw slums as the solution not the problem, and invented the myth of "self-housing" as a form of entrepreneurship and grassroots capitalism, see Davis, *Planet of Slums,* 70–94.

73. Peace, "Prestige Power and Legitimacy," 35.

74. Peace, 35.

75. Peace, 40.

76. Berry, "City, Country, and Class."

77. Agbola, *The Architecture of Fear.*

78. Apter, *The Pan-African Nation,* 231, 283.

79. Apter, 283.

Conclusion

1. "Lagos will not spoil": the city's defiant unofficial motto.
2. "Lagos: The Megacity Battling for Water."
3. Kazeem, "Lagos Is Africa's 7th Largest Economy and Is About to Get Bigger."
4. When I was in Uganda in 2010, the housegirls of the family I was staying with in Gulu understood and could speak Nigerian pidgin English from watching the Nigeria television channel "Africa Magic" nightly.
5. BBC Minute, "London to Lagos."
6. Quote in heading: Digest Africa, "Lagos, a City of Shanty Towns and Millionaires." First sentence of section: Woetzel et al., *A Blueprint for Addressing the Global Affordable Housing Challenge*.
7. For an overview of the different population estimates for Lagos, see Fox, Bloch, and Monroy, "Understanding the Dynamics of Nigeria's Urban Transition." Africanpolis's estimate of 10.6 million for 2010 was based on newer methods of satellite imagery and remote sensing and is closer to UN and Nigeria National Population Commission's figures than the widely cited 17 and 23 million estimates calculated and promoted by Lagos State.
8. Quoted in Roland Igbinoba Real Foundation, *The State of Lagos Housing Market*, 2:44.
9. McKinsey Global Institute, *A Blueprint*, 29, 182; Woetzel et al., "Tackling the World's Affordable Housing Challenge."
10. Roland Igbinoba Real Foundation, *The State of Lagos Housing Market*, 2:85. This figure is based on a population estimate of 16 million for 2016.
11. UN News, "Nigeria Must Act to Stop Housing Crisis and Forced Evictions."
12. Roland Igbinoba Real Foundation, *The State of Lagos Housing Market*, 2:88.
13. Steffen Wetzstein points out in "The Global Urban Housing Affordability Crisis" that "the world's largest cities capture two-thirds of McKinsey's Global Institute's 'Affordability Gap'" (3161).
14. See Wetzstein, "The Global Urban Housing Affordability Crisis"; Gyourko, Mayer, and Sinai, "Superstar Cities"; and Dobbs et al., "Urban World: Mapping the Economic Power of Cities."
15. Between 2007 (prerecession highs) and 2016, the price of New York condos rose nearly 30 percent, while the price of townhouses rose nearly 60 percent. See Nonko, "Manhattan Home Prices Have Increased Dramatically in a Decade." On the financialization of housing, see Soules, *Icebergs, Zombies, and the Ultra Thin*.
16. Roland Igbinoba Real Foundation, *The State of Lagos Housing Market*, 2:65–66.

Notes to Pages 203–207

17. Figures from Roland Igbinoba Real Foundation, *The State of Lagos Housing Market*, 2:53, 54, 61, 98, 132–33.
18. "Lagos Living."
19. Goodfellow and Owen, "Thick Claims and Thin Rights," 426.
20. Goodfellow and Owen, 409.
21. Bierschenk and de Sardan, *States at Work*, 221, quoted in Goodfellow and Owen, "Thick Claims and Thin Rights," 413.
22. Pratten, "The Precariousness of Prebendalism," 246, quoted in Goodfellow and Owen, "Thick Claims and Thin Rights," 414.
23. Scheye, "Heart of Africa's Organised Crime." Export restrictions meant Nigerians looking to stash and launder money have turned to Lagos real estate for decades; see Goodfellow and Owen, "Thick Claims and Thin Rights," 413.
24. Akinyele, "Contesting for Space in an Urban Centre," 109–34.
25. Olawoyin, "Nigeria: Otodo-Gbame"; Joy Ike and Esiebo, "They Came While We Were Asleep"; Amnesty International, "Nigeria: Deadly Mass Forced Evictions Make Life Misery for Waterfront Communities"; JEI Press Release, "Over 30,000 Homeless after Police Use Demolition by Fire."
26. Salvaire and Mitchell, "It's Like a Civil War."
27. Amnesty International, "Nigeria."
28. Oserogho & Associates, "Property Taxes in Nigeria."
29. Lagos State Development and Property Corporation, accessed August 4, 2018, http://www.lsdpc.gov.ng/.
30. Gurran and Phibbs, "Are Governments Really Interested in Fixing the Housing Problem?"
31. Sawyer, "Piecemeal Urbanisation at the Peripheries of Lagos"; see also "Lindsay Sawyer," https://www.africancentreforcities.net/people/lindsay-sawyer/. In "Planning, Anti-planning and the Infrastructure Crisis Facing Metropolitan Lagos," Matthew Gandy found that only 10 percent of Lagos was connected to municipal water system (378). See also van Zeijl, *Do-It-Yourself Society, on Life in Lagos*.
32. Obiefuna et al., "Land Cover Dynamics Associated with the Spatial Changes in the Wetlands of Lagos," 671.
33. Obiefuna et al., 671.
34. "Why Flooding in Nigeria Is an Increasingly Serious Problem."
35. Obot et al., "Evaluation of Rainfall Trends in Nigeria for 30 Years."
36. Komolafe et al., "A Review of Flood Risk Analysis in Nigeria."
37. Adelekan, "Vulnerability of Poor Urban Coastal Communities to Climate Change in Lagos."
38. Akoni and Olowoopejo, "50% Hospitalized Lagosians Suffer Water-Borne Diseases."

268 Notes to Pages 207–212

39. Adetayo, "Lagos: Profits Over Preparation."
40. Gaestel, "Things Fall Apart."
41. Obasi, "Okunde Blue Waters Scheme."
42. Onuoha, "A 50-Mile Island Built to Save Lagos's Economy Has a Worrying Design Flaw."
43. Morshed, "The Aesthetics of Ascension in Norman Bel Geddes's Futurama," quoted in Hassanain and Martina, "Architectures of the (Un)Inhabitable."
44. Wetzstein, "The Global Urban Housing Affordability Crisis," 3162.
45. Wetzstein, 3163. The mid-2000s "housing crisis" (an "over"-accessibility of homeownership) that triggered the 2008 financial crisis and the contemporary "housing crisis" (an under-accessibility of housing) that came in its aftermath as banks were bailed out and homeowners were foreclosed on (allowing a reconcentration of real estate and wealth) illustrates that current economic policies are out of sync and not working for anyone besides those who hold housing stock already. See Dayen, "Banks Got Bailed Out, Homeowners Got Sold Out."
46. Aalbers and Christophers, "Centring Housing in Political Economy," 374; Christophers, "For Real: Land as Capital and Commodity," 143. See also Schneider, "The American Housing Crisis Might Be Our Next Big Political Issue."
47. See Davis, "Insecure and Secure Cities."
48. Makhubu, "This House Is Not for Sale," 58.
49. The situation in Lagos is similar to how Miami's "current housing boom is tied to foreign buyers' parking cash in condos; much of the cash is derived from commodities like oil, which makes it a city that is literally drowning as a result of the combustion of the fossil fuels that made [luxury real estate buyers] rich" (Crist, "Besides, I'll Be Dead").
50. Makhubu, "This House Is Not for Sale," 58.
51. Makhubu, 58.
52. Makhubu, 60.
53. Makhubu, 61–62.
54. Makhubu, 62.
55. Makhubu, 66.
56. Makhubu, 69.
57. Harrison, *The Dominion of the Dead*, 37.
58. Harrison, 37.
59. Makhubu, "This House Is Not for Sale," 58.
60. Makhubu, 61.
61. Within the brackets, Harrison writes that this fact, "when we reflect on it, unsettles our everyday conception of the house as natural shelter or dwelling place" (*The Dominion of the Dead*, 38).

Notes to Pages 213–221

62. Harrison, *The Dominion of the Dead*, 40.

63. Harrison, 40.

64. Harrison, "Hic Jacet," 359.

65. Makhubu, "This House Is Not for Sale," 63.

66. Deleuze and Guattari, *Anti-Oedipus: Capitalism and Schizophrenia*.

67. On this counterpoint, see Scott, *Against the Grain*, who argues that settling in sedentary houses in order to pursue agriculture was a strategy humans used to gain control over reproduction through building patriarchal houses that subjugated women, captives, and slaves. This was the case in Lagos for many enslaved individuals who found new freedoms and opportunities to break loose from bondage through the ownership of land at the end of the nineteenth century. Gradually, white cap and other powerful families in Lagos chipped away at land rights of former slaves. By the 1930s, descendants of slaves had lost the ability to securely own property in Lagos; see Mann, *Slavery and the Birth of an African City*, 276.

68. Ferguson, *Give a Man a Fish*, xiii.

69. Shasore, *Possessed*.

70. Albert, "Crisis and Individuation," 230. As Jason Hickel writes, "Investors can effectively conduct moment-by-moment referendums on decisions made by voters or governments around the world, bestowing their favor on countries that facilitate profit maximization while punishing those that prioritize other concerns" (quoted in Albert, "Crisis and Individuation," 230–31).

71. As Hassanain and Martina write, "Whitney Bauman offers a poignant observation that connects spatial conquest to an act of divine creation. Bauman argues that a key underpinning of the legal fiction of terra nullius was the Christian doctrine of creatio ex nihilo (creation out of nothing). This doctrine of a divinely mandated human dominion over nature—a theology in which 'humans mimic the power of the Creator God'—provided 'a justification for the colonial concept of individual property,' and the underlying cause of the present ecological crises" ("Architectures of the (Un)Inhabitable"). See Bauman, "Creatio Ex Nihilo, Terra Nullius, and the Erasure of Presence," 356.

72. Mbembe, "Ruth First Lecture 2019," emphasis added.

73. Ogundiran, *The Yorùbá*, 82.

74. To be clear, in Lagos, this involved increasingly exploitative forms of slavery by the nineteenth century, a reality that underscores the need for iterating ideas for the institution of ilé to protect vulnerable members.

75. Harrison, "Hic Jacet," 362.

76. Hassanain and Martina, "Architectures of the (Un)Inhabitable."

77. Hassanain and Martina.

78. Hassanain and Martina.

79. Lal, *African Socialism in Postcolonial Tanzania;* Croese, Cirolia, and Graham, "Towards Habitat III."

80. This is not to say that Lagos State governors have not made real improvements in some areas of the city's infrastructure. In the last decade, in addition to land reclamation and levees, Lagos State has expanded and upgraded drainage systems in core urban areas to combat flooding. These efforts are part of real improvements achieved by several successive governors to raise revenues and to invest in the city's infrastructures and services. Lagosians have noticed these state actions and have paid taxes at higher rates than they have historically.

81. "Deplorable Housing in Nigeria, Grave Breach of Human Rights."

82. See Adetayo, "Lagos: Profits Over Preparation."

83. Bowman, Myers, and Southwood, "The Housing Theory of Everything."

Bibliography

Archives Consulted

The British Library
Harvard Map Collection
Lagos State Record and Archives Bureau
The National Archives, Kew, UK
Nigerian Federal Survey Department
Nigerian National Archives at Ibadan
Nigerian National Library at Yaba
Nigerian National Museum at Lagos
Schomburg Center for Research in Black Culture, New York Public Library

Unpublished Theses and Articles

Aboutorabi, S. Mohsen. "Problems of Housing in Lagos: The Sociocultural Dimension of the Provision of Housing for the Urban Poor in Lagos." PhD diss., The Glasgow School of Art, 1986.

Alonge, Marjorie Moji Dolapo. "Afro-Brazilian Architecture in Lagos State: A Case for Conservation." PhD diss., Newcastle University, 1994.

Animashaun, Idris. "A Historical Study of the Development and Growth of Medical and Health Services in Lagos, 1873–1960." MA thesis, University of Lagos, 2011.

Brown, Spencer Hunter. "A History of the People of Lagos, 1852–1886." PhD diss., Northwestern University, 1964.

França, Nara Muniz Improta. "Producing Intellectuals: Lagosian Books and Pamphlets between 1874 and 1922." PhD diss., University of Sussex, 2013.

Gbadegesin, Olubukola A. "Picturing the Modern Self: Politics, Identity, and Self Fashioning in Lagos, 1861–1934." PhD diss., Emory University, 2010.

Godwin, Tony. "The Brazilian Influence on Buildings in Lagos." Unpublished article, 1974.

Hopkins, Anthony G. "An Economic History of Lagos." PhD diss., University of London, 1964.

Mann, Kristin. "A Social History of the New African Elite in Lagos Colony, 1880–1913." PhD diss., Stanford University, 1977.

Okpala, Donatus C. Ifebueme. "The Potentials and Perils of Public Urban Land Ownership and Management: A Case Study of the Lagos Executive Development Board (Nigeria), 1928–1972." PhD diss., MIT, 1977.

Sawada, Nozomi. "The Educated Elite and Associational Life in Early Lagos Newspapers: In Search of Unity for the Progress of Society." PhD diss., University of Birmingham, 2011.

Shaw, Joanne Nagel. "Historic Buildings of Lagos, Nigeria." Unpublished manuscript, 1980. Oak Grove Library Center, Northwestern University.

Published Works

Aalbers, Manuel B., and Brett Christophers. "Centring Housing in Political Economy." *Housing, Theory and Society* 31 (2014): 373–94.

Abiodun, Josephine Olu. "Problems in Nigerian Cities." *Town Planning Review* 47 (1976): 339–47.

Abrams, C., S. Kobe, O. Koenigsberger, M. Shapiro, and M. Wheeler. "Metropolitan Lagos [an edited selection of the Report *Metropolitan Lagos* (UN Department of Economic and Social Affairs, 1964)]." *Habitat International* 5 (1980): 55–83.

Achebe, Chinua. *No Longer at Ease.* New York: Anchor, 1994.

Adekemi, Ogundiran, and Enisan Olugbenga. "Challenges of Housing Delivery in Metropolitan Lagos." *Research on Humanities and Social Sciences* 3 (2013): 1–9.

Adelekan, Ibidun O. "Vulnerability of Poor Urban Coastal Communities to Climate Change in Lagos, Nigeria." *Environment and Urbanization* 22 (2010): 433–50.

Adelusi-Adeluyi, Ademide. "'Africa for the Africans?' Mapmaking, Lagos, and the Colonial Archive." *History in Africa* 47, no. 1 (2020): 275–96.

———. "Historical Tours of 'New' Lagos: Performance, Place Making, and Cartography in the 1880s." *Comparative Studies of South Asia, Africa and the Middle East* 38, no. 3 (2018): 443–54.

Aderibigbe, A. B. "Early History of Lagos to about 1850." In *Lagos: The Development of an African City,* edited by A. B. Aderibigbe and J. F. A. Ajayi, 1–26. Nigeria: Longman, 1975.

Adetayo, Ope. "Lagos: Profits Over Preparation." The Sinking Cities Project. Accessed March 27, 2024. https://unbiasthenews.org/.

Adewoye, Omoniyi. "The Tijani Land Case (1915–1921): A Study in British Colonial Justice." *Odu* 13 (1976).

Adichie, Chimamanda Ngozi. "Still Becoming: At Home in Lagos with Chimamanda Ngozi Adichie." *Esquire,* April 29, 2019.

Adshead, S. D. "The School of Civic Design at the Liverpool University." *Landscape Architecture Magazine* 1 (1911): 105–9.

Agbiboa, Daniel E. "Stomach Infrastructure: Informal Transport, Electoral Politics, and the Precariousness of Patronage in Lagos." In *Transport, Transgression and Politics in African Cities: The Rhythm of Chaos*, edited by Daniel E. Agbiboa. Abingdon: Routledge, 2018.

Agbola, Tunde. *The Architecture of Fear: Urban Design and Construction Response to Urban Violence in Lagos, Nigeria*. Ibadan: IFRA, 1997.

Agbola, Tunde, and A. M. Jinadu. "Forced Eviction and Forced Relocation in Nigeria: The Experience of Those Evicted from Maroko in 1990." *Environment and Urbanization* 9 (1997): 271–88.

Agiri, Babatunde A. "Architecture as a Source of History: The Lagos Example," In *History of the Peoples of Lagos State*, edited by Ade Adefuye and Babatunde A. Agiri, 341–44. Lagos: Lantern Books, 1987.

Agiri, Babatunde A., and Sandra Barnes. "Lagos Before 1603." In *History of the Peoples of Lagos State*, edited by Ade Adefuye et al., 18–32. Lagos: Lantern Books, 1987.

Ahonsi, Babatunde A. "Nigeria: Glimpses and Interpretations from an Informed Lagosian." In *Under Siege: Four African Cities: Freetown, Johannesburg, Kinshasa, Lagos: Documenta 11, Platform 4*, edited by Okwui Enwezor et al. Ostfildern-Ruit, Germany: Hatje Cantz; New York: Art Publishers, 2002.

Aina, Tade Akin. "The Construction of Housing for the Urban Poor of Lagos." *Habitat International* 12 (1988): 31–48.

———. "Petty Landlords and Poor Tenants in a Low-Income Settlement in Metropolitan Lagos." In *Housing Africa's Urban Poor*, edited by Philip Amis and Peter Lloyd, 87–101. Manchester: Manchester University Press, 1990.

Aizenman, Nurith. "Is It Insulting to Call This a Hut?" *NPR*, November 12, 2017. https://www.npr.org/.

Ajayi, J. F. A. "The British Occupation of Lagos, 1851–1861: A Critical Review." *Nigeria Magazine* 69 (1961): 96–105.

———. *Christian Missions in Nigeria, 1841–1891: The Making of a New Elite*. Harlow: Longman, 1965.

Akinsemoyin, Kunle, and Alan Vaughan-Richards. *Building Lagos*. Jersey: Pengrail, 1976.

Akinyele, Rufus T. "Contesting for Space in an Urban Centre: The Omo Onile Syndrome in Lagos." In *African Cities: Competing Claims on Urban Spaces*, edited by Francesca Locatelli and Paul Nugent, 109–34. Leiden: Brill, 2009.

Akoni, Olasunkanmi, and Monsuru Olowoopejo. "50% Hospitalized Lagosians Suffer Water-borne Diseases—LASG." *Vanguard*, March 16, 2017. https://www.vanguardngr.com/.

Akyeampong, Emmanuel. *Between the Sea and the Lagoon: An Eco-Social History of the Anlo of Southeastern Ghana, 1850 to Recent Times.* Athens: Ohio University Press, 2002.

———. "Commerce, Credit, and Mobility in Late Nineteenth-Century Gold Coast: Changing Dynamics in Euro-African Trade." In *African Development in Historical Perspective,* edited by Emmanuel Akyeampong, Robert H. Bates, Nathan Nunn, and James A. Robinson, 231–63. Cambridge: Cambridge University Press, 2014.

Aladeojebi, Gbade. *History of Yoruba Land.* South Africa: Partridge, 2016.

Albert, Michael J. "Crisis and Individuation: Mapping and Navigating the Planetary Crisis Convergence." PhD diss., Johns Hopkins University, 2020.

Amnesty International. "Nigeria: Deadly Mass Forced Evictions Make Life Misery for Waterfront Communities." Amnesty International, November 17, 2017. https://www.amnesty.org/.

Anderson, David M. "Master and Servant in Colonial Kenya, 1895–1939." *Journal of African History* 41 (2000): 459–85.

Anderson, David M., and Richard Rathbone, eds. *Africa's Urban Past.* Oxford: James Currey, 2000.

Apter, Andrew. *The Pan-African Nation: Oil and the Spectacle of Culture in Nigeria.* Chicago: University of Chicago Press, 2005.

Aradeon, David. "Planning Lagos: The Unmaking of Tradition." *African Quarterly on the Arts* 1 (1996): 72–85.

Arendt, Hannah. *The Origins of Totalitarianism.* New York: Harcourt Brace Jovanovich, 1976.

Atkinson, G. Anthony. "African Housing." *African Affairs* 49 (1950): 228–37.

———. "Mass Housing in Rapidly Developing Tropical Areas." *Town Planning Review* 31 (1960): 85–102.

Awe, Bolanle. *Nigerian Women in Historical Perspective.* Lagos: Sankore, 1992.

Ayeni, M. A. O. "Living Conditions of the Poor in Lagos." *Ekistics* 43 (1977): 77–80.

Baker, Pauline H. *Urbanization and Political Change: The Politics of Lagos, 1917–1967.* Berkeley: University of California Press, 1974.

Balogun, F. Odun. *Adjusted Lives: Stories of Structural Adjustments.* Trenton, NJ: Africa World Press, 1995.

Barber, Karin. "Documenting Social and Ideological Change through Yoruba Oriki: A Stylistic Analysis." *Journal of the Historical Society of Nigeria* 10 (1981): 39–52.

Barnes, Sandra. *Patrons and Power: Creating a Political Community in Metropolitan Lagos.* Manchester: Manchester University Press, 1986.

Bauman, Whitney. "Creatio Ex Nihilo, Terra Nullius, and the Erasure of Presence." In *Ecospirit,* edited by Laurel Kearns and Catherine Keller, 353–72. New York: Fordham University Press, 2007.

———. *Ecospirit.* New York: Fordham University Press, 2007.

Bibliography

BBC Minute. "London to Lagos: Why Repats Are Making the Move." *BBC*, undated. http://www.bbc.co.uk/.

Beardsley, John, ed. *Cultural Landscape Heritage in Sub-Saharan Africa*. Cambridge, MA: Harvard University Press, 2017.

Beier, Ulli. *Art in Nigeria*. Cambridge: Cambridge University Press, 1960.

Berry, Sara S. "City, Country, and Class: Work, Migration, and Class in Western Nigeria: A Reinterpretation." In *Struggle for the City: Migrant Labor, Capital, and the State in Urban Africa*, edited by Fred Cooper. Beverly Hills: Sage, 1983.

———. *Cocoa, Custom and Socio-Economic Change in Rural Western Nigeria*. Oxford: Clarendon, 1975.

Bhabha, Homi K. *The Location of Culture*. 2nd ed. Abingdon: Routledge, 2004.

Bierschenk, Thomas, and Jean-Pierre Olivier de Sardan. *States at Work: Dynamics of African Bureaucracies*. Leiden: Brill, 2014.

Biersteker, Thomas. *Multinationals, the State, and Control of the Nigerian Economy*. Princeton, NJ: Princeton University Press, 1987.

Bigon, Liora. "Between Local and Colonial Perceptions: The History of Slum Clearances in Lagos (Nigeria), 1924–1960." *African and Asian Studies* 7 (2008): 49–76.

———. "Bubonic Plague, Colonial Ideologies, and Urban Planning Policies: Dakar, Lagos, and Kumasi." *Planning Perspectives* 31, no. 2 (2016): 205–26.

———. "The Former Names of Lagos (Nigeria) in Historical Perspective." *Names* 59 (2011): 229–40.

———. *A History of Urban Planning in Two West African Colonial Capitals: Residential Segregation in British Lagos and French Dakar, 1850–1930*. Lewiston, NY: Edwin Mellen Press, 2009.

———. "Tracking Ethno-cultural Differences: The Lagos Steam Tramway, 1902–1933." *Journal of Historical Geography* 33 (2007): 596–618.

Blier, Suzanne Preston. *The Anatomy of Architecture: Ontology and Metaphor in Batammaliba Architectural Expression*. Chicago: University of Chicago Press, 1994.

———. "Vernacular Architecture." In *Handbook of Material Culture*, edited by Christopher Tilley, Webb Keane, Susanne Kuechler-Fogden, Mike Rowlands, and Patricia Spyer, 230–53. London: Sage, 2006.

Bloch, Sean. "Statis and Slums: The Changing Temporal, Spatial, and Gendered Meaning of 'Home' in Northeastern Kenya." *Journal of African History* 58 (2017): 403–23.

Bourdieu, Pierre. *Distinction: A Social Critique of the Judgement of Taste*. Translated by Richard Nice. Cambridge, MA: Harvard University Press, 1984 [1979].

———. "The Forms of Capital." In *Handbook of Theory and Research for Sociology of Education*, edited by John G. Richardson, 241–58. New York: Greenwood, 1986.

———. "The Kabyle House or the World Reversed." In *Algeria 1960*, translated by Richard Nice, 133–53. Cambridge: Cambridge University Press, 1977.

Bowman, Sam, John Myers, and Ben Southwood. "The Housing Theory of Everything." *Works in Progress*, September 14, 2021. https://www.worksinprogress.co/.

Braimoh, Ademola K., and Takashi Onishi. "Spatial Determinants of Urban Land Use Change in Lagos, Nigeria." *Land Use Policy* 24 (2007): 502–15.

Bremner, G. A., ed. *Architecture and Urbanism in the British Empire*. Oxford: Oxford University Press, 2016.

Brenner, Neil, and Christian Schmid. "Planetary Urbanization." In *Urban Constellations*, edited by Matthew Gandy, 10–13. Berlin: Jovis, 2011.

Brown, Christopher. *Moral Capital: Foundations of British Abolitionism*. Chapel Hill: University of North Carolina Press, 2006.

Brown, Spencer H. "Colonialism on the Cheap: A Tale of Two English Army Surgeons in Lagos, Samuel Rowe and Frank Simpson, 1862–1882." *International Journal of African Historical Studies* 27 (1994): 551–88.

"Bulldozing History: The Destruction of Heritage in Lagos." *Economist*, June 15, 2017.

Bunn David. "'Our Wattled Cot:' Mercantile and Domestic Space in Thomas Pringle's African Landscapes," in *Landscape and Power*. 2nd ed. Edited by W. J. T. Mitchell, 127–73. Chicago: University of Chicago Press, 2002.

Burton, Richard Francis. *Wanderings in West Africa from Liverpool to Fernando Po*. Vol. 2. London: Tinsley Brothers, 1863.

Callaci, Emily. *Street Archives and City Life: Popular Intellectuals in Postcolonial Tanzania*. Durham, NC: Duke University Press, 2017.

Carland, John M. "Public Expenditure and Development in a Crown Colony: The Colonial Office, Sir Walter Egerton, and Southern Nigeria, 1900–1912." *Albion: A Quarterly Journal Concerned with British Studies* 12 (1980): 368–86.

Carsten, Janet, and Stephen Hugh-Jones. *About the House: Levi-Strauss and Beyond*. Cambridge: Cambridge University Press, 1995.

Cell, John W. "Anglo-Indian Medical Theory and the Origins of Segregation in West Africa." *American Historical Review* 91 (1986): 331.

Chang, Jiat-Hwee. *A Genealogy of Tropical Architecture: Colonial Networks, Nature and Technoscience*. London: Routledge, 2016.

Christophers, Brett. "For Real: Land as Capital and Commodity." *Transactions of the Institute of British Geographers* 41 (2016): 134–48.

Coker, G. B. A. *Family Property Among the Yorubas*. London: Sweet & Maxwell; Lagos: African Universities Press, 1966.

Cole, Patrick. *Modern and Traditional Elites in the Politics of Lagos*. London: Cambridge University Press, 1975.

Cole, Teju. *Known and Strange Things: Essays*. New York: Random House, 2016.

Bibliography 277

———. "One Night in Lasgidi," *Paris Review*, July 7, 2015.

Coleman, James S. *Nigeria: Background to Nationalism*. Berkeley: University of California Press, 1965.

Collins, Jessica. "Makoko Floating School, Beacon of Hope for the Lagos 'Waterworld.'" *Guardian*, June 2, 2015.

Colonial Reports—Annual, No. 554, Southern Nigeria, Report for 1906. London: His Majesty's Stationery Office, 1908. https://libsysdigi.library.illinois.edu/ilharvest/Africana/Books2011-05/3064634/3064634_1906_southern_nigeria/3064634_1906_southern_nigeria_opt.pdf.

Colonial Reports—Annual, No. 920: Report for 1915. London: His Majesty's Stationery Office, 1917. https://libsysdigi.library.illinois.edu/ilharvest/Africana/Books2011-05/3064634/3064634_1915/3064634_1915_opt.pdf.

Colonial Reports—Annual, No. 1114, Nigeria, Report for 1921. London: His Majesty's Stationery Office, 1922. https://libsysdigi.library.illinois.edu/ilharvest/Africana/Books2011-05/3064634/3064634_1921/3064634_1921_opt.pdf.

Colonial Reports—Annual, No. 1569: Annual Report on the Social and Economic Progress of the People of Nigeria, 1931. London: His Majesty's Stationery Office, 1932. https://libsysdigi.library.illinois.edu/ilharvest/Africana/Books2011-05/3064634/3064634_1931/3064634_1931_opt.pdf.

Colonial Reports—Annual, No. 1625: Annual Report on the Social and Economic Progress of the People of Nigeria, 1932. London: His Majesty's Stationery Office, 1933. https://libsysdigi.library.illinois.edu/ilharvest/Africana/Books2011-05/3064634/3064634_1932/3064634_1932_opt.pdf.

Colonial Reports—Annual, No. 1688: Annual Report on the Social and Economic Progress of the People of Nigeria, 1933. London: His Majesty's Stationery Office, 1934. https://libsysdigi.library.illinois.edu/ilharvest/Africana/Books2011-05/3064634/3064634_1933/3064634_1933_opt.pdf.

Comaroff, Jean. "Invasive Aliens: The Late-Modern Politics of Species Being." *Social Research* 84 (2017): 29–52.

Comaroff, Jean, and John Comaroff. "Africa Observed: Discourses on Imperial Imagination." In *Of Revelation and Revolution*. Vol. 1 of *Christianity, Colonialism, and Consciousness in South Africa*, edited by Jean Comaroff and John Comaroff, 86–125. Chicago: University of Chicago Press, 1991.

Cooper, Frederick. *Africa since 1940: The Past of the Present*. Cambridge: University of Cambridge Press, 2002.

———. *Decolonization and African Society: The Labor Question in French and British Africa*. Cambridge: Cambridge University Press, 1996.

———. *On the African Waterfront: Urban Disorder and the Transformation of Work in Colonial Mombasa*. New Haven, CT: Yale University Press, 1987.

———, ed. *Struggle for the City: Migrant Labor, Capital and the State in Urban Africa*. Beverly Hills, CA: Sage, 1983.

Cowell, Alan. "Lagos, Oil Boom Fading, Scarred by Vast Growth." *New York Times*, May 22, 1983.

Crinson, Mark. "Imperial Modernism." In *Architecture and Urbanism in the British Empire*, edited by G. A. Bremner, 198–238. Oxford: Oxford University Press, 2016.

Crist, Meehan. "Besides, I'll Be Dead." *London Review of Books*, February 22, 2018. Review of *The Water Will Come: Rising Seas, Sinking Cities and the Remaking of the Civilised World*, by Jeff Goodell. Carlton, Australia: Black Inc., 2017.

Croese, Sylvia, Liza Rose Cirolia, and Nick Graham. "Towards Habitat III: Confronting the Disjuncture between Global Policy and Local Practice on Africa's 'Challenge of Slums.'" *Habitat International* 53 (2016): 237–42.

Crouch, Christopher. *Design Culture in Liverpool, 1880–1914: The Origins of the Liverpool School of Architecture*. Liverpool: Liverpool University Press, 2002.

Crowther, Samuel. *A Vocabulary of the Yoruba language*. London: Seeleys, 1852.

Curtin, Philip D. *The Image of Africa: British Ideas and Action, 1780–1850*. 2 vols. Madison: University of Wisconsin Press, 1964.

———. "Medical Knowledge and Urban Planning in Tropical Africa." *American Historical Review* 90 (1985): 596–97.

da Cunha, Marianno. "Brasileiros Nagos em Lagos no peculo XIX." *Cultura* 23 (1976): 30–35.

———. *From Slave Quarters to Town Houses: Brazilian Architecture in West Africa*. Sao Paulo: Livraria Nobel S.A., 1985.

Daré, Abi. "Beaten, Raped and Forced to Work: Why I'm Exposing the Scandal of Nigeria's House Girls." *Guardian*, March 17, 2020.

D'Aruria, Viviana. "In the Laboratory and in the Field: Hybrid Housing Design for the African City in Late-Colonial and Decolonising Ghana (1945–57)." *Journal of Architecture* 19 (2014): 329–56.

Davis, Diane E. "Insecure and Secure Cities: Towards a Reclassification of World Cities in a Global Era." *MIT International Review* 1 (2008): 30–41.

Davis, Mike. *Planet of Slums*. London: Verso, 2006.

Dayen, David. "Banks Got Bailed Out, Homeowners Got Sold Out—and the Feds Made a Killing." *Fiscal Times*, March 11, 2016. https://www.thefiscaltimes.com/.

De Boeck, Filip. "Inhabiting Ocular Ground: Kinshasa's Future in the Light of Congo's Spectral Urban Politics." *Cultural Anthropology* 26 (2011): 263–86.

———. "'Poverty' and the Politics of Syncopation: Urban Examples from Kinshasa (DR Congo)." *Current Anthropology* 56 (2015): S146–S158.

Deleuze, Gilles, and Felix Guattari. *Anti-Oedipus: Capitalism and Schizophrenia*. Translated by Robert Hurley, Mark Seem, and Helen R. Lane. New York: Viking, 1977.

Bibliography

Demissie, Fassil, ed. *Colonial Architecture and Urbanism in Africa: Intertwined and Contested Histories.* Surrey, UK: Ashgate, 2012.

"Deplorable Housing in Nigeria, Grave Breach of Human Rights—UN Rapporteur." *Sahara Reporters,* September 23, 2019. http://saharareporters.com/.

Derricourt, Robin. *Inventing Africa: History, Archaeology and Ideas.* London: Pluto Press, 2011.

Digest Africa. "Lagos, a City of Shanty Towns and Millionaires." *World Weekly,* March 23, 2017. https://www.theworldweekly.com/.

Dike, Onwuka K. *Trade and Politics in the Niger Delta, 1830–1885: An Introduction to the Economic and Political History of Nigeria.* Oxford: Clarendon Press, 1956.

Dobbs, Richard, Sven Smit, Jaana Remes, James Manyika, Charles Roxburgh, and Alejandra Restrepo. "Urban World: Mapping the Economic Power of Cities." McKinsey & Company, March 1, 2011. https://www.mckinsey.com/.

Donadio, Rachel. "Le Corbusier's Architecture and His Politics Are Revisited." *New York Times,* July 12, 2015.

Donley, Linda W. "A Structuring Structure: The Swahili House." In *Domestic Architecture and the Use of Space: An Interdisciplinary Cross-Cultural Study,* edited by Susan Kent, 114–26. Cambridge: Cambridge University Press, 1990.

Doris, David T. *Vigilant Things, Yoruba Anti-Aesthetics, and the Strange Fates of Ordinary Objects in Nigeria.* Seattle: University of Washington Press, 2011.

Drayton, Richard. "Where Does the World Historian Write From? Objectivity, Moral Conscience and the Past and Present of Imperialism." *Journal of Contemporary History* 46 (2011): 671–85.

Drew, Jane, Maxwell Fry, and L. Humphries. *Village Housing in the Tropics, with Special Reference to West Africa.* London: Percy Lund Humphries, 1947.

"Dual Responsibility." *Daily Service,* November 23, 1955.

Duckworth, E. H. "An Appeal for Beauty." *Nigeria* 34 (1950): 222–26.

Duerksen, Mark. "The Koolhaas Effect: Hot Air over Lagos." *Johannesburg Salon* 7 (2014). http://jwtc.org.za/test/mark_duerksen.htm.

———. "Making Africa's Megalopolis: A Visual-Spatial History of Lagos." Infographic. Africa Center for Strategic Studies, accessed May 2024. https://africacenter.org/wp-content/uploads/2023/02/hds_poster_duerksen.compressed.pdf.

Dumett, Raymond. "The Campaign against Malaria and the Expansion of Scientific Medical and Sanitary Services in British West Africa, 1898–1910." *African Historical Studies* 1 (1968): 153–97.

Dunn, Cyril. "Facade by Lagos Lagoon." *Observer,* January 29, 1956.

Echeruo, Michael. *Victorian Lagos: Aspects of Nineteenth Century Lagos Life.* London: Macmillan, 1977.

Elden, Stuart, Eleonore Kofman, and Elizabeth Lebas, eds. *Henri Lefebvre: Key Writings*. London: Bloomsbury, 2006.

Elias, T. Olawale. *Nigerian Land Law and Custom*. 3rd ed. London: Routledge and Kegan Paul, 1962.

Elkins, Caroline. "Looking beyond Mau Mau: Archiving Violence in the Era of Decolonization." *American Historical Review* 120 (2015): 852–68.

Elleh, Nnamdi. *Architecture and Politics in Nigeria: The Study of a Late Twentieth-Century Enlightenment-Inspired Modernism in Abuja, 1900–2016*. London: Routledge, 2017.

Engels, Frederick. *The Housing Question* (1872). Marxists Internet Archive. Accessed July 4, 2016. https://www.marxists.org/archive/marx/works/1872/housing-question/.

Euba, Titilola. "Dress and Status in 19th Century Lagos." In *History of the Peoples of Lagos State*, edited by Ade Adefuye and Babatunde A. Agiri, 142–63. Lagos: Lantern, 1987.

Falola, Toyin. "Pawnship in Colonial Southwestern Nigeria." In *Pawnship in Africa: Debt Bondage in Historical Perspective*, edited by Toyin Falola and Paul E. Lovejoy, 245–66. Boulder, CO: Westview Press, 1994.

———. *The Political Economy of a Pre-colonial African State: Ibadan, 1830–1900*. Ile-Ife: University of Ife Press, 1984.

Fathy, Hassan. *Gourna: A Tale of Two Villages*, 2nd ed. New York: Prism, 1989.

Faulkner, Simon, and Anandi Ramamurthy, eds. *Visual Culture and Decolonisation in Britain*. Burlington, VT: Ashgate, 2006.

Feldman, Hannah. *From a Nation Torn: Decolonizing Art and Representation in France, 1945–1962*. Durham, NC: Duke University Press, 2014.

Ferguson, James. *Give a Man a Fish: Reflections on the New Politics of Distribution*. Durham, NC: Duke University Press, 2015.

———. *Global Shadows: Africa in the Neoliberal World Order*. Durham, NC: Duke University Press, 2006.

Fernandez, James W. "The Feeling of Architectonic Form: Residual and Emergent Qualities in Fang Cult and Culture." In *The Visual Arts: Graphic and Plastic*, edited by Justine M. Cordwell, 104–37. The Hague: Mouton, 1979.

"FG Vows to Punish Collaborators in the Demolition of 'Ilojo Bar'—a National Monument in Lagos." *Bella Naija*, January 30, 2017. https://www.bellanaija.com/.

Foucault, Michel. *The Order of Things: An Archeology of the Human Sciences*. New York: Vintage, 1994.

Fourchard, Laurent. "Between World History and State Formation: New Perspectives on Africa's Cities." *Journal of African History* 52, no. 2 (2011): 223–48.

———. "Lagos, Koolhaas and Partisan Politics in Nigeria." *International Journal of Urban and Regional Research* 35 (2010): 40–56.

———. "Lagos and the Invention of Juvenile Delinquency in Nigeria, 1920–60."

Bibliography

Journal of African History 47, no. 1 (2006): 115–37.

Fox, Sean, Robin Bloch, and Jose Monroy. "Understanding the Dynamics of Nigeria's Urban Transition: A Refutation of the 'Stalled Urbanisation' Hypothesis." *Urban Studies* 55 (2017): 950–51.

Frearson, Amy. "Kunlé Adeyemi's Floating School Suffers 'Abrupt Collapse.'" *Dezeen*, June 8, 2016. https://www.dezeen.com/.

Frey, William, and Zachary Zimmer. "Defining the City." In *Handbook of Urban Studies*, edited by Ronan Paddison, 14–35. London: Sage, 2001.

Frobenius, Leo. *The Voice of Africa*. Vol. 1. London: Hutchinson, 1913. https://library.si.edu/digital-library/book/voiceofafricabei01frob.

Fry, E. Maxwell. *Fine Building*. London: Faber and Faber, 1944.

———. "Slum Clearance in the Town." *Highway* 26 (1934): 8–10.

———. "Town Planning in West Africa." *African Affairs* 45 (1946): 197–204.

Fry, E. Maxwell, and Jane Drew. *Tropical Architecture in the Dry and Humid Zones*. London: B. T. Batsford, 1964.

Gaestel, Allyn. "How Long Is Now? Lagos' Fast-Evolving Architectural Landscape." *ICWA*, December 12, 2015. http://www.icwa.org/.

———. "Things Fall Apart." *Atavist Magazine* 76 (2018). https://magazine.atavist.com/.

Gale, Thomas S. "Ségrégation in British West Africa." *Cahiers d'études africaines* 20 (1980): 495–507.

Gandy, Matthew. *The Fabric of Space: Water, Modernity, and the Urban Imagination*. Cambridge, MA: MIT Press, 2014.

———. "Learning from Lagos." *New Left Review* 33 (2005): 36–52.

———. "Planning, Anti-planning and the Infrastructure Crisis Facing Metropolitan Lagos." *Urban Studies* 43 (2006): 371–96.

Gbadegesin, Olubukola A. "'Photographer Unknown': Neils Walwin Holm and the (Ir)retrievable Lives of African Photographers." *History of Photography* 38 (2014): 21–39.

Geary, Christraud M. "Early Images from Benin at the National Museum of African Art, Smithsonian Institution." *African Arts* 30, no. 3 (1997): 44–93.

George, Abosede. *Making Modern Girls: A History of Girlhood, Labor, and Social Development in Colonial Lagos*. Athens: Ohio University Press, 2014.

Gilroy, Paul. *The Black Atlantic: Modernity and Double-Consciousness*. Cambridge, MA: Harvard University Press, 1995.

Glazer, Nathan. *From a Cause to a Style: Modernist Architecture's Encounter with the American City*. Princeton, NJ: Princeton University Press, 2007.

Godlewski, Joseph. "Alien and Distant: Rem Koolhaas on Film in Lagos, Nigeria." *Traditional Dwellings and Settlements Review* 21 (2010): 7–19.

Godwin, John, and Gillian Hopwood. *Sandbank City: Lagos at 150*. Lagos: Kachifo, 2012.

———. "View from Lagos, Nigeria." *Architectural Review*, October 25, 2013.

Goerg, Odile. "From Hill Station (Freetown) to Downtown Conakry (First Ward): Comparing French and British Approaches to Segregation in Colonial Cities at the Beginning of the Twentieth Century." *Canadian Journal of African Studies* 1 (1998): 1–31.

Goodfellow, Tom, and Olly Owen. "Thick Claims and Thin Rights: Taxation and the Construction of Analogue Property Rights in Lagos." *Economy and Society* 49, no. 3 (2020): 406–32.

Gore, Charles. "Neils Walwin Holm: Radicalising the Image in Lagos Colony, West Africa." *History of Photography* 37 (2013): 283–300.

Gramsci, Antonio. *Selections from the Prison Notebooks.* Edited and translated by Quentin Hoare and Geoffrey Nowell Smith. New York: International Publishers, 1971.

Griffin, Donald W. "Urban Development in Africa: The Case of Lagos." *California Geographer* 8 (1967): 37–46.

Gurran, Nicole, and Peter Phibbs. "Are Governments Really Interested in Fixing the Housing Problem? Policy Capture and Busy Work in Australia." *Housing Studies* 30 (2015): 711–29.

Gutkind, Paul. "African Urban Studies: Past Accomplishments, Future Trends and Needs." *Canadian Journal of African Studies* 2, no. 1 (1968): 63–80.

Guyer, Jane. "Describing Urban 'No Man's Land' in Africa." *Africa: The Journal of the International African Institute* 81 (2011): 474–92.

———. "Household and Community in African Studies." *African Studies Review* 24 (1981): 87–137.

Guyer, Jane, LaRay Denzer, and Adigun Agbaje, eds. *Money Struggles and City Life: Devaluation in Ibadan and Other Urban Centers in Southern Nigeria, 1986–1996.* Portsmouth, NH: Heinemann, 2002.

Gyourko, Joseph, Christopher Mayer, and Todd Sinai. "Superstar Cities." *American Economic Journal: Economic Policy* 5 (2013): 167–99.

Hair, P. E. H. "The Cowboys: A Nigerian Acculturative Institution (Ca. 1950)." *History in Africa* 28 (2001): 83–93.

Hallen, Barry. *The Good, the Bad, and the Beautiful: Discourse about Values in Yoruba Culture.* Bloomington: Indiana University Press, 2000.

Harris, Richard, and Garth Myers. "Hybrid Housing: Improvement and Control in Late Colonial Zanzibar." *Journal of the Society of Architectural Historians* 66 (2007): 476–93.

Harrison, Philip. "On the Edge of Reason: Planning and Urban Futures in Africa." *Urban Studies* 43 (2006): 319–35.

Harrison, Robert Pogue. *The Dominion of the Dead.* Chicago: University of Chicago Press, 2003.

———. "Hic Jacet." In *Landscape and Power.* 2nd ed. Edited by W. J. T. Mitchell, 349–65. Chicago: University of Chicago Press, 2002.

Hassanain, Ola, and Egbert Alejandro Martina. "Architectures of the (Un)Inhabitable." Disembodied Territories. Accessed January 12, 2024. https://

Bibliography   283

disembodiedterritories.com/.

Heap, Simon. "'A Bottle of Gin Is Dangled before the Nose of the Native': The Economic Uses of Imported Liquor in Southern Nigeria, 1860–1920." *African Economic History* 33 (2005): 69–85.

———. "'Their Days Are Spent Gambling and Loafing, Pimping for Prostitutes, and Picking Pockets': Male Juvenile Delinquents on Lagos Island, 1920s–1960s." *Journal of Family History* 35 (2009): 1–23.

Hecker, Tim. "The Slum Pastoral: Helicopter Visuality and Koolhaas's Lagos." *Space and Culture* 13 (2010): 256–69.

Heidegger, Martin. "Building, Dwelling, Thinking." In *Poetry, Language, Thought*, translated by Albert Hofstadter. New York: Harper & Row, 1971.

Henderson, J. W. "Housing in Lagos, Nigeria." *Housing Review* 7 (1958): 9–11.

Herskovits Kopytoff, Jean. *A Preface to Modern Nigeria: The "Sierra Leonians" in Yoruba, 1830–1890*. Madison: University of Wisconsin Press, 1965.

Hinchcliffe, Tanis. "Pandora's Box: Forty Years of Housing History." *London Journal* 41, no. 1 (2016). https://www.tandfonline.com/.

"Historical Background." LSDPC official website. Accessed July 11, 2018, http://www.lsdpc.gov.ng/his.php.

Hitchins, Stephen. *Fry, Drew, Knight, Creamer Architecture*. London: Lund Humphries, 1978.

Hobson, J. A. *Imperialism: A Study*. New York: James Pott, 1902.

Home, Robert K. *Of Planting and Planning: The Making of British Colonial Cities*. 2nd ed. Abingdon: Routledge, 2013 [1997].

Hooper, Michael. "Public Participation: Simple Conceits versus Complex Realities." In *Metropolis Nonformal*, edited J. Bridger and C. Werthmann, 104–7. New York: Applied Research and Design, 2016.

Hopkins, Anthony G. "Economic Imperialism in West Africa: Lagos, 1880–1892." *Economic History Review* 21 (1968): 580–606.

———. "The Lagos Strike of 1897: An Exploration in Nigerian Labour History." *Past & Present* 35 (1966): 133–55.

———. "Property Rights and Empire Building: Britain's Annexation of Lagos, 1861." *Journal of Economic History* 40 (1980): 777–98.

Huxley, Elspeth. *Four Guineas: A Journey through West Africa*. London: Reprint Society, 1955.

Iliffe, John. *The African Poor: A History*. Cambridge: Cambridge University Press, 1987.

Immerwahr, Daniel. "The Politics of Architecture and Urbanism in Postcolonial Lagos, 1960–1986." *Journal of African Cultural Studies* 2 (2007): 165–86.

Irving, Robert Forsyth. *A Collection of the Principal Enactments and Cases Related to Titles to Land in Nigeria*. London: Stevens and Sons, 1916.

Jack, W. Murray. "Old Houses of Lagos." *Nigeria Magazine* 46 (1955): 96–117.

Jackson, Iain, and Jessica Holland. *The Architecture of Edwin Maxwell Fry and*

Jane Drew: Twentieth Century Architecture, Pioneer Modernism and the Tropics. Farnham, UK: Ashgate, 2014.

Jasanoff, Maya. *The Dawn Watch: Joseph Conrad in a Global World.* New York: Penguin, 2017.

Jean-François, Edvige, and Chris Giles, "Lagos' Afro-Brazilian Architecture Faces Down the Bulldozers." *CNN*, July 19, 2017. http://www.cnn.com/.

JEI Press Release. "Over 30,000 Homeless After Police Use Demolition by Fire and Bulldozer Working in Dead of Night Destroy Otodo Gbame Community Despite Subsisting Injunction." November 10, 2016. http://www.hic-gs.org/news.php?pid=6954.

Johnson, Samuel. *The History of the Yorubas from the Earliest Times to the Beginning of the British Protectorate.* Edited by Dr. O. Johnson. Lagos: C.M.S. Bookshops, 1921.

Jones, Adam, and Peter Sebald. *An African Family Archive: The Lawsons of Little Popo/Aneho (Togo) 1841–1938.* London: British Academy, 2006.

Joseph, Richard. *Democracy and Prebendal Politics in Nigeria.* Cambridge: Cambridge University Press, 1987.

Joyce, R. B. *Sir William MacGregor.* Oxford: Oxford University Press, 1971.

Joy Ike, Ijeoma, and Andrew Esiebo. "'They Came While We Were Asleep': Lagos Residents Tell of Brutal Evictions." *Guardian*, May 31, 2017.

Kaplan, Robert D. "The Coming Anarchy." *Atlantic*, February 1994.

Kazeem, Yomi. "Lagos Is Africa's 7th Largest Economy and Is About to Get Bigger with Its First Oil Finds." *Quartz Africa*, May 5, 2016. https://qz.com/.

Keazor, Ed. "The 100 Greatest Nigerians We Never Knew Pt 1." SlideShare, April 12, 2013. https://www.slideshare.net/.

Kimmelman, Michael. "School at Sea." *New York Times*, May 24, 2013.

King, Anthony D. *The Bungalow: The Production of a Global Culture.* Oxford: Oxford University Press, 1995.

Kirk-Greene, A. *Britain's Imperial Administrators, 1858–1966.* London: Palgrave Macmillan, 2000.

Klonk, Charlotte. "Myth and Reality of the White Cube." In *From Museum Critique to the Critical Museum,* edited by Katarzyna Murawska-Muthesius and Piotr Piotrowski, 67–79. Farnham, UK: Ashgate, 2015.

Koenigsberger, Otto. *Manual of Tropical Housing and Design.* London: Longman, 1974.

Komolafe, Akinola Adesuji, Suleiman Abdul-Azeez Adegboyega, and Francis Omowonuola Akinluyi. "A Review of Flood Risk Analysis in Nigeria." *American Journal of Environmental Sciences* 11 (2015): 157–66.

Koolhaas, Rem, and Bregtje van der Haak. "A Discussion on Koolhaas's Research with the Harvard Project on the City on Lagos, Nigeria." OMA,

Bibliography 285

July 5, 2002. https://web.archive.org/web/20150907183243/http://www
.oma.eu/lectures/lagos-infrastructure-and-improvisation/.

Koolhaas, Rem, and the Harvard Project on the City. *Mutations*. Barcelona:
ACTAR, 2000.

Kopytoff, Igor, ed. *The African Frontier: The Reproduction of Traditional African
Societies*. Bloomington: Indiana University Press, 1987.

Krapf-Askari, Eva. *Yoruba Towns and Cities: An Inquiry into the Nature of
Urban Social Phenomena*. Oxford: Clarendon Press, 1969.

Kuper, Adam. "The 'House' and Zulu Political Structure in the Nineteenth
Century." *Journal of African History* 34 (1993): 469–87.

Kus, Susan, and Victor Raharijaona. "Domestic Space and the Tenacity of Tradition among Some Betsileo of Madagascar." In *Domestic Architecture and
the Use of Space: An Interdisciplinary Cross-Cultural Study*, edited by Susan
Kent, 21–33. Cambridge: Cambridge University Press, 1990.

"Lagos Living: Solving Nigeria's Megacity Housing Crisis." *BBC*, January 23,
2017. https://www.bbc.com/.

"Lagos Slum Scheme: For Whose Benefit?" *Daily Service*, November 21, 1955.

"Lagos Slums Must Be Cleared; It Is National Pride to Do So: Says Ribadu."
West African Pilot, March 16, 1956.

"Lagos: The Megacity Battling for Water." *CNN* online video, May 23, 2017.
http://www.cnn.com/.

Lal, Priya. *African Socialism in Postcolonial Tanzania: Between the Village and the
World*. New York: Cambridge University Press, 2015.

Landau, Paul S. "Empires of the Visual: Photography and Colonial Administration in Africa." In *Images and Empires: Visuality in Colonial and Postcolonial Africa*, edited by Paul S. Landau and Deborah D. Kaspin, 141–71.
Berkeley: University of California Press, 2002.

Laotan, A. B. "Brazilian Influence on Lagos." *Nigeria* 69 (1961): 156–65.

Larkin, Brian. *Signal and Noise: Media, Infrastructure, and Urban Culture in
Nigeria*. Durham, NC: Duke University Press, 2008.

Law, Robin. "The 'Hamitic Hypothesis' in Indigenous West African Historical
Thought." *History in Africa* 36 (2009): 293–314.

———. "Trade and Politics behind the Slave Coast: The Lagoon Traffic and
the Rise of Lagos." *Journal of African History* 24 (1983): 321–48.

Lawal, A. A. "The Politics of Revenue Allocation in Nigeria: The Early Phase,
1900–1935." *Historical Society of Nigeria* 12 (1984): 51–64.

Lawal, Babatunde. "Some Aspects of Yoruba Aesthetics." *British Journal of Aesthetics* 15 (1974): 239–49.

Le Roux, Hannah. "Building on the Boundary: Modern Architecture in the
Tropics." *Social Identities* 10 (2007): 439–53.

———. "The Networks of Tropical Architecture." *Journal of Architecture* 8

(2003): 337–54.

Lévi-Strauss, Claude. *Race and History*. Paris: UNESCO, 1952.

———. *The Way of the Masks*. Translated by S. Modelski. London: Jonathan Cape, 1983.

Lindsay, Lisa. "Domesticity and Difference: Male Breadwinners, Working Women, and Colonial Citizenship in the 1945 Nigerian General Strike." *American Historical Review* 104 (1999): 783–812.

———. "No Need . . . to Think of Home? Masculinity and Domestic Life on the Nigerian Railway, c. 1940–1961." *Journal of African History* 39 (1998): 439–66.

———. "'To Return to the Bosom of their Fatherland': Brazilian Immigrants in Nineteenth-Century Lagos." *Slavery and Abolition* 15 (1994): 22–50.

———. *Working with Gender: Wage Labor and Social Change in Southwestern Nigeria*. Portsmouth, NH: Heinemann, 2003.

Liscombe, Rhodri Windsor. "Modernism in Late Imperial British West Africa: The Work of Maxwell Fry and Jane Drew, 1946–56." *Journal of the Society of Architectural Historians* 65 (2006): 188–215.

Livsey, Tim. "State, Urban Space, Race: Late Colonialism and Segregation at the Ikoyi Reservation in Lagos, Nigeria." *Journal of African History* 63 (2022): 178–96.

———. "'Suitable Lodgings for Students': Modern Space, Colonial Development and Decolonization in Nigeria." *Urban History* 41 (2014): 664–85.

Losi, John B. *History of Lagos*. Lagos: African Education Press, 1967. First published 1941 by Tika-Tore.

Luig, Ute, and Achim von Oppen, eds. "The Making of African Landscapes." Special issue, *Paideuma* 43 (1997).

Mabogunje, Akin L. "Land Reform in Nigeria; Progress, Problems and Prospects." Report for Presidential Technical Committee for Land Reform, 2007. https://www.oicrf.org/-/land-reform-in-nigeria-progress-problems-prospects.

———. *Urbanization in Nigeria*. London: University of London Press, 1968.

———. *Yoruba Towns*. Ibadan: Ibadan University Press, 1962.

Macaulay, Herbert. *The Lagos Land Question*. Lagos: Tika-Tore, 1912.

Macdonald, Helen. *H Is for Hawk*. New York: Grove Press, 2016.

MacGregor, William. "A Discussion on Malaria and Its Prevention." *British Medical Journal* 2 (1901): 680–90.

———. "Lagos, Abeokuta and the Alaka." *Journal of the Royal African Society* 3 (1904): 464–481.

———. "A Lecture on Malaria." *British Medical Journal* 2 (1902): 1902.

Makhubu, Nomusa. "'This House Is Not for Sale': Nollywood's Spatial Politics and Concepts of 'Home' in Zina Saro-Wiwa's Art." *African Arts* 49 (2016): 58–69.

Bibliography

Mann, Kristin. "African and European Initiatives in the Transformation of Land Tenure in Colonial Lagos (West Africa), 1840–1920." In *Native Claims: Indigenous Law against Empire, 1500–1920*, edited by Saliha Belmessous, 223–48. Oxford: Oxford University Press, 2011.

———. "Interpreting Cases, Disentangling Disputes: Court Cases as a Source for Understanding Patron-Client Relationships in Early Colonial Lagos." In *Sources and Methods in African History: Spoken, Written, Unearthed*, edited by Toyin Falola and Christina Jennings, 195–218. Rochester: University of Rochester Press, 2010.

———. *Marrying Well: Marriage, Status and Social Change among the Educated Elite in Colonial Lagos*. Cambridge: Cambridge University Press, 1985.

———. "Owners, Slaves and the Struggle for Labour in the Commercial Transaction at Lagos." In *From Slave Trade to "Legitimate" Commerce: The Commercial Transition in Nineteenth Century West Africa*, edited by Robin Law, 144–71. Cambridge: Cambridge University Press, 1995.

———. "The Rise of Taiwo Olowo: Law, Accumulation, and Mobility in Early Colonial Lagos." In *Law in Colonial Africa*, edited by Kristin Mann and Richard Roberts, 85–107. Portsmouth, NH: Heinemann, 1991.

———. *Slavery and the Birth of an African City: Lagos, 1760–1900*. Bloomington: Indiana University Press 2007.

Marafatto, Massino. *Nigerian Brazilian Houses*. Lagos: Istituto Italiano di Cultura, 1983.

Marchal, Jules. *Lord Leverhulme's Ghosts: Colonial Exploitation in the Congo*. London: Verso, 2017.

Marchand, Trevor H. J. *The Masons of Djenné*. Bloomington: Indiana University Press, 2009.

Marris, Peter. *Family and Social Change in an Africa City: A Study of Rehousing in Lagos*. Evanston, IL: Northwestern University Press, 1962.

———. "Motives and Methods: Reflections on a Study in Lagos." In *The City in Modern Africa*, edited by Horace Miner, 39–54. New York: Praeger, 1967.

Marsh, Bill. "Overpopulated and Underfed: Countries Near a Breaking Point." *New York Times*, June 15, 2017.

Martin, Phyllis. *Leisure and Society in Colonial Brazzaville*. Cambridge: Cambridge University Press, 1995.

Matthew, Theresa. "Designing Better Affordable Housing in New York." *Citylab*, June 25, 2018. https://www.citylab.com/.

Maudlin, D., and B. L. Herman, eds. *Building the British Atlantic World: Spaces, Places, and Material Culture, 1600–1850*. Chapel Hill: University of North Carolina Press, 2016.

Mayne, Alan. *Slums: The History of a Global Injustice*. Chicago: University of Chicago Press, 2017.

Mbembe, Achille. *Critique of Black Reason*. Translated by Laurent Dubois. Durham, NC: Duke University Press, 2017.

———. "Ruth First Lecture 2019: Blacks from Elsewhere and the Right of Abode." *New Frame*, October 19, 2019.

Mbembe, Achille, and Sarah Nuttall, eds. *Johannesburg: The Elusive Metropolis*. Durham, NC: Duke University Press, 2008.

———. "Writing the World from an African Metropolis." *Public Culture* 16, no. 3 (2004): 347–72.

McGrew, Roderick E. *Russia and the Cholera, 1823–1832*. Madison: University of Wisconsin Press, 1965.

Meacham, Standish. *Regaining Paradise: Englishness and the Early Garden City Movement*. New Haven, CT: Yale University Press, 1998.

Meek, C. K. *Land Tenure and Land Administration in Nigeria and the Cameroons*. London: Her Majesty's Stationery Office, 1957.

Meier, Prita. *Swahili Port Cities: The Architecture of Elsewhere*. Bloomington: Indiana University Press, 2016.

Melly, Caroline. *Bottleneck: Moving, Building, and Belonging in an African City*. Chicago: University of Chicago Press, 2016.

———. "Inside-Out Houses: Urban Belonging and Imagined Futures in Dakar, Senegal." *Comparative Studies in Society and History* 52 (2010): 37–65.

Miescher, Stephan F. "Building the City of the Future: Visions and Experiences of Modernity in Ghana's Akosombo Township." *Journal of African History* 53 (2012): 367–90.

———. *A Dam for Africa: Akosombo Stories from Ghana*. Bloomington: Indiana University Press, 2022.

Miller, N. S. *Lagos Steam Tramway, 1902–1933*. London: Fowler, 1958.

Mitchell, W. J. T., ed. *Landscape and Power*. 2nd ed. Chicago: University of Chicago Press, 2002.

Morshed, Adnan. "The Aesthetics of Ascension in Norman Bel Geddes's Futurama." *Journal of the Society of Architectural Historians* 63, no. 1 (2004): 74–99.

Morton, David. *Age of Concrete: Housing and the Shape of Aspiration in the Capital of Mozambique*. Athens: Ohio University Press, 2019.

Myers, Garth. *African Cities: Alternative Visions of Urban Theory and Practice*. London: Zed Books, 2011.

———. *Verandahs of Power: Colonialism and Space in Urban Africa*. Syracuse, NY: Syracuse University Press, 2003.

Ndibe, Okey. *Never Look an American in the Eye: Flying Turtles, Colonial Ghosts, and the Making of a Nigerian American*. New York: Soho Press, 2016.

Nelson, Steven. *From Cameroon to Paris: Mousgoum Architecture In and Out of Africa*. Chicago: University of Chicago Press, 2007.

Bibliography

Newell, Stephanie. *Histories of Dirt: Media and Urban Life in Colonial and Postcolonial Lagos.* Durham, NC: Duke University Press, 2020.

Nicolson, I. F. *The Administration of Nigeria, 1900–1960: Men, Methods, and Myths.* Oxford: Clarendon Press, 1969.

"Nigeria Must Act to Stop Housing Crisis and Forced Evictions: UN Rights Expert." UN News, September 24, 2019. https://www.un.org/.

Nikuze, Alice, Richard Sliuzas, Johannes Flacke, and Martin van Maarseveen. "Livelihood Impacts of Displacement and Resettlement on Informal Households: A Case Study from Kigali, Rwanda." *Habitat International* 86 (2019): 38–47.

Njoh, Ambe J. *Planning Power: Town Planning and Social Control in Africa.* London: UCL Press, 2007.

Nonko, Emily. "Manhattan Home Prices Have Increased Dramatically in a Decade." *Curbed,* February 2, 2017.

Nwafor, J. C. "Physical Environment, Decision-Making and Land Use Development in Metropolitan Lagos." *GeoJournal* 12 (1986): 433–42.

Nwanunobi, C. Onyeke. "Incendiarism and Other Fires in Nineteenth-Century Lagos (1863–88)." *Africa: Journal of the International African Institute* 60 (1990): 113.

Obasi, Sebastine. "Okunde Blue Waters Scheme: Huge Investments Threatened as Environmental Disaster Looms." *Vanguard,* June 25, 2018.

Obiefuna, Jerry N., Peter C. Nwilo, Ajiri O. Atagbaza, and Chukwuma J. Okolie. "Land Cover Dynamics Associated with the Spatial Changes in the Wetlands of Lagos/Lekki Lagoon System of Lagos, Nigeria." *Journal of Coastal Research* 29 (2013): 671–79.

Obot, N. I., M. A. C. Chendo, S. O. Udo, and I. O. Ewona. "Evaluation of Rainfall Trends in Nigeria for 30 Years (1978–2007)." *International Journal of the Physical Sciences* 5 (2010): 2217–22.

Ogbeche, Danielle. "Lagos Lagoon Hungry, Angry: Ifa Priests Urge Oba of Lagos to Appease Gods." *Daily Post,* March 25, 2017.

Ogundiran, Akinwumi. *The Yorùbá: A New History.* Bloomington: Indiana University Press, 2020.

Ojo, G. J. Afolabi. "Traditional Yoruba Architecture." *African Arts* 1, no. 3 (1968): 14–17, 70–72.

———. *Yoruba Cultures: A Geographical Analysis.* London: University of London Press, 1966.

———. *Yoruba Palaces.* London: Athlone Press, 1966.

Ojo, Sanya. "Making Markets with the Dead: Residential Burial among the Yoruba." *Journal of Consumer Behavior* 16 (2017): 591–604.

Okafor, Obidike, interview with Emeka Udemba. "When Are You Coming Back to Our Street?" *Contemporary And* 2 (2014): 14.

Okolo, Abraham. "The Nigerian Census: Problems and Prospects." *American Statistician* 53 (1999): 321–25.

Okonta, Ike, and Oronto Douglas. *Where Vultures Feast: Shell, Human Rights, and Oil.* New York: Verso, 2003.

Okorafor, Nnedi. *Lagoon.* London: Hodder & Stoughton, 2014.

Okutubo, Taiwo. "Kalakuta Acquired." *Daily Times,* April 29, 1977.

Olawoyin, Oladeinde. "Nigeria: Otodo-Gbame—Evicted by Lagos Govt, Stranded Residents Struggle, Die in Crowded Slums." *Premium Times,* May 13, 2018. https://allafrica.com/.

Olinto, Antonio. *The Water House.* Translated by Dorothy Heapy. New York: Carroll & Graf, 1970.

Olukoju, Ayodeji. "Accumulation and Conspicuous Consumption: The Poverty of Entrepreneurship in Western Nigeria, ca. 1850–1930." In *African Development in Historical Perspective,* edited by Emmanuel Akyeampong, Robert H. Bates, Nathan Nunn, and James A. Robinson, 208–30. Cambridge: Cambridge University Press, 2014.

———. *Infrastructure Development and Urban Facilities in Lagos, 1861–2000.* Ibadan: Institut français de rechereche en Afrique, University of Ibadan, 2003.

———. *The Liverpool of West Africa: The Dynamics and Impact of Maritime Trade in Lagos, 1900–1950.* Trenton, NJ: Africa World Press, 2004.

———. "Population Pressure, Housing and Sanitation in West Africa's Premier Port-City: Lagos, 1900–1939." *Journal of the Australian Association for Maritime History* 15 (1993): 91–106.

———. "The Segregation of Europeans and Africans in Colonial Nigeria." In *Security, Crime and Segregation in West African Cities since the 19th Century,* edited by Laurent Fourchard and Isaac Olawale Albert, 263–86. Paris: Karthala; Ibadan: Institut français de recherche en Afrique, 2003.

———. "The Travails of Migrant and Wage Labour in the Lagos Metropolitan Area in the Inter-war Years." *Labour History Review* 61 (1996): 49–70.

Oluwasegun, Jimoh Mufutau. "Managing Epidemic: The British Approach to 1918–1919 Influenza in Lagos." *Journal of Asian and African Studies* 52 (2017): 412–24.

Omezi, Giles. "Lagos: City of Concrete." In *Urban Constellations,* edited by Matthew Gandy, 108–12. Berlin: Jovis Verlag GmbH, 2011.

Onagoruwa, Olu. "What Are Your Property Rights within the Law?" *Sunday Times,* April 10, 1977.

Onuoha, Mimi. "A 50-Mile Island Built to Save Lagos's Economy Has a Worrying Design Flaw." *Quartz Africa,* March 18, 2017. https://qz.com/.

Oserogho & Associates. "Property Taxes in Nigeria." January 2, 2014. http://www.oseroghoassociates.com/.

Bibliography

Oshodi, Lookman. "Housing, Population and Development in Lagos, Nigeria." *International Development, Urban Infrastructure and Governance Blog*, November 24, 2010. https://oshlookman.wordpress.com/.

Osinulu, Damola. "Painters, Blacksmiths and Wordsmiths: Building Molues in Lagos." *African Arts* 41 (2008): 44–53.

Owomoyela, Oyekan. "The Good Person: Excerpts from the Yoruba Proverb Treasury." Accessed June 19, 2018. http://yoruba.unl.edu/yoruba.php-text =7&view=0&uni=0&l=0.htm.

Packer, George. "The Megacity: Decoding the Chaos of Lagos." *New Yorker*, November 13, 2006.

Parker, John. "The Cultural Politics of Death and Burial in Early Colonial Accra." In *Africa's Urban Past*, edited by David M. Anderson and Richard Rathbone, 205–21. Oxford: James Currey, 2000.

Peace, Adrian. "Prestige Power and Legitimacy in a Modern Nigerian Town." *Canadian Journal of African Studies* 13 (1979): 25, 27–51.

Peel, J. D. Y. *Religious Encounter and the Making of the Yoruba*. Bloomington: Indiana University Press, 2000.

———. "Urbanization and Urban History in West Africa." *Journal of African History* 21 (1980): 269–77.

Peil, Margaret. *Lagos: The City Is the People*. London: Belhaven, 1991.

Percy, Mark. "Thoughts on Building in Tropical Africa." *West Africa Builder and Architect* (1964): 52–53.

Peterson, Jon A. *The Birth of City Planning in the United States, 1840–1917*. Baltimore: Johns Hopkins University Press, 2003.

Poole, Deborah. *Vision, Race, and Modernity: A Visual Economy of the Andean Image World*. Princeton, NJ: Princeton University Press, 1997.

Pratten, D. "The Precariousness of Prebendalism." In *Democracy and Prebendalism in Nigeria: Critical Interpretations*, ed. W. Adebanwi and E. Obadare, 243–58. New York: Palgrave Macmillan, 2013.

Pyla, Panayiota I. "Hassan Fathy Revisited: Postwar Discourses on Science, Development, and Vernacular Architecture." *Journal of Architectural Education* 60, no. 3 (2007): 28–39.

Quayson, Ato. *Oxford Street, Accra: City Life and the Itineraries of Transnationalism*. Durham, NC: Duke University Press, 2014.

Radcliffe, Kendahl, Jennifer Scott, and Anja Werner, eds. *Anywhere but Here: Black Intellectuals in the Atlantic World and Beyond*. Jackson: University Press of Mississippi, 2015.

Rayner, T. C. "Land Tenure in West Africa." In *Reports on Land Tenure in West Africa*, edited by T. C. Rayner and J. J. C. Healy. West Africa Pamphlet no. 19, 1898.

"Removing to the New Homes." *Daily Times*, December 13, 1955.

Report of the Lagos Town Planning Commission with Recommendations on the Planning and Development of Greater Lagos. Lagos: Government Printer, 1946.

Report of the Tribunal of Inquiry into the Affairs of the Lagos Executive Development Board for the Period 1st October, 1960 to 31st December, 1965. Lagos: Federal Ministry of Information Printing Division, 1968.

"Reports, &c., From Drs. Stephens and Christophers, West Coast of Africa." In Reports to the Malaria Committee of the Royal Society. Third Series. London: Harrison and Sons, St. Martin's Lane, 1900.

Report with Recommendations on the Planning and Development of Greater Lagos. Lagos: Government Printer, 1946.

Richards, Thomas. The Imperial Archive: Knowledge and the Fantasy of Empire. London: Verso, 1993.

Robinson, Jennifer. Ordinary Cities: Between Modernity and Development. Abingdon, UK: Routledge, 2006.

Rogan, Bjarne. "An Entangled Object: The Picture Postcard as Souvenir and Collectible, Exchange and Ritual Communication." Cultural Analysis 4 (2005): 1–27.

Roland Igbinoba Real Foundation for Housing and Urban Development. The State of Lagos Housing Market. Vol. 2. Lagos: Pison Housing Company, 2016.

Ross, Ronald. "Sanitary Affairs in West Africa." In Affairs in West Africa, edited by E. D. Morel, 153–69. London: William Heinemann, 1902.

Sada, P. O., and A. A. Adefolalu. "Urbanisation and Problems of Urban Development." In Lagos: The Development of an African City, edited by A. B. Aderibigbe, 79–107. Ikeja: Longman Nigeria, 1975.

Salvaire, Côme, and Charlie Mitchell. "'It's Like a Civil War': In Lagos, Land Clearances Can Be Fatal." Fabric, December 1, 2016. https://www.citymetric.com/fabric/.

Sato, Shohei. "'Operation Legacy': Britain's Destruction and Concealment of Colonial Records Worldwide." Journal of Imperial and Commonwealth History 45 (2017): 697–719.

Sawyer, Lindsay. "Piecemeal Urbanisation at the Peripheries of Lagos." African Studies 73 (2014): 271–89.

Scala, Giambattista. Memoirs of Giambattista Scala. Translated by Brenda Packman and edited by Robert Smith. Oxford: Oxford University Press, 2000.

Schatz, Sayre P. Nigerian Capitalism. Berkeley: University of California Press, 1977.

Scheye, Eric. "Heart of Africa's Organised Crime: Land, Property and Urbanization." ENACT Policy Brief, May 9, 2019. https://enact-africa.s3.amazonaws.com/site/uploads/2019-05-10-urbanisation-policy-brief-001.pdf.

Bibliography 293

Schneider, Benjamin. "The American Housing Crisis Might Be Our Next Big Political Issue." *Citylab*, May 16, 2018. https://www.citylab.com/.

Schneider, Jürg. "Portrait Photography: A Visual Currency in the Atlantic Visualscape." In *Portraiture and Photography in Africa*, edited by John Peffer and Elisabeth L. Cameron, 35–66. Bloomington: Indiana University Press, 2013.

Schoenauer, Norbert. *6,000 Years of Housing*. New York: Norton, 2003.

Scott, Heidi V. "Colonialism, Landscape and the Subterranean." *Geography Compass* 2, no. 6 (2008): 1853–69.

Scott, James C. *Against the Grain: A Deep History of the Earliest States*. New Haven, CT: Yale University Press, 2017.

———. *Seeing Like a State: How Certain Schemes to Improve the Human Condition Have Failed*. New Haven, CT: Yale University Press, 1998.

Seaton, Beverly. *The Language of Flowers: A History*. Charlottesville: University of Virginia Press, 1995.

Seriki, E., and E. Pullybank. *Visitors Guide to Lagos*. Lagos: published by West African Book Publishers, printed by Academy Press, 1975.

Seun, Adetiba Adeamola. "Malaria and Sanitation in Colonial Lagos: A Historical Appraisal." *History Research* 3 (2015): 65–71.

Shasore, Olasupo. *Possessed: A History of Law and Justice in the Crown Colony of Lagos, 1861–1906*. Lagos: Q Books, 2014.

Silverstein, Paul A. "Of Rooting and Uprooting: Kabyle Habitus, Domesticity, and Structural Nostalgia." *Ethnography* 5, no. 4 (2004): 553–78.

Simone, AbdouMaliq. *For the City Yet to Come: Changing African Life in Four Cities*. Durham, NC: Duke University Press, 2004.

———. "People as Infrastructure: Intersecting Fragments in Johannesburg." *Public Culture* 16, no. 3 (2004): 407–29.

———. *The Surrounds: Urban Life within and Beyond Capture*. Durham, NC: Duke University Press, 2022.

Simone, AbdouMaliq, and Edgar Pieterse. *New Urban Worlds: Inhabiting Dissonant Times*. Cambridge: Polity, 2017.

Simpson, Rowton Stanhope. *A Report on the Registration of Title to Land in the Federal Territory of Lagos*. Lagos: Federal Government Printer, 1957.

Sklar, Richard L. *Nigerian Political Parties: Power in an Emergent African Nation*. Princeton, NJ: Princeton University Press, 1963.

Sluyter, Andrew. *Colonialism and Landscape: Postcolonial Theory and Applications*. Lanham, MD: Rowman & Littlefield, 2001.

Smith, Constance. *Nairobi in the Making: Landscapes of Time and Urban Belonging*. Suffolk, UK: Boydell & Brewer, 2019.

Smith, Robert. "The Canoe in West African History." *Journal of African History* 11 (1970): 515–33.

———. *Kingdoms of the Yoruba*. London: James Currey, 1988.

—. *The Lagos Consulate, 1851–1861*. London: Macmillan, 1978.

Soja, Edward. *Thirdspace: Journeys to Los Angeles and Other Real-and-Imagined Places*. Malden, MA: Blackwell, 1996.

Soules, Matthew. *Icebergs, Zombies, and the Ultra Thin: Architecture and Capitalism in the Twenty-First Century*. Princeton, NJ: Princeton Architectural Press, 2021.

Soyinka, Wole. *Myth, Literature and the African World*. Cambridge: Cambridge University Press, 1990.

—. *The Open Sore of a Continent: A Personal Narrative of the Nigerian Crisis*. Oxford: Oxford University Press, 1996.

Spitzer, Leo. "The Mosquito and Segregation in Sierra Leone." *Canadian Journal of African Studies* 2 (1968): 49–61.

Stallard, George, and Edward Harrison Richards. *Ordinances and Orders and Rules Thereunder, in Force in the Colony of Lagos on December 31st, 1893*. London: Stevens and Sons, 1894.

Stern, Robert A. M., David Fishman, and Jacob Tilove. *Paradise Planned: The Garden Suburb and the Modern City*. New York: Monacelli Press, 2013.

Stoler, Ann Laura. "Colonial Archives and the Arts of Governance." *Archival Science* 2 (2002): 87–109.

Strother, Z. S. "Architecture against the State: The Virtues of Impermanence in the Kibulu of Eastern Pende Chiefs in Central Africa." *Journal of the Society of Architectural Historians* 63 (2004): 272–95.

—. "'Breaking Juju,' Breaking Trade: Museums and the Culture of Iconoclasm in Southern Nigeria." *Anthropology and Aesthetics* 67/68 (2016/2017): 21.

Sule, O. R. A. "The Deterioration of the Nigerian Environment: Problems of Solid Wastes Disposal in the Metropolitan Lagos." *GeoJournal* 3 (1979): 571–77.

Swanson, Maynard W. "The Sanitation Syndrome: Bubonic Plague and Urban Native Policy in the Cape Colony, 1900–1909." *Journal of African History* 18 (1977): 387–410.

Táíwò, Oyè. "Headedness and the Structure of Yorùbá Compound Word." *Taiwan Journal of Linguistics* 7 (2009): 27–51.

Taylor, R. W., ed. *Urban Development in Nigeria: Planning, Housing, and Land Policy*. Aldershot, UK: Avebury, 1993.

Tew, Mervyn. *Report on Titles to Land in Lagos*. Lagos: Government Printer, 1947.

"They Oppose Clearance: Postpone the Scheme." *Daily Service*, November 21, 1955.

Tigidam, Perez. "The Fernandez House in Lagos: Relic of an Afro-Brazilian Past." *Nerve*, December 18, 2015. http://thenerveafrica.com/.

Uche, Chibuike Ugochukwu. "Foreign Banks, Africans, and Credit in Colonial Nigeria, c. 1890–1912." *Economic History Review* 52 (1999): 669–91.

Bibliography

Uduku, Ola. "Modernist Architecture and 'the Tropical' in West Africa: The Tropical Architecture Movement in West Africa, 1948–1970." *Habitat International* 30 (2006): 396–411.

Uher, Francis. "Aerial Views of Lagos." *Nigeria* 38 (1952): 109–21.

Van Onselen, Charles. *Studies in the Social and Economic History of Witwatersrand, 1886–1914*, vol. 1 *New Babylon* and vol. 2 *New Nineveh*. London: Longman, 1982.

Vlach, Michael. "The Brazilian House in Nigeria: The Emergence of a 20th-Century Vernacular House Type." *Journal of American Folklore* 97 (1984): 3–23.

Waters, Chris. "Review of *So Clean: Lord Leverhulme, Soap and Civilization*." *Victorian Studies* 52 (2009): 149–50.

Watson, Vanessa. "Shifting Approaches to Planning Theory: Global North and South." *Urban Planning* 1 (2016): 32–41.

Watts, Michael. "The Shock of Modernity: Petroleum, Protest and Fast Capitalism in an Industrializing Society." In *Reworking Modernity: Capitalism and Symbolic Discontent*, edited by A. Pred and M. Watts, 21–63. New Brunswick, NJ: Rutgers University Press, 1992.

Wetzstein, Steffen. "The Global Urban Housing Affordability Crisis." *Urban Studies* 54 (2017): 3159–77.

Wheatley, Paul. "The Significance of Traditional Yoruba Urbanism." *Comparative Studies in Society and History* 12, no. 4 (1970): 393–423.

White, Louis. *The Comforts of Home: Prostitution in Colonial Nairobi*. Chicago: University of Chicago Press, 1990.

Whiteman, Kaye. *Lagos: A Cultural History*. Northampton: Interlink, 2014.

Whitford, John. *Trading Life in Western and Central Africa*. Liverpool: The "Porcupine" Office, 1877.

"Why Flooding in Nigeria Is an Increasingly Serious Problem." *Conversation*, August 15, 2017. https://theconversation.com/.

Woetzel, Jonathan, Sangeeth Ram, Jan Mischke, Nicklas Garemo, and Shirish Sankhe. *A Blueprint for Addressing the Global Affordable Housing Challenge*. N.p.: McKinsey Global Institute, 2014. https://www.mckinsey.com.

———. "Tackling the World's Affordable Housing Challenge." McKinsey & Company, October 1, 2014. https://www.mckinsey.com/.

Zeijl, Femke van. *Do-It-Yourself Society, on Life in Lagos*. Amsterdam: Ambo Anthos, 2022.

———. "Telling New Stories of Ilojo Bar: An Invitation." Legacy 1995, n.d. https://mcusercontent.com/f66694a4deeb825a673c0b934/files/bcd4119b-0055-b84a-aaf9-6addb6b998e6/telling_new_stories_of_ilojo_bar_an_invitation.pdf.

Index

àbàgbọn chiefs, 34

Abeokuta: Lagos migrants from, 117; missionary outpost founded (1846) at, 36

Abidjan, 82

Abuja, Nigerian capital relocation to, 32, 195–96

Accra: Colonial Office's West African Building Research Station in, 148; Ga perception of graveyard burial in, 243; Ronald Ross's description of houses at, 90; segregation at, 82

Aerial photographs of Lagos: early (1920s), 31, 112–13, 140; imprint of colonial segregation as seen through, 96

African: architecture, 23, 26, 151; cities, 6–7, 17, 19, 220, 226; houses, 13–16, 23–27, 214–15; housing, 17–18, 25, 96–97, 114, 125–26, 128; landscapes, 18–23, 25–26, 31–32, 85, 97, 151, 227, 241

Afro-Brazilian influence on Lagos architecture: Alakoro example of, 90, 92–94; artisans and craftsmen and the, 61; debate on, 62–64; Ebun House and twentieth-century examples of, 107; plastered patterns of, 11, 64; *The Water House* and the, 10

AG (Action Group), 158, 183

àkárígbéré chiefs, 34, 228

Akyeampong, Emmanuel, xi, 236

Alakoro Swamp: MacGregor Canal construction and, 79; reclamation of, 88–90; residential houses at, 90–91, 97–98; results of reclamation at, 245

Allada, 33

Amodu Tijani v. Secretary, Southern Provinces, 118

Apapa, 157, 183, 193, 196; colonial seizure of and subsequent litigation over, 118–20; Lugard and colonial Lagos's expansion to, 105; map (3.5) of, 133–34, 135

architecture: modernism, 32, 145–47, 163–64, 215, 251, 257; monumental, 21, 25; vernacular, 23, 25; Yoruba (*see* Yoruba: architecture)

archives: critical studies of, 12, 168–71; historic maps and photographs as, 8, 11–12, 28–29; houses and landscapes as, 27–28, 213, 216; landscapes as, 29, 170–71

aso ẹbí, 64, 238. See also *ẹbí*

Atlantic World, 6, 172, 227, 233

Awori, 2, 33–34, 97, 139, 178, 180, 182, 213, 217–18

baálẹ, 2, 19, 33–35, 100, 219

bàbá ìsàlẹ, 50, 59, 64, 232

Badagry, 4, 35; first "storey house" relocated to Lagos from, 62; José Fernandez fleeing to, 54; missionary outpost founded (1842) at, 36; ọba Kosoko's exile to, 37

Barber, Karin, 60, 236

Barnes, Sandra, 174, 178–83

Batammaliba houses, 26

Bathurst, 82

Beier, Ulli, 23, 151–52

Benin (country), xii, 26

297

298 Index

Benin, Bight of, 11, 35–37, 43–44
Benin, Kingdom of, 15, 21, 33–34, 36, 139
Benin City, 15, 20
Bigon, Liora, iii
Blier, Suzanne, xi, 26
Bourdieu, Pierre, 23, 25, 50–51, 226, 232
Brazilian Quarter (Oke Ite), 39, 237
British National Archives, 78, 112, 132, 169–70
British planners, 91, 95, 114, 138, 166
British West Africa, 82, 148, 242, 249–50
bungalow(s), 2, 7, 13, 76, 79, 91, 106, 109, 148, 149, 214

capital, 6, 32, 175, 202–3, 205, 209, 215–16, 221; cultural, 51–52, 58, 64; economic, 51–53, 56, 59, 73; moral, 232
Carter, Bridge, 118, 129
Carter, Gilbert, 123
Caxton House, 53, 59
Central Lagos, 32, 67, 110, 136–37, 154, 156–57, 160–63, 168–70, 189, 261. See also Lagos
Central Lagos Slum Clearance Scheme, 154, 159, 260
channel, Lagos, 25, 33, 42–43, 47, 79, 140, 229; deepening of, 30, 40, 43, 75, 214, 229; mapping of, 39–40
chiefs, white cap, 34, 118, 120, 133, 205–6, 228. See also idéjọ chiefs, land ownership of; ọmọ onilẹ
Church Mission Society (CMS), 38, 62, 70
Clifford, Hugh, 110, 120, 122
climate change, 201, 207, 210–11, 222
Cole, Patrick Dele, 49–51, 53, 60, 68
Colonial and Indian Exhibition in London, 45, 47, 52, 73
Colonial Office, 81, 84, 88, 92, 96, 105, 108–10, 118, 120, 145, 148–49, 245–46
Colony of Lagos, 46–47, 49, 66, 68–70, 240. See also Lagos
Conakry, 82
conspicuous consumption, 60, 181, 241
Cooper, Frederick, 141, 151–52, 165, 257–59
Corbusier, Le, 146–47, 251, 257
courtyards, 2, 24, 34, 36, 67, 126, 165
Crown grants, 55–56, 58, 68–70, 74, 98, 100–101, 136–37, 235, 239, 247
Crowther, Samuel Ajayi, 36, 168, 230, 231

Dahomey, 21, 26, 33, 139
Dakar, 82
decolonization, 141, 143, 168–69, 171
Djenné-Djenno: masons of, 226–27; urbanism of, 25–26
Doherty House, 53, 55
dominant class, 51, 57, 110, 174, 179, 231
Drew, Jane, 32, 145, 147, 149, 208

ẹbí, 34. See also aso ebi
Ebun House, 55, 107
Ebute Metta, 105–6, 114, 120, 219, 238
Egba, 50
Egerton, Walter, 82–83, 86–88, 90, 101, 103–4, 108, 116, 243
Èkó, 1–2, 47, 102, 120, 200; Awori landscapes of, 213; etymology of, 2; ilé architecture of, 34–35, 219; kingdom of, 34–36; origins of, 32–33
Eko Atlantic, 203, 207–8
eléèkó, 115, 120–21, 125, 129, 131, 132–33
Elephant House, 53, 55
Elias House, 65, 238
elite status, 49, 51, 58, 231–32
Epe, 90–91, 187
European reserves, 76, 80, 82, 87, 105
European surveyors, 5, 78
evictions, 1, 12, 47, 68–69, 160, 165, 190, 206–7, 260, 265

"face-me-I-face-you" tenements, 3–4, 7
Faji, 39, 57, 60
family property, 61, 68, 97, 99–100, 136–37, 161, 185–87; legal tenets of, 247
Federal Survey Department of Nigeria, 119, 144
fee simple title, 55–56, 68, 99, 239
FESTAC (Festival of Black Arts and Culture), 175–76, 178, 184, 188, 193
Fourchard, Laurent, 112, 225, 250–52, 254–55
freehold rights, 100, 136–37, 157, 173, 181, 185, 187, 191
Freetown: governing colonial Lagos from, 230; Ronald Ross's description of houses at, 90; segregation at, 82
Frobenius, Leo, 19–22, 24, 26, 225
Fry, E. Maxwell, 5, 32, 145, 147–55, 158, 164, 168–69, 187, 208, 215

Gandy, Matthew, 112
Garden City, 79, 84, 123, 244

Index

Glover, John Hawley, 41, 70, 72, 191, 230, 235; 1859 map produced by, 37–38, 40, 228–29

Godwin, John, xii, 122, 229

Government House, 41, 74–75, 80–81, 104, 106, 108, 242, 246

Gropius, Walter, 146–48, 166

Gropius House, 146

habitus, 51, 232

Harrison, Robert Pogue, 29, 210, 212–13, 218, 220–21, 225

homelessness, 16, 35, 125, 129, 160, 212

Hopkins, Antony Gerald, 59, 101

Hopwood, Gillian, xii, 54, 122, 229

House at Ikoyi, 148–49

household(s), 16, 31, 34–36, 130, 158, 161, 180, 202. See also *idile*

houses: archetypes of in colonial Lagos, 97–99; axis mundi of in postcolonial Lagos, 174, 179; colonial, 106–9; Lagos studies and, 7, 11, 13, 32, 66, 98, 210, 212, 214–16; literature on, 13–16, 18, 22–27; materiality of, 26, 34, 36, 39–40, 59, 61–62, 64, 67, 71, 90–92, 109, 152, 196–97, 203; meanings and forms of, 2, 10, 29, 115, 197, 209–22; new uses of in Lagos Colony, 47, 56; role of in consolidating elite status in Lagos, 49, 52, 73. See also *ilé*

housing: colonial attention to, 126, 157; crisis of, 203, 208–9, 221–22, 268; land and, 53, 56, 179, 181, 191, 203, 205, 209, 216; problem of, 143, 150, 185; shortage of, 12, 16, 18, 68, 95, 117, 173, 201; stock of, 4, 11, 66, 127–28, 174, 185, 192, 204, 206, 209; studies and theories of, 16–18, 21–22, 208–10, 216, 222

housing question, the, 13, 16, 209

huts, pejorative views of, 14–15, 22, 31, 40, 82, 224

Ibadan, 19, 50, 60, 82; Frobenius's 1910 visit to, 19. See also University of Ibadan

Iddo Island, Awori settlement of, 33–34, 139, 213

idéjọ chiefs, land ownership of, 34–35, 74, 98–99, 102, 104, 118, 186, 228

idile, 180, 183

ìgá, 53, 57, 63, 120, 125

igá idunganran, 38

Ijebu, 35, 50, 59, 117, 139

Ikeja, 179, 183, 187

Ikoyi, 3, 131, 133, 140, 183, 189, 203; African request for return of, 121; desegregation of, 110, 157; forfeiture of to Crown, 103–5; Government Reservation Area at, 4, 76–78, 80, 108–10, 116, 118. See also House at Ikoyi

ilé: *agbo*, 34; *alapako*, 62; *ilẹ̀-*, 213; importance of in Lagos history, 11, 33–35, 228; *petesi*, 62; *temi*, 34, 228; *tiwo*, 34; Yoruba concept of, 218–21

Ilé-Ifẹ, 33, 86

Ilojo Bar (Fernandez House), 44; history of, 53–54, 234

Ilorin, 152

imperialism, 79, 107, 170, 227, 243

Isale Eko, 4, 38, 125, 151, 192

Jaekel House, 106–7, 250

Johannesburg, 8–9

Johnson, Samuel, 19, 21, 24

Joseph, Richard, 174, 176, 179, 262

Kabyle House, 23–24

Kano, 78, 82, 131

King, Anthony, 13, 226

Koolhaas, Rem, 5, 111–12, 115, 250–51

Lagos: bombardment by Britain, 15, 37, 44, 228, 230; dredging the sandbar, 10, 44, 72, 75, 229; house styles, 41, 44, 53–54, 58, 61, 65–66, 74–75, 98, 214; housing crisis, 12, 209, 220; landscapes, 5, 42, 44, 46, 86, 90, 193, 198; mainland, 76, 86; population, 66, 96, 115, 184, 225, 230, 263. See also Central Lagos; Colony of Lagos; Èkó; Native Council

Lagos Consulate, 40, 54

Lagos Island, 31, 33–35, 37, 46, 73, 76–77, 79, 104, 117, 119, 124, 126, 133, 136, 151, 160, 162

Lagos Lagoon, 42, 139–41, 256

Lagos State, 2, 4, 179, 187–88, 190–91, 205–7, 216

Lagos Town Council, 122, 133

Lagos Town Planning Ordinance, 122, 133

300 Index

land: expropriations, 87, 205; family, 98–100; grabs, 132, 189; grants, 54, 101; monetization of, 38, 54–55, 67; rights, 31, 86, 99, 132, 136, 228, 269; shortages of in Lagos, 11, 56; tenure, 97, 136, 204, 248, 256, 259; value, 66, 102, 185

landed chiefs, 34, 74, 101–2, 218, 228. See also ìdéjọ chiefs, land ownership of

landlords, 4, 29, 32, 66, 69, 122, 127–28, 134, 136, 181, 196

landowner(ship), 34, 50, 72, 74, 80, 137, 181–83, 191, 203, 256, 259

"Land Question," 97, 101, 104, 116, 250

landscapes, 13–15, 18–19, 24, 26–30, 41, 153, 211–12, 214, 216, 220–22, 224; African, 9, 14, 18, 22–23, 25, 31–32, 85, 97, 151, 153, 227, 241; Black, 77, 80, 83, 90, 108, 241; historical production of, 10, 13, 29–30, 43–44, 77; urban, 9–11, 22, 219

Land Use Act, 191–92, 221

Lawson, William, 40, 45, 47–49, 53, 56–57, 59, 73–74, 88, 95, 214, 220, 231; 1885 map by, 51–53, 58–59, 66, 214, 220, 233, 245

LEDB (Lagos Executive Development Board), 141; 1940s schemes of, 132–36; 1950s schemes of, 154–63; 1960s schemes of, 165–66; creation of, 115–16, 121, 253; early schemes of, 127–29; legacy of, 168; original authority of, 122–24, 259; transformation of into the LSDPC, 187, 189

Lekki, 4–5, 200, 203, 205

Lévi-Strauss, Claude, 24–26, 226, 257

Lewis v. Bankole, 97, 247

Lindsay, Lisa, 128, 157–58

Liverpool, 83, 97, 147, 149

Liverpool School of Architecture, 83, 147

LSDPC (Lagos State Development and Property Corporation), 166, 187–90

Lugard, Frederick, 83, 86, 90, 101, 105–6, 109, 115–16, 120

Macaulay, Herbert, 31, 80, 94, 103–4, 114, 116, 118, 120–22, 125, 129, 131–32

MacGregor, William, 81–82, 84, 86, 94, 100–101, 105

MacGregor Canal, 77–78, 80–83, 88, 100, 104–6, 110, 124, 243

Makoko, 2–3, 113, 138, 202, 208

Makoko Floating School, 112, 207–8, 211, 251

Mann, Kristin, 6–7, 42, 49–51, 54, 56, 68–69, 227, 231–35

Maputo, 27

Marris, Peter, 158, 160–63, 168, 170

Mbembe, Achille, 1, 8–9, 17, 210, 217–18, 221, 223–25, 243–44

Mushin, 173, 178–79, 182–84, 186, 192–94, 196

National Archives of Nigeria, 124, 127

Native Council, 84, 100. See also Lagos

NCNC (National Council of Nigeria and the Cameroons), 158–60, 165, 260

New Gourna, 23

Nigeria: amalgamation of, 10, 102; British colonial, 10, 106; independence of, 12, 140, 168; military government of, 180, 183, 188, 193; nationalism and, 80, 103; postcolonial petro-state of, 173–79

Nigerian Civil War, 183, 185

Nigerian General Strike, 128

Nigerian Youth Movement, 132, 158

NNDP (Nigerian National Democratic Party), 115, 121, 132, 158–59, 165

Nollywood, 201, 211–12

ọba, 15, 34, 36, 38–39, 60, 73, 102, 120–21, 131, 134, 137; palace of, 33, 73, 107, 178

ọba Dosunmu, 40, 54, 69–70, 230

ògáládé chiefs, 34, 228

Ojo, G. J. Afolabi, 24

Oko Awo, 117, 121, 123–28, 138

Oko Faje, 38–39

Olaiya House, 53

ọlọfin, 34, 235

Olosa, 140, 256

Olowogbowo, 38, 51

Olukoju, Ayodeji, 6, 125, 129

Oluwa, Chief (Tijani), 118, 120–21

ọmọ onilẹ, 186, 205, 256

Orange House, 44, 51, 53, 57, 60, 63

Otondo Gbame, 205–6

Ouidah, 35

Oyo, 60, 64, 117, 131

Payne, J. A. Otonba, 51, 52, 53, 59, 62, 64, 73

Peel, J. D. Y., 42, 71–72, 240

Index

plague, 31, 81, 115–16, 121, 123, 259
property: private, 44, 55–56, 66, 74, 206; rights, 16, 35, 47, 53, 55–56, 66, 74, 190, 218

real estate, 11, 35, 56, 64, 68, 175, 179, 181, 184, 215–16, 267–68
rehousing estates, 157, 160, 162–63
Report on Titles to Land in Lagos (Tew), 132, 136

SAPs (structural adjustment programs), 175, 195, 200
Saros, 38, 46, 61, 64, 238
Savage House, 53, 65
Scala, Giambattista, 39, 61
segregation, 12, 14, 17, 74, 82, 85–87, 96, 105, 109–10, 116, 241–42
seigneurial rights, 98, 102, 118
Shitta Bey Mosque, 65, 238
Sierra Leone, 36, 47, 49, 54, 65, 230
Silva House, 53, 55
slave(s), 35, 36, 57, 61, 68–69; former (*arota*), 36, 54, 56, 70, 74, 98–100, 137, 235, 239, 269; trade, 36, 102
slavery, 35–36, 54, 56, 61, 69, 71, 80, 100, 233, 235, 248
slum clearance, 113, 116, 129, 132, 134, 154, 156, 158, 160, 162, 165–66, 171, 260
sobrados, 61–63, 107
social reproduction, 11, 128, 218–19
Soyinka, Wole, 9, 168
structural adjustment programs. *See* SAPs
Surulere, 157, 160, 163, 189, 261, 265

Taiwo Olowo, 53, 57–60, 62, 64–65, 70, 214, 235–36, 238, 241

terra nullius, 14, 269
Tew, Mervyn, 132; *Report on Titles to Land in Lagos*, 132, 136
Tew Legislation, 136, 186, 206
Tinubu Square, 53, 62
Treaty of Cession, 40, 102, 116, 118, 133, 191, 228, 252
Tropical Modernism, 32, 178; origins and principles of, 141–43, 149–50, 169; urban planning and, 154–56, 178, 259–60

University of Ibadan, 23, 152, 226
urban and town planning, 16, 86, 141, 154, 220, 243; modernism and, 145; professionalization of, 77–79, 83, 246
urbanism, 25; colonial, 168; plotted, 207
usufructuary rights, 97, 118, 136–37, 252

Victoria Island, 42, 105, 154, 189, 203

Water House, 55, 61, 237
Water House, The (Olinto), 10, 249
Whitford, John, 40–41
Wright, Joseph, 36

Yaba, 2–3, 105, 114, 120, 127, 129, 131, 219
Yoruba: architecture, 20, 23–24, 62, 64, 90, 152, 237, 245; culture, 21, 24, 33, 60, 131, 236; houses, 7, 20–21, 24, 62, 66, 226; landscapes, 94, 213, 221; Oriki poetry, 237–38; palaces, 244, 250; urbanism, 19, 21–22, 33, 225, 228, 244; wars, 47, 237
Yorubaland, 19–23, 33, 35–36, 38, 56, 61, 64, 71, 221